Thresholds of Peace

Thresholds of Peace

Four Hundred Thousand German Prisoners
and the People of Britain
1944–1948

MATTHEW BARRY SULLIVAN

HAMISH HAMILTON · LONDON

First published in Great Britain 1979
by Hamish Hamilton Ltd
Garden House 57–59 Long Acre London WC2E 9JL

Copyright © 1979 by Matthew Barry Sullivan

British Library Cataloguing in Publication Data

Sullivan, Matthew Barry
    Thresholds of peace.
    1. World War, 1939–1945—Prisoners and
    prisons, British
    I. Title
    940.54'72'41   D805.G7

    ISBN 0–241–89862–5

Printed in Great Britain by
Ebenezer Baylis & Son Ltd,
The Trinity Press, Worcester, and London

For Elizabeth

truest of wives
truest of critics

Contents

Illustrations

Foreword and Acknowledgments

There was no peace treaty between Germany and the Allies after the Second World War, for even West Germany was not a fully sovereign state till nine years after the Third Reich was destroyed. All the more important, therefore, has been what is sometimes called 'person-to-person peace' and the myriad human acts through which true peace is founded, enemies are reconciled and constructive relations between nations developed. There was a unique opportunity for this between the British people and the 400,000 German prisoners of war held in Britain, in some cases for more than three years after hostilities had ended. It was for them at first a traumatic time, for the bitterness of defeat was compounded by 'non-fraternisation' which lasted no less than nineteen months. One pillar of the present study is, therefore, their crises and search for personal, social and political renewal. The other is the attempt on the part of the British to guide or assist this renewal, both officially and unofficially. In this context any discussion of war crimes trials has been judged to be out of place.

My thanks go in many directions: first of all to Herbert Sulzbach who pressed me to take up the theme. When I had already written a letter declining, a guardian spirit showed me in his unmistakable way how wrong I was; I tore up the letter and the project from then on greatly expanded. I found myself entering an area which was, as regards Germany, largely unexplored: that low point or *Stunde Null* from which West Germany began the purging of its past and the amazing recovery of its free institutions and national dignity. All too little attention has been focused on this important time of transition as against the evils of the Nazi state. Twenty-five years ago, as editor responsible for Gerald Reitlinger's grim classic *The Final Solution*, I waded with him through a historical country as hateful as the scene of the present study is hopeful. Not least am I grateful for the opportunity to help restore the balance.

When the British and American Quakers were together given the Nobel Peace Prize in 1947, their contribution to promoting brotherhood among men was defined at the award ceremony in Oslo as 'the silent help from the nameless to the nameless'. In this book I have deliberately named hundreds of names, mostly very obscure, who provided the groundwork of the story. For this is a story as well as history. I am in debt to hundreds of you who have assisted me to gather and uncover material. All over Britain and in several corners of Germany you have talked freely into my tape-recorder, trusting my discretion; you have fished into your memories and turned up old diaries, cuttings and photographs. You have corresponded with me, sometimes at great length, and put me in touch with further correspondents: I am most grateful to all of you, especially those who have sustained me with their patience and good wishes.

I have tried to be faithful to the life in the material collected, to check details and to provide a sound structure from contemporary documents. But there are incidents the truth of which I cannot vouch for, and others where those who took part give diametrically opposed versions. 'It was a claustrophobic time,' one POW said to me, 'and experiences from it move into it that are definitely second-hand, stories you've heard so often they become your own.' Even diaries can be suspect, their ink and paper showing that they were written up afterwards, though not always with intent to mislead.

Except for a few who wished to remain anonymous all those who have helped are listed at the end, though by no means all the material sent in could be used—for reasons of space or repetition. If I single out certain people here it is because they went to great trouble to help me, in most cases commenting, sometimes sharply, on work in progress: Alexander McLeod Murray, Herbert Hartwell, Kurt Schwederski, Rudolf Halver, Fritz Borinski, Charles Cranfield, Siegfried Bandelow, Urban Forell, Kurt Blohm, Karl Gursky, Werner Jentsch, G. D. Friedrich, Kelvin Osborne, Herbert Schmitt, Horst Woetzel, Gunter d'Alquen, Herbert Sulzbach, Charles Stambrook, Ted Rees, C. M. L. Clements. Above all, Henry Faulk has been an exemplary friend and ally. Having himself written a standard but deliberately impersonal work on a similar theme, he unlocked for me without stint his own store of unprinted knowledge and stories, combed my text meticulously for weeds and extracted not a few thistles, corrected many misapprehensions, and accepted disagreements in the best liberal spirit.

I must also thank two citizens from Hamburg for some financial support—Dr Erich Leverkus and Herr Alfred Toepfer, donor of the Hanseatic Scholarship I had received in 1938. A third benefactor wishes to remain anonymous. My neighbour, Anna-Brita Snodin, kindly translated for me a chapter of Birger Forell's only book from the Swedish; and Joan Bligh, also of Jordans, patiently and tactfully and with valuable comments turned an unsightly typescript into presentable pages.

Matthew Sullivan
Jordans, Buckinghamshire
July 1978

All translations in the text from the German are by the author, except for the lines of Brecht at the head of Chapter Seven, which are by Christopher Middleton. Copyright permission is acknowledged for this extract out of *Gedanken über die Dauer des Exils* from Surkamp Verlag; for Günther Eich's *Inventur* in *Abgelegene Gehöfte* from Hanser Verlag.

Certain German words are used in the text untranslated:
    Attentat (attempted) assassination, always refers to the bomb plot against Hitler on July 20th 1944
    Filzung frisking and confiscating
    KZ (Konzentrationslager) concentration camp
    Heimat Homeland (the deeper, female counterpart to Fatherland)
    Landser common soldier, somewhat equivalent to 'Tommy'
    Waffen-SS (Waffen = weapon, arms) front-line fighting SS
    Allgemeine-SS (Allgemeine = common, or general) concentration guards, special commandos, etc.
    Wehrmacht armed forces, combining all three services
The SS ranks—*Standartenführer, Scharführer*, etc.—are normally translated into their Wehrmacht equivalents.

PART ONE

Meine jungen Kameraden, ich weiss dass es schlimm ist wenn es einem Soldaten gesagt wird 'du hast verloren'. Aber ich sage Euch eins: es ist besser für Deutschland, besser für uns, dass wir verloren haben. Nämlich hätten wir gewonnen, so hätten wir uns selbst verloren.

(My young comrades, I know that it is a sad thing for a soldier to have said to him 'You have lost'. But let me tell you this: it is better for Germany, better for us, that we have lost, because if we had won we would have lost ourselves.)

> General Johann Theodor von Ravenstein, Commander of the 21st Panzer Division, on 8 May 1945 at Grande Ligne Camp, Quebec.

You accuse me of being pro-German. You could not have made a bigger mistake. I am pro-humanity.

> Major Boughton, Commander of Norton Camp.

Die Jahre des Wiederaufrichtens nach ungehaurem Einsturz, da sind die guten Wachstumsjahre der Völker. Zwar erkennen nur immer wenige besonnentätige Geister die Vorteile der Niederlage, aber auf diese wenigen kommt es an, und während andere geniessen, anklagen, verfluchen und aufwühlen oder der Menschheit vorschrieben, wie sie sich von nun an zu entwickeln habe, bereiten jene still die Zukunft vor; sie haben alle schon den Untergang gefühlt und sind nun den Bestehenden gegenüber sehr frei . . . Verwirklichen wollen sie, was ihnen die innere Stimme rät, wärs auch das kleinste Ding . . .

(The years of reconstruction after a total collapse—these are the good growing years of a people. It is true that only a few actively thoughtful spirits recognise the advantages of a defeat, but all depends on these few, and while others indulge in the pleasures of complaining, cursing and agitating, and prescribing the path that humanity must travel, these ones are quietly preparing the future. are unbound by prevailing circumstances . . . They only wish to bring about what their inner voice tells them, if only in the smallest matter . . .)

> Hans Carossa
> *Der Arzt Gion* 1931.

I

Surrender

Hands up! Hände hoch!
Moments of fear and hope. Moments of anger, shame, intense relief.

Egypt, July 1942. The New Zealand 2nd Division made a surprise night attack on the Ruweisat Ridge south of Alamein. I was liaison officer with an Italian unit. We were quickly overrun and I was caught from behind by a sergeant who grabbed me out of a hole. We'd been short of water for some time, and after a while the chap, noticing I was bleeding a bit from a wound, gave me a cup of tea and shared it with me—the best drink of my life. I was well treated. I wish I could have met that wonderful New Zealand sergeant again and thanked him for the drink that revived me. But I heard after the war that he was later killed in action.

Normandy, July 1944. There was I, a Bavarian farmer, with a wagon and four horses driving through France, and the wagon full of ammunition, and I sees the English coming. What do you do, Fritz? I just says 'Whoa', lets go of the reins, puts my hands up. Do you think I'm going to get blown up with that lot behind me!

Near Metz, August 1944. Tank attack by the Patton army against our bunker. All the others were wounded, so I went out and indicated that we wanted to surrender. 'Stop firing—we are wounded,' I called out, as they had come quite close. The stretcher-bearers arrived quickly, which was good, or some of our men would not have survived. Then, to my astonishment, they asked me if I wanted to go back to the bunker and go on fighting. They didn't want to use the pause to deal with the wounded to force our surrender. A joke? I don't think so.

Belgium, August 1944. Shit! I thought, and put my hands up. We had only rifles and a few grenades left against the oncoming tanks and lorry-borne infantry; the maquis too had us in crossfire. I had a fist-sized wound in my left calf. An English medical orderly gave me some dope, then an officer with 'Horse Guards' on his battle dress came to interrogate me. Well, at least I, as a colonel, was entering captivity in a manner appropriate to my rank! Some soldiers carried me in a blanket into a peasant's house, and put me on the carpet in the best room. The nice farmer's wife brought me some schnapps. A few hours later an English ambulance took me to the Belgian hospital at Hechterinen. I saw some wounded Belgians who had fought on our side. A maquis leader came and berated them. Later I heard them being shot in the courtyard of the hospital. The Belgians, mostly Flemings, were good to us. A nun remarked, 'The Germans are a clever people—only they've always got to be making war.'

Moments of transition, of thankfulness to be alive, of satisfaction at having fought well. Moments of tension, terror, confusion.

Alsace, August 1944. The American tank men shot into the sand beside us. They could easily have killed us all. Some of us shot back from our fox-holes—a panic reaction. Then the commander opened his hatch, told us to climb up, and we were taken, sitting on the outside of the tanks, eastwards towards Germany on the only transport available.

Gothic Line, Italy, end of 1944. A platoon of Grenadier Guards has just repulsed a German raid. They are unwinding, pleased with their success, as they have had no casualties, but the enemy have left three wounded behind. The guardsmen, from being killers at one moment turn, as their custom is, at the next into kindly nurses, putting the wounded men on to stretchers with an encouraging, 'All right, Fritz, we'll soon get you off to the rear.' Suddenly a shot rings out. One of the Germans still has a weapon concealed under the blanket and, at point-blank range, wounds a guardsman. The platoon commander, hearing the shot, turns round, and, as his men tense up to deal with the Nazi bastard, shouts out sharply, 'Hold it!' The desire for quick revenge subsides. The German will be dealt with in the correct manner. An act of morality and of obedience.

Erschaffenburg, Easter Day 1945. We destroyed our top secret radar documents and someone put a white towel up out of the cellar. The Americans seemed just as frightened as we were. 'Don't shoot—Nikt schiess, Kamerad!' We crawled out of the cellar.

Holland, end of April 1945. I was a real wild one, eighteen years old, at the end of my strength after being on those last moment commando-style raids. After an action—it was dark—I went to a point of rendez-vous on a farm where I expected to meet the rest

of my unit. I met my captors instead. I was terrified as they disarmed me. One of them said, 'Put your hands behind your head
and walk towards that light.' I expected to be shot. Instead I fell
into a ditch. There were more Canadians there. I was frightened
and tried to make friends and ingratiate myself and said something
like 'German prisoners play football in England, yes?' When they
saw I still had a knife on a lanyard they hit me. After that I was
taken to a POW cage in a state of total physical and mental
exhaustion.[1]

*Hands stretched to the sky, an unconscious act of prayer as well as sub-
mission, a cry for life, not certain to be accepted. And, if accepted, life has
been given back to you. You will survive! The unknown ordeals ahead are
nothing to this fact. No longer is it 'Kill or be killed'. But then the
adrenalin subsides and a reaction sets in. You have the prisoner's sullen
face, the face of defeat, of exhaustion—but also of change. One world has
ceased to be, another not yet begun.*

Mass surrenders are different. There is no intense momentary
face to face drama, rather a mood of corporate numbness. But not
always. The first mass surrender of Germans in the West was at
Tunis in May 1943, when nearly a quarter of a million troops,
Germans and Italians in equal numbers, suddenly gave in. To the
British victor, General Alexander, 'It was like Derby Day. Men
who a short time before had been fighting like tigers now seemed
transformed into a cheerful, docile crowd, resigned to the accept-
ance of their fate.' As they waited in droves to be taken into the
cage on the Massicourt Road, a German band arrived, complete
with instruments, and stood in a square playing soothing Viennese
music.[2] Lord Alexander's first biographer, Nigel Nicolson, who
was also there, described Hitler's African divisions giving themselves up 'with strange unconcern, almost gaily, like a defeated
team after a hard-fought Rugby match, demanding baths and a
celebration tea.' These sporting images sprang from mutual respect between worthy opponents, an attitude frowned on heavily
by General Eisenhower, Commander-in-Chief in North Africa,
and the Americans.* Members of the 7th Armoured Division,
who had fought a ding-dong battle with the Afrika Korps up and
down the desert for two and a half years, did in fact mingle with
the enemy for a while, exchanging cigarettes and sweets. In

* See page 221.

general, the troops on both sides looked at each other with 'passionless curiosity'.

Hans-Georg Moschallski of the élite Hermann Goering Division was given no order to surrender. He heard on the BBC that the 'last round-up' was taking place. His unit had been driven back to the coast, disgusted at the sudden lack of leadership and at being left in the lurch. Their eye-hold was a smudge on the horizon out over the shimmering blue sea, the Isles of Pantelleria, the nearest point of Europe. They had hoped for an armada to take them back to continue the war.* Instead five Englishmen turned up on an armoured gun carrier to lead them to the assembly point, shouting 'Snell, snell'. Once there, 'a tank rolled up and there in the turret was a Tommy. He called, "Kamerad, kennst du Knäckebrot?" (Friend, have you ever had crispbread?), holding a packet of the famous stuff up in his hand; in this way he got us to trot behind the gun carrier.' Treatment was good, but the Germans had prudently hidden away their watches and decorations against souvenir hunters, while Moschallski himself smashed his retina camera on a rock. It was during the eight-day transport by the Sahara railway to Casablanca that he and many others first came to doubt whether Germany would win the war. 'When I saw the miles of war supplies parked along the railway lines—millions of barrels of petrol, tanks, guns and lorries—my heart sank to my boots.'

The spirit of the war in Europe was different. Booty was the privilege of the victor, and in most units a prisoner was fair game. Filching personal effects became almost routine. When Rudolf Bradatsch, a Petty Officer in the Marines, was surrounded on the Dutch island of Vlissingen a comrade who had been taken prisoner in the First World War reassured him: 'You need not bother to conceal anything—the English are always *korrekt*.' Bradatsch found they must have greatly changed. Everything was taken from them—knives, money, pens, family photos, watches, down even to his pocket handkerchief. Their haversacks containing bits of food were emptied. Hans Freiberger, captured near Arnhem, was left with a pencil stump which became his most prized possession. Leutnant Goersdorf in Normandy hid his grandfather's watch and his ring in his top boots. When they were discovered the

---

* Field Marshal Rommel repeatedly, but in vain, begged the Führer to allow him to evacuate his best Afrika Korps troops back to Italy, which he guaranteed he could then hold against an Allied invasion.

Canadian captain asked why he had done that. He pointed to the lighter brown circle on his wrist where his watch had recently been, for which insolence he was given twenty-four hours fatigue duty and forbidden to speak to his comrades. It was the common lot, it seems, of Germans, after a few camps and a few friskings, to be skint of possessions. The new mood of the war made for this. In fact, the Geneva Convention on Prisoners of War does permit anything to be removed that can assist a man to escape, such as knives and watches, though all such items should be handed in and signed for. To their frank astonishment thousands did, in fact, find little bags containing their valuables handed back to them by the British at repatriation.

Cadet Elmar Tremmel took part in the retreat from the Russians as they advanced across North Germany. After days by cart and lorry, with the 'Cossacks' just behind, his remnant encountered the Americans driving East. 'Throw down your arms and keep going,' they were told, 'but stay off the main roads.' Then Tremmel had a shock at his first meeting with Yankee support troops: some were decorated with watches right up to the elbow. He thought, 'Good Lord! America is supposed to be such a rich country!' GIs indeed, when an enemy officer had his hands up, were known to take his watch off before they took his pistol. Occasionally an officer would keep his watch, perhaps by protesting vehemently in the name of the Geneva Convention, or insisting that, as a doctor, he needed one. The adjutant of General Eberling was captured in West Holland. When both were taken to Canadian headquarters, he was a bundle of nerves, hungry and exhausted. A big sergeant came to take his watch off his wrist. As an automatic reaction, he cracked the edge of his right hand down on the man's fingers. He apologised abjectly, explained his action —and kept his watch. Everyone took watches, but the GIs were the worst—so much so that it was said the letters US stood for *Uhrensammler* (watch-collectors).

Capture by Polish troops, understandably, was always feared; but when Pastor Halver was stripped of all his personal effects, an officer afterwards apologised and allowed him to retrieve his Bible and photos from a heap; and later on, when his men got drunk, he protected the prisoners from their threatening behaviour. The Canadians were perhaps the roughest of the invaders and, out of a surplus of raw physical energy, became notorious for their habit of wanton destructiveness. But it depended on the unit. A

Canadian with a Polish accent pointed a sten-gun at Nikolaus Manthey, hiding in a cellar, and called out almost amiably, 'Komm'raus. Vil besser in England.' Karl Gursky, a young Lutheran pastor called up as a paymaster, got cut off from his unit in the confusion of the retreat and joined up with a horse-drawn field hospital commanded by a veterinary colonel. He recalls how 'Canadian tanks entered the village and we surrendered immediately. The Canadians were very proud to have captured a high officer and treated us with courtesy. I was asked to interpret and soon discovered they were very disappointed our colonel was only a vet. We officers had to stay under guard in a villa, and were astonished at the civil way in which we were treated. The lady of the house was allowed to give us dinner—she had asked this hoping that her own husband might also find such gentlemanly opponents. She served us with an excellent wine and the colonel made a short speech in which he thanked us for our services to the German people and begged us not to despair in this dark epoch of our history. Of course, we guessed that after this first heart-warming reception, bitter weeks and months and even years would follow.'

If the Canadians were unpredictable victors, Germans captured by Americans also had many surprises. Hugo Staudinger, with whom Patton's men offered to continue the interrupted fight as though it were a ball-game, had heard them on the intercom talking to each other in his own language with Bavarian or Swabian accents—they were Americans of German descent. Paul Seufert took part in a last stand in the Ardennes:

The fanatical new commander of our bunker was less determined now that we should hold out to the last man. 'We'll pull back now,' he said, and without waiting to know whether anyone followed him, he heaved himself out of the trench and protected by his white camouflage dashed off. It's likely he was shot down fairly soon. We could have put up a white towel, but it's doubtful whether it would have been seen in the dim light and the snow. An anxious, highly unpleasant night, and next morning an uncanny stillness. Perhaps the Americans had retired in the night. Our look-out reported smoke from Bunker 143. We had no idea who was occupying it. Finally, since no one else would, I held up the white flag in my hand and marched rapidly towards the bunker. Twenty metres before I reached it two soldiers came out from behind a fir tree and pointed their carbines at my chest. I found a few morsels from my school English and offered our surrender. I was rather disappointed with this first close encounter with Americans. Before me stood two undersized men in middle age and both bearded. One wore a woollen cap, the other presented a luxuriant growth of hair. In leather waistcoats and pullovers and without any indication of rank or unit, they appeared to be more like woodcutters, poachers or smugglers than proper soldiers. I was told they were the so-called 'Sing-Sing' paratroops—volunteers from the famous prison earning remittance with a stint at the front.

About the same time Colonel Freiherr von der Heydte, commander of the last parachute drop ever made by the Wehrmacht, awoke in a high fever. He saw a steel-helmeted soldier at the foot of his bed. 'Strange,' he thought, 'Germans always take their helmets off when entering a house.' He remembered that in the Ardennes, cut off and at the end of his strength, he had sought refuge with a German family in Barogne. The soldier spoke German with a strong American accent. He had a small book in his hand and was a priest. 'Do you want to confess?' The colonel said he had done so before being dropped and had no occasion for sinning since. He then lost consciousness again, and next time he awoke he was in hospital and surrounded by war reporters. One of them asked him what he thought of Sepp Dietrich (Commander of the First SS Panzer Korps). He answered 'To me he's just a drunken sergeant', and passed out again. He was fairly soon nursed back to health, his life being saved by the penicillin the Americans gave him, at that time unknown in Germany.

When in 1936 T. E. Lawrence's *Seven Pillars of Wisdom* appeared in German, the back of the jacket high-lighted the passage describing the behaviour of the German contingent in October 1918 at the Battle of Deraa where the Turkish 4th Army was finally routed. Printed in bold type, the words were both longed-for admiration from abroad and an inspiration to the new Germany: 'I grew proud of the enemy which had killed my brothers. They were two thousand miles from home, without hope and without guides, in conditions bad enough to break the bravest nerves. Yet their sections held together, in firm rank, sheering through the wrack of Turk and Arab like armoured ships, high-faced and

silent. When attacked they took position, fired to order. There was
no haste, no crying, no hesitation. They were glorious.'[3] In 1945
the Germans, though often respected as tough defensive fighters,
inspired no such words. Final scenes lacked all nobility. Far off in
Connecticut Thomas Mann, enduring with an agonised empathy
the ordeal of his country, wrote of 'the dazed fatalism' with which
total defeat was faced.*

Most soldiers have fantasies about what will happen to them if
they are taken prisoner, optimistic or fearful according to temperament, and Nazi propaganda was easily able to use the demand for
unconditional surrender to work up their fears. Even early in the
war a young submariner might be told that if captured by the
English he would have a swastika branded on his forehead. The
more naive ones believed it. By the end many officers were sure
that, after a thorough interrogation, they would simply be killed
—that was the final propaganda line. Certainly no German looked
forward to being in the hands of the French, even in the African
theatre. A Corporal Schmidt, one of the lucky wounded to be
flown out of Stalingrad, found himself a few months later being
transported across Algeria in an open lorry. They had no water
all day. When, at high noon, the French guards stopped for re-
freshment they gave them none and shot at some Arab boys who
were surreptitiously handing them up cans of water, killing one.
When the Leclerc Division advanced on 25 August 1944 to the
centre of Paris, Karl Sandig was a member of General von
Cholditz's staff at the Hotel Majestic. As they were marched out
of the Kommandatur bunker, they were not at first protected from
the fury of the civilian population. Acts of such viciousness took
place that today Professor Sandig prefers not to rake over scenes
which can only burden Franco-German relations. Germans who
fell into the hands of the Resistance were usually shown mercy,
but often not if they had been involved in punitive operations
against civilians. The Indian Legion of the Wehrmacht, wretched
adventurers and misfits who knew they had been swindled by the
Nazis, were so employed. When thirty survivors surrendered to a
Communist group near Bordeaux they were immediately shot, and
their officers would have been but for the timely arrival of a
British captain, who showed great courage and stubbornness in
saving their lives. One of these officers was Heinrich von Trott zu
Solz, brother of the executed 20th July conspirator. He was for-

* *Dr Faustus*, Ch. 46.

tunately advised to hide this fact when he was caged with other German prisoners. Otherwise, they would probably have killed him as a traitor.[4]

War is like that and becomes more vindictive, more murderous as it progresses. Yet Leutnant Herbert Walter, interpreter on the staff of an Army Corps that was overrun in Picardie, was captured in quite a different style. 'We were all surrounded by a combined unit of British and Free French. I climbed out of my fox-hole and, as I walked forward, I was accosted by a quite elderly Frenchman wearing a Resistance arm-band.

"Est-ce-que vous êtes Chrétien?" he said to me.

"Mais oui; je suis catholique."

"Ah, moi aussi! Mais alors, nous devrions être amis—et nous ne sommes pas!"

He offered me a cigarette, helped me to carry my baggage and took me to our assembly point.'

The French, a most civilised but volatile people, often behaved individually with decency to German prisoners. But, understandably, public behaviour was often virulent and nasty, and the usual explosion of hatred in the liberated populations was a deep shock especially to younger German soldiers. Paul Seufert, having surrendered to the Sing-Sing volunteers, trudged all day through the Ardennes snow, helping to carry the German wounded; then, at the French frontier, they had to run a gauntlet of screaming abuse and insult, of which the mildest were the familiar 'sales Boches' and a gleeful 'Les Russes à Berlin!' Only slowly did it dawn on the dumbfounded Seufert what it felt like to be an occupied nation. Beside him Corporal Lerse had tears of shame streaming down his cheeks. Hubert Walter, his liking for the French having just been confirmed, was soon observing the women of Arras turn round as they went by, bend over and lift their skirts. Werner Düttmann, the twenty-three-year-old cadet officer who had survived when Patton's tank-men shot not at him but into the sand beside him, was soon being transported through Nancy. 'We had to get out of the trucks and march through a long crowd throwing stones at us. One lot were standing on a bridge spitting down at us, thought to have been let out of the local jail to join in the fun. We were in a rage and the Americans had to let off warning shots to protect us.' Twenty-two-year-old Willi Wolf of the Third Parachute Division was captured by Belgian maquis after a bold attempt to reach

home after his unit was overwhelmed at St Lo. Handed over to
the Americans, he wondered whether the black truck drivers were
drunk or taking evading action against the stone-throwing villagers. Later when they were marched to the station at Compiègne,
a hostile mob of men, women and children accompanied them,
and as they were waiting for the train to move off, showered it
with stones. When these landed in the open trucks the Germans
threw them back again and since the French were in a solid row
even hit children in their mothers' arms once or twice. The
journey to Cherbourg took four days and it would have been easy,
says Willi Wolf, to escape, but the word had gone round that they
would be hunted down with a price on their heads. At some
bridges and tunnel entrances people would be waiting to throw
missiles down at them and it seemed that the black guards were so
angry that they were not just shooting into the air to warn them
off. All the way through these negro soldiers were ready to do
trade—they never just took things. A postcard-size nude woman
fetched the high price of two blocks of chocolate; a silver parachutist's badge was much coveted and fetched two chocolate bars
and a packet of cigarettes. The former was divided round and
eaten slowly in tiny pieces; then came the solemn moment of the
smoke, the guards giving them a light. So weak were they from
hunger that with one pull for a few seconds the world around
would disappear into darkness.

The ebullient Bavarian artist, Leutnant Josef Huber, experienced the explosion of hatred at Le Havre, due in part at least to
the very high civilian casualties caused by the British bombing
and bombardment of the inner harbour.* He remembers how his
unit surrendered after being in cross-fire at the waterworks outside the city. 'The comrade next to me had been killed and blood
drenched my uniform as I held him in my arms. Then all prisoners
were herded into the cemetery. A French resistance man, wearing
a tricolour arm-band and carrying a carbine, got my watch. I

* This was the occasion when the well-known playwright William
Douglas Home, then an artillery captain, refused to obey an order on
the grounds that the bombardment was inhuman, the civilian population not having been given a chance to evacuate. He was court-
martialled and given a year's imprisonment. Major Dr Gunther
Geisseler, chief of intelligence on the German side, likewise condemns
the British conduct of the siege, and argues reasonably that it was
chiefly this which caused the feelings of the French to burst bounds:
they blamed the Germans for the high casualties.

complained of this to the English colonel who spoke German. He said, "Be happy he didn't take your life too." I'd kept a box of paints right through the war. A Canadian NCO wanted them. I said, "Never!", and gave him 5,000 francs—which were no more use to me. For the first three hours we were kept under guard at the cemetery. I had with me a large bunch of keys of the fortress and I amused myself by going round and putting one on top of each grave. Then we were marched by resistance men in a column down a long line of civilians. I was right in front, clutching my paints, and beside me was my friend Everling, also an artist. There was a ciné camera every hundred yards or so. Then the first woman came and spat in my face. We were meant to hold our hands high, but I wouldn't and held them up in front of me. One of the resistance men then clapped me on the elbows with the butt of his rifle, but I was so mad that I sloshed at him and he left me alone. By the end I was grey-white from head to toe with the slime of their spit. Afterwards I was standing with my uniform drenched with my friend's blood and now streaked with mucus. The English colonel came up to me and said, "What happened?" I told him. He said, "Go through that gate and you'll find some boards", and with these we scraped the spit off ourselves.'

One way to maintain morale was by effrontery and cheekiness. Horst Woetzel, an artillery lieutenant happy to surrender near Wesel, recalls being transported in an open lorry across Belgium, along with some paratroop and Luftwaffe officers. 'Their arrogance was astonishing. One or two stood up in front wearing a monocle just provoking the population.' And why not a bit of cheekiness sometimes? Leutnant Goersdorf was waiting at an assembly point in Dieppe Harbour. In the heat of the day an American negro sentry had drowsed off. A German private crept up to him and succeeded in removing the bolt from his rifle. They then threw pebbles at him to wake him up. The fellow, terrified at what had been done to him, had to buy back the bolt for his rifle with several packets of Lucky Strikes. Equally good for Leutnant Goersdorf's morale was when he saw, or believed he saw, a French mother put her two small sons over her lap and spank them for throwing stones at the prisoners.

For centuries the Low Countries have been the cockpit of European wars. Twenty-five years earlier in November 1918 they had also been the scene of great German armies in retreat. Then the Armistice only required them to retire behind the line of the Rhine and there demobilise; they still had fight in them and marched back in good order. The home front had collapsed before the western front and the legend of the stab in the back was born. This time, the Allies would pursue them remorselessly to the heart of their homeland and link up with the dreaded Russians. The longer this took the more the devastation would resemble the Thirty Years War of the seventeenth century. For a while, indeed, it seemed that a quick thrust to the Ruhr might bring the end by Christmas; for the laborious break-through in Normandy became a sudden break-out, with the Wehrmacht, forbidden tactical retreats, now in headlong flight. In an encircling movement a single American division took 4,000 prisoners in three days. On the northern flank the tanks and armoured cars of the Brigade of Guards and the 11th Armoured Division drove forward with a speed unparalleled in any war; racing over the battlefields of 1914–18 in a few hours, they reached Brussels in three days and Antwerp in four on 4 September. During these exuberant hours their main hazard was 'delaying tactics' by the jubilant populations. In their wake huge numbers of prisoners were herded in. General Eberbach, Commander of the VIIth Army, and his staff were overrun outside Amiens, in his pocket a fresh order to defend the line of the Somme which had already been crossed. Further south, the entire German 1st Army from South West France might have been cut off, had it not been for the delays completing and celebrating the liberation of Paris.

Leutnant Karl Heinz Knoop was a platoon commander in the pell-mell retreat of General Blaskowitz' XIXth Army from the Mediterranean coast after the Allied landings. At Lyons their train was bombed and strafed by the RAF. They lost their supplies and many were killed when the ammunition trucks blew up. Taking cover in pine woods by day, Knoop's company moved only by night, for fear of partisans picking up stragglers. Orders reached them to give cover to tank units of the Waffen-SS retreating from Normandy to defend the town of Montargis. It was not even on their poor map; when they found it, it was in the hands of Patton's army. A mere seventeen were now left of the original three hundred and twenty and they only had rifles to use against tanks. A sensible French civilian came up and said to them, 'Mais pourquoi se suicider? Rendez les armes!'—which they did.

The problem of dealing with hordes of prisoners now became acute, and certainly they fared worse than, say, the British captured four years earlier at Dunkirk. But memory is highly selective, and it is hard to judge whether the conditions they were subjected to were often as bad and as widespread as numerous interviews and accounts assert. The more philosophical, naturally stoical, or cynical witness passes over incidents that one more sensitive will dwell on. Leutnant Knoop, an unusual man who eventually became a Quaker, British and a male nurse, went through extreme emotions at the time of capture. A regular soldier, he had only recently been promoted in the field by Field-Marshal Rommel himself from sergeant. But when taken prisoner he denied his rank, more than half believing the desperate Nazi propaganda of the time that he would be interrogated and then shot. But his intense relief at surviving soon turned sour when they were all 'treated as the lowest criminals by the Americans'.

There were not many American GIs who had that frequent 'we're-all-in-it-together' feeling of the front-line Tommy towards the captured enemy. There was a world of difference in the very sound of the words 'Jerry' and 'Kraut'. The prescribed American attitude was, in fact, to be stern and superior; on the receiving end, it could seem punitive. Black soldiers were never like this. When Werner Düttmann was taken to an unwired collecting point in the rear he and his fellow-prisoners had literally to lie low for a day and a half. If they so much as got up to pee they were shot at. It was raining and there was no food for them. But at night black soldiers came across to them crawling so as not to be seen by their officers, bringing food, cigarettes and blankets. Such stories are not infrequent. Werner Kuwertz of the Waffen-SS, captured in the Ardennes, was taken to an American-run camp in France. 'The tents were on top of snow and we walked about at night to keep warm. We got blankets, built small stoves out of tin cans and were given our swill each morning and evening. It thawed and we were ankle-deep in mud. It must have been a sugar-beet field, as we were able to fish roots out of the mud and cook them in water. We lived in little tent communities, each fighting for its rights. Some died of dysentery and there were cases of frost-bite. The Poles in the watch-towers were pretty trigger-happy, and shot at us if we left our tents at night. Then a lot of black guards took over. They did what they could for us. They let us go out and gather firewood, and there was a hole in the fence where they put their potato peel and other rubbish, and we fished it out.'*

How can the feelings of this multitude of disarmed, despondent and mainly sullen men be adequately described or imagined? They were not only captured, they belonged to a soon to be defeated nation. They were not only defeated, they were hated. And finally they were humiliated. In 1945, after the war was over, they were handed the usual card to be filled in and sent through the Red Cross to tell their relatives that they were safe, wounded or un-wounded, in Allied hands. But when they read the card they found a word gratuitously added—to rub in that this was different from 1918. EIN MITGLIED DER GESCHLAGENEN WEHRMACHT SUCHT SEINEN NAECHSTEN ANGEHOERIGEN (A member of the *defeated* German army seeks his next-of-kin.) Why should the Allies, and especially the British who they liked to think were fair opponents, seek to humiliate them like this in front of their families? German pride had been deliberately insulted. It was sometimes debated whether it was even honourable to sign such a card. Not a few tore them up.

But any prisoner who thought for a moment was at least grate-ful he had been captured in the west and not by the Russians. If in the next weeks and months many had a bad time from hunger, cold and wet, they knew it was not much good protesting and talking about the Geneva Convention. The logistical problems of feeding not only the Allied armies but also, eventually, liberated populations on the verge of starvation, as in Holland, were immense; and many prisoners realised this. For Werner Düttmann it was a time when comradeship broke down. 'I had been living in

* The relationship between German POWs and black Americans would make an intriguing study, especially in view of the Nazi doctrines with which so many of the former were imbued. Dr Erich Leverkus remembers how in camps in the Southern States the blacks were socially inferior to the Germans, who nevertheless called them Mr So-and-So, which the whites never did. 'As guards, drivers and sometimes as co-workers in the fields they were always merry and positive towards us, which helped a lot.' Leverkus believes that they had a natural sympathy for fellow under-dogs. General von Ravenstein in his Canadian POW camp also found the black guards especially considerate and believed it was because they were anxious to prove that they were as civilised as other people. Both explanations are surely wide of the mark. A black American who served in France comments that his race are 'generally a very forgiving people'. Certainly most blacks have a more feeling nature than most whites; also it was not 'their war'. (Author.)

two worlds. On the one hand, there was the welcome end to the
Third Reich. Part of one wished to sweep the road clear for the
Allies to reach Berlin. On the other hand, we were fighting soldiers
who were trained to stop them. It was a schizophrenic situation.
Then we came to the transit camp, near Chartres I think. We'd
heard of the Morgenthau Plan and a rumour went round that we
would all be castrated; some believed it. The mood was one of panic
and anger—a sort of end-of-the-world feeling. Not enough food,
not enough latrines. Esprit de corps vanished. I felt I was among
beasts and was terribly depressed.' A catch-phrase became current
at this time: 'Comrades don't exist any more—they all fell at
Stalingrad.'

In the final phase the Wehrmacht were a disintegrating ruck.
As if by chemical reaction, the adhesive ceased to bind. For one
thing, not only had Hitler by the end thrown in schoolboys and
older men, but the Wehrmacht had tried to integrate an astonishing number of nationalities, far more than Napoleon's armies ever
had. In Toft Hall Camp, Knutsford, in 1947, where all odd bodies
were collected, the prisoners claimed to comprise no fewer than
thirty-eight nationalities, though the British only admitted to
twenty-six.[5] A bag of prisoners might contain Alsatians, Slovenes,
Hungarians and Rumanians, not all of whom were racial Germans
who volunteered or were conscripted, or could even speak German. There were Poles and Czechs of dubious nationality in 1939
who were forced into fighting for Hitler and were anxious to
redeem themselves and their country by putting on an Allied
uniform. There was the Indian Legion, and an Albanian Legion;
there were Danes and Dutchmen, Latvians, Estonians, Lithu-
anians, Hungarians, Rumanians, Belgians, French and Norwegians, largely to be found in the Waffen-SS, though many,
especially the Alsatians, were far from being volunteers. And—
the largest class—there were the Austrians. Hitler had made
sure that there would be no separatist movements within his
armies, forbidding his fellow-countrymen, whom he deeply dis-
trusted, to make up all-Austrian formations and having them
distributed throughout the *Wehrmacht*. When taken prisoner,
they were often the first to cut the swastika badge from their uniforms. Hans Freiburger remembers his disgust in the camp at
Enghien, months before the end of the war, when his Austrian
comrades-in-arms separated themselves off and were put in a
separate compound. These were the people who had gone wild

with enthusiasm when Hitler summoned them 'home into the Reich' in 1938. Now, encouraged by the British, they were deserting the ship. It was a bitter blow to his young, still ardently Nazi heart, the first sign of the disintegration of the German nation.

Lastly there were the Russians. Their presence in the *Wehrmacht* was already known to Allied Intelligence, but little was known about their background. They were no strangers to POW cages, being mostly survivors of the millions of prisoners taken by the Germans in the invasion of Russia. Four years later the stories of those who still survived would be picked up by Alexander Solzhenitzyn in *The Gulag Archipelago*: how in their typhus-ridden starvation camps they had boiled shoe leather to keep alive, while outside the camp gates smoke rose from a field kitchen; how there would be a bellyful of kasha for anyone who signed up to help the Germans.[6] Whether for this or because they genuinely hated Stalin and Communism, hundreds of thousands became *Wehrmacht* auxiliaries, being known as *Hiwis* (an abbreviation of *Hilfswillige*—willing to help). After the Stalingrad disaster they were joined in 1943 by fellow countrymen who had made one of the most amazing treks of modern times—the Cossacks, Caucasians and semi-nomad people from the Kalmuk Steppes who had naively welcomed the *Wehrmacht* as liberators from Stalin's oppression. To save their lives the Germans took these collaborators with them when they retreated. Across the frozen Sea of Azov, across the Ukraine they came with their women and children, priests, horses and cattle. The end of the trek for many would be Tolmezzo in North Italy.

Meantime, all the Russians who joined the Germans as POWs or refugees—there were a million all told—were being transformed into fighting units. They would become, they were told, the spearhead of a liberation army to free Russia from Bolshevism. When in late 1943 a small proportion deserted back to the Soviet armies, Hitler had most of them transferred to the West—some 800,000—where they could prove their worthiness against Russia's Allies. They came either as *Hiwis* or as *Osttruppen*. The former were attached to German units, six per company, or to Luftwaffe bases for menial tasks and lived a life of 'brutalised drudgery'. As to the *Osttruppen* there were no fewer than eighty-two battalions of them operationally employed mainly to plug gaps in the Atlantic Wall. The High Command may have used the Russians cynically and as a desperate remedy, but a few Russophile

Germans in the *Wehrmacht* and Civil Service did their best for them as commanders and welfare or liaison officers. The *Osttruppen* had their own staff officers with a headquarters at Lyons; they were sent on to attend German training courses and could receive German decorations. At the eleventh hour they were allowed their own medical and welfare organisation and, to maintain their morale, even a few Russian nurses wearing national dress. Then the invasion came.

Some of the *Ostbatallionen* fought well, some mutinied, some gave themselves up. By a month after D-Day 1,200 had been ferried across the Channel; by October 16,000. They were the strangest, hardiest and most tragic prisoners ever to come to English shores. The brief and unbelievably luxurious haven of a camp in Britain was only another twist of their fortune, another stage on the way to a dreadful fate. For they had fought against their country on the losing side. Nearly all were segregated away, the Soviet Military Mission being, naturally, given access to them; and so were some émigré groups. Nikolai Tolstoy has described their hopes, anguish and despair as they vacillated in their feelings between on the one hand fear and hatred of communism which their priests encouraged, and on the other a Slav fatalism and intense love of Russia which inclined them to want to return whatever the cost. In the event, they had no choice—even those who had never been Soviet citizens being remorselessly sent to Russia with the rest. Their authentic tragedy surely makes them victims, not so much of Yalta as of war itself and ultimately of Hitler's evil designs on their country.[7]

In this huge conglomeration of prisoners there was no longer cohesion, but by no means was there a total collapse of morale. The military hierarchies remained and the oath to the Führer; a certain solidarity would be recovered or reimposed by force in the POW camps. The German nation has a capacity for endurance, and the Prussian an almost Roman capacity to endure defeat tight-lipped and unflinching. The older ones also had been through it, if not so thoroughly, once before. Along with the paratroops, the toughest, the most defiant were the Waffen-SS. They stuck together in affliction, but among them now began a tortured debate about how it was they had reached such a bitter end of the road.* To the rest of the *Wehrmacht* they were an alien body, disliked

* See below p. 290.

for their arrogance and pretensions to an elite, though they won a grudging respect for fighting capacity and high morale. A sense of their dark presence pervaded any scene where they were. And they were very pervasive, for over a million had been enlisted in the Waffen-SS by the end of the war, 300,000 being killed. They should, however, be generally distinguished from the more sinister Allgemeine-SS, although both were integrated into one over-all system under Himmler. The latter were responsible for the horrors of the Concentration Camps; the former, though they took part in 'pacifications' and atrocities enough, were normal fighting units; and latterly a great many had been conscripted or conned into joining. Their fate as prisoners of war will receive a chapter on its own.

For almost all prisoners the ordeal of defeat was to be long drawn out. Most would be kept in uncertainty for nearly two years before they even knew the date of their release. For the present, it was a relief that heroics were over. Some lived for a while on simple gratitude at being a survivor, others saw their fate as the lesser evil. For Leutnant Wallmann, who had no chip on his shoulder, it was a matter of having 'learned as soldiers to make the best of small blessings in adverse circumstances'. If defeat prised open human weakness, the ones who survived best were those who found a strength in themselves which they did not think they possessed. But the sting was often at the tail end. As prisoners of war they might go through hunger, hardship, despair, acute anxiety about their families, but they were in one way isolated from the worst. It was not till they returned home that the full reality of belonging to a defeated and prostrate country hit most of them.

2

Transit

O Lord our God and God of our Fathers, we pray that, in this moment of victory, we may remember the legend handed down to us by our Doctors: that when after crossing of the Red Sea Miriam raised her soul in exultation and the angels at the throne of Thy Glory began to take up the refrain, Thou didst rebuke them saying: 'What! My children are drowning and you would sing!'

Hebrew Prayer For Our Enemies[8]

The stream of prisoners backwards along the path of the liberators reached its first peak during the Battle of Normandy. By mid-July 1944, 49,000 had been ferried to Britain; by the end of the year 145,000; by the end of the war 200,000. Until more camps were built and the Italian prisoners of war were repatriated, the rate had to slow down. As a result the eleven British-run camps in Belgium were over-full, reaching in the summer of 1945 a total of 200,000, although the inspectors of the International Red Cross estimated that their capacity was not much over 150,000. Yet, fantastic as it may sound, those held at this time in Belgium and Britain combined only comprised about one tenth of the grand total of 3,700,000 German prisoners and 'surrendered enemy personnel' who in one way or another were in British hands during 1945. But of these only half a million were detained as POW after 1945. With important exceptions the rest were released in Germany, many in time for the harvest of 1945.*

At first the British and American governments worked on a fifty-fifty basis and for the first months after D-Day half the POWs taken in France were sent across the Atlantic, half across the Channel, regardless of who captured them. But in Britain the totally unexpected numbers put a huge strain on all departments involved. War Office documents of the time show a continual concern that under the circumstances it would not be possible to

* POW statistics are discussed in the Appendix.

2

fulfil the requirements of the Geneva Convention.[9] Accommodation was greatly extended, but largely through a process known as 'wintering' tented accommodation. Since this and the maintenance and building of camps were not the province of the War Office but of the Office of Works, it is likely that bureaucratic delays held matters up. In any case the British government felt itself unable to keep to the original fifty-fifty arrangement with the USA which in the end accepted no fewer than 175,000 extra Germans who were held 'on the account of the UK as British prisoners'. The return of these men to Britain and not to their homes in 1946 later caused much ill feeling.

Typical of those shipped to America was Paul Seufert. After his surrender in the snowy Ardennes and traumatic crossing of the border from Belgium, his first night in France was in the dungeon of an old fort without straw or blankets. The next day goods waggons took them to an empty factory building at Namur. He had his first interrogation, registration, medical examination, the taking of finger-prints and warm food, the feeding of thousands passing off efficiently and quietly. The prisoners could wash and shave and begin to gather self-respect again. This lasted two days; then came a further long rail journey to Attichy on the Aisne. It was dark as they panted from the station uphill for an hour. Going through the gates they were soon in a tented camp, ankle deep in mud—it was still January. The little straw available was wet or damp. With one blanket available for four men, they lay pressing on each other like herrings for protection from the cold. There were 8,000 prisoners in this camp, with more arriving continuously. Hungry and freezing, Paul Seufert remained eight days, and once more was packed into a convoy of lorries. When it slowed down through Rheims, to his relief both the Gothic pile of the cathedral looked intact and the inhabitants almost ignored them. The camp was in the docks beside a big warehouse. Work parties were sent in to the dirty work of sorting out waggon loads of filthy uniforms, blankets, coats and equipment of all kinds. There was a smell of rot and decay, for most of the uniforms had come off dead or wounded, often with blood on them. The old hands in the camp had cornered the softer jobs in the laundry, tailoring and saddlery section. A high rate of work was maintained by the overseers—Poles and Czechs in American uniforms—with a continual 'Let's go' on their lips. Prisoners, weakened with hunger and cold, kept collapsing and a doctor would pronounce them to be Unfit 1, or Unfit 2—available for light duties or for none. There was one area where jumbled piles of steel helmets, German and Allied, had to be sorted out, along with cooking utensils, cutlery and flasks of all the warring nations. There were rusty rifles, sidearms and parts of machine guns and even occasionally live cartridge cases. On one occasion, when Seufert was off sick, a trip mine which had been flung among the equipment exploded, causing several deaths. Posted back to Attichy, Seufert dreaded his return but found the place transformed. There were metalled roads through the camp. Food and accommodation were unrecognisably better. He was put to work in the forest of Compiègne as a woodsman, so lightly guarded that flight would have been easy. Ten days later, he was in a long train of cattle-trucks, bound for America.

There was a marked difference between American-run and British-run camps, as was discovered by Paymaster Karl Hildebrand, who kept his amused eyes wide open. He had bad luck, as he succeeded in reaching his home-town in South Germany just before the Americans arrived. On a house-search they discovered his uniform hanging up on a door. 'Where is this man? Find him!' He was hauled out of a nearby pub, made to put his uniform on again and sent to Kreuznach, one of the American *Rheinwiesenlager* —giant open air camps set up during the spring and summer of 1945 on the banks of the Rhine. They often had something of a wild-west atmosphere. 'I was staggered,' remembers Hildebrand. 'German soldiers going on guard duty are given so many rounds and if they cannot account for every one, they are put on a charge. The trigger-happy American fills his pocket with ammo as he goes on duty and shoots it into the air or at a tin. *Freude am Schiessen*— he just likes shooting! Empty cartridge cases everywhere. They used to shoot right across the camp at a target on the hillside, and one or two of us got hit by ricochets. We were pretty short of food and very short of water. But when a German canteen worker had a baby in the camp, she was completely deluged with bars of chocolate. The blacks behaved towards us best. They didn't just take your watch—they offered you money. "How many jewels?" they'd say. "Twenty stones; OK, twenty dollars." '

At Kreuznach there were a lot of SS. A good few managed to get civilian clothes, slip away and start a new life under-cover. Everyone went through the arms-up parade to discover whether they had the tell-tale blood-group mark tattooed under the left bicep. Anyone with a scar or even a mole near this position was suspected of trying to get rid of the brandmark. At Kreuznach Hildebrand found a general levelling down. 'I saw one lieutenant-colonel who had taken off his insignia, so much as to say "We are all democrats now". At the next camp I saw him with it sewn on again. This was at Rheinberg near Wesel; the journey there in a cattle truck took a whole week. All we had was beetroot and a large tin of sugar! At Kreuznach we were once given five pounds of cheese and no bread. *Sehr amerikanisch*! The British had just taken over Rheinberg from the Americans and were bringing in a bit of order, getting frame huts erected and so on. The Commandant made us a speech. "I am now the manager of a hotel with 12,000 non-paying guests." He gave out that prisoners should salute officers of the detaining power who were equal or superior in rank. When some of us did it very vigorously to him, he was delighted, and said to the first few "Release him at once. He can go home."* Provided we brought back some little attaché case which he paid for, we were allowed out on parole into the town of Wesel. It was May 1945, and there were still goods in the shops. He trusted us as gentlemen!' Paymaster Hildebrand eventually reached the forest camp at Jabbecke. 'We could hear the steamer horns at Ostend. The camp was well-run, very *korrekt*, the food was all right, but the red-tape and "bull"—three times as bad as ours. A hammer was missing and we were paraded four times and searched. We had to give up our knives and forks—too dangerous for POWs to carry! Soon we got a whole new set—Sheffield this time, much better than ours! One commandant got a big shallow hole to be dug in the middle of the camp—to hold water for fire-hoses; the next had it filled in as a parade area.' Prisoners rarely know the why and wherefore of what happens around them or to them; they feel they are being moved about from camp to camp by unseen forces. And they have no right to be told. From the point of view of the victors the more distance between the out-siders, themselves, and the insiders the better. There was, too, the strict non-fraternisation order.

Camp 2231 at Enghien, fifteen miles south-east of Brussels, held 20,000 men, including several thousand Hungarians. For the Adjutant, Captain J. A. Dent, it was just a job of work to do. The British staff comprised eight officers and thirty NCOs; the guards were Belgian and the internal administration of the camp was entirely in the hands of the Germans, except as regards punish-

* A nice but unlikely story.

ments. 'The prisoners,' Captain Dent remembers, 'were well-
behaved and subdued. Apart from boredom, I would say that their
lot was uncomfortable, but not unlike the life they had been living
for the last five years. It was a tented camp, probably crowded in
the bell tents, but tolerable enough. Medical wards, cook-houses,
latrines and washing facilities were about the same as in the British
army. The weather was fine, rations for the prisoners arrived
promptly, small work parties were sent out each day to help with
road building, gardening, clearing rubble, etc. in the local town
and its environs. The attitude of the British of all ranks was
entirely proper, it seems to me. There was no pronounced anti-
German feeling; rather "these were the sods who had buggered
up our lives over the past five years and they could stay prisoners
till kingdom come, but they'd better continue to behave themselves"—that was the general feeling.' There was some small
trouble with the Belgian guards who used to go black-marketing,
one suicide, one successful attempt in three escapes, one charge of
homosexuality against a medical orderly and an occasional theft
between the prisoners. The Commandant was unimaginative, but
a character. There was little crime, but whenever an offender was
brought to him, relates another officer, Captain Tunbridge, 'he
always gave the maximum penalty, twenty-eight days, and always
made the same identical speech to the defendant, which went:
"Stealing is a despicable crime, but when you steal from a comrade
that is the lowest form, and the reason that your nation has been
defeated is that you are a low-down, despicable race." And all for
pinching a bar of soap!'

Two worlds which barely impinged on each other—but
Enghien was one of the better camps, and the British remoteness
didn't matter. At Overisje, some twenty miles east across the
battlefield of Waterloo, it did, with shocking results later in the
year.* But if already in the spring of 1945 it was an unpleasant,
over-large camp and difficult to run, outsiders were not idle. Karl
Gursky, the paymaster-pastor who had been allowed by the
Canadians to enjoy a last dinner after capture in a private house,
remembers how, when the prisoners were floundering about in
the mud, some lorries driven by the Belgian YMCA turned up,
stacked with duck-boards. A major made a speech of thanks, saying he had been a member of the YMCA in his youth and how
much this act of Christian neighbourliness meant to them. For the

* See below p. 31.

good Gursky it was a 'sermon without words'. What they did not
know, and what the British staff did not know, was that the duck-
boards had been liberated from a British Forces depot. An English
member of the YMCA whose job was the welfare of British troops
had obtained and quietly diverted them through his Belgian colleagues to what he felt was a greater need.

Vilvoorde was a very volatile camp and the extremest rumours
prevailed. One was apparently filtered in by Belgian Communists
through parties which were sent outside to work: namely, that
such prisoners had a right to protest at being used as sweated
labour. The Communists and Stalin, who was all behind the
German workers, would put things right. Soon could be heard
booming through the camp massed male voices in a new version
of an old refrain:

> Es geht alles vorüber, es geht alles vorbei
> in einigen Wochen macht Stalin uns frei.
> (Everything passes, everything goes by—in a few
> weeks Stalin will set us free.)

The British authorities got worried and asked for officers to go
round and counter this propaganda, promising them in a somewhat panicky manner early repatriation.[10] At the very same time,
seventy miles away, a nineteen-year-old lance-corporal, Bernhard
Harms, was learning a very different refrain which spread around
the camp at Zedelgem:

> . . . und wir tragen unser Schicksal mit Geduld
> Denn an der ganzen Scheisse sind wir selber Schuld.

which might be rendered:

> Let's put up with our fate without a fuss
> The bloody mess we're in is only due to us.

'It was,' says Harms, later a Studien-Direktor, 'a spontaneous try
at coping with the sobering end of the war. Changes of heart
were taking place and older men rummaging in their pre-Nazi
past. It had nothing to do with either Christian penitence or the
then much debated question of Germany's collective guilt. But
this attitude didn't last long when we realised we weren't going
home for years.' Harms went on to spend the hard winter at
Jabbecke where he, like everyone else, suffered from hunger, boredom, homesickness and disgust at the way the German camp staff

grew fat and the rest were gradually reduced to skin and bones. But he also managed to attend and pass with a high rating a course in the youth education compound.

As more and more prisoners went over to Britain, the Belgian camps were kept topped up. Some arrived from America in 1946 and were either handed over to the Belgians or kept for a while in the British-run camps before joining the labour force in Britain. Some comprised the large remnants from North Germany who were not cleared for early release. Cadet Tremmel and Karl Schneider have grim memories of a journey in January from Holstein, in cattle trucks without even straw to keep them warm. When the Salzgitter camp was dissolved in December many of the 2,000 prisoners, who were largely SS, imagined they would be released. Instead the Commandant told them that, to his regret, they were being sent to an unknown destination. They were put into trucks under heavy guard, fifty per waggon. At Cologne they learned that the destination was Belgium and, as the train was leaving the city, they began to smash planks, break out of the waggons and jump to the ground. The guards opened fire and restored order. When the train reached Berchem there were said to be fifty missing. The large contingent, full of angry and violent men, was therefore kept at the double for the two or three miles to the camp. The civil population threw stones and bottles at them and, once in the camp, the Belgian guards belaboured them with rifle butts. Among the Belgian guards at this camp some of the Germans recognised former comrades in the Waffen-SS Viking Division.

Sagas of long journeys cooped up in cattle trucks and goods-waggons come again and again into prisoners' stories. Some scored the ordeal up against the victors, others accepted it as the fortune of war. How many of them have since become aware—they could hardly have known at the time—that they were being transported in waggons possibly used not so long before for a very different purpose: going east and not west, still more crowded and stinking, with guards infinitely more ruthless, and speaking the German language, waggons from which at the end of the journey the dead would be removed and the pathetic living herded more coldly than cattle to a grisly segregation and selection? For these very waggons might once have carried a cargo of despised, derided and doomed men, women and children: Jewish people being transported to the death camps.

'The stern of the landing-craft opened like a barn door, the hold filled up rapidly with grey figures. I'd always wanted to travel and see England, and it was happening without cost to myself, and I was being removed from the theatre of war, from the hellish fighting in Normandy. In Southampton we were received with tea and pastries and soon after herded into heated passenger trains on the way to Kempton Park.'

For many prisoners the hoped-for journey to Britain (or America) was an adventure in itself. It would be by landing-craft, steamer, freighter and sometimes, for the wounded or a VIP, by air. Many, as they stepped on board, recalled the marching song of 1940, 'Wir fahren gegen Engelland' (We're sailing against England.)* At Ostend someone at the quay had a record of it and played it ironically as the Germans trooped into the Liberty Ship that took them to Harwich. Horst Woetzel, who appreciates the English sense of humour, still chuckles about it. Every kind of soldier, he remembers, was crammed into the hold, all dirty from the red rust, all thirsty. He observed with amazement how officers, real militarist types, were at once prepared to exchange their decorations for cigarettes. After the reception in Belgium he was strangely moved by the cool matter-of-fact way the military and the harbour workers at Harwich didn't stare at them. Pastor Halver, coming by a different route, found a less favourable contrast. 'At Dieppe they threw stones at us, at Southampton they looked through us as if we were glass.' Was the reception so different or was it the same scene through different eyes? The painter, Karl-Josef Huber, remembers Southampton because a Frenchwoman screamed at them, 'You've been drinking all our champagne, dirty Boches!', which the crowd took good-humouredly; Peter Brugger remembers it because he saw for the first time ordinary working women wearing painted lips and finger-nails during the day—unthinkable in Nazi Germany or besieged Europe. Willi Wolf was positively shocked when he saw a big-bellied woman with a baby in her arms and a cigarette in her mouth. The next stage of the journey—the prisoners could hardly believe it—was always in a passenger train with upholstered seats and, in winter, heated. On occasions, though, prisoners were marched from the boat in a double column which divided in dif-

* This rousing song from the First World War remained a favourite with the *Wehrmacht* long after Operation Sea Lion was finally cancelled in 1941.

ferent directions. Friends who were side by side never met again.
Werner Düttmann crossed in a flat-bottomed landing craft through
a storm. 'A lot of us were so miserable we wanted it to sink. There
was a Russian next to me who took off his cossack hat to be sick
into. And then at Southampton we were put into a train with
tables in the carriages, and English soldiers came along and put a
bowl of porridge in front of each of us. I was in heaven!'

The wounded had the best of treatment and transport, being
handled alongside the Allied wounded. When the irrepressible
Prussian veteran, Colonel Borcherdt, whose vanity was satisfied
when he was able to surrender to an officer of the Household
Brigade, was routed onwards, he was all eyes for the quality of the
opposition. 'In the ambulance we passed Montgomery's Army on
the way east. My God, what a splendidly uniform lot of vehicles
they had! With no anxiety from the air, they were driving along
as if it were peace time.' Slung up in a hammock and with a
maquis guard who was sick most of the way, he was air-lifted
from Brussels to Caen. Again, he was amazed at the absence of
air-raid precautions and at the way the traffic control, without any
officer on duty to shout orders, proceeded with perfect smooth-
ness. The uniformed women drivers impressed the old warrior too
—and from this he gathered that the English had mobilised themselves more for total war than the Germans. At tented general
field hospital No. 107 the food was excellent, the white bread a
matter for astonishment; so was an English lieutenant who turned
out next morning to be a Scot and, when he put on his kilt, had
nothing on underneath. Borcherdt was taken out to a Dutch hospital ship at the Mulberry harbour, and lay incongruously beside
a wretched *Hiwi* all the way over. At Tettern he was put in a
wheelchair, his wounded leg throbbing and stinking, for interrogation. 'Of course I gave them no military information, but I
did say that a war between England and Germany was madness.
"You don't know the Russians," I told them. That didn't go
down well.'

Rumours, as we have seen, were puffed up like balloons; they
were sustained by fear of the worst, which Nazi propaganda had
been working at assiduously. The eighteen-year-old commando who
was sure the Canadians were about to shoot him when they made
him walk towards the light, later lay in a shed at Dunkirk waiting
for embarkation. An officer nurse (Queen Alexandra's Auxiliaries)
walked between the rows in which Allied and German stretcher

2*

cases were mingled and put a tin of fifty Players and a bar of chocolate on each man's chest. He tried to draw her attention, terrified that he would be charged with false possession or misrepresentation. One of the orderlies brought him his uniform, as he could be a walking case, but then an English doctor came and said, 'Put his pyjamas on over his uniform.' This was done and he was carried on a stretcher tucked round with a blanket. It was being said that Belgians were tipping prisoners into the water as they carried them on board. He presumed that he was in pyjamas so that they wouldn't be able to tell him apart from a British soldier. There was another possible explanation: perhaps it had happened once, or it had happened by accident, launching the fearful rumour. A sensitive man, suffering from delayed shock, could have a paranoiac fear of being such a victim. On the other hand, the Europe of 1945 had become brutalised. Old scores could be paid off 'by mistake on purpose' and there would be no investigation, no names taken. War is the father of viciousness as well as the mother of lies.

The last big contingent of prisoners to arrive at Southampton were the occupation troops from the Channel Isles who held out from the invasion of Normandy to the end of the war, no attempt being made to invade the islands. Islanders and Germans endured a winter of mounting starvation. When the British sent, by a Swedish ship, a food parcel for each inhabitant, Colonel Schwettar upheld the agreement by which the food was for the inhabitants alone, and he was obeyed. As a result, among those who arrived up the Solent in mid-May were many hundreds of severely undernourished German soldiers who were sent to Naburn Hospital Camp, York, originally set up for the Americans. Here, reports Karl Heinz Knoop, a German staff of ninety doctors, orderlies and nurses, under the excellent Colonel Wild, RAMC, nursed them back to strength; but some three hundred and sixty could not be made fit for work and were repatriated.[11]

The extremes set a mark on any collective experience. The 200,000 who had to spend the winter of 1945–6 in Belgium can never forget their ordeal.[12] The capacity of the eleven camps, nearly all tented, was (as later admitted) only 150,000 and a good proportion of the prisoners were either over fifty or under eighteen, from Hitler's last desperate call-up. Others arrived weak and hungry from badly-run American Rhine-bank camps. Karl

Schneider, transported from the reserved military area in Schleswig in January, remembers Berchem for the cold and wet, along with a severe shortage of drinking and washing water. The daily ration could be as little as a tin of watery soup, tea and two slices of bread. The men grew beards and had faces like Kaffirs from the smoke from the little stoves they made out of tin cans and the lights in their crowded tents when fuel was available. At roll-calls they had to introduce themselves to their mates, so unrecognisable did they become. Tin cans were also rammed down into the water-logged clay soil to make a road through the camp mud. But the edges of the metal wrenched all the nails from their boots; so they had to develop a comical walk rather like storks to avoid this happening. Even Berchem was better than another tented camp—the notorious Overisje. Here there were 60,000 men in twenty compounds, with Belgian guards and British guard-dogs round the four-and-a-half mile perimeter. In the autumn of 1945 the inspectors from the International Red Cross made a cautious report indicating inadequacies, especially of water. In December and January two hundred died of dysentery, after which a sharper report was put in. The reduction of the ration from three to two thousand calories had come with the cold weather; two blankets per man and the limited coal provided were cruelly inadequate to combat cold and damp in the tents sunk a foot into the ground. Men didn't have a change of clothing all winter, and their underclothing turned into tatters. Some broke mentally; Cadet Elmar Tremmel remembers, 'We had no proper kit and our boots were disintegrating. All we could think and talk about was food—the menus we would eat one day. People even got crazed and started giving away rations. There had to be an order not to eat grass. POWs arrived from America with plenty of cigarettes—if we took two puffs of one we had to lie down. When we were shown pictures of the concentration camps we at least could say, "They had huts to live in, we only have tents." ' (At this time the horrors of the K2 were part of the 're-education' syllabus used by the Allies—see below, Chapter Six.)

Tremmel was one of the 79,000 who went across to Britain from the British camps in Belgium between March and August 1946. On board the SS *Aarhus* he acted as interpreter for one of the decks. 'A huge staff-sergeant of marines looked me up and down and said, "How old are you?" I told him, "Nineteen". "Good Lord, you're only a youngster!" He was so shocked at my condition that there were tears in his eyes as he spoke. The British brought us food on the quiet; "officially we are not allowed to give it you, but we'll leave it here." At Tilbury we waited for the goods train. They almost had to push us into the coaches that pulled up alongside the quay. This was our train, with cushioned seats! Packets of biscuits and cups of tea! Luxury of the highest order! We heard afterwards that officers in the Belgian camps had been court-martialled for selling food and clothing on the black market.'

This was not exactly true, but articles and letters in the press and questions in Parliament about the shocking state of affairs did impress POWs with good will as an example of democracy at work, even if slowly. Early in the year conditions had been improved in the worst camps with more blankets and fuel being provided and extra food for the sick. But this did not prevent the death toll from malnutrition, exposure and disease rising to 565 by May. The full scale of the suffering only came into the open when some of the early 'white' repatriates to Germany who passed through the Belgian camps talked to a correspondent of the Observer. At the same time MPs in Britain heard about the severe undernourishment of POWs arriving in Britain. The Minister of War was pressed to investigate. Six weeks later explanations were given in Parliament. The main fault had been with high officers who left the administration of supplies to inexperienced juniors. Without proper supervision from above, these men had been careless about sending in correct indentures. Euphoria at the end of the war, frequent shifting of officers partly due to demobilisation and an unprecedented number of prisoners led to what the War Office admitted to be 'an unpardonable contravention of our duties under the Geneva Convention'. A contributory factor was that on top of the generally reduced rations the German camp staff, while eating well themselves, were selling off part of them on the Belgian black market. Whether British connivance at this —there were of course some bad types in back areas of the army— was hushed up or not is hard to say. But it could be that somewhere along the line the policy of remote control allowed a certain willingness to 'let the Germans stew in their own juice for a while' to creep in here and there.

There was something of this attitude for a while at Neuengamme, to which Captain Tunbridge was posted from Enghien as adjutant in October 1945. (Neuengamme was one of the former

Konzentrationslager which the British turned into civilian internment camps.) Here conditions were similar to Vilvoorde with men
dying of hunger oedoema and many suicides. The British Commandant didn't really want to know, while the Assistant Director
of Medical Services at Hamburg, a colonel in the Medical Corps,
was a Hun-hater and knowingly prevented the truth coming out.
Tunbridge tells how, though only adjutant, he managed to get
directly through to Sir Evelyn Barker, the British Corps Commander in Schleswig-Holstein, who immediately visited Neuengamme. Next day all necessary supplies were delivered.[13] Captain
Tunbridge's comment thirty years later is pertinent: 'The British
hate injustice and there is usually someone who feels strongly
enough to act, because it is never *policy* to treat people inhumanely.
How different it was in the Third Reich when the policy *was* to be
brutal. Given the weak, unfeeling side of human nature, it is easy
to see how Belsens arise.'

Genuine diaries of POWs in Britain for the early stages at least
seem to be rare. It was against regulations to have one when captured as it might betray military secrets; so they were often destroyed. If outspoken, a diary could even lead to the writer's death
if it fell into the hands of the super-Nazis. Prisoners also feared
they might be confiscated on posting to another camp. Consequently diaries often turn out to be a 'late work', written from
memory or from notes taken at the time. The journal of Father
Josef Jansen which covers nearly four years of captivity belongs
to this last category, composed after his return home under the
title *Rabauken, Bakaleuten und Menschen 'Guten Willens' in West
England 1944 bis 1948* which might be rendered as 'Toughs,
Creepers and Men of Good-will in West England 1944–1948'. Its
value lies less in objectivity than in the way a Catholic priest from
the Lower Rhine identifies himself with the fate and many of the
views of the ordinary *Landser*.

Described later by an English friend as a short man of average
build with a smile all over his face, Father Jansen was serving
when captured as a corporal clerk in the Bakery Company of the
325 Infantry Division and also as a deputy divisional chaplain.
(This was the covert way by which the High Command arranged
for the presence of chaplains in the field, which was not permitted
by Hitler in the latter part of the war.) He ministered as required
to three SS Divisions for burials and occasional confessions. Being

a man with a certain authority, he was also used to protect the French population from molestation by the German troops, and to smooth out any 'incidents'. He had moreover had foisted on him responsibility for political education of his company: since it consisted mainly of middle-aged men, it was felt they would stand him, but not any Nazi indoctrination. In the early part of the war, Father Jansen had had to do service with the Landesschütz (a kind of Home Guard) who provided guards in prisoner of war camps in his neighbourhood. He had thus gained a close impression of the conditions of various captives who were by no means always well treated. The English, he says, were comparatively well off because of the Red Cross parcels, but he felt real pity for the Russians. Such a man was Father Josef Jansen, who now became prisoner himself.

After the great tank battle at Falaise our division, still 800 strong, reached the Brussels area on 2 September, being routed via Antwerp to Denmark to refit. During a night march from Ternath, where our train had been severely bombed, my legs gave way from nervous exhaustion. I dropped out, accompanied by Lance-Corporal Jaeger, a salesman in civvie life. We spent the night in a harvest field which was strafed at dawn by low-flying aircraft. Our own transport, hurrying to catch up the retreat, refused to stop any more. Though the Belgian population had already beflagged their houses for the liberation, they were very decent to us, offering us coffee and showing us on our way. Some others soon stopped us and told us not to go further as the bridges were destroyed and Brussels had been evacuated [by the Germans] the previous day. We certainly had nothing to fear from the English and Americans, but much from the resistance fighters, who, without waiting to find out whether they were armed or not, were blasting any uniformed Germans off the road. (We had lost all our equipment when the train was bombed near Ternath.) I would have found refuge with a priest, but I felt responsible for my companion and did not do so. What with the enemy flags and the curious glances of the locals it was like picking our way through a minefield. We tried putting ourselves under the protection of the Belgian police, but they insisted they were a civilian body. '*Met uw verdommde Krieg hebbe e nix to dun,*' they said in Flemish, but of course if we as civilians had any special wishes . . . well, that was asking! Since

the Normandy battle we'd been dry, so we said we'd like a glass
of good Brussels beer and a Butterbrot. '*Dat zult je hebben*', and
immediately we were brought just that from a near-by pub. It
might be our last meal on earth, we thought, as the gendarmerie
couldn't protect us any more. In half an hour, however, we
were fetched in a car by the Young Christian Workers' Union
and declared prisoners.

The treatment at the Vilvoorde and Brussels camps was very
friendly. The Belgians were somewhat embarrassed as to what
to do with so many prisoners, and they themselves were suffering from food shortage. At the Vilvoorde Agricultural School
we were given some soft fruit, then at the assembly camp at
Halle we were roughly sorted out according to place of origin.
The population flocked to stare and make faces and throat-
cutting gestures at us, as though they owed this to their new
masters, with priests, too, unfortunately taking part. Towards
evening a thousand of us were taken back into the city to the
Ecole Militaire where we were herded into the lecture halls
between the tables and benches. The commandant, Major
Vanhooven—I was the only priest he could discover in the confused mass of prisoners—greeted me as someone who could
give the prisoners the spiritual succour he presumed they
needed. He regretted I could only have a room with an armchair and table, and a carpet to lie on, which I had to share with
a dozen others who revealed themselves as Alsatians wanting
to have nothing more to do with us Germans. I was content
enough, as the major, who was full of the best intentions towards his camp, promised to come and see me daily. He seemed
to have a horror of the bulk of the prisoners—mostly SS. But
he put a sergeant at my disposal, a young Belgian of the Young
Christian Workers who used to come and chat happily in our
room with his musket, a kind of sporting gun, between his
knees. This sergeant had access to all parts of the camp and I
got him to take me to the sick and wounded, most of them
youngsters in the SS or the Work Corps. The SS men's first
question was 'Will I be shot?' With the sergeant's help I could
ease their fears at least as far as the Belgians were concerned,
but we would soon be handed over to regulars and our fate
decided then. I could remind a few of God and religion and
even heard a few confessions.

Quite a number, however, were anyway at permanent war

with the 'papists' and rejected me completely. One group of SS officers, who had probably heard of me through the Belgian commandant, asked for me to come, and I was allowed to visit them, though they were under the closest possible guard. Windows and doorways were blocked up with boards and barbed wire, I had to go past three guards with sten guns, and there were machine guns outside both windows. There in a room which had no furniture were standing five men, a major, a captain, a doctor and two lieutenants, all in the SS. 'Herr Pfarrer, what right have they to keep us like this? We're regulars! We're not allowed even to speak to each other!' They had no sense of any guilt and no charge had been made against them. They were not in the least interested in spiritual succour, only wanted someone to speak to. 'Are they going to shoot us—then why not at once?' Two of them were very frightened indeed of dying, and I could reassure them all a little. After all, I was a prisoner myself, though the Belgians were associating with me in a friendly manner on the basis of our common faith. The prior of the Dominicans in Brussels visited me almost daily, bringing books, combs, soap and such things to our room. He found me a small mauve woollen cross to sew on to my tunic, and a portable Mass-set to replace the one I'd lost in Normandy, though two days later an English padre who was going up to the front took it off me. Commandant Vanhooven at this became all the more friendly, letting me celebrate Mass in a church close by, a single guard taking me there and back, after I had breakfasted with the local priest. Finally, he was concerned to get me a decent uniform and cloak to replace my own, torn and dirty from the hedges and wire of Normandy, and had me taken with some others to an old German clothing store, but it turned out to be one for women air force auxiliaries. But it was his goodwill that counted.

When finally their lordships the British turned up to take us over, the commandant had a long personal talk with me. He was a fine man and a good Catholic, had twice escaped from German captivity himself, the last time via Sweden to England. He tried to console me over the state of my country—perhaps I'd have the opportunity to see foreign lands, England, Canada, Australia or some such place! He would gladly go and greet my relatives if he had the chance; the same promise was made to my Luxembourg sergeant who seriously wanted to smuggle me

out of the camp, as he couldn't bear to see me mixed up with all
those SS, Russians and Poles. But he breathed a sigh of relief,
and so did the Dominican prior, when I made it clear that it was
my duty to stay and minister to my comrades in captivity.

We were now taken over by a Canadian regiment, the Hamp-
shires, a very raw soldiery. They at once removed our money,
fountain pens, watches and anything else of worth and took us
in goods-trucks to Enghien without any breakfast or food on
the way. There was the usual hostile performance from the
population. We were standing herded tightly against each other,
and very thirsty, when the train suddenly halted and there were
our Canadian guards sitting on the roof and *selling* water to the
prisoners: one beaker-full, five Belgian francs. This enabled us
to establish that only the non-German prisoners—Poles,
Russians, *Hiwis* etc. had money. We Germans had none as it
had been taken off us. So, according to plan, we went on being
thirsty. After three days at Enghien we were transported to
Dieppe, where the rations were minimal; still worse, there was
almost no water. We hadn't yet been registered and were just a
mass, thousands of us. For a day and night sixty of us were
locked in a cattle truck, half of us being Poles who had a sensible
spokesman; straight away he and I agreed on a demarcation
line across the middle of the waggon, though we would on
occasion visit each other's territory. For instance, the Poles
bored a hole through the side of the waggon as a loo, and let us
reach this 'hole in Poland' along a 'corridor'. Our rations—
corned beef, biscuit and water—were shared out after negotia-
tions in which each side was allowed the veto. Our food thus
happily lasted till evening. But then there was nothing more till
the following evening. As a Catholic priest I was respected by
the Poles, but there was no general conversation between us.
By dawn we were rolling through the Normandy countryside.
The train stopped now and then, but the Canadian guards
wouldn't let us climb down. The population, which had always
been quite friendly to Germans, took pleasure in putting one
over on the British guards by passing fruit to us without the
guards noticing. Whole baskets and sacks were emptied through
the high ventilating slots in the trucks.

We were amazed at the quick recovery of the railway system
since our retreat. At one station I succeeded in getting into conversation with a French railwayman and handing him a message

to be passed on via a French family I knew. He promised to do this—though he would have to wait for six to eight weeks because of censorship, and because there was still no postal or railway communication for civilians.

On the second day at midday we were marched uphill to the Dieppe camp through an abusive, spitting population, which had been singled out two years before at the time of the Dieppe raid for praise for their friendliness to Germans. Well, we now knew what they really felt. The camp was a huge area surrounded by minefields—escapers and animals that ventured into them demonstrated the dangers. Beyond, there was barbed wire fencing which also criss-crossed the camp. The food (we had to wait twenty-four hours after our arrival till the following evening) was good as to quality, but meagre in volume—six biscuits per man for two to three days. In addition, a teaspoonful of jam or honey, a dessertspoon of sugar and a slice of tinned meat or cheese, all to last two to three days. Worst was the water ration—a mugful to last three days. Most of us began to form tent communities, and kept the water in two cooking canteens, one for drinking, the other for washing for all eight men. We had been searched again at the camp entrance and, by showing the guards a rosary or family photos, some had been allowed to keep a razor and blade, and perhaps a comb. Conversation with the prisoners was strictly forbidden to the guards. There were not enough tents for everyone by far. The September nights were cold and the second half of the month rainy. I had neither cloak nor blanket. Many dug themselves fox-holes and showed others how to do it. Stealing went on of course and somewhere there was always a brawl going on, or someone was being beaten up. Later on, the English liked to remark 'The German is the German's worst enemy'. Thieves and ration-cheats, when caught, were mercilessly pilloried by their comrades and made to march through the camp with placards round their necks. As night approached, 'closing time' was called out by one of the guards and a burst of machine-gun fire streaked across the camp one metre above our heads. If anyone got in the way it was his fault. (Also, if rough-houses got out of hand the machine-gun opened up. If there hadn't been a great shortage of water, we would probably have got doused with a power hose.) We took note of this, and went about doubled up around this time. The Canadian soldiers who, except on duty, were very keen on

barter—souvenirs exchanged for chocolate or cigarettes—
proved to be real cattle-drovers when we had to be moved,
using sticks, whips and pistol shots. These last were at least in
the air, but they made the more exhausted of us crumple up.
When my tent mates were incompatible or drizzle penetrated
the canvas, I used to get up at night with a few others and try
to keep warm by walking or running round the compound.
After a few circuits, one was dog-tired, found a place to collapse into and slept as long as one could.

Now and then, attempts were made at roll-calls to sort the
prisoners according to age, which led to rumours that those
capable of work were being handed over to the Russians. In the
end the German NCOs pulled things together, that is, the
genuine sergeants. Quite a few had falsified their paybooks and
had got themselves 'promoted', but none obeyed and few
believed them. They got us into groups of a hundred, which
eased supervision and the roll-call. The day passed with telling
stories, dirty jokes, queuing for water, barter or improving the
accommodation. Chaplains were neither recognised as such nor
required. But there was an emergency field-hospital and
dressing-station in one corner with some German medical
orderlies. The separating out of officers and men meant there
were no doctors in our compound—a real grievance.

Everyone was hoping to cross to England and I joined the
fortunate ones on 31 October 1944. First, another body search:
combs, razor-blades, knives—everything else had gone—and
we were marched down to the harbour of Dieppe and waited
from before noon to evening for a landing craft that was bringing men on leave back from England, and was to take us over.
We got our first slices of snow-white bread—we didn't believe
our eyes! (Later in England, when we had a slice of this bread
morning and evening, we found it didn't agree with the German
stomach, and our camp baker was allowed to mix in rye as
well.) There were Poles on the foredeck, we were at the stern.
No one was allowed to leave the hold. Our guard was kindly.
When I said I might be sea-sick, he allowed me to reach my
head over the edge and kept a look-out. Then he gave me some
advice: it was best if you lay in your hammock—each of us had
one!—and tried to doze off. At midnight he woke me out of a
bleary sleep with two bars of chocolate. 'Take them, they are
good for sea-sickness.' He did all this quietly, so that the others

didn't wake. In return I gave him my belt that hadn't yet been filched. This pleased the good lad who then gave me some cigarettes, real riches in those days.

When we were doled out our rations in the morning there was more trickery by the Germans (or could it have been the Tommies who liked their jokes?): we got double corned beef, the Poles double biscuits and no meat. There was a great shindy from the Poles; we just laughed. Nothing to do about it! But who did best in the long run, when we became desperately thirsty and the tea ran out, was debatable. From Newhaven a train took us to Kempton Park, near London, where there was a race course with large spectator stands.*

* Father Jansen's journal continues on page 43.

3

Interrogation

During the fighting in North Africa an accurate German battery was harassing a British position. A raid was made and a German sergeant who was directing the fire from a forward observation point was captured. Here was a man for immediate interrogation as he was bound to possess a great deal of local tactical information. The German gave name, rank and number, as required by the Geneva Convention, and said nothing more. But a Canadian interrogator famed for his quick results was on the spot and took over. He began quietly, then with more menace, and finally laid into the prisoner with threats and abuse. But verbal bullying had no effect. As the interrogation was being conducted near a farmhouse, there was a convenient pig-sty at hand. 'Get in there,' the captain snapped at the sergeant. He always kept strictly to the rules and never laid hands on a prisoner; but there was no rule against burying a man up to his middle in pig manure. This was done, but with no more success. There was one ploy left. The sergeant was taken to a wall and blindfolded; a soldier standing nearby meaningfully clicked over the bolt of his tommy gun and the captain waited for the effect. The sergeant at last spoke out. 'Herr Hauptmann, I have something to say.' 'Well . . .' said the interrogator aggressively, confident that he had broken his man. 'Herr Hauptmann, please take the bandage away from my eyes.' A soldier did so. 'Well, what are you going to tell me now?' 'I wish to look into the eyes of the men who are going to shoot an unarmed man.' The triumphant sergeant was then sent unscathed to the rear. The story[14] may be a tall one, and it doesn't answer one question: was the sergeant extraordinarily brave, or did he know perfectly well that the whole affair was a bluff?

The relationship between prisoner and interrogator is nothing if not dramatic. It is at once intensely human and a denial of the human. The probe and parry can have the excitement of a duel, vital information and loyalty being the personal stakes. Each confrontation is a test of nerve, endurance and moral superiority.

Placate the angry father-figure a little and he will leave you alone, that is the temptation on one side; and on the other, to overplay the bluff and give away your weak hand.

Forward interrogators had to get rapid results. Quick, clever verbal frisking; the cold, sinister approach; the big bravura act— all these were tried, with different degrees of nastiness. And every interrogator attempted to show if he could that so much was already known that a tiny piece of information would not constitute a betrayal. Americans could be both more primitive and warmer than the British. Werner Düttmann was told to dig a grave and was confused enough to think it was more than a ploy. Hugo Staudinger, who also surrendered to Patton's army, was impressed by the decent and somewhat naive Jewish immigrants who interrogated him. 'I come from Germany and want to go back there. Pity there had to be a war over Danzig.' The interrogation of Colonel von der Heydte, the parachutist captured in the Ardennes, by the refugee novelist Hans Habe, was the beginning of a friendship.

In Britain the handling of POWs to obtain information or voluntary collaboration with the war aims of the Allies took place in centres lying in a segment of the Home Counties between southwest and north of London. Kempton Park, the general sorting house, and Ascot Park, a camp mainly for friendly Germans, were south of the Thames; in South Buckinghamshire were Wilton Park and Latimer House and twenty-five miles further east in Middlesex was Trent Park, these last being the three direct interrogation centres where more sophisticated methods were employed. In Brondesbury, a London suburb, was an old nunnery lived in from 1945 onwards by prisoners who worked with the BBC or who had clerical jobs to do with the camps and re-education. Far away in North Buckinghamshire was the Black Propaganda set-up, run by Sefton Delmer, the creator of 'Soldatensender Calais' for which only a tiny handful of prisoners ever worked. The interrogation centre in Kensington, known as 'The London District Cage', was the most feared of the places where prisoners were 'processed'.

All POWs from the Continent were channelled quickly in and out of Kempton Park. Good barrack-room obscenities in perfect German might greet the de-trained prisoners as they were herded through a barbed-wire tunnel under the railway on to the race

course: *Ich trete dich in die Eier!* (I'll boot you in the balls!). The
buildings were in a tatty state. The cavernous areas under the
stands were ideal for the big delousing parades at which every
prisoner was squirted with DDT; the stables and loose boxes were
sleeping quarters, while the suites overlooking the course were
used by the staff for interrogation. Captain Lawrence Green,
whose task it was to unearth prisoners who might broadcast for
the BBC, sat in the royal box. He describes the Commandant,
Lieutenant Colonel Dennison, as an excellent and sympathetic
man who allowed no monkey tricks on prisoners, but he may have
had trouble maintaining correct military smartness and behaviour
in such a backstage unit. Leutnant Bruno Ulrich was 'shocked at
the sight of the filthy uniform of the officer on duty. The sergeant,
noticing my distress at this, gave me my first English cup of tea.'
If, on the other hand, as Colonel Borcherdt, Father Jansen and
others suggest, aggressive Jewish refugees now and then acted up
the part of the traditional Prussian NCO, barking orders and
throwing their weight about, perhaps they were just having their
own back in a fairly harmless way. Lawrence Green recalls one or
two sergeants who were actors and probably homosexual. Green
also comments on the blatant removal into their private possession
of the best items from the kitbags or boxes belonging to a draft of
U-boat prisoners. At the same time, it is clear that many Germans,
and especially officers, had a psychological shock when they found
themselves ordered about by obvious Jews in British sergeants'
uniforms—probably Austrian refugees. There were, in fact, only
very few of them and the only Jewish officer, according to Green,
was the doctor; but so strong was the anti-Semitic conditioning
of Nazi Germany and also often the guilt of feeling this that
POWs passing through saw nothing to remember but Jews at
Kempton Park. Notable among these was Father Jansen, who
may also have had the additional complex about Jews that
Catholic doctrines can encourage.

They knew all about the different divisions that had been
involved in Normandy and Flanders. We were put into loose
boxes according to our *Wehrmacht* units. A speech was made
at us in good German. The guard personnel, especially the
officers, were Jewish emigrants; our division was given the
name 'Marmeladedivision' because we had left few dead and
wounded but all our jam behind in the retreat—a slander to

start off our democratisation! As the host-land, England welcomed us, so far as we were worth it. We would have to work. Gradually we would have removed from us all those bad German things that had to do with militarism and Hitler. The Nazi-German language was bad German; we should learn English as soon as possible, England anyway had more to offer, so 'Get rid of your gear and your uniforms. Throw it all away, comrades, and have everything new. You'll sleep in beds with sheets and eat off china plates—perhaps.' [This became a POW slogan]. The young Jewish soldiers—almost all were NCOs— threw an occasional punch or kick, or boxed our ears. Our people didn't defend themselves. In the main, it gave the impression of a large department store. One saw officers wearing silk neck scarves, and always with creases in their trousers, which one never saw with combat troops. English soldiers—the guards who had brought us there and would accompany us further—went out of their way to show us sympathy and cheer us up. 'Take it easy, German', they'd say, or 'Good luck'. For all one's understanding of what these emigrants from Germany had had to go through (they were not the only sufferers under the Hitler regime), I was sorry that they seemed to want to retaliate with 'an eye for an eye and a tooth for a tooth', without making any distinctions, without asking or knowing how an individual German might feel towards them. During the Hitler period I helped many Jewish friends, as far as was in my power; as chaplain at Walbeck, Kreis Geldern (1932–8), I never allowed any Jew who called in at the priest's house before crossing the frontier to go away without help, comfort and food. Because of the Jews I have been ashamed since 1938 to be a German. And this was the thanks! I certainly wasn't the only one among the prisoners who thought like this; there were doctors, lawyers, sensitive philosophers and artists, educated men who were definitely not anti-Semitic, until the experience of the Jew-Camp at Kempton Park. A pity! All the same, I must say that this was the only bad experience with Jews during my captivity and that later I learned that among all nations, the Jews as well, there are good and bad people, and that the bad ones are often responsible for the sufferings of the good ones.

Jews with a remarkable attitude were also not exceptional: Victor Gollancz, Lieutenant Spelmans, interpreter officer at

Bury, Fräulein Margaret Rosenberg in the Lake District camps, the industrialist at Knutsford who from 1947 onwards paid for fatherless German boys to go to the university, and others. Nor must I omit the Jewish friends I had in Germany.

After a shower-bath at which I got a cane across my naked back, we received our effects back again, except 'valuables retained for safe-keeping'—they had been checking through our clothes and 'luggage' while we bathed. They showed us the bag they had put them in and explained, 'We have taken these things off you, your pay-book among them. They will be returned to you, but we can't tell you when.' I never saw them again. It was like a magician's performance—but much more genuine!

At Kempton Park quite a few Germans decided to co-operate with the British and for a variety of motives. They included some young soldiers, fair weather Nazis and even SS men who quickly could be 'indoctrinated into democracy' and served on the camp staff. Others, politically motivated, were looking for an opportunity to help bring down the tyrant of their country—not that that sort of patriotism was understood by their comrades, to whom they were just traitors. Others, like Father Jansen himself, found a middle way. His final experience at Kempton Park was 'a confidential interview with an extremely friendly Jewish captain' (or he saw him as Jewish) about where he was to be sent next. It faced him with a formidable challenge—but this belongs to a later part of his tale.

The art of the interrogator often involved helping such a person to overcome his scruples about co-operating, which might well increase as defeat approached. An honourable man might feel that to change over late in the day put him among the opportunists. Such a man was Hubert Walter, who at capture had his luggage carried for him by the elderly Frenchman. At his first interrogation he refused in the proper manner to give more than his name, rank and number. 'You won't talk with us then?' 'No, sir.' 'That remains to be seen!' This straight-looking Catholic lieutenant, speaking good English, was an obvious case for treatment as a possible co-operator. He was sent to Ascot Park and with him, but separately, was sent the diary that had been found on him, written when he was interpreter at the POW camp at Lamsdorf in Silesia where, it was claimed, British personnel had been maltreated. The diary, moreover, contained the name of the commandant there, Graf Fink von Finkelstein, who was on the list of possible war-criminals. 'I was made to stand in front of a row of intelligence officers with only my pants on. They told me that my situation was compromising and dangerous and they advised me that my best way out was to help end the war by speaking on the radio along with Peter Coelestin on "Soldatensender Calais". If I refused I might be taken to a distant island and not see my family for a very long time. I couldn't help chuckling to myself at the picture they painted of this far-away place of banishment, because I knew they did not really mean it. But it was a strange way to get me to co-operate. A Bavarian Leutnant now on the British side was put in my cell. "It was a mistake to keep that diary!" he told me. Then a walk with a most pleasant British officer. Soft treatment, then hard again. All the while my thoughts were running like this: As a Catholic I could not wish Hitler to win the war, for I knew what would happen to the Catholic Church if he did. But to make a big protest now against him when I could do it in safety was not right for me. I should have done it, if at all, earlier.'

Three decades later Hubert Walter, D. Phil., at seventy still looking an oak of a man and without a crack in his big, deep voice, could still ponder whether he should have done more to resist Nazism in his own country. But his thoughts usually come to rest on a single historical fact: the Pope made a concordat with Hitler.

Kempton Park was also a place where Russians captured in German uniform were interrogated by officers of the Soviet Military Mission, headed by General Ratov. Lawrence Green recalls the arrival of survivors of the Caucasian Division from Italy, wretchedly clothed and stinking to heaven. Few British had sympathy for these men who had gone over to the invaders of their country, either to save their lives or to try to bring down their government. They simply appeared as tools of Hitler's grand design for Europe. But then the Soviet interrogators were seen or heard using physical methods, and a Russian POW was found bound hand and foot in a hut, without food. Colonel Dennison then tried to assert his proper authority, at which, according to Green, the Soviet Mission then appointed a more senior officer to whom Dennison might not give orders. It is said that General Ratov, after a severe dressing-down from General Firebrace, head of the British-Russian Liaison Group, for allowing these things to happen on British soil, was soon sent home.

Ascot Park was the camp for friendly enemies, a rather jittery collection of victims of persecution, cosmopolitans and international drifters who found themselves in the wrong uniform; Germans with good connections in England; anti-Nazi prisoners, like Heinrich von Trott zu Solz, at risk from their own comrades; men like Hubert Walter who might, it seemed, be weaned into talking on the BBC; and those who were willing, or indeed eager, to do so. Now and then Ascot also housed an obvious 'good sort' like the E-boat commander captured off the coast of Belgium in 1944, Charlie Mueller, who might be courted and made use of. An opposite number on the British side was the artist and ornithologist, Lieutenant-Commander Peter Scott, who commanded a flotilla of motor torpedo boats. He was summoned to meet Charlie Mueller at Ascot. They got on famously, compared notes on naval actions, and the German gladly agreed to comment on the draft of the official history of MTB operations which Scott was then writing. It included an analysis of German tactics, in which Scott expressed surprise that the Germans had not yet tried an attack by concentrated boats on the south and east coast shipping lanes, as this would be difficult to counter. Suddenly, and without his interrogators being consulted, Mueller and a high officer were repatriated as part of an exchange. Scott was worried and sure enough, before long the east coast convoy route was attacked by massed E-boats for the first time.

At Ascot the team of speakers on the BBC made their own little community. Most of them were protégés of 'Captain Holt', a brilliant and attractive idealist from Munich. His real name was Waldemar von Knoeringen, a member of the old Bavarian aristocracy. During the Weimar republic he had been an ardent member of the Socialist Workers Youth Movement and an active member of the 'Reichbanner'. In 1933 he emigrated to Czechoslovakia where he continued opposition to the Nazis and, as a member of the movement 'Neubeginn', organised contacts with trade unionists. When Czechoslovakia was overrun in 1939 he came to Britain where he had a valuable friend in Richard Crossman. With his high position in the Political Warfare Executive Crossman was able to use Knoeringen's talents, for instance, by getting him to analyse the political content of letters sent home by captured members of the Afrika Korps. Knoeringen immediately saw the possibility of using some of these men on the air and persuaded Crossman to send him to North Africa in 1943 to talk to prisoners in the camps. This he did with success under the cover-name of Captain Holt, creating round him in Algiers a nucleus of anti-fascists and representatives of the 'other Germany'. They were brought to Ascot in 1944 and joined by occasional POWs from the invasion of Europe. They spoke up passionately and anonymously for, as they put it, the honour of their country, for Germany against Hitler and for the ten thousand anti-fascists who were their fellow-prisoners.

As the war drew to a close a diary-keeping Englishman, Henry Swanzy, used their late-night programme as his 'window on Europe' and through it experienced 'the tragedy of Germany that overhangs all our days, a thing longed for but terrible.' He wondered whether the famous prophecy of Goethe to Eckermann was coming true: that one day the barbarians would use the iron railings round Wieland's grave to forge shoes for their horses. He heard their special programme for Good Friday, 30 March, and a voice choked with emotion speaking the first verse of the Passion hymn, 'O Haupt voll Blut und Dornen', then music and reading on the theme of deliverance and redemption through defeat. His diary records that on Easter Day they broadcast a recording of the war-silenced bells of Cologne Cathedral, a sermon, and a long scene from *Faust* where Helena restores harmony to the tortured world. 'The voices sounded really beautiful behind the furious jamming.' Throughout April the prisoners pleaded with their audience to be clear-sighted, brave and determined and thus help their country by surrendering now; officers spoke of their oath of loyalty as worthless; they commented, with personal memories, on Belsen, Buchenwald, Sachsenhausen; they spoke of their own inner struggles; they berated the playwright Gerhart Hauptmann* because, having never opened his mouth against the Nazis, he broke silence to protest against the Dresden raid; they attacked the Nazi corruption of youth and doctrines that divided the world into friends and enemies, the latter to be *zerschmettert* (crushed to pieces). On 5 May, overcome by their feelings, they described the scenes of surrender on the Luneburg Heath, referring to the reported stony faces of the German generals 'as though they had lost a game of chess'.† All this in the sonorous plangent emotion of the German language. On 7 May they gave their names for the first time. Hans

* Very old, he died soon afterwards.
† But see page 225.

Seikel from Saxony had a message for his parents, and Wilhelm
Brandt for his wife, Margot, bidding her not to hate. On 10 May
they reported the British victory celebrations, being surprised at
the absence of any 'mailed fist', and went on to play Bach and
recite Hölderlin.

Many of this Ascot group, true Germans in their own eyes,
traitors in most of their comrades', went to work in the Foreign
Office's 're-education' programme, mostly on publications, for
in the camps they would have been totally rejected. On 22 May
Henry Swanzy heard them 'discuss their personal futures, with
considerable naiveté'.

The London District Cage in Kensington was on the opposite
end of the spectrum to Ascot Park. It was set up by Lieutenant-
Colonel Scotland, a man with some outer characteristics of a
gentleman, a grizzled head and a tight, clenched appearance. This,
with his penetrating gaze and the Afrikaans tang to his far from
perfect German, made him a feared figure to his prisoners. He had
been one himself in the First World War, suffering a long spell of
solitary confinement in German South West Africa. He knew
from experience what enables a man to hold and what makes him
break. Under him the London Cage acquired a formidable reputation.[15] No one was physically touched, but it could be a traumatic
experience for a burly submarine petty officer or an SS corporal to
be confronted hour after hour by the diminutive Major Kettler,
with his slightly deformed body, boring into him with his quick
mind and dynamic energy. 'Der Giftzwerg' (the poison-dwarf)
was the POW nickname for Kettler. 'He had great professional
pride,' remembers Ken Morgan, his colleague till 1944, 'He would
rather break his heart and his larynx than fail to break his man.
When he was done with him he would throw it off with a laugh.'
There were no microphones at LDC, which resulted in less subtle
methods being used than elsewhere. But in no interrogation
centres were brain-washing techniques employed, nor truth drugs,
hypnotism, long solitary confinement or starvation diet. This
kind of treatment was forbidden by the Geneva Convention, and
POWs could have reported it to the Protecting Power (Switzerland). It was also regarded as useless by good interrogators,
and hankered after only by lazy or bad ones.[15a] Morgan himself,
who like many interrogators was a teacher of languages, looked
steelier than he was. 'I found it much harder to get my blood

up than "Scottie' who was motivated by past experiences or Kettler who had his own reasons for enjoying these battles. A whole submarine crew would suddenly arrive, just fished up out of the sea. Living comfortably in London, it was a real emotional strain to make oneself hard, to work oneself up into the required state of anger and annoyance. Fortunately for me, other methods were also necessary: jig-saw work on the small details picked up in an interrogation or scrutinised out of the POWs papers; or playing on some factor like a man's family situation or his Christian background, appealing to something sentimental in his nature perhaps.'

LDC was also used by Free Poles, Free Danes and Free Norwegians and also as a practical training ground for intelligence officers down from Cambridge and other intelligence schools. Its frightening reputation was its chief asset. This was spread by rumour but was also due, in contrast with everywhere else, to the seedy atmosphere of the old mansion with its many rooms and corridors and peeling paint; and to the behaviour Colonel Scotland expected from the other rank staff. Fritz Wenzel, a U-boat Lieutenant, was taken there from the civil atmosphere of Trent Park. 'Their tone was very harsh and even brutal. I shouldn't have liked an extended cure at their hands. I get naturally obstinate and resentful if anyone bawls at me, and I shouldn't have had much to laugh at with them, for they were bawling all the time.'

When the war ended LDC became the 'War Crimes Investigation Unit'. Colonel Scotland had a new mission: to track down SS killers of prisoners and civilian hostages. So in addition to its harsh atmosphere, the 'Cage' in its cool pursuit of justice became a hot-house of guilt, defiance and fear. The methods remained the same—*korrekt* according to SS-Captain Herbert Christiansen—but some nasty characters were being sent for examination and the outcome now might be a jail sentence or even death. To make the bully feel small gave great pleasure to certain interrogators. Treatment of witnesses depended upon who they were and how they reacted. General von Senger, one-time Rhodes scholar at Oxford, was among the several generals taken there to write comments on alleged atrocities in his area of command. 'We were not badly treated,' he says, 'only the food was, as usual, inadequate.' The parachutist Colonel von der Heydte spent ten days doing the same and clearing himself of charges. When he, quite properly as an officer, refused to undertake fatigue duties, a sergeant took him into the guard room and treated him to a drink; and on Sunday an Irish captain came into his cell, read Mass for him alone and afterwards produced a bottle of whisky which they shared. But the warm-hearted, outgoing Friedrich August Freiherr von der Heydte was the sort of man to whom those things happened. He subsequently found his stay at Trent Park 'one long holiday', but that was after the war ended.

At Trent Park or 'Cockfosters' the atmosphere was even during the war extremely civil. The cell block, including high-fenced exercise yards and raised watch towers, was adjacent to the mansion which belonged to Sir Philip Sassoon, connoisseur and man of affairs. The interrogating officers lived here and in the cottages and had use of the large park. The 'guests', as they were always referred to by the British among themselves, were usually officers, at first mainly from the Navy and the Luftwaffe. U-Boat Leutnant Fritz Wenzel describes how, to his great delight, his old friend and comrade, Hans Engel, joined him in his cell. They had a great deal to say to each other but naturally took the precaution of talking softly and frequently changing position. They also had a good look round the walls, but 'despite the most meticulous search, we never succeeded in finding any trace of a microphone; so, perhaps we were over-cautious.' They were not, but again and again prisoners were lulled out of a suspicion they had been instructed to exercise. The brilliant device of incorporating a microphone in the electric light fitting was, in fact, never detected by any prisoner. At Trent Park the 'guests' were now and then invited into the officers' mess in the big house for a drink and a game of bridge. This did not happen to Fritz Wenzel; the game played with him was an hour's pleasant walk in the park with a British naval officer. They chatted about many unimportant things and it was clear the Englishman was very well informed. Apparently he especially wanted to know whether the U-Boat ace Commander Kretschmer had another boat and what another shipmate was doing. The two parted on the best of terms, Wenzel of course giving nothing away—unless afterwards to the listening socket in his cell. Why otherwise was he at Cockfosters for a month? Not just so that he could catch up on his reading from the excellent library!

The most remembered character at Cockfosters was Ian Munroe

whose *nom de guerre* was 'Lord Aberfeldy'. A delightfully outgoing and intelligent Scot, he was the prototype of the officer and gentleman and his contribution to the war was to act this out to the full. He took his guests on walks, to restaurants, galleries and shops in London, disarming not a few with the snob appeal of his assumed title. The unspoken implication of 'gentlemen of the world unite' was well employed by the calmly ruthless directors of the operation. Unconsciously perhaps they were already united—at least against a man like Hitler.*

In 1942 the main body of CSDIC (Combined Services Direct Interrogation Centre) was moved twenty-five miles west from Trent Park to Latimer House. This was a large mock-Jacobean country house overlooking the valley of the Chess, with a park and a pretty ornamental lake complete with swans. There was a detachment at Wilton Park a few miles away, which also housed MI 19, the unit responsible for briefing and de-briefing military agents. At both places the same cell system as before, but improved, was erected, while Trent Park continued to function as a long stay unit, mainly for generals and senior officers who, unknown to themselves, were of considerable intelligence value.

The Latimer House complex was now the hub of the operation, and no part of the information web was more important than the hut where a battery of monitors wearing earphones kept constant watch on the cells. In front of each was a turn-table with a smooth disc on it; if anything significant was being said they lowered the magnetic arm on to the disc. Corporal and sergeant secretaries in the three services, who might sit a wall's width from the prisoners but never saw one, then transcribed what had been recorded for use in further interrogations or in intelligence reports. The monitors, who had the rank of sergeant, were nearly all Jewish refugees from Germany and Austria. Their room was part of the hutted central complex and highly secret, but interrogators would go there to get the measure of a prisoner they were about to see or after talking to him to hear what he said about him: he might even brag to his cell-mate about what he had refused to give away. The monitors' room had the letter M on the door and was known as 'Mother'. Mother was always listening. It was also sometimes referred to as 'Pandora's Box'.

* See also page 222.

There were many ways of getting men to talk. In the early days there were obedient, peasant-like soldiers who could be told: 'You are a soldier.' 'Ja, mein Hauptmann.' 'And a soldier must always obey his officer. Is that not so?' 'Ja, mein Hauptmann.' 'You no longer have a German officer who gives you orders. I have taken his place.' 'Ja, mein Hauptmann.' 'When did your unit arrive at the front?' But such a compliant subject would hardly possess valuable intelligence. It is even told that a dumb-ox type could be made to give away some small details in the following way. 'Are you in the 51st Regiment?' 'Nein.' 'Are you in the 52nd?' 'Nein.' 'The 53rd?' Silence.

But the general method at Latimer and Wilton Park was a sophisticated mixture of cunning and bluff, of softening a man with kindness and wearing him down, and, if necessary, hinting at or threatening other possible methods. Each service had its leading interrogator. Wing-Commander Felkin, a former business man with a good scientific mind, had charm, patience and a sixth sense. He worked best late at night. Over a glass of whisky in Room A, which was fitted out like a sitting-room, he would spin his web. He knew his Germans and he would supplement friendly persuasion by leaning forward to give a touch on arm or leg. His technical interrogations were often crucial in the 'Battle of Boffins', from that of the key captive after the Bruneval Raid on a German radar post in 1941 to the piecing together of tiny pointers to rocket development in Germany. His team contained several hard-talking businessmen with a good knowledge of German industry; their task was to keep the 'Bombers' Baedeker' up-to-date. One of them, Captain P., a kindly man and a good actor, had a somewhat Slav appearance and was used occasionally for the ultimate threat, held in reserve if it came out that the prisoner had done service in the East. 'I am very sorry, but we sometimes receive lists from our Russian Allies of German officers they want to interrogate. We hope there is nothing in it, but we have no alternative but to let a representative of the Russian military mission in Britain come and see you.' The verbal threat might work; if not, Captain P., putting on a very convincing Russian-German accent with his KGB uniform, was taken to the prisoner's cell. His English interrogator, also there, then appeared as his only friend in the world against the threatening red tabs and the stony unblinking Slav-looking face. At the 'London Cage', when a prisoner refused to open up, his file was sometimes stamped ostentatiously with the

3

letters NR. He was then told that it meant 'Nach Russland' (To Russia). In fact, the letters stood for NOT REQUIRED.[16] Sent back to his cell, he might soon ask for a further interrogation. But this bluff was usually called.

Sometimes a collaborating prisoner or a refugee trained for the act would be put in a cell as a stooge. He might warn his companion not to talk and to hide their conversation from a possible microphone turn on the tap. Later in the exercise yard he might get him to talk more freely. Discovering where the prisoner lived, the stooge might be withdrawn for an ostensible interrogation, and be re-briefed with all kinds of information about the prisoner's local town and its personalities. In this way, he would establish a *bona fides* with the naturally suspicious prisoner. Ploys like these had many permutations.

Pilot Officer Geoffrey Forrest saw his first prisoners of war lounging on the edge of the barbed wire 'cage' just outside Alexandria: a handful of magnificent but surly young blonds, incongruous giants beside their small swarthy companions. They were racial Germans from South Tyrol called up into Mussolini's army and captured at Alamein. A little later Forrest, a navigator, happened to go on attachment to a forward base at Benghazi just after it fell to the Eighth Army. Wandering around the bombed houses he found a set of the new *Encyclopaedia Italiana* in mint condition. For a book-lover here was booty indeed, but what use to him? He made it into a huge parcel and at the next opportunity took it to the officer on duty at the Alexandria cage, hoping it would not be rejected as Fascist (which it was only mildly). It was his first act of peace. A year later, since he could speak German, he was seconded to Air Intelligence and found himself at Latimer House. Being an unaggressive man, he was used mostly on the easier prisoners, as a befriender and for report writing. He remembers taking prisoners on the 'depression' trip round London.

We went by car and the driver was always an ATS girl who was fair, buxom and pretty with a large beauty spot on her cheek. She was known to us just as 'Carmichael' and was part of the treatment. She never spoke to or answered the prisoner who was always aware of her and whose confidence was being undermined as he was driven through large areas of London without any bomb-damage at all, totally belying Goebbels' propaganda. The carefully chosen route always led to Harrods. A stroll through the elegant and still well-stocked store—especially the food halls—was well calculated to shake morale. London life looked astonishingly normal and the sight of all the different Allied uniforms in the street and a table for two at a good restaurant or at the thé dansant at the Piccadilly Hotel (though not for dancing) continued the softening-up process. Carmichael was waiting to take us back. When next day the prisoner was faced with his tough-type interrogator, it was reckoned he would be more malleable.

Early January 1945. The Luftwaffe's Last Fling.* Wing Commander Felkin (to the prisoners 'Oberst King') is greatly improved in humour. A Group Commodore captured in the big attack by seven hundred fighters on New Year's Day is due to arrive at Latimer—the first ever. Felkin has also unearthed details of a coming intruder operation by German night fighters and has sent Carmichael with urgent papers over to Bomber Command. There have never been so many 'guests'. All the cells are full; fifty German names have been chalked on the blackboard in the main office with their units, interrogators and report editors. 'Like the good old days of the Battle of Britain', says someone, and another, speaking of their morale, 'Like the good old days of the Afrika Korps.' A yellow standard hangs on the wall with a complicated device to symbolise the unit's activities: the shield is emblazoned with lions couchant in the form of fuselages; the base is runways crossing each other with dispersal tracks curving away like the base of an octopus. 'Yes,' thinks Forrest, who is officer on late duty, 'We suck and squeeze and frighten our guests just like an octopus.'

An interrogator is sitting with a young fighter pilot and rings Forrest. 'Would you look something up about a Leutnant Eichdorf?' He passes back the information in the card index: 'On 9 September he was in the 2nd squadron of Fighter Group II.' In the silence the faint buzz of the scrambler box can be heard. Felkin, delving into his papers, biting his nails, keeps twisting round to look at the blackboard. For once he does not retire for the night session in Room A with a bottle of whisky under his arm. At 11.15 an American interrogator returns from an I. room.

* Based on Geoffrey Forrest's journal.

'I got him all right.' 'How did you do it?' says Felkin. 'Oh, I had to talk to him like a sick horse for an hour and a half. Then he gave up.' 'Good man!' The officer who asked about Eichdorf comes back. 'Thanks for the dope, Forrest! He came clean after that. He just saw we knew everything and packed up—he's the kind who then goes on and tells you everything. He'd had eight hours of us today and got tired, I suppose. But he didn't know much.'

A long conference next day builds up a picture of the New Year's Day raid: a brave show, well-planned, but poorly executed because of the inexperience of the pilots. The Group Commodore arrives. He turns out to be an Austrian, very truculent and Nazi. At first Felkin leaves him largely to his minions. Forrest is sent to make pleasant conversation with him, if he can. When politics come up he bursts out: 'I'd rather fight to the last drop of my blood and die in the snow, than live again those days of poverty and unemployment.' He gets very rude, the sergeant in Mother calls to his neighbour, 'Come and listen to this.' Forrest leaves the cell, convinced that this embittered, contemptuous man will one day become a maquis fighter in his defeated country. The Commodore keeps up his aggressive front: he hopes that the Russians will arrive in Austria before the Yankees and accuses the American pilots of shooting at German aircrew who bale out. This makes the two American interrogators at Latimer bristle to get at him, which they do, and blow so much air about him that he apologises for his general behaviour.

A V.1 rocket lands on West Hampstead Station. This with the bad weather causes traffic delays and late arrivals. Some of the girls in the unit manage to ski down the slope to the lake. In his cell the Commodore is still trying to hold out against the undermining techniques. Only the chief has any success with him, slowly and subtly, with whisky at night and the jaunt to London, which begins to do the trick. 'The old boy was really put out by that.' Felkin keeps his team informed of progress. 'We ought to invent a new word for the boomerang effect of propaganda.' 'Boomeranda,' suggests Forrest. Felkin's second ploy is to make himself appear to be the Commodore's friend against the unpleasant Americans who want, he pretends, to have him court-martialled. The third, and decisive, factor is the filing system of information. 'Wing-Commander King speaking,' he rings the duty officer. 'Please look up and describe the photo of Leutnant

X.' The records reveal a man with fair hair and thick lips. Felkin turns to the Austrian. 'Your friend has thick lips and likes kissing.' The Commodore is staggered. 'My God, yes! He can never go on an operation without sleeping with a woman first!' Soon after this, around midnight on 21 January and three weeks after capture, the prisoner stops resisting.

Why does he cave in? Is his coming clean just the reverse side of his truculence? Did he have a soft centre like many Viennese and fall for Felkin's charm? Felkin's explanation is that basically he admires England. Or is it, wonders Forrest, having at first completely misjudged the man, that he admired what is strong and has power over him, and which at this moment appears to be so clever in the person of Oberst King?

Imagination can follow the Group Commodore to his next camp. His fellow officers rib him. 'Kept you a long time, old boy!' He boasts about how he got an excellent meal in London out of Oberst King and how he pulled the wool over his eyes. 'In any case, they always keep senior officers longer. His whisky was excellent!' He is told 'We always collect as much information about interrogations as possible; will you write a report?' 'Can't be much use now, can it?' 'So you think we've lost the war, do you?' In the mess he feels the cold looks of the North Germans, their suspicion that, as an Austrian, he is bound to be unreliable as a bed-fellow anyway. One of his cell mates at Latimer arrives. 'Oh, yes, the Commodore spent hours with Oberst King, late into the night, too.' With news of the battle front in Germany itself, fear of the future eats away at the old trust between fighting men, begins to forget his secret defeat, persuades himself that, with the Luftwaffe disintegrating, he gave nothing away of importance. No one will remember . . . Felkin dies in 1958; only Geoffrey Forrest's journal fragment and odd moments in his own dreams will hold the truth about his loss of integrity and his short, curiously intimate relationship with 'Oberst King'.

It was, of course, largely a game and on both sides air-crews especially were briefed on the tricks likely to be played on them. With so many Allied airmen escaping home the British had much more detailed information about the German set-up at Oberursel near Frankfurt than the Germans had about Latimer; indeed no German got home after 1941, but they could infer that similar methods were used. But even if played according to rules, games are unpleasantly exposing for those who don't like them, or who lose their cool or quail before people who shout at them; who don't mind much if their side doesn't win, or give up trying when it is losing. Those who defended themselves best simply by refusing to talk shop at all were the ones most admired by their interrogators, especially if they were affable at the same time. There was always that one simple way of winning, as the sergeant in the pig-sty may have known: keep mum.

Forrest's most memorable prisoner was the captain and navigator of a Dornier reconnaissance plane shot down in the Atlantic in the spring of 1944. This Hauptmann was an unusual enough fish for Felkin to keep him at Latimer for quite a long time—for gossip value rather than direct military information, of which he gave little. He was a good talker, only intermittently aware of the bugging, and would draw out any cell mate usefully. Slim, dark, urbane and with an alert presence, he was the opposite of a Nazi. He had been on the edge of the Stefan George circle in Berlin, the poet who had died in Italy in voluntary exile in 1933. The Hauptmann's love of France and civilised, rather austere attitudes, confirmed the George connection. Forrest happened to have a new bilingual edition of the poet and lent it to the German. They discussed how the Nazis had wanted to bring George's body home and inter it with national solemnity in one of Germany's great cathedrals and how his friends and disciples had prevented such a travesty.* They talked about nature, history, literature, but not much politics.

On the London 'drepression' trip and on country walks a tentative, almost furtive amity grew up between them. For form's sake the conversation would start on air matters (a report had to be written after each meeting) but soon they were discussing other things. Once Forrest told him of his last experience in Germany before the war. It was in June 1939, late at night in a cellar waiting room at Cologne Station. There were three men drinking at a near-by table. Suddenly two Gestapo men arrived, led by a third, an obvious informer, who indicated one of the men at the table. The man was seized and as he was marched away struggling he called out continually, 'Ich habe nichts gesagt.' (But I said nothing.) He kept shouting this down the wide tunnel under the platforms, till out of hearing. 'For me that's what the war's

* Three of the von Stauffenberg brothers, including Klaus, who attempted to assassinate Hitler, attended his death-bed.

about,' Forrest ended. The Hauptmann nodded gravely. Standing there by a stile on a peaceful hillside in beechy Buckinghamshire, the point of the story hardly had to be made.

One day the German had a personal request. 'I have been writing a journal. It will be taken away from me when I leave here. Will you keep it for me till after the war? I'll put my address on it. I have written some poems in it—one for you, too.' Forrest gladly agreed, and promised to keep the contents to himself. Not long after this he went on a short leave and, on returning, found that his friend had gone. To Felkin he had become a squeezed lemon and immediately discarded. He left the George poems behind and a hurried good-bye note. The guard sergeant-major told Forrest, 'He also left a pile of ashes in his cell. Do you know what he was burning?'

4

Three Essential Men

In 1945 German prisoners of war in British hands, as everywhere, faced a bleak and unknown future. For all but a few, release was out of sight, although their repatriation was required by the Geneva Convention as soon as peace was signed. But it never was signed—between Germany and the Allies. The general attitude to these hundreds of thousands of men is summed up by the last lines of Auden's poem *Spain*:

> History to the defeated may say alas,
> but cannot help or pardon.

There were many who both thought and acted the opposite. Among them were a refugee from Nazi Germany, a Scottish grammar school master and a Swedish pastor. The oldest of these was the German refugee, Herbert Sulzbach. He was already fifty and a sergeant in the British army when, in January 1945, with high hopes and not without trepidation, he entered a prisoner of war camp in Scotland that was seething with defiance. At first sight there was little in his background to prepare him for a call so late in life. But it is interesting that he was born and brought up in Frankfurt-am-Main: there used to be no Jews so patriotic and proud of belonging to German culture, to which they contributed so much, as the assimilated Jews of the big cities. Cut off from their religion and racial foundations, they became, it was commonly said, more German than the Germans. Herbert Sulzbach's family were wealthy without being ostentatious. A Sulzbach bank had been founded in 1856 and Herbert's grandfather, Rudolf, became one of the founders of the Deutsche Bank; offered a title of nobility by Kaiser Wilhelm II, he refused it, and died worth 33 gold millions. Herbert's father, Emil, was an amiable, cultured man, 'the most modest millionaire I have ever met', says his son. Herbert's mother, also a full Jew, was a Berliner. She was fashionable and smart, loved life and loved spending money. She had an English governess for her son, but though the young Herbert

did not like Gertrude Stone (a dreadful snob), she loyally kept up
with him and, when in 1940 he was interned in the Isle of Man,
his wife went to live in her house. With his happy nature, Herbert
was an easy going schoolboy without ambition and at the Goethe-
Gymnasium where the upper bourgeoisie of Frankfurt sent their
sons he failed his final exam. After a consolation trip round Africa
he was sent to learn banking.

In August 1914 this *jeunesse dorée* ended abruptly. As with thousands of others, putting on his country's uniform liberated the
young Sulzbach from a life of little challenge. Within four weeks
he was marching towards Armentières through lanes of German
dead. Commissioned in 1916, he took part in thirty-five engage-
ments and, fortune's child, never had a scratch. There was no
more patriotic or dedicated gunner in the German army. He filled
thirteen diaries in a terse, unsentimental style, celebrating the
fraternity of arms and accepting the realities of war, though he
would look up with envy at the fliers whom he hoped in vain to
join: they could fight it out in a cleaner, more chivalrous way.
Respecting the brave enemy and hating all traitors, he came
through strangely uncontaminated by the violence around him.
The armistice of 1918 shocked his German soul deeply, but it was
a consolation when his division, marching back behind the Rhine,
was pelted with flowers by the people of Bonn. At home in Frankfurt he wore his uniform for the last time as he went to be de-
mobilised and wrote the last words in his diaries: 'I felt as though
I were going to my own funeral.' The next uniform he would put
on was that of a British private twenty-two years later.

He was soon desk-bound, apprenticed to Sulzbach, Dreyfus and
Co. In 1920 when the French marched into the Rheinland he
walked about meaningfully in his medals. Before long he settled
in Berlin where his father set him up as partner and manager of a
small fancy-paper factory. But this gay, companionable Frank-
furter hardly had his heart in it—much more to his taste was the
theatre or expeditions to the country or horse racing. He married
as his second wife an actress, Beata Scherk, niece of the conductor,
Otto Klemperer. He travelled on business and pleasure. He read
books. He was an indefatigable correspondent and writer of letters
to the press, not failing to attack the Nazis, though he expected
when Hitler came to power that the whole 'schwindel' would soon
be over. Interest in the Great War had revived; so he got out his
fading diaries and offered them to a publisher who brought them

out in 1934 under the title *Two Living Walls*. Their soldierly, patriotic spirit suited the feeling of the time and even Nazi papers reviewed them enthusiastically, ignorant of who the author was. But, being a Jew, he began to face difficulties at the factory. A subsidiary company at Slough seemed to offer the basis of a new life, so he emigrated to Britain in 1937. The following year he returned to fetch his wife and her sister—a brave act since he suspected, rightly, that he was on a black list. The removal men showed him where in his furniture he could safely hide some currency, but he did not dare to risk it. His faith in a humane Germany was further confirmed when they said farewell to the braver members of their friendship circle. A local policeman, for all the swastika in his badge of office, forged his wife's passport and then risked his job by coming to the little party they gave in a pub. This man, Wachmeister Oetzel, whose name Herbert Sulzbach was to celebrate again and again in later life, became for him the symbol of the permanent and true Germany.

The Slough business went bankrupt. In 1940, along with those refugees who, like him, were technically 'enemy aliens', Sulzbach was interned. The Isle of Man filled up with talented artists, musicians, writers and actors, and he joined one of the cultural committees. Meanwhile, his flat in Hampstead was bombed. There was only one way men in his situation could support the war—in the Pioneer Corps. In October, intensely proud to be wearing the King's uniform, he joined up and was sent to 229 Company at Didcot. While digging trenches or ditches he would refer with humorous, unbitter irony to 'my friends' as the bombers came over. In the meantime he got in touch with Captain Basil Liddell Hart, the well-known military expert and historian. Liddell Hart showed interest in Sulzbach's book and in certain contacts he had had with Ludendorff and others. Believing his talents were wasted, he tried through his private connections to get him transferred to the Intelligence Corps or a post with the BBC, but to no avail. In January 1942 Sulzbach was asking him about the possibility of the formation of a Free German Force, but in the following month it was 'I have a so-called easy job, cleaning the dining-room. But even the four to five hours of scrubbing are too much. I feel so dead tired and unable to do anything afterwards and feel worse from week to week.' He was now as Devizes on the edge of Salisbury Plain, and here he saw his first Nazis for six years, prisoners working in the fields. It was for him a traumatic experience. 'I didn't see them as people at all. I only saw the swastika on their uniforms.' In 1944, when interpreters were being sought for POW camps, he applied at once. He was sent on a course, promoted to staff-sergeant, and posted to Comrie in Scotland in the New Year.

It was the time of the Ardennes Offensive, Hitler's last desperate fling in the West which caught the Allies off-guard. At the same time V rockets, the promised secret weapon, were landing on England. The camps in Britain, which had been sullen and depressed after the battle of Normandy, suddenly erupted into defiance. In Comrie, Nazi elements already in control stepped up their reign of terror. A certain Sergeant Rosterg, a robust man of thirty, strong enough to stand up for his anti-Nazi opinions, arrived there from Devizes. He could read English fluently and was asked to translate the newspaper reports about the Ardennes Offensive which had now been halted. He made it clear he was glad as that meant the war and the Nazis would soon be finished. That night he was beaten up in his hut, and his diary fished out of his kit-bag. Senior Cadet Pallm-Koenig who led the *Rollkommando* (raiding party) discovered some defeatist anti-Hitler remarks, and read them out, and added another invented crime that Rosterg had betrayed an attempt at a mass-escape from Devizes which was foiled by the British. 'The penalty of this is death,' said Pallm-Koenig, handing him a thin cord. 'Do it yourself, to save us the trouble.' Why Rosterg did not then ask for asylum from the British is a mystery. Two days before Christmas the *Rollkommando* came for him at midnight. Having worked up a lynching spirit, they put a cord round his neck and, with a grim hundred-strong cortege, dragged him across the camp to the lavatories where they strung him up. The Polish guards found him a few hours later.[17] At the time of Sulzbach's arrival a murder-squad from Scotland Yard was questioning all the occupants of two huts, but was defeated by a wall of silence. As the terror control of the camp grew stronger, Sulzbach's innocent and optimistic nature recoiled from what he saw. He was affected by the fact that Rosterg might even have been one of the men he had so strongly rejected at Devizes. But the whole situation at Comrie wounded his German soul to the depths. His reaction, moreover, coincided with the wave of gut hatred of Germany that was mounting at this time, caused by the prolongation of the war and then by the revelations about the concentration camps.

Other idealists and believers in 'another Germany' were dis-
orientated at this time, one the perhaps best-known British Jew,
Victor Gollancz. This left-wing publisher and philanthropist had
been the main opponent during the war of the views of Lord
Vansittart who led the campaign for a punitive treatment of
Germany.* In his book *Shall Our Children Live or Die?*, Gollancz
corrected Vansittart's narrow view of history and, while deeply
aware of the Nazi evil, made an impassioned plea against becoming infected by their spirit of hatred. But the revelations of the
death camps and the calculated mass murders of the 'final solution'
were so far beyond any evil he had imagined that he had a spiritual
and nervous crisis. He retired with his wife to the Scottish Highlands taking with him as always a suitcase full of books. They
were a selection of Christian and Jewish mystical writings. He
came through his crisis, returned to work and re-entered the
humanitarian battle on behalf of the suffering people of Europe
and especially of prostrate Germany. The outcome of those weeks
of meditation and renewal was two-fold: the foundation in the
autumn of the movement 'Save Europe Now', and the making of
one of the best spiritual anthologies of the century, *A Year of
Grace*.[18]

Sulzbach's crisis was different: it was a straight case of virus
infection, for at Comrie he was actually in close contact every day
with violent Nazis. He also had on his mind the fate of his relatives
in Germany. In March he was sending portions of his diary to
Liddell Hart. The arrogance of the prisoners, he wrote, was
beyond belief. Vansittart was right, and so was hatred of such
people. 'Our camp has about 4,000 German POWs and nearly all
are fanatics. I always used to say that there may be 10 per cent
decent Germans, but you could not find 400 decent chaps here.
Out of 100 letters they write home, 95 contain the sentence "We
trust in our beloved, our Iron Führer. Even if the situation is not
good now, final victory is certain." I always wish I could invite all

* Author, playwright and diplomat, Vansittart was Permanent Under-
Secretary of State for Foreign Affairs 1930–38, and then Chief Diplomatic Adviser to the Foreign Secretary till his retirement in 1941 when
he was given a peerage. His immensely popular book *Black Record* tried
to show by a highly selective reading of history that the Germans were
more disposed towards aggression and violence than any other people:
they were the 'butcher-birds' of Europe and should be dealt with
accordingly. Goebbels remarked once that the Englishman's attacks on
Germany were worth ten divisions to the *Wehrmacht*.

soft people of this country here for a few hours, *all* of whom would become hard, very hard. The first thing after having arrived here that impressed me were the Poles. A Polish company is doing guard duty here; many of them speak German ... I never met such hatred as these Poles have against those Germans ... The soft ones of this country should be forced to listen to the stories of these Poles here. They have their own camp Gestapo here. They find out if a man is anti-Nazi, or half-critical of German victory, or who may say a word of doubt against the God-Führer. There is nothing human left in them, they are just beasts. Some German asks that he be taken out of the compound as he fears to be hanged, some are badly beaten up and shout for help. I myself can only see one way out of the next war: to keep Germany occupied until that generation of Germans is dead. The bad Nazis in our hands should not go back for a long time.'

Thirty years later it is beyond Herbert Sulzbach to recall the depth of the crisis of faith he went through at Comrie, nor is he the man to want to relive the past. For a period he rejected the people who had rejected him, and even identified himself with the Polish guards; they too were victims of the vicious side of his own people. As the end of the war approached Comrie was still dominated by fanatics living on in their fantasies of ultimate victory. They put the notice-boards with both the Allied communiqués out of bounds; they refused to read the daily papers which told of Hitler's death, some even believing that the *Scotsman* and the *Glasgow Herald* came in special editions prepared to deceive the prisoners. They answered Sulzbach's 'Do you know that' circular about the capitulations with counter-questions such as, 'Do you know that the U-boat blockade is forcing England to her knees, and that the English population is demonstrating against the government?'

But, with the final unconditional surrender on all fronts, the world even of the ultra-Nazis began to fade away, except for those whose fantasies had become pathological. In May a different Sergeant Sulzbach was writing to Liddell Hart: 'My job is the most interesting I can imagine,' and in September, 'I could tell you many things, interesting, exciting, awful, also touching little happenings'; and to his commandant and the Foreign Office later in the year: 'We have the chance of a life-time to re-educate all POWs ... The soil is prepared for the adoption of a new way of life.' By 1946 he had not only reverted to his real self but was becoming an inspiration and even father-figure to one-time ardent Nazis at the 4,000-strong officers' camp at Featherstone Park. Men of the Waffen-SS would say that he saved their sanity and faith in humanity, and Otto Erxleben, now a farmer in Kent, could proclaim in 1976, 'Even now, if it were necessary, I would sell half my cows and drive over half the world just to be able to talk to Herbert.'

Henry Faulk, the Scottish grammar school master, was hobbling on sticks when he first encountered German prisoners of war. His leg had been smashed in a motor-bike accident late in 1943 and prevented him landing in Normandy with the D-Day troops. Thousands of Germans learned to respect this challenging yet kindly man: a Scot to the core, with more than a little granite in him; powerfully built with a squarish face and a square stance; cool blue eyes of the born questioner that creased into the twinkle of the natural story-teller; the set jaw that could relax into a quick, infectious grin. He could dominate a room and exhaust a subject, but, having no small talk, could sink into the background, unobserved but acutely observant. He would have been a good fighting officer; he was more valuable doing battle with and for the mind.

Faulk's family had been farmers for generations. His father was the first to break out of the mould, leaving home as a lad to go to sea, and working among other things on the Canadian Pacific Railway. Returning home, he married and had a small business in Dundee. 'He was', wrote his son, 'one of the most intelligent and physically powerful men I have met. He dominated our close-knit family in an atmosphere that must have been a curious blend of Victorianism, authoritarianism, Calvinist and liberal thought in every field, from politics to religion. The individual was insignificant and neither father nor his many friends talked of themselves, though all had led interesting lives; the community and mankind were both topic and aim.'

Faulk remembers little of his childhood. 'One took life for granted and my memory only begins to function cohesively after I went to work and had concrete subject matter to handle.' He went to the Harris Academy in Dundee, found school easy and interesting, and went on to study French and German at Glasgow University. Having to spend a year in each country—an enlightened policy only adopted much later by some English universities

—Faulk found himself in Berlin during the elections of March 1933. As part of a vast throng, he watched the results being flashed up on the Ullstein Building in the Friederichstrasse—with the Nazis still only getting 47.3 per cent of the votes. He also looked on as Nazi thugs beat up a teenage Jewish boy. 'I was', he says, 'unpolitical at the time. I saw the Germans as people and as bearers of the language, but the effect on me of that incident must have been powerful, if unconscious.' He was still the silent, alert observer with the slightly clenched jaw and remained so when, three years later, as a school master, he brought a party of school-boys to Freiburg-im-Breisgau. Carried away with the group enthusiasm, they returned—as so many did in those early days of Nazi power—'plastered with swastikas'. Faulk was curious to know more. When the Mayor of Freiburg, a fanatical early Nazi, an *alter Kämpfer*, said it was possible for a foreigner like Faulk to go to an *Arbeitsdienst* Centre, he seized the opportunity and went through part of a normal course of the compulsory Labour Service at Heidelberg. What a privilege for the young Scot, the Mayor would have thought, and how impressed he will be by the strength and fervour of our national revival! In fact, he was providing him with an insight into methods of group-manipulation that he would try to undo among Germans of the same age group a decade later. Nazism pursued him home, for he was now on the mailing list for the Nazi youth magazine, *Wille und Macht*. Its very title 'Will and Power' and its nationalist and militarist outlook made a strong negative impression on Faulk. His sense of empathy with other human beings was violated.

Looking back over the years, Faulk believes that it was this capacity for empathy that underlay his actions in life, rather than any motivation. 'I am convinced', he has written, 'that one is born with a certain degree of empathy that is fostered or inhibited or distorted in the first years of rearing, rather than any so-called principles.' In his case it clearly was fostered in his Dundee home and through it he became an effective schoolmaster. Consequently, he was never inclined to see life through national or political, but rather more through sociological, eyes. He was, therefore, un-touched by the wave of anti-German feeling that swept through Britain at the end of the war. He expected virtually all the prisoners coming through his hands to be Nazis, but he also accepted them as soldiers and as men showing fortitude in adversity. But he knew very little about them.

Although in a reserved occupation, Faulk had joined up at the beginning of the war 'as much from a sense of need as of duty'. After being on the last war-time intake of officers at Sandhurst, he did a spell with the Cameron Highlanders and, because of his languages, became an intelligence officer. Then came the fateful accident which saved him from the Normandy beaches. After a long spell in hospital, he was posted to the Other Ranks POW camp, at Aberlady near Edinburgh, as interpreter. He spoke the language flawlessly with that tang that always gives the Scot an edge over the Englishman in speaking German. At Aberlady in that summer of 1944 the best method to maintain good order, as Faulk saw it, was to make this an internal responsibility of the Germans. To his surprise, all the prisoners there were anti-NCO; they were fed up with being bawled at and being kicked around. So none of the sergeant-majors wanted to be camp leader. Faulk had his remedy for this. 'I lined them up, gave each one as he stood to attention the command, "Arms bend, open hand!" and into each open hand I put a piece of screwed up paper. Then came the order, "Open papers!" Then: "Who has the paper with the cross on it?" and, when I got the answer, "You are the camp leader." Dead silence! Then one man—and only one—slowly grinned and said clearly, "*Das war gut!*" ' Faulk was hardly aware at this time of the tensions and was only mildly surprised when the Nazis tried to take over the hospital section. There was no question at this camp of sending men out on working parties, although this was allowed under the Geneva Convention. For one thing, they would not co-operate, for another the population were frankly frightened of men they imagined to be dangerous. Another part of Faulk's job was to sort out the thousands of non-Germans captured in Wehrmacht uniform, conscripts whom it was usually possible to turn around and put into British uniform for service on the Allied side.

From Aberlady Faulk was posted to Wandsworth Common. This had been an untented assembly point for Allied troops just before D-Day, and was now a huge barbed-wire cage containing a thousand and more POWs, including some hundreds of Russian *Hiwis*, captured in France. Faulk recalls some remarkable characters among them. One had been a strong man at a circus, and people would congregate to watch him lift a railway sleeper in each hand (instead of two men per sleeper) and throw them nonchalantly on to a railway truck. Another was 'the only survivor of a battalion from a remote corner of the Soviet Union. No one spoke his language, he was too dull to learn Russian from the others, and simply watched their faces intently, his expression moulding itself from laughter to seriousness according to what he saw. He spoke to no man, and understood no man—one of the saddest cases I knew.'

Wandsworth was a rough camp with tents for a few, slit trenches for most. Vermin spread fast and by September the area had been reduced to mud; even the small British staff were living in trenches covered with corrugated iron. It was here that Faulk had a chance to discover his lion-tamer qualities. The German sergeant-major in charge decided to hold a parade to show that his men, at least, had not lost morale. The Russians were looking on from the side when one of them, a cheeky or curious teenager, walked forward and stood a few paces behind the sergeant-major, gawking up at the bawling German, who turned round and saw him there. 'Clear off.' The Russian boy, not understanding a word, just nodded and grinned. The sergeant-major went up to him, put his hand on his face and pushed him over into the mud. Delighted, the German ranks roared with laughter. At this, a second Russian came forward, went up close to the German. 'What did you do that for?' The answer was a gesture showing him that he would receive the same treatment. But this Russian was made 'of steel and concrete' and, with a single blow, knocked the sergeant-major cold. The first that Faulk, who was on the edge of the camp, knew of this was when he saw the corporal on duty running as fast as he could off the field. 'What's wrong?' 'There's a riot going on. I don't want them to get my revolver.' Faulk seized his two walking sticks and hobbled towards the ruck. He arrived just as Russian reinforcements were turning up, carrying bricks and planks, and some spiral metal rods used for holding down barbed wire. At the top of his extremely powerful voice he yelled, 'Stop!' 'I represented authority,' he writes, 'and it was an internationally understandable word. The riot stopped at once and the participants disappeared like snow in the hot sun—all but one German who stood his ground and glared defiance. I hobbled towards him at once and he, too, made off. The sergeant-major was still lying there on the ground; otherwise, I would not have been able to identify the first culprit.' Faulk, using a Volga German as interpreter, held an immediate enquiry, there on the edge of the common. The German sergeant-major with his twisted face could barely speak, while the Russian vividly relived his part in the affair in mime. 'I gave them both a rather nominal twenty-eight days, but the camp was dissolved before that was up because of the scandal about the vermin.' In the meantime, a party from the Russian Military Mission—the toughest characters Faulk ever saw in his life—had come down to screen their people. On the evening before their departure—the *Hiwis* believed they were on their way to their homes—they raided the German part of the camp for musical instruments and danced and sang all night.

From Wandsworth Faulk was posted to Camp 181 at Carburton in Nottinghamshire, again as interpreter. The Commandant was a Lieutenant-Colonel Ellison of the Grenadier Guards. 'It was', Faulk says, 'a normal Nazi society,' but, unlike officer camps, without political control. The men with the war about to be lost were edging towards something new, and he began to talk to them not as soldier to soldier but as man to man. 'I didn't attack Nazism directly but spoke about my impressions of pre-war Germany at, for instance, the Heidelberg *Arbeitslager*. I told them what I thought and said I was prepared to discuss what they thought—as a basis for looking into the future.' So much and so swiftly did Faulk change the atmosphere that when the War Office asked for volunteers for outdoor working parties 100 per cent put their names down, whereas in every other Midland camp there had been total refusal.

This success led Faulk to a bold stroke. In that last February of the war at the officer camp at Bridgend in South Wales there was a mass escape. Sixty-nine men tunnelled out; unfortunately for them it was a security area and all were rounded up, but not without considerable panic in the vicinity. The War Office reacted sharply: the officers of Bridgend were a potential menace. The majority were to be sent to Carburton, which would be turned into a high security camp, and they were to be left to stew for a while in their own juice. Faulk undertook to go one better. Before the camp was evacuated in readiness, he handpicked 250 other ranks and asked them if they would stay behind as orderlies, cooks and medical staff to the influx of some twelve hundred officers described by the War Office as 'ardent Nazis'. He interviewed each one personally and asked them if they would support his plan to keep the newcomers under surveillance. Faulk's previous success with them was supplemented by the natural anti-officer attitude of the average Landser in captivity and all volunteered to go along with him. In addition he won over five of the Carburton commissioned ranks: a dentist, and two doctors, and the two padres. One of these was Father Theo Lotz, a rare case of a Catholic padre who was also an officer. An immensely tall Jesuit and an outspoken, tolerant and humorous man, he later became Monsignor Lotz, chaplain of Cologne University. The stage was now set for an unique confrontation.[19]

The officers from Camp 11 set off in the morning of 23 March, marching heavily guarded to Bridgend Station. They arrived at Worksop late in the evening and marched again the five miles to Carburton. As they swept into the camp their aggressive morale confirmed Faulk's expectations. Because of the black-out it was almost dark and there were only two hand-lamps for the reception and search. Faulk, speaking his faultless German, gave directions for some of them to sit on a bench. '*Ach der!*' a large bully of a man sneered as he pushed his way through. 'Oh him! In three days the little deserter will be dancing to our tune.' The word was going round that Faulk, whose name sounds exactly like 'Volk', was either an emigrant or a hateful turncoat. The Germans took over the camp according to a pre-arranged plan. Colonel Lemke, the senior officer, was installed in the heart of the compound, but the real power lay with the adjutant who, according to Faulk, was a political officer. How many of the 1,300 were convinced Nazis is hard to say, but the war was still on and their outer cohesion was maintained by a mixture of group loyalty and fear of reprisals. As officers most also felt affronted as they gradually realised that the camp staff had been worked on by the British—to many they were simply informers and traitors.

Next morning Colonel Lemke, his adjutant and his interpreter called on the Commandant. Asking the other two to leave the room, Ellison, every inch a gentleman, said through his interpreter, 'I understand you consider it your duty to escape. Mine is to keep you from doing so.' He stood up, extended his hand and said, 'Good luck!' Some irrepressible hot-heads had meantime decided to pull the cross off the chapel which, constructed out of scrap material, had been the pride of earlier inmates. Faulk was told of this and had a car headlight beamed on to the cross and sentries posted nearby. As they could no longer get at the offensive symbol, they determined on the next night to urinate and defecate inside the chapel, but made off when spotted by the waiting

British guards. Colonel Ellison was deeply shocked at the turn of events, and gave Faulk a free hand in the battle for ascendancy which now began in earnest. Blandly and politely Lemke and his adjutant asked for a meeting with their formidable opponent. In view of the strain on the staff of such a big camp, suggested the adjutant, would it not be better if they took over the commissariat and also all the personal accounts of the officers?* This, Faulk knew, was a ploy already used in Bridgend to harass anyone politically suspect: their cards were marked but their goods retained. When this was seen through the stratagems grew more sinister. There were two railway officials captured in France who ranked as officers; at Bridgend they had dared to send a permitted postcard to their wives instead of, as 'recommended', to Hitler for his coming birthday in April. For this act of civil courage they had been severely beaten up. On arrival at Carburton one had gone straight to sick quarters, the other had asked for asylum with the other ranks. 'It is surely unfitting,' the adjutant told Faulk, 'for an officer not to be with his fellow officers. Please see that he comes over to us.' Faulk heard through his loyal staff that it was intended to do him quietly in.

It happened that as well as twelve priests and pastors there were fourteen doctors among the newcomers. Those who were senior to the two 'loyalists' now marched into sick quarters to take over, but could be legally rebutted, as by the Geneva Convention the two already there were under orders of the holding power. Next a mammoth sick parade was ordered so as to prove more doctors were needed. When a long queue formed, laughing and joking, Faulk said he would dismiss them but the two doctors insisted they would treat each man even if it took all day—all they wanted was more pills. As a result the camp spent an extremely restless night! That put an end to the sick queues; instead half a dozen burly young men were instructed how to feign symptoms that required prolonged treatment. The two doctors and most of the camp knew that they had also been instructed to wreck the sick quarters during the night and beat up certain of the patients. They appealed to Faulk who had the six driven in ambulances to a military hospital where, to their chagrin, they were kept on observation and a strict diet for six days.

The Nazi leadership was now desperate to assert its authority against Faulk. The Catholic chaplain, Father Lotz, was con-

* Officers still received pay but in the form of canteen vouchers.

demned to death at a *Fehmgericht* (secret court). Faulk says that he virtually ordered him to stay in the camp as his flight would be a victory for the extremists. That night when he was due to be hung his hut was boarded up, bolts were put on his door and he was provided with a whistle. He blew it once but, despite the speed of the guard nearby, the attackers disappeared. Faulk's final stroke was to confront Colonel Lemke next day without his adjutant with a warning that he personally would be held responsible before the law for any acts of violence that took place. He was sufficiently scared to call the camp on parade and tell them, 'If these things go on I will myself hand the culprits over to justice.' He then dissolved the special court and the raiding squad. Throughout the whole battle of nerves the camp staff, regarded by most of the officers as traitors or communists, stood firm. These men, who had known years of fighting and one at least of whom was an SS-man, had developed their own new group identity and were not to be overawed. When some officers appeared in the kitchen they were met by the quiet menace of a huge cook swinging a giant ladle. When the camp office was entered and the staff threatened, a clerk named Beck stood on a chair and made such a sincere and impassioned speech against Nazism that the visitors disappeared without a word.*

All this took place over some ten eventful days during which the staff made a list of those who they thought were fully behind the Nazi leadership in the battle for ascendancy. The majority of officers may not have been actively involved but most were certainly affronted by the way that in their eyes Faulk had 'manipulated' the other ranks against them. Siegfried Bandelow, one of the junior officers and a member of the theatre group from Bridgend, says that they tried for the fun of it and to obviate boredom, to hoodwink Faulk by planting 'gags' and tall stories among the 'informers'. But it is unlikely that the other ranks were deceived. After years of front line fighting they were very much

---

* There is a sad supplement to this story. Beck was repatriated early as a White to the French zone of Germany, and picked up as a war-criminal, a case of mistaken identity. Beck in despair gave the French authorities Faulk's name as a referee and actually got a letter out to him. With great difficulty because of the conditions in Europe at the time Faulk got as far as the town where he was imprisoned. An officer at the prison, however, brought him to a dead stop with 'Pourquoi vous en faites-vous? Ce n'est qu'un Boche.' Faulk was not allowed to see Beck and knows nothing of his subsequent fate.

men in their own right and by this stage the average *Landser* tended to be anti-officer anyway, which the latter bitterly resented. The drama ended on 4th April when without warning 250 selected officers—Bandelow among them—were ordered to parade with their gear. Cocky and flattered at being singled out, they were marched—except for a few injured—the five miles to the neighbouring camp at Carburton. A month later with the capitulation defiance, with a few exceptions, ceased; by the end of the year quite a few of the 250 were enjoying the congenial atmosphere of Featherstone Park, the 'camp of confidence'.

Captain Faulk was now a man marked for promotion. At Carburton he had demonstrated a double gift: he could reach the minds and feelings of those who were open to discussion, and he could confront and outwit the fanatical loyalists. His success in this and in getting 100 per cent volunteers for a labour force led Midland Command to call him in whenever a new camp was being founded. Through Major Kettler who saw him at work at Carburton his fame reached Wing Commander Hitch, head of the embryo unit which had been set up by the Foreign Office for the political re-education of German prisoners of war. As a result this sympathetic and formidable Scottish schoolmaster was given the chance of his life.

Sweden, that most aloof of countries, has become with Switzerland the arch-neutral of Europe. Geography and the proximity across a narrow sea of two warring nations twice this century strengthened her wish to remain uninvolved. Two Swedes of the post-war world have, however, caught the headlines and the public imagination. The first was Count Folke Bernadotte who, with a fleet of buses, entered Germany in the last weeks of the Third Reich and, with the surprising agreement of Himmler who was trying to curry favour with the Allies, rescued several thousand captives from probable death. Three years later he was assassinated while a United Nations mediator in Palestine. But the character and personal claims of this unfortunately vain man have not withstood the scrutiny of historians.[20] Dag Hammerskjöld— public servant, mystic and scholar—was a quite opposite type: deeply self-questioning to the point of selflessness. His role as the first Secretary General of the United Nations and as a fearless man of peace is a matter of history. He too died violently.

A third Swede who worked for international reconciliation is, however, almost forgotten, even in his own country. There were no outer dramas in his life and the press was hardly aware of him. He was Pastor Birger Forell.[21] Three times he was drawn from his native country into the orbit of Germany and each time when that country was being subjected to tyranny or defeat—in 1919 to 1920, in 1929 to 1942 and from 1944 till his death. Each time his involvement was more complete. The third occasion began when he was asked to become special minister to the German prisoners of war in Britain. The invitation came from Dr George Bell, Bishop of Chichester, and led to his playing a unique role as a bringer of hope to the camps, as a doer of good works and as an instigator of enterprises. History may well find that Forell was one of the most remarkable men of peace of his times. Significantly the chief inspiration in his life came from Mahatma Gandhi; and it was a former German prisoner of war, when Rektor of Münster University, who suggested he should be given the Nobel Peace Prize.

Forell's origins were humble. He was born in 1893 in the small town of Södehamn 150 miles north of Stockholm. To the west lies thinly populated farmland and forest, to the east the Gulf of Bothnia, shimmering in summer, in winter frozen in its motion all the way over to Finland, except where the ice-breakers keep a channel open for the iron-ore ships from the north. The community around Söderhamn—farmers, fishermen and workers in the wood industry—was close-knit in a Lutheran way, but without the social hierarchy of further south. From early on young Forell was determined to rise beyond these limiting circumstances. His father, chauffeur to the owner of a pulp-mill, had to pinch and scrape to send him to commercial school, after which he had to fend for himself. His nineteenth summer was an important time: he spent it with his books and his maternal grandmother, Greta Maria Jannsen. This old lady with calm, smiling ways and an inner radiance of life, was then seventy-four. She lived, except in winter, in a hamlet in the remote forest wilderness of Ljusdal. From her he had learnt how to pray; especially with her he felt the closeness of the grace of God and the nearness of Christ. Those long still months of 1913 with her were her last on earth and she died there at Ljusdal under his care. It was surely through her that he received the spiritual call that would take him till his thirty-fifth year on a remarkable and far spiritual journey.[22] The first stage was to qualify to study theology, which he began to do four years later at Uppsala.

Uppsala at that time, and until his death in 1930, was dominated by the towering figure of that great European, Archbishop Nathan Söderblom, one of the chief architects of the growing movement of Christian unity. But this prince of the Protestant church, who was to have a strong influence on Forell's life, did not become his guiding star. In 1916 Professor Rudolf Otto of Marburg published one of the most famous and seminal books of the century: *Das Heilige* (A Sense of the Holy). In it Otto proclaimed that there is one essential experience common to all religions, namely a sense of the numinous; and this sense of the numinous was the very spirit of God and all men could respond to it. A profound reverence should, therefore, be felt towards all the great religions between which there was a deep inner bond. Otto had not only experienced this bond of the numinous himself, but had many personal links with other religions, especially in Asia. Forell read Rudolf Otto's book and knew that there was only one thing he must do: sit at the German's feet. His professor enviously gave him leave to interrupt his studies, he borrowed money from a relative and set off.

It was 1919. Forell was filled with compassion for a country in the humiliation of defeat, hunger and civil strife. He went first to Tübingen and then spent a year at Marburg, drinking in Otto's teaching not only in lectures and seminars but during country rambles and private talks. Otto opened many other doors to him and, indeed, was so taken with Forell that he was soon asking him to become secretary to the Religious League of Mankind which he had just founded. Forell, with his degree still to complete, had to decline, but he was beginning a life as a man with a wide web of human relationships, mainly working quietly in the background. Archbishop Söderblom himself found him a most useful adviser about the broader Lutheran scene and procured him his first post at the Swedish Legation pastorate in Rotterdam—in essence a mission to Swedish seamen. He stayed there five years, visiting the merchant fleet at sea during the summer, for the rest of the year residing—he was now married to a pastor's daughter—in the harbour district of Rotterdam. But the wider work in the ecumenical movement continued, as did his support for Otto, with whom he attended the historic First Universal Christian Conference on Life and Work at Stockholm in 1925.

With Otto, Forell had been mainly taken up into the realm of elevated thought and feeling, but his mentor was now to lead him to the crucial experience of his life which would root him solidly in the world of practical action. He invited him to be his companion on a journey to India during the winter of 1927-8, to further the Religious League of Mankind. They visited the Ramakrishna Mission, the Buddhist League of Young Men, the Maharaja of Mysore, and had a reception with the Viceroy. But the main event was a conference at which some thirty representatives of the main religions of India, and so of the world,—Hindus, Muslims, Buddhists and Christians—came together at Gandhi's ashram at Achmedabad. The object was to further an International Federation of Religions.

At that time Gandhi was already world-famous. He had not only brought hope and cohesion to the down-trodden masses of his countrymen; his technique of passive civil disobedience had fundamentally changed the political and social state of affairs under the British Raj. Based on the Mahatma's deep spirituality and respect for all human beings, it was an entirely new method of transforming an explosive situation by peaceful means, of bringing freedom and social betterment without violent revolution. The three-day conference held under his charismatic guidance—the first of its kind ever to take place—was thus an important historical event. When it was due to start Professor Otto was ill and Birger Forell, then aged thirty-five, went as his representative.

Forell has left us in his only book one of the clearest acknowledgements by any Westerner of Gandhi's genius and spirituality. His description captures the austere yet colourful charm of the setting, beginning with his dismay, on arrival at the station, at finding young women waiting to carry his baggage. He protested, but they easily hoisted it on their heads and carried it gracefully to the ashram, which lay in a sandy, almost treeless, plain beside a dried-up water course. Forell was ushered into a room in which some two hundred people were already sitting, mostly cross-legged. 'I did not,' he writes, 'at first recognize Gandhi who was indistinguishable from the mass. Then when I did, he felt my eyes upon him and looked up at me. . . . There is nothing impressive about his physical person, with a body emaciated through fasting, vigils and work. His face, hardly beautiful, his rather large shaven skull, his protruding upper lip accentuated by a dark moustache— these are hardly noticed when one meets his clear, kind, scrutinising eyes. There is nothing in his manner that signifies the public person. When, at the end of the session, he passed down the row we opened for him, he saluted in all directions, but almost timidly, showing the degree to which he had kept his soul uncontaminated by those attractions of popularity that have a disastrous effect even on people of genius.'

The congress discussed Otto's proposals for co-operation between the major religions and the theme of the first session was the need for a world-wide spiritual revival and return to the spirit of love as the only possible foundation for living in harmony together. Excellent, but not unusual sentiments, comments Forell. Fortunately, the conference did not remain at this level, but on the second day developed into a profound discussion of missionaries and the problem of conversions. Gandhi's standpoint, which he made very clear, was shattering to many Christians present: an international religious society could not by definition be missionary. Its aim should rather be that its Christian members become better Christians, its Muslim members better Muslims, its Hindu members better Hindus, and so on. In that way they would find each other better. Any direct, conscious effort to try to convert others through more or less intellectual means was wasted spiritual force; and every organised mission ran the danger of developing into a religious imperialism, which was a danger to religion itself. Gandhi's close American friend, C. F. Andrews, a large, bearded Franciscan-looking man, wearing a white Indian robe, and the second figure at the conference, asked humorously if Gandhi would allow Christian missionaries to go to cannibals or animists in Africa. Gandhi warded off this sally with a light touch: if all missionaries were to come in the spirit of his good friend, that would be all right. The true task of the missionaries in Gandhi's final definition was *to serve, to serve, and yet to serve*.[23]

Today these sentiments seem unexceptionable; fifty years ago they were original and challenging in the extreme. Forell recorded them with obvious approval. But, more important still for him, were two private meetings he had with Gandhi who, one can assume, discerned at once the quality and capacity of his guest. He even gave up his usual hour of meditation to Forell, and sitting at his spinning wheel, put him at ease with his light child-like laugh and by asking him for a short lesson in the correct pronunciation of Swedish names. Then, it seems, Gandhi opened himself, so that Forell saw the real force of his nature. It was the opposite of the harmonious 'holy men' he had found among the Buddhists; a man, rather, who was committed to outer action, totally involved in a struggle both with the world as it was and inwardly with himself, and achieving at the same time a marvellous lightness of spirit. Before leaving, Forell was touched by a small incident. At one of the receptions he noticed a tall, lanky Englishman who, without seeming important, went and sat near the Mahatma to drink tea. He was C. N. Broomfield. Their respect and affection for each other had begun during the trial in 1922 when Broomfield, the District Judge, had reluctantly sentenced the Mahatma to six years imprisonment for civil disobedience, of which he served two.

The artery of influence that had flowed out from Gandhi has had an immeasurable effect, spiritual, political and social, on our age. But it is not always recognised. The triumphs of non-violence must, by definition, be slow-working and unspectacular. They happen through the gradual irrigation of feelings and the quiet persistence and bravery of individuals. Their positive result is often the absence of a violence that otherwise would have taken place, and the absence of something is never news. For this reason, stories of peace-making, of the drawing-off of the poisons of war, of the reconciliation of enemies do not receive much attention from journalists, political analysts or even historians. The Nobel Peace Prize, it is true, does something to remedy this, but the concept of the 'peace worker' has been much abused and is often far removed from the ideal and the condition that Gandhi himself set: that the bringers of peaceful change must themselves be without violence and at peace within themselves.

This was pre-eminently the case with Birger Forell. The next year was the hardest in his life for his visit to India had been cut short by bad news. One of his young sons had already died; now the second had suddenly succumbed to a virus and he hastened home to comfort his wife, Calise. Soon afterwards he met a surprising opposition from his Archbishop. The Swedish pastorate in Berlin—the ideal post for Forell, if ever there was one—had become vacant. Söderblom put difficulties in his way because he sensed that Forell was drawing apart from the Swedish Church, and might even have a loyalty to a world wider than protestantism. Forell, characteristically, went to beard the lion of Uppsala and found him oddly nervous and embarrassed. But, eventually, since there was no other serious candidate, Forell was given the post and, ten years after his first encounter with Germany, began his second which was much deeper and more testing. It was 1929, the world slump about to begin, the triumph of Hitler on the horizon. He knew all too clearly what that triumph would mean to the true Germany he loved all the more because it was under threat. In those violent March days of 1933 (when Henry Faulk too was in Berlin) he wrote a last frank letter to Otto—afterwards he was too aware of censorship. 'The very foundation (*Bestand*) of the German nation is now at stake.'

As minister to the Swedish Embassy, Forell had diplomatic status, which gave his parsonage in the Landstrasse in Berlin-Wilmersdorf immunity from search. Primarily, he was there for the 1400 Swedes living in Berlin, but, as the creeping power of Nazism tried to move in on all walks of life, his house became a focus for sustaining resistance to the Gestapo and helping its victims. The front door was usually under surveillance, and attempts were made to bug the building, but distinguished visitors came and went; so did occasional people wanted by the Gestapo, for there was a large garden and a backway in and out. Opposition figures like Bishop Dibelius and Dietrich Bonhoeffer were entertained at the parsonage; and from England Dr Nathaniel Micklem from Oxford and Dr Bell, Bishop of Chichester, who were both deeply concerned to give succour where they could during the Nazi attack on the Church. The latter had been one of the first Englishmen to draw attention to the menace of Nazism not only to the world, but to the true Germany. At the World Council of Churches at Oxford in 1937 he said, 'The most important thing happening in the world is the destruction of Christianity in Central Europe.' His empathy with sufferers under Hitler was as strong as Forell's.

Later on, in the prisoner of war camps in Britain, non-Nazis who had met him or known of his activities in Berlin, would button-hole him. On occasion these activities brought him into direct confrontation with the Gestapo. He did not hesitate to sit it out in their dread headquarters in the Albrechtstrasse till he could meet a high enough official to reverse a decision on a refused exit permit. Forell's inner force, coupled with a shrewd use of his diplomatic status, frequently nonplussed the bully mentality. But Sweden was still politically isolated, weak, and liable to invasion, and would remain so till after Stalingrad and the turning of the war against Germany. Ships still sailed down the Gulf of Bothnia carrying the high-grade ore needed for Hitler's war machine. Forell undoubtedly took risks, possibly too many, for he was recalled in the spring of 1942 to be minister at Boras, a textile town in Southern Sweden with a population of 25,000. His last act with his diplomatic passport was to take to Sweden for safe-keeping some secret files of the Confessing Church in Germany, which he had been hiding in the parsonage attic.

Forell now entered on a rare, relatively peaceful interlude in his career. But it did not last for long—a bare two years. Early in 1944 the Bishop of Chichester sent his letter of invitation. Dr Bell had already made himself a thorn in the side of the British Government by his speeches in the House of Lords against the Allied policy of indiscriminate bombing of German civilians; and he had met Dietrich Bonhoeffer secretly in Stockholm in 1942 in order to convey facts of the German resistance to the British government. Always the long-term Christian strategist, this 'turbulent priest' as Anthony Eden, the Foreign Minister, called him,[24] was now looking ahead to after the Allies had won the war: a devastated Germany must be brought back into the community of nations, and what was more important than to reach, with a message of hope and faith for the future, the hearts and minds of the young men who would return to rebuild their country? No one, he knew, could do this more acceptably and with more love than Birger Forell. Coming from Dr Bell, such a request and challenge could hardly be rejected. Calise, the three assistant pastors at Boras and his own bishop made it easy for Forell to accept.

The assignment was, in the first place, for one year. He arrived in England in April 1944. The plan was that he should work for the War Prisoners Aid of the World Alliance of YMCAs, which already in four continents—but not in Russia—was providing welfare for prisoners of war: books, writing material, paints, musical instruments and scores, footballs and even seed-packets. The operation was financed from American and world-wide YMCA funds and by the Church of the Brethren in the USA. The Swedish charity Help for War Victims and his own congregation at Boras also gave direct support to Forell.

Before the invasion of Europe there were still very few camps in Britain—most prisoners were sent to Canada or Australia. Forell, whose base was a small flat in Great Russell Street a few steps from the YMCA building, could get around all of them in a few weeks. After the invasion of Normandy they increased rapidly, and by the autumn he was writing to Archbishop Eidem:

'This is an SOS. There are not just 70,000 but 100,000 and the War Ministry reckons there will soon be 150,000 prisoners here. Yesterday I was in a camp of 5,000, living in very primitive conditions and there are many such.' Forell, who always travelled with his car crammed with musical instruments, goes on: 'In half an hour I had assembled a small band. My few Bibles were literally torn from my hands. There really is a chance here of a "mission to the heathen". Fellow countrymen, wake up and see! This can be your great opportunity.' Forell was hoping that, while Switzerland, always ready to help bind the wounds of war, would take over similar work in France and Belgium, Sweden would take on the lion's share of welfare in Britain, for it was better, he felt, for this to be done by neutral nations. At first Sweden, to his deep disappointment, sent no one, though later several came. But he did find the ideal assistant in the Reverend Dr Herbert Hartwell. This Christian convert and one-time member of Pastor Niemoeller's congregation at Dahlem, had under the name of Hirschwald been the youngest judge in the highest court in Berlin. Dismissed by the Nazis, he had continued to work for the Confessing Church, until warned through Dr Bell that he was about to be arrested. With the Bishop's assistance, he and his family left by the last emigrants' train from Berlin in 1939. He had then trained as Congregational Minister under Dr Micklem at Mansfield College, Oxford, and had been uniquely ordained 'for the Ministry of the Word and Sacraments in the prisoner of war camps in Britain'. Utterly modest, deeply caring, and a most hard-working organiser, he was the perfect helpmeet for Forell.

At the other end of the POW welfare axis was the YMCA representative, John Barwick, former manager of a travel agency. He was impulsive, brash, immensely energetic and helpful, and very American. Barwick could not abide the sensitive, deceptively mild Hartwell and wanted to get rid of him. Hartwell, on his side, was offended by a man who, in his eyes, seemed to think that providing footballs was the essential part of his work. Forell, who was well above the personal animosities that riddle even charitable agencies, and had plenty of humour, could work equally well with both. He made patient use of Barwick's good-heartedness, realising that, if the reasons for an action were spelt out, Barwick would be endlessly helpful. Also, as he confided to his diary, 'It is liberating to be able to talk to someone who both thinks of what you want, *and* can open coffers.'

As the work increased, a joint committee for welfare of prisoners of war was formed. This eventually included the YMCA, the International Red Cross, a Joint Committee for Education, World Student Relief and the Society of Friends (Quakers), the last of these being for Forell especially and always 'a very present help in trouble.' But no one was so active or had so many ideas as Forell. To the POW Division at the War Office he put forward various schemes, most of which eventually bore fruit: for a special camp for theological students and another for teachers, for a printing unit run by prisoners—all these to be supported by the YMCA. The colonel who was the brain behind POW operations at the War Office, impressed and was impressed by Forell; he advised him not to depend on the authorities too much but to take on as much as possible himself. 'You have made a good start—you're doing fine!' Forell was for ever on the search for books in German, proposing that the libraries left by the Wehrmacht in France be gathered in and distributed to the camps; this happened, but to the benefit of the Germans held in France and Belgium. Two young women, Jewish refugees from Germany, combed for him the second-hand bookshops in London, above all good quality literature, but nothing too erotic: a young officer had remarked to him, 'It's hard enough for us, anyway!'. But Forell's main occupation was visiting the camps, and very often the hospital camps. Nothing ever hardened his compassion for the wounded, for the man in Sheffield without a leg who didn't dare write to his wife that he was a cripple, for the eighteen-year-old Austrian conscripted into the SS, who had come to realize what that now meant: 'His eyes burned with horror as he told me what he had seen in the East.' Many at this camp were sick with anxiety about their relatives as the bombing got worse and the Russians began to enter their country. 'It is shattering,' Forell wrote, 'to go through the wards with their dozens of bandaged men, with arms and legs shot off, and not to have a violin to play them a chorale of Bach.* I sat beside a twenty-year-old boy from Cologne, who had just heard he had no hope of seeing again. He held my hand for half an hour. We spoke little, but I still feel the pressure of his hand . . . The sympathetic head doctor stood the whole while beside the

* Forell was very musical, but he had not had time to play his violin for many years.

bed. "Ah, how helpless we are at such times," he said when we were outside. We shook hands, each looking in the other's eyes, and understanding one another.'

No one who met Forell could ever forget him, although, as with Gandhi, the initial impression could be misleading. 'I saw three figures approaching from the distance. Two were extremely tall and imposing, as Swedes are. The third was insignificant and, by comparison, almost ugly. It was a shock to me that this was the person about whom I had heard so much. But when he began to speak he was the only man there.' This was the first impact made on Helene von Koenigswald, artist wife of Forell's German biographer. She sketched him but, she says, could not begin to convey the animation and fascination he exercised in conversation. Ronald Howe first saw him in the corridors of the YMCA Centre in London. 'My first impression was one of total quiet and colourlessness. Later, I began to observe his quality of awareness and compassion; at conferences he was the one who noticed if someone had not settled down and quietly talked to him between the sessions.' But to Dr Hartwell he was 'always impressive and very masculine; his eyes and face very much the mirror of what was within. He was essentially a man of action rather than words, speaking at length about future plans only: a man who lived exclusively from his inward spiritual resources.'

At the end of the account of his visit to Gandhi, Forell records the farewell message that the Mahatma gave to the 1928 congress. He set it down like a programme for his own life. 'We all have much to give each other, and we all need to pray for guidance and light in order to serve truth. We need to teach ourselves each day that we cannot live without each other, and life can only be fulfilled in serving love. Our minds tell us that love is the law of life itself, but it is so difficult to act accordingly, but if we believe that God is the one that works in everything, we must also have the courage to approach him in spite of our frailness. Let us, therefore, each one of us pray in the secret of our own chamber that God make us all to be his able servants.'

Forell's son, Professor Urban Forell, has passed on a story he can only have heard from his father who, quite early on, had to go to the War Office in Whitehall to meet some senior official. This personage asked him what his intentions were with the German prisoners.

'I suppose, Padre, you'll follow the Vansittart line.'

'No,' said Forell, 'I would never accept such nonsense.'

'But how will you deal with them?'

'I will treat everyone as if he were my own son.'

There was a silence, till the surprised Englishman said, not unsympathetically, 'Padre, I wouldn't know what's best myself.'

5

1945: Time of the Leper

This is my cap,
this is my coat,
here is my shaving kit
in a linen bag.

A tin-can is my plate
also my mug,
I have scratched my name
on the tin.

This is my notebook,
this is my ground sheet,
this is my towel,
this is my thread.

Stock-list, Günther Eich (1945)

Stripped of all power, all rights, of its dignity as a nation and of most of its manhood, Germany was reduced in 1945 to a bedrock of existence. The state itself had ceased to exist, while its leaders had committed suicide, fled or were awaiting trial. Every corner of the land was occupied. Over four million had died fighting or were missing, and 600,000 in air-raids; another possible fourteen million—the equivalent of the population of Scandinavia—were being expelled from the Sudetenland and the lost territories of the east; of these two million would die in the process. Seven million more were prisoners, two million of these in Russia. Four million houses had been destroyed or heavily damaged. Never in European history had a great nation been laid so low. Not since the Thirty Years War had there been such devastation. Günther Eich's well-known poem written in an American camp in Germany describes in a language which is itself stripped to a bare minimum the condition of the country in 1945. Life had to begin again at the elementary level, like someone learning to talk again after a severe breakdown.

If Germany was reduced to this state, the vast majority on the Allied side and still more so in the liberated populations of Europe was glad. The Germans were being taught a lesson, hopefully for all time, that playing the master race and militarism bring terrible retribution. But there were still fears and doubts. It was natural for a virile nation to revive a second time and seek revenge: how could the world be sure that unless held firmly down they would not start the whole thing over again? Lord Vansittart's book *Black Record* appeared to have been borne out. Churchill's pithy rhetoric was bandied about as if it was a statement of permanent historical truth: 'That dangerous combination of warrior and slave', and again, 'The German is either at your feet or at your throat'.[25]

It is difficult to reconstruct the mood of 1945. Today the older citizens of the Federal Republic do not like to recall the emasculated state of their country only half a lifetime ago, when hatred was directed at them as indiscriminately as had been the mass bombing. Historians trying to recapture from witnesses the truth about those days find whole areas of experience blotted out, relegated to unconscious memory. And on the victor's side it is not entirely comfortable to remember the wave of moral righteousness which, in partnership with Stalin's Russia, conveniently found in one nation the root cause of the century's chief troubles. As the revelations of the death camps became known it was tempting to see the whole German people as guilty because—and it seemed so obvious—they had willed Hitler to power and gloried in his triumphs. 'The Germans are moral lepers, and should be treated as such until we are certain that the race has been purged and redeemed', wrote John Gordon in the *Sunday Express* a fortnight before the end of the war and went on, 'The Germans in my view should be outlawed from the civilised world until the present generation of Germans is dead. The account against them is so great that it cannot be repaid in a generation.'

Already in 1941 the *Daily Express* had voiced the view 'Whether you like it or not, vengeance on Germany is becoming the aim of all Europe'. Four years later it was inevitable that the Beaverbrook press took the lead in whipping up the genuine mood of revulsion in Britain. Forell picked this up in his journal: 'It seems that there is a distinct propaganda to make the whole German people out as criminals and sadists.' Even the moderate press assumed that virtually all the Germans who had fought for Hitler were dyed with his doctrines. In truth the British and the Americans had themselves become tinted, if not stained, by the very evil they were fighting against: the totalitarian idea, which sees people not as individuals but in the mass. And the catch phrase of the war, 'The only good German is a dead German', could not be unlearned overnight.

The mood of the Anglo-Saxons, let it be said, was one less of vindictiveness than righteousness—a righteousness that was much more fierce on the part of the Americans than the British. This did not come as a surprise to the many German refugees settled in America. In 1940 Professor Karl Brandt prophetically warned the young Adam von Trott zu Solz—the German Foreign Office official then on a conspiratorial journey to America, who was hung for his part in the 1944 *Attentat*—of the terrible thoroughness with which America would enter the war. 'The Puritan character is still alive here,' he said, 'and once America is roused to war you will see it in all its harshness and fury. In such moments they judge men as the children of light or the children of darkness with no half-shades. They will be merciless to Germany.' So it was to be. Only a ruthless policy would teach Germany a permanent lesson. Unconditional surrender to start with; and then a Carthaginian peace, with reduction of Germany to a nation of mainly farmers and artisans incapable of waging modern war. The logical Morgenthau Plan advocating this course was published in August 1944. Though Roosevelt abandoned it as impolitic, if not too severe, its spirit remained and no other plan took its place. Even Cordell Hull, the milder Secretary of State, advocated that Germany's standard of living should be kept down, and only raised as a change of heart appeared.[26] Churchill's very characteristic idea (in 1941) of the future of a defeated Germany was of a nation 'fat but impotent'.[27]

The cornerstone of the Allies' preliminary policy was 'non-fraternisation'. It was a method of putting into coventry a people who had deeply offended against the moral code of nations. The British Army put up two huge signboards at the Dutch–German border at Hengelo: 'You are now entering Germany'. Under one was added 'Here ends the civilised world'; under the other 'Behave as conquerors'—which was Eisenhower's directive. The many Germans who surprisingly and genuinely greeted Allied troops as liberators had a rude shock. Fraternisation even with confirmed anti-Nazis was forbidden. The American Forces newspaper *Stars and Stripes* pronounced, 'If in a German town you bow your head to a pretty girl or pat a blonde child, you bow to Hitler and his reign of blood.'[28] The British approach to non-fraternisation was more rational. Goronwy Rees, then a colonel in Military Government, has said,[29] 'Behind the order there were really two motives. One was fear which was a false fear, that in some way the Germans would try to influence British troops. That was not true at all because they were only too willing to be influenced themselves by any kind of idea one was able to put to them. The other motive was to avoid giving deep offence to the people in England to whom it would have been shocking, if after five years of war and after what they had been told of the behaviour of the Germans in Europe, British troops on entering Germany had behaved as they always do—being friendly, anxious to be taken into people's houses, to become part of the family.'

The Allied experts on Germany, both in military intelligence and political warfare, had in fact completely misread the situation in the Third Reich during the final phase of the war. They reckoned that Germans defending their homeland would obey exhortations to fight to the last, that the 'Alpine Redoubt' would have to be reduced, that the Hitler Youth were all latent 'Werwolfs'. Because the tyrant had not actually been toppled, the truth about internal resistance and disaffection had been ignored; so had the yearning of the average German for peace. Excessive sacrifices had been demanded in the name of patriotism. That deeply evocative word *Heimatland*, signifying love of hearth and home, of landscape and local culture, had come, in George Steiner's memorable phrase, to mean 'a place for which, perhaps too often, a man is supposed to die'.[30] With the moral collapse which had started with the defeat at Stalingrad came fissures which rent the whole fabric of the Nazi state, so that even SS leaders, including Himmler himself, were secretly negotiating with the enemy. The physical collapse and Hitler's suicide only finalised the internal disintegration. Golo Mann, Thomas Mann's distinguished son, like his father a refugee in America, visited his country immediately after the war ended. In his *History of Germany 1919–1945* he writes, 'The evil spell lasted no longer than the magician. With incredulous astonishment the Allies found that in a country that had been ruled for twelve years by National Socialism there were in fact no National Socialists.'[31] At first sight one thinks he is being ironical—but not so. Active belief in Nazism, fundamentally a nihilistic philosophy of life, could only be sustained by national successes and had no more to offer.

If in Germany itself the Third Reich was now a bad dream, relived again and again at the de-nazification tribunals and the war crimes courts, in the Allied prisoner of war camps the situation was quite different. Here Germans were still in uniform, comrades living in more or less military formations that were self-contained, almost tribal societies. The group mentality was still paramount, and the most obvious way to preserve self-respect was to present a solid front to their gaolers who were, in general, impressed by disciplined behaviour. Basically the POWs were stateless human beings, at the disposal of their conquerors; they would have to work, to be sure, in reparation for damage caused in the war, and this many of them could accept, knowing well that forced labour had been exacted by their own side when they were winning. If they were a work force, their guardians also saw them as available to be worked upon, that is to say politically, to free them from the Nazi infection. At the Teheran Conference of November 1943 the Allies had decided that after defeat the Germans should be de-militarised, de-nazified and democratised. The first two aims implied boards of inspection and judicial panels, the third something much more difficult: an educational attempt to reach the hearts and minds of the Germans with ideas, doctrines and example. The word 're-education' had already become current for such a policy and programme which were unprecedented in European history for one nation to impose on another.

It was in many ways an unfortunate expression. It seems that it was first used in letters to the press in 1941 by writers of Vansittart's persuasion, suggesting that a body of Englishmen take up residence in Germany after the war and dedicate themselves to this self-sacrificing task. In the House of Commons on 27 May 1943, R. A. Butler, the Minister who was at the time preparing the famous Education Act that bears his name, used the word very judiciously. 'In my opinion,' he said, 'and that of my colleagues, the best way to start the re-education is by means of an overwhelming military defeat, so that [Germany] may learn once and for all that the evil doctrines which have inspired her philosophy and her leaders for many years and have had such terrible results shall not be allowed to occur again. While we should teach first of all that war does not pay, we should also be wise to realise that re-education of a people comes better from inside that people themselves ... We may then hope eventually to start such a leaven in the country that a real self-education and re-education arises.' This measured statement by Butler at least implied the existence of civilised Germans who would lead the change of heart. But such an attitude, which clearly distinguished between the Nazis and others, became increasingly rare as the war progressed, and vanished from the government front bench. Butler himself did not deal any more with the matter. Certain Bishops in the House of Lords maintained this line as did thoughtful socialists like Kingsley Martin, editor of the *New Statesman*, and Richard Stokes MP, the genial and rich industrialist who was so much the keeper of the conscience of the Labour Party at this time. In September 1943 Stokes quoted a memorable speech that General Smuts, the wisest elder statesman of the Commonwealth, had recently made in Johannesburg when he spoke of the 'revolt of the German soul itself' and of 'another Germany which must have passed through hell in witnessing the brutal and savage inhumanity of its people.'

The increasing attitude of grouping all Germans together as Nazis, a mistake Stalin never made, drew a cogent reply from one of the most distinguished German refugees, Professor Gerhart Leibholz, who held a post at Oxford and was later a member of the Supreme Constitutional Court at Karlsruhe. He wrote in July 1944, 'The implication of losing this war and the consequences of a Nazi collapse will extend so far beyond man's range of sight that forces may well be forthcoming in a much shorter time than most people realise today to satisfy the desperate need for faith, without which the re-education in post-war Germany cannot be based ... We know that there are tens of thousands in Germany who refused to compromise with the regime and who have gone through the fires of persecution. History will show that their struggle is no less heroic than that of like-minded people in occupied countries ... In addition, there are hundreds of thousands, yes, even millions of German people who have kept their faith in defiance of the Nazi regime—even if they have done so in silence ... They also will have a part to play in re-educating Germany. I even doubt the correctness of the generally held view that the entire young generation which has gone through ten years of Nazi tyranny must be considered lost.'[32] Leibholz's intuition about the true state of his country, assisted by information obtained through his being married to the twin sister of Dietrich Bonhoeffer, has been vindicated by recent studies. But in 1944 it had no chance of a hearing; letters he wrote to *The Times* and the *Manchester Guardian* were refused publication. Indeed, the views of even the best-known refugees about the state of their country and its future were totally ignored in Whitehall as in Fleet Street. For one thing, they tended to point out embarrassingly that the war was an ideological struggle in which the attitude of Russia was far different from that in the west.

The 20th July plot, if rightly assessed, could have given credence to Leibholz. Instead, it brought from Churchill disparaging words in the House of Commons that only strengthened the totalitarian hard-liners. He said of the conspirators who had tried to get rid of Hitler and all his works, 'The highest personalities in the German Reich are murdering each other, or trying to.' How far Churchill's discernment was blinded by the God of War, how far by faulty advice and how far he may have wanted to allay the Russians' fear of the West making a separate peace with Germans who overthrew Hitler, it is hard to say. Bishop Bell, who listened to the debate, wrote to Leibholz, 'I heard Churchill . . . but he is living in a world of battles only.' Later, Churchill the historian, having become acquainted with the documents of the German resistance, characteristically made amends in words of deep feeling—proudly reproduced in a West German parliamentary publication:

> In Germany there lived an opposition which grew weaker and weaker through its sacrifices and an unnerving foreign policy, but which belongs to the noblest and greatest that has ever been produced in the political history of any people. These men fought without help from within or without, driven only by the restlessness of their consciences. As long as they lived they were invisible and unrecognisable to us because they had to hide. But in their dead, the resistance became visible. These dead do not have it in their power to justify everything that happened in Germany. But their deeds and sacrifices are the foundation of the reconstruction. We hope for the time when this heroic chapter of German domestic history will find its just valuation.[33]

If attitudes became harder in Britain in 1945, across the Channel the popular image of the German nation was, not surprisingly, much more extreme. The poet, Stephen Spender, whose book *European Witness* provides a valuable mood picture of the summer and autumn of 1945, wrote: 'Sometimes when people in occupied countries speak of the Germans one has the sensation of a sob and fury of despair . . . One has the impression that one is not talking about human beings, one is talking about the monstrous, the unutterable.' On the continent of Europe there were initially no human bridges between Germany and the Rest.

Among the Powers Britain alone tried to reach her prisoners with a comprehensive programme of re-education. The Cabinet ruling setting it in motion was dated 18 September, 1944: 'Agreed that the Political Warfare Executive should undertake the re-education of German Prisoners of War and that all possible steps should be taken to facilitate their work'. Immediately two men were given the task of implementing the Cabinet instruction. One who remained Controller of the PW Division till its closure was Wing Commander E. H. Hitch, a large, amiable man who had come up through the world of merchant banking and public relations. More of a contact maker and co-ordinator than an initiator, Hitch had till then worked as an assistant deputy director in PWE (Political Warfare Executive); a realist in international relations, he was without the usual prejudices about Germans although he did not know their language. Hitch's Chief Executive Officer and the man generally acknowledged to be the 'Father of Re-education' was the worldly-wise and somewhat world-weary Cyrus Brooks, who also had been in PWE. Sharper and far shrewder than Hitch, he had been a teacher of English in Germany in 1914 and had been interned for the duration; later he had made a name for himself as a translator of authors such as Erich Kästner and Alfred Neumann, and as a writer of detective stories. There was an air of mystery about this quiet, pipe-smoking *Literat* and observer of human nature. To Norman Roffey he was 'an oriental-looking man who said little, smiled a lot, but with a definite twinkle: one's idea of a man in charge of spies.' To Birger Forell who came up against him more as a watch-dog 'he was no one's fool—a sort of *Detektivfigur*, rather suspicious, but not unsympathetic.'*

The structure which Hitch and Brooks eventually evolved consisted of a Controller (Hitch himself) and posts for three executive officers: for re-education which was filled by Brooks, for a field officer to direct the all-important work in the camps, and for an administrative officer. There were sections to administer Lectures

* See below p. 262.

4*

(there were eventually well over 200 lecturers), Publications, Literature, English Teaching, Visual Aids (including films) and Statistics. There was a branch directorate which fulfilled roughly the same functions in the Middle East and North Africa where some 100,000 prisoners were held. The all-important Field Section covered the supervision of training advisers the screening of prisoners into the different categories of White, Grey and Black,* and also 'information'. This which consisted largely of the vital but very difficult task of putting the re-education policy across to the War Office and to the often sceptical or hostile camp commandants.

It was not at all easy to find a team qualified to man such a structure. The PW Division was low in order of priority for good German speakers; these were in short supply quite apart from the needs of Military Government in Germany and the fast expanding Control Commission. In the scramble to find staff, most unlikely people applied and were turned down, or perhaps should have been. Hitch and Brooks recruited journalists, men who had been intelligence officers or in psychological or political warfare, academics, broadcasters with BBC or 'Black' radio experience, quite a few of these being high-calibre but often temperamental refugees, or, as the prisoners called them with a sting in the word, 'Emigranten'. In the first six months during which the PW Division was something of a Cinderella, continually moving to another office building, it hardly surprisingly did not get far off the ground.

There was extremely little theory or experience to aid the re-educators. Cyrus Brooks had himself been responsible for a first rather superficial psychological study of prisoners.[34] Among some 300 captured in 1940—mainly airmen—he discovered only one confirmed anti-Nazi. He was astonished to find how far Germany and Hitler had become for these young men a single concept. He concluded that the really dangerous Nazi was not the sadist of the special SS battalions, but the ordinary decent German who talked a great deal about honour, who believed in Hitler's omniscience and kindness and who, insulated from the outside world and subjected to constant propaganda, absorbed ideas and slogans and repeated them like a litany. After the Normandy landings a British report laid more emphasis on the relation of age to National Socialist conformity, the group from 26 to 35 containing the most fanatical elements—these being the men who up to the end tried

* The terms A, B, C and C-plus were also used.

to maintain control by threats and violence both in the disintegrating armies and in the POW camps. A far more professional
study was put together at the same time by a group of American
psychiatrists. It set out to assess enemy morale, reaction to Allied
propaganda, and potential attitudes to defeat. Their report
separated Hitler as a symbol and National Socialism as a creed.

The Allies, it stated, had been putting the wrong question,
namely, 'How on earth could the majority of Germans accept
National Socialism?' The assumption was that it meant the same
thing for the Germans as it did for the Allies, that is, a policy of
domination, militarism, conquest, oppression, persecution and
sadistic cruelty. If, said the report, that had been so, it would have
meant a motivation which would have distinguished Germans most
dangerously from all other people. The investigators found that
POWs valued National Socialism chiefly for its social and economic
achievements, and laid twice as much stress on economic stability,
social welfare and elimination of class conflict as on national power.
The attitude of various age groups was, moreover, decisively different. Those under thirty had twice as much trust in Hitler as
older men; and half those over thirty were ready to fix responsibility on Hitler for starting the war. The final conclusion was that
Germans would have to live through a deeply traumatic experience and learn to grasp the real nature of National Socialism
before they could dispel the resistance to reality caused by the
pipe-dream of Hitler. Had this balanced study been in the hands
of the intelligence officers who did the early screening of prisoners,
a great many absurdities and injustices would have been avoided.[35]

Another source of advice came from the anti-Nazi prisoners
presided over by 'Captain Holt' at Ascot. Hitch found a handful
of these men invaluable in helping him and his staff to reach the
minds of the men in the camps. But in reality re-education was not
founded on a theory, nor did it work to a plan. This was as well,
for otherwise it would not have had the kind of success it had. It
was rather a politically activated policy for which a structure had
to be created. Within this framework a disparate body of
men, including refugees, set out to discover how a defeated army
could be helped to prepare a democratic future for their shattered
country. 'We all,' writes Henry Faulk, 'had a common humanitarian view of mankind. To some of us that was called Christianity; to others it meant Human Justice; to others who were atheists
it was Respect for Man'. Re-education could have been a total

failure. In the event, there was one man who not only believed in it strongly but had the ability and capacity, the nerve and the verve, to direct the practice of it in the camps: Faulk himself. His bold initiative at Carburton and success at the setting up of several of the Midland camps had brought him the OBE. He was rapidly promoted through major to lieutenant-colonel and appointed—to give him his clumsy original title—Executive Field Officer of the POW Branch of the Political Intelligence Department of the Foreign Office. Saved by his motor-bike accident from seeing action in the war, he must have been, at thirty-seven, one of the freshest officers in the British Army. With his great energy he at once became the dynamo and the key figure of the whole extraordinary and unlikely operation on which he laid his pragmatic and Scottish stamp. To a hostile challenger two decades later on the nature and value of the re-education programme he wrote in its defence:

> The real inventor of re-education, both as an intention and a method, was the British public. Briefly, the British public was immensely afraid of future wars and was convinced that Nazism was a political form of nationalism and that aggressive nationalism was a peculiar German disease. It, therefore, looked for a way of preventing another war, and the suggestions varied from the violence of a Vansittart to the popular demand for re-education. There is no other word in English so apt to describe what was intended by the public, namely the cultivation in the POW of a new and co-operative attitude to humanity. . . . Re-education wasn't meant to be *Hochnäsigkeit* [arrogance]. It was essentially the belief that Germans were better than Nazi doctrines that blinded them to morality by politics and was an attempt to give them a chance to see that.[36]

While the war still raged, most camps remained militant, and it could require a good show of courage on the part of the British to enter some of them. The atmosphere could be palpable, like that of a hostile tribe confronting an anthropologist with dark looks, impenetrable thoughts and secret customs. One did not always have to go inside a camp to sense this dammed-up, male and alien force. Every Sunday at Warth Mills, Bury, where 4,000 were packed into an old textile mill, the whole complement of the camp stood out in the open and sang the strident Nazi anthem, the

Horst Wessel song, at full voice. It could be heard two miles away.

The arrival of the V1 pilotless bomber in English skies caused great excitement among prisoners and an upsurge of morale. Here was Hitler's secret weapon which, with the V2 rocket, would change the course of the war. On 24 December those at Doncaster racecourse were woken by a noise in the sky—flying bombs on a northerly course. Large numbers formed into a column and marched round the big perimeter—the camp was on the racecourse—singing 'Deutschland über Alles'. The guards fired warning shots and searchlights focussed on the marching men till a troop of guards entered the camp and drove them back into their tents. Attempts to break out were frequent but not nearly so successful as by the British in Germany; for one thing, the chances of getting across the Channel were almost nil. By March 1945 there had been 420 escapes, but only four men were still at large. Prisoners frequently say that a bold Luftwaffe crew got into an RAF station, seized an aircraft and flew back to the fatherland, but this never happened.* The present author has been told of escapes at Devizes and Doncaster; of tunnels discovered at Lodge Moor, Crewe Hall and Shap Wells; of successful escapes at Swanwick, Bridgend and Belfast. The men at the last camp, believing that neutral Eire would be a safe asylum, got across the border, but were soon back in Belfast, in the cooler. The mass break-out of sixty-seven men at Bridgend in February 1945 was unique and caused great alarm in the Glamorgan countryside. (Somewhat imaginative German films and English radio programmes have been based on it.)[37] All the missing men were rounded up within a week. As this was an officers' camp in a security area, and with a high morale, it was decided to send most of them to a more tightly guarded camp. Instead, as we have seen, the majority of them came up against the formidable Henry Faulk at Carburton.

It is difficult to assess the number of killings by *Roll-commando* (death squads) of so-called traitors. The case of Sergeant Rosterg at Comrie is the best documented. Prisoners recall, though the facts are hard to check, similar events at Carlisle, Dover and at Canadian camps. Hans Freiberger writes of a man who stuck up for his democratic opinions at Doncaster and was found in a lavatory strung up and daubed with swastikas—the culprits being soon discovered. In early April 1945 at Glen Mills, Oldham, a

* See below page 134.

man rushed into the German administration office. 'Come quickly!' Major Militz hurried to the fire-tank in the centre of the camp which was surrounded by a mob of prisoners. With difficulty he forced himself to the rim of the tank where he found an exhausted staff-sergeant swimming. Each time his fingers touched the edge they were knocked away, so that he would have eventually drowned. The Major enabled him to climb out just as some guards, alerted by the noise, arrived on the scene. The staff-sergeant, the compound leader and several others were then taken into protective custody. The guilty men were soon identified and all posted away—paratroops being the main culprits.[38]

Camp 176 at Glen Mills was where Father Josef Jansen first landed. His last interrogation at Kempton Park, it may be remembered, was a confidential one with a friendly captain. This officer considered his possible availability to take part in broadcasts. 'Instead of this,' Jansen wrote in his memoir, 'they decided to use me, as the till then oldest padre captured, for re-education purposes in camps dominated by SS and paratroops. It was emphasised that it was a very tough assignment, that I would have to maintain comradely relations even with the SS, since I too was a prisoner; but that if the worst came to the worst I would always be protected. Fortunately, I never needed this protection, although I was in some of the "worst" camps in England.' Glen Mills was the first of these, and here he at once found himself midway between the 'bullies and creepers' of the title he gave his memoirs. The picture that follows is a much shredded version of the account he has written.

It is October 1944 when Jansen arrives at Glen Mills, the last in a row of huge mills with tall chimneys all around. The building is several storeys high with but a single staircase and has several long spinning halls, some of which can hold a thousand men. The main windows are all permanently painted over because of the black-out. Every ten minutes an LMS train roars by on the embankment above the camp. Well over four thousand men are here at first and before wash-rooms are provided the conditions are appalling. There are only twelve lavatories and two taps, towards which a thick mass of men is forcing its way up and down the 'martyrs' stairs' all the time, and often in vain as the taps don't always run. There are extra delays because of the dozen Muslims* in the camp

---

* Jansen calls them *Russen und Mongolen*—they were probably unsegregated *Hiwis*.

whose ritual ablutions are respected, ten of them forming a human barrier round the two who are washing. Time is passed carving objects from bits of wood, such as the cross pieces of the American 'lend-lease' beds, blades being made from old iron hoops. But it is against the camp rules and for this and other misdemeanours culprits are locked in a big room. Food is sent in but the English 'forget' to empty the lavatory buckets, so that by the third and fourth day the conditions are unbearable; Father Jansen complains of the danger to health. (Quite gratuitously, he adds that at his next camp, Warth Mills at Bury, he learned from reading Vita Sackville-West's book on St Joan of Arc that the English knew about such tortures already in 1429 and applied them.) There are searches when everyone has to stand out in the open in the cold and wet and all sorts of things are filched; on one occasion even part of his portable Mass-kit is missing till the English chaplain intervenes and apologises. Things improve as Father Jansen finds Catholic friends and helpers, especially an idealistic artist from Osnabrück, Hans Helmkamp, 'a Franciscan type', who makes rosaries of the kind called Franco-rings out of old toothpaste tubes. But the rings are toothed and, convinced that they might be used for knuckle dusters, the English start looking for them. Jansen himself is interrogated about them and production stopped. A Berlin artist called Menzel creates a gripping picture, 'The Prisoner on his Cross'. The crucified soldier sees daemonic figures advancing on him which torment him more than his cross—fears for the future, dread of evil-minded comrades, of being grilled by interrogators. For those first two or three months Jansen himself longs for sleep; as with many others, it brings him dreams of escape, home-coming, *Heimat*. But then the dreams stop and he dreads bedtime because, lying half awake, all kinds of terrors come back from the combat time—tanks slithering softly towards him, explosions, nerve-shattering interrogations, senseless shouting of incomprehensible, frightening orders. Becoming horribly nervous, he longs each night for the reality of a fresh day. Even though Jansen is sleeping now with the kitchen and camp staff, he is not spared roll-calls in the middle of the night and in all weathers, when they might have to stand to attention for half an hour or an hour.

He has his duties to fulfil. Out of 1,300 registered Catholics in the camp, 800 come to Mass on Sunday and a thousand a month take communion. He instructs four converts brought to him by

Hans Helmkamp, the artist, and in March they are confirmed by
no less a person than the Papal Nuncio himself, Monsignor
Godfrey, who makes a visit. Jansen, who is without a Catholic
Bible, prepares his sermons, gives talks on Christian attitudes, on
the Psalms, Job, the prison letters of St Paul, on the history of the
Popes (from memory). He is put in touch with the Reverend
Philip Reynolds from St Patrick's Church, who brings him an altar
cloth and chalice and, 'seldom enough', the host. For their relationship has been deliberately fouled up by the machinations of the
camp spokesman, SS Sergeant-Major Fedor Typpner, a born
intriguer, who tells Father Reynolds that Jansen has no wish to
see him, and when he doesn't turn up says to Jansen, 'The fellow
isn't coming any more though I asked him to—you see how
reliable the English are.' Healing influences begin coming in from
outside: from Pastor Forell, 'a dear friend and counsellor'; in
evangelical church aid from Sweden, Switzerland and Norway;
from Quakers and the Salvation Army; and even, briefly, from
Evita Perón's Argentine relief.* Another very friendly interpreter
officer is mentioned, Captain Agnew, a Scot and former British
consul in Wuppertal. But Jansen's portrait of the Commandant,
Lieutenant-Colonel Stoddard, is far from friendly, and they frequently clash. When Jansen and the Protestant chaplain agree on
two texts to go on either side of the altar in the chapel (which had
been erected previously by Italian prisoners), they need the
approval of both the camp spokesman and Stoddard. Back comes
the former with the news, 'Not approved. You've got to put on
one side the text "Who does not work, neither does he eat" and
on the other "Who won't eat must die" '. They put neither up,
but Jansen isn't surprised; Stoddard has let it be known he has a
sister married in Moscow and he sympathises with 'the
Bolsheviks'.

Each Sunday morning Stoddard carries out the obligatory inspection of the whole camp. When he arrives in each room the
Germans stand stiffly to attention at the foot of their beds till he
says, 'Stand at ease!' which he often forgets to do. First he lets his

* Reconstruction aid to Europe sent by Argentina immediately after
the war was considerable and predated Marshall Aid. Father Jansen,
writing in 1947, may have identified it with Evita Perón because of her
highly publicised tour of Europe in that year. She was not however
invited to Britain because the Argentine state was considered fascist and
sanctuary was given there to many Nazis.

eye rove round the room with his escort, adjutant, interpreter, camp spokesman and so on, quaking in his rear. He then observes to the last centimetre whether knife, fork and spoon have been laid on the kit-bag according to the regulations, and whether each blanket has been folded in the precise manner. After looking at each object he gazes at the person, trying to divine what his thought and attitude might be. Then, haughtily and mostly without a word, he leaves the room, though sometimes he says just to his escort, 'I am satisfied. These people are in better condition than I expected. I hope the improvement will be maintained.' [Such inspections were familiar to most British service men of the time, but they amazed many a German by being more Prussian than the Prussians.]

When the war ends an order goes out to scrape the blackout paint off the main windows with razor blades (the work parties that do this become the nucleus of the later gangs that go outside the camp); when some practical jokers—or patriots?—instead cut swastikas into the paint, guards come and smash the windows right in so that for weeks there is no protection from wind and weather. All the while up till now Father Jansen has been playing his tricky game with the camp leadership. The 'creepers' are the worst element in the camp; even the British don't respect a bad German. He finds it advisable to go along with the 'toughs' to a certain extent. The very radical Austrian SS and other SS men themselves come and ask his moral judgment of men they 'want to see falling over the banisters'. 'You might be partly right,' he tells them, 'but that doesn't mean . . .' He takes rapid precautions, warning the victims and, if necessary, asking 'Tommy' for asylum for such people, or that they be sent away, without of course betraying anyone. He is constantly in danger of being pilloried as a tale-bearer, but this is another mine-field he learns to pick his way through, and in his time at Oldham no one is, he says, actually killed. The camp leaders even mock him a bit: 'Your bishop wouldn't like the way you make up to the SS, would he?' (His bishop happened to be the newly-made Cardinal von Galen, famous for his stand against Hitler.) 'Ah well, we'll allow you are no bishop, and might even be a comrade among traitors, a human being among human beings.' This makes him feel better, but his conscience pricks him a good deal as to whether he has done right. He has no one to appeal to, no confessor. Because of the language difficulty, he can tell none of this to an English priest.

Father Jansen ends his vivid account of Glen Mills by going back to the brilliantly managed Christmas hoax of 1944, an astonishing case of mass hypnosis. It was before Stoddard became commandant and when the camp was firmly in the hands of the redoubtable SS Sergeant-Major Typpner, who was later unmasked by the British. Here is the story, unconfirmed, as Father Jansen tells it:

The camp leadership had succeeded in getting the prisoners to boycott and eventually remove the official loudspeaker on which announcements, war bulletins from both sides etc., were given out. Word was then put about that there was a radio in the office of the camp leader and anyone wanting to hear not lies but the true situation could listen to it. Those who did so did not realise that what they heard was entirely fabricated news which was being relayed into the set: von Rundstedt's Ardennes Offensive had been a triumphant success. From this the wildest rumours began to build up in the camp: that the Germans had won back the Channel coast, including Calais, that parachutists had landed on British soil; the Führer was with his troops and a new type of shell (*Glasperlengranaten*) was clawing Allied bombers out of the sky, and a new type of glass dust putting their engines out of action. On the day before Christmas we all woke up to a tremendous explosion—a V1 had landed in Manchester. (This was the only fact in the whole swindle and got in quite by accident!) The last news was given out on Christmas Eve; under pressure of the invading troops the King had abdicated, the Queen had been installed as Regent and called on Oswald Mosley, the English Nazi leader, to form a government. 'Good evening, everyone! German troops, after occupying London, are advancing on the Midlands.' There was vast excitement in the camp. Everyone believed this nonsense— a case of mass psychosis. 'Our SS men have surprised the guards,' came a fresh rumour, 'and with Tommy guns under their arms have taken over the surveillance of the camp.' A swastika flag had been sewn together, probably with the aid of the stage people, and was flying from the top of Glen Mills. The whole camp was seething with enthusiasm. Everyone remained awake that night—a Protestant service had been arranged for eleven o'clock, a Catholic Mass for midnight. Someone reported to me that one of the assistant interpreters, a

Czech whom everyone disliked, was about to be lynched. At once I set out to stop such craziness and with some friends made for the interpreter's office, to find that the interpreter himself and all his English officers were off celebrating with the commandant. This was it! They had already stripped the Czech of his jacket and bound his hands and were about to haul him on a cord over the open door and attach the cord to the door-handle. I succeeded, mainly with the aid of some SS of cadet rank (especially Wolfgang Schmidt from Oldenburg), in stopping the affair, proposing 'a proper court martial after the liberation'.

Matins on Christmas morning went off splendidly, though in my sermon I had to warn against over-hasty action: as prisoners it was up to us to behave in a disciplined manner. The Commandant (Stoddard's predecessor), an elderly good-natured Irishman, attended with members of his staff and afterwards came up as far as the altar steps to thank me for the celebration and for my sermon which he had had translated for him. There were tears in his eyes, though perhaps only from the effect of alcohol. He let it be known through the camp leader that for his part he knew no details of any German advance, but suggested that the senior men in each of the galleries should, if they wished, come and listen to his own radio.* It seems that the English themselves, or at least the ordinary soldiers, were rather puzzled and didn't trust their own reports. At any rate, on Christmas Day there was no more phoney news and we spent it hob-nobbing with the guards who wanted only one thing—to be demobbed and sent home. The following day, a Bank Holiday, was spent playing cards, chess and similar games. Only on the 27th [January] when I entered the sick quarters did the senior doctor say, 'Wasn't that a dirty trick—the whole thing was invented!' I was brought down to earth with a bump like everyone else. Only a few fanatical Hitlerites still believed in it —the same ones who never accepted any bad news, like Hitler's death, or the end of the fighting. We gradually learned to laugh at these thick-heads.

The consequences of the affair came somewhat later. The Commandant had already been moved away and some of the guards replaced by military police, when on 7 February we were

* Surely a perfect example of Germans reacting to a piece of cool English irony in deadly seriousness.

told to parade out in the cold for four or five hours on the camp road. Captain Agnew, the interpreter, advised me and the Protestant padre, Hans Joachim Kremer, to stay on the edge of the parade or at least among the medical orderlies—which was very well meant. The camp road was in a hollow and all around and above us was a triple cordon and machine-guns mounted all around. We had to stand there till it was past dark. The behaviour of the ordinary soldiers was either restless, ironic or indifferent, as one had come to expect, especially with the SS and our international comrades—there were still Russians and Poles and also Spaniards among us. Suddenly there was a report. Everyone stiffened and very soon we heard that a soldier on the lower road had been shot. He had apparently gone menacingly towards a guard, who had put a bullet in him. A chalk mark was put round the spot, and no one was allowed to go near. The whole camp reacted to the news by spontaneously and all together singing, 'I had a comrade'. Nothing more. If the English believed a revolt would break out, they were mistaken. They didn't have to bring the machine-guns into action. Immediately we were marched back into our quarters, passing the dead man who lay with his hands in his pockets, his head smashed and bloody—it turned out he was in fact a medical orderly, by name Paul Hartmann. The *Manchester Guardian* reported 'a revolt by a few Nazi soldiers, of which one man has been the victim'. Being a Protestant he was buried by Pastor Kremer.

So ends Pastor Jansen's account of Glen Mills, Oldham. Its value lies not in objectivity but in the way a robust, rather wry Catholic priest reflects the mood of the time, and himself is buffetted by, and even briefly submerged by, events.

For Petty Officer of the Marines Rudolf Bradatsch, and many others like him, Hitler's birthday each April was a day of days, a cause for celebration and gratitude, and always a public holiday. But Hitler's last birthday on 20 April 1945, which Bradatsch spent in the Hayes POW camp at Swanwick, was the worst day of his life.

We were assembling for the usual roll-call when the English sergeant arrived on the parade ground, looked up and on the mast between the big marquees spotted a swastika flag. The alarm was given, the guard strengthened, the machine-guns manned on the watch-towers, and we found ourselves surrounded by soldiers with fixed bayonets. It was demanded that the culprit come forward. When no one emerged, the guards began to shout and rave at us—up till then we'd always got on well with them. They divided us up into groups and began a game with us that lasted nearly all day. One group had to sing, another to stand to attention, another were chased through the camp as if a horde of Indians were after them. After a while, we were paraded again, the same question asked, and again no one came forward. In the second part of the circus we had to dismantle the wooden flooring of the tents and pile them in heaps outside the camps, then the same with the duck-boards which criss-crossed the whole camp. The little flower-beds which prisoners had made round their tents were trampled to bits. Next the mess-tents and their tables and benches had to be added to the heap. Then individual groups had to advance across the whole camp picking up every match stick and piece of paper on the ground. Everything had to be done at the double. The camp was on a hill at the bottom of which were heaps of stones and heavy concrete blocks: we had to carry these to the top of the hill and then to the bottom again.

The guards urged us on with shouts and an occasional bayonet prick, for which a few had to have medical attention. We had not even had any tea that morning, and it was now afternoon. As a petty officer of twenty, I was one of the youngest, and quite a sportsman, but there were men ten and twenty years older than me. What infuriated me most was the attitude of the officers, both English and German, who stood watching it all in the top part of the camp and never intervened. Hatred in our hearts against the English was only stirred up, and many who were not Nazis became so on that occasion. And what hatred the English must have felt for us to have punished us like that—and all because of a flag! In the event, an older prisoner came forward as the culprit—which he wasn't; he simply wanted to make an end of the whole *Spiel*. Only when we had re-erected the whole camp did we get anything to eat. Later on elsewhere, in my capacity as editor of a camp magazine and clerk in the pay office, I often talked the case over with English officers, and they never wanted to believe that their own people could have sunk so low.

Were the events at Swanwick due to hatred? This seems most improbable, especially since previous relations were good. It is more likely to have been due to anger and fear, leading to panic: if these bloody Germans are not given the medicine they respect, heaven knows what they will be up to next! The mass break-out at Bridgend had happened only a few weeks before. Then, having over-reacted, face would have been lost if the harassment was called off before someone confessed. The whole affair speaks badly for the Commandant.

Two officer camps in North England present a remarkable contrast. The first, Camp 17 at Lodge Moor above the grimy edge of Sheffield, consisted mostly of hutments from the First World War, but a high proportion of the POWs had to live at first under canvas, especially officers of the Waffen-SS. Bruno Ullrich of the Medical Corps recalls the winter of 1944-5: 'We lived in our clothing day and night, and our uniforms became like cardboard. Food was prepared in galvanised dustbins, which led to a good deal of gastro-enteritis.' There was a compound for other ranks as well; Kurt Jaeger remembers how five of their sergeants kept back a fifth of the cold rations supplied to them per hundred men, and when discovered were made to walk round the camp with a placard round their necks which read, 'I have continually stolen from my comrades.' There was a special compound for officers who had been in the civil service. Kurt Schwederski, as a member of the judiciary,* was automatically suspect. 'We were treated as criminals, photographed and finger-printed, the result being sent to the Allied centre in Paris. We were told we might be kept an indefinite time and some of us saw ourselves interned in St Helena for years!' The guards were often officious, the sergeants now and then made use of their swagger-canes, and the camp was ruled largely by keeping the punishment cells full. Yet, though Lodge Moor was the most continually unhappy camp in Britain, the Commandant, Lieutenant-Colonel Jackson, was thoroughly approved of by the War Office. Camp 191 at Crewe Hall, on the other hand, was no less Nazi in character but was a mainly contented camp and its Commandant, Lieutenant-Colonel Lord Napier and Ettrick, was greatly liked and respected. Yet he was removed.

* In Germany a judge is a profession started young, not a status achieved.

Crewe Hall had originally been set up brand-new for American forces before D-Day and only needed to have perimeter wire, watch-towers and special lighting added. With access to the grounds, the lakes, the rhododendron walks and even parts of the big house, some 1,400 German officers found themselves in clover. Among them were many interesting and talented men and there was soon a wide programme of activities, academic, vocational and cultural. There was a theatre company of 175 which in a year and a half put on 223 performances of 88 different programmes.

The first concerts were put together with scores written out from memory. There was a choir of 95 and the YMCA gradually provided more instruments. At the end of 1945 a complete performance of Bach's B Minor Mass took place. They played football, boxed, and even laid on a circus. The small, bright-eyed Major, Dr Kurt Sandig, a future Heidelberg professor, who underwent the horrific surrender at the Hotel Majestic in Paris, became full-time director of studies and himself gave lectures on business economics. He was particularly gratified with the then high quality of English toilet paper for use in note-taking—until the YMCA began sending in enough writing material. Dr Kurt Blohm, previously lecturer in English at Liverpool University, press attaché in Brussels and intelligence officer, naturally took over the courses in English. But the feelings of Major Dr Günther Geisseler, the formidable lawyer who would defend Alfred Krupp von Bohlen at the second Nuremberg trial, were mostly of frustration. 'A caged lion just walks up and down and doesn't experience the environment . . . But it was important to observe what happens to the behaviour of men at a collapse, though there are things which I prefer to expunge from my memory, like the violations of the Geneva Convention by the British, against which I protested. We were living in a time of transition, during which our relations with each other were much more important than those with the custodian power. Friendships started which have lasted since then. But what I remember with most pride from Crewe Hall is that for the first time in my life I worked with my hands and completed a baker's apprenticeship.'

Over this caged, talented and nationalistic society Lord Napier presided with benevolence. Lowland Scot and thirteenth holder of his title, a member of the exclusive Royal Company of Archers (the King's bodyguard in Scotland), he had in 1939 raised his own battalion of the King's Own Scottish Borderers, though he was not asked to command it in action. For three years he had languished as Assistant Adjutant General at the War Office, till he was appointed in 1944 to be commandant of a German POW camp at Denny in Stirlingshire. Here he had been given the nickname, on account of the excellence of the conditions, of 'Lord Navycut and Porridge'. Lord Napier's trim, springy figure in trews, russet jacket and forage cap, lean alert face with a thin moustache, clipped speech and hearty laugh made an indelible impression on the Germans. (Being a Lowland Scot he never wore a kilt, though prisoners apparently remember him doing so.) Groups of officers would accompany him on walks round the lake or between the rhododendrons, drinking in his stories about the British army, the Abdication and Churchill. He always kept *Distanz*, never shook hands, but treated everyone man to man, with respect. The urbane Dr Blohm, who spoke such excellent English and gave the right social signals, he especially approved of and made him 'my interpreter', in preference to the refugee German whose job it was. When the cook-house orderlies purloined the raisins meant for the morning porridge in order to make schnapps, he had Dr Blohm and others come and taste it; and when an orderly gave away the construction of an escape tunnel and asked for asylum, he gave it a professional inspection. 'As your Commandant I must condemn your tunnel; as a Colonel of Pioneers, I must admire its construction.' When he put those responsible into solitary confinement, he remarked to Dr Blohm, 'I rather like these young fellows for not wanting to be cooped up in this camp.' He visited them in their cells, nonchalantly dispensing cigarettes and demonstrating how to split matches to make them go further. Since the cells were without baths he sent down a bath-tub of his own and, so the story goes, had it announced that he hoped no further attempt escapes would be made or he would have to go on having no bath. The same informant says that he was on the prisoners' side when some security searches were rather harshly carried out. On one occasion the search lasted nearly all day, during which the POWs had to stay outside on parade without food. Lord Napier stood with them in the yard all the while, occasionally handing out cigarettes and himself going without food as long as they did. When SS-Leutnant Cremer, who had his bunk next to the Lutheran padre, drank all the communion wine, Lord Napier roared with laughter, had him in, stopped his cigarettes and procured more wine. 'But look after it this time!'

'My dear Dr Blohm,' he would say, 'you know we'll be fighting on the same side one day.'

This benevolent style soon had the British staff talking about 'the Nazi Lord'—though to the Germans he appeared to be just a super-gentleman. Certainly he had, like many commandants, little idea of what Nazism was, though there were some nasty eruptions of it in his camp. When the captain of a naval lighter captured at Brest (not a member of the Kriegsmarine) made himself objectionable by defeatist talk, some naval lieutenants decided to act. Believing that the chivalrous British would understand their motives, they severely beat up the traitor. Lord Napier dealt with the culprits and, feeling let down by the camp leader, Lieutenant Colonel Unger, demoted him, which left the way for the only full colonel in the camp to take his place. This was none other than the irrespressible Prussian veteran, H. G. Borcherdt of the Luft-waffe, who had recently arrived after recovering from his calf wound in Belgium. There were no more eruptions. In his family memoirs Borcherdt describes how he dealt with the situation. 'I told Lord Napier that he was responsible for the outer security of the camp while I would be for peace and order inside it. But it would help if any convinced democrats or supporters of the unfortunate 20th July were removed. "Quite," said the Lord. To the officers I said, "I don't want 50, 75, 150 or 175 per cent soldiers, but 100 per cent ones, all faithful to their oath. We will all without exception from now on use the German greeting" [Nazi salute]. As my deputy I appointed Korvettenkapitän Winter, U-Boat Chief in Brest, wearer of the Knight's Cross and long on Admiral Dönitz' staff.' [He was a thorough reactionary]. One day a bishop arrived at the gates. Borcherdt felt he knew exactly how to deal with him. 'I met him and requested him not to hold any services, on the grounds that the Archbishop of Canterbury had blessed bombers before they took off for Germany'.*

The patriotic, boastful yet amiable colonel was neither a dyed-in-the-wool Nazi nor a typical Prussian. Four generations in his family had won the Iron Cross. Cavalry reservist turned flier in the First World War, working hard as a moorland farmer be-tween the wars before going back into service with the Luftwaffe ground troops, he lacked that rather stiff self-control that marks the true Prussian; he was too ebullient, too humorously provoca-tive with his captors. He survived on top and enjoyed life, by

* Untrue—Nazi propaganda.

swinging with the pendulum, but in his own idiosyncratic way. Half in jest, he said to Dr Blohm, 'When the Kaiser abdicated I was all for him; when the Nazis came in I was all for the Weimar Republic; and now at the end of the Third Reich I am a Nazi! Odd, isn't it?'

And odd things did happen in and around Crewe Hall. One day Lord Napier announced, 'You officers don't get enough exercise. We'll all go on a route march together.' Only those who gave their parole were allowed to go. So, one fine day in early spring, most of the fourteen hundred marched through the gates out on to the country roads. The villagers of South Cheshire watched with astonishment as the long grey-green column, articulated into companies of a hundred and only lightly guarded, snaked through the countryside, now and then breaking into staccato singing. The Commandant accompanied them throughout, and as they returned to camp requested that they all parade in front of the proud Borcherdt, who though his calf wound was still troubling him, had determinedly taken part. As they marched past with Dr Blohm standing a few paces behind Borcherdt, Lord Napier himself joined in giving the normal military salutation. All the Germans raised their arms in the Nazi manner—though not, to Colonel Borcherdt's saddened eye, putting up much of a show. How could they, with news from the war and the Fatherland continually worse? Nevertheless, spirits were artificially kept up by holding a loyal parade on Hitler's birthday—this happened in many camps; Borcherdt even laid on a funeral service when Hitler's death was announced ten days later. Brief though it was, it may have been unique, as Borcherdt likes to believe it was.

Lord Napier announced the end of the war in characteristic manner. He summoned the Colonel, Commander Winter, the compound leaders and Dr Blohm to his office. In his clipped way he said, 'Gentlemen, your armies have capitulated. That is all. Gentlemen, thank you.' As they walked out of the room, he felt that something more was required, and called out, 'Dr Blohm, stay behind a moment, will you.' He fished into his hip-pocket and pulled out a small silver whisky flask. 'For your consolation,' he said, handing it to him. 'But bring the flask back!' Dr Blohm found Borcherdt and Winter and they consumed the whisky together. (Borcherdt's version of the story is more dramatic: Lord Napier, after making the announcement, threw something on to the table which he at first thought was a revolver in its holster, for use by anyone who wished. It was, in fact, a whisky flask. But this appears only to have happened in the colonel's enlarged memory.)

Not long after the quixotic Lord Napier was removed, announcing it to his camp leader with the words, 'I think I have treated you well—I almost deserve the Iron Cross!' But it is doubtful whether any of the Germans could begin to understand the special manner and sense of humour of the Border aristocracy. Lord Napier's style certainly verged on the eccentric for a commandant of enemy prisoners of war, but it was wonderfully refreshing to most of them and they never forgot him.

Borcherdt's style was equally inappropriate to the new stage of re-orientation and political re-education. He inevitably did the wrong thing. Having once, so as to put an end to discord, ordered everyone to give the Nazi salute, he now on the same grounds ordered everyone to take the swastika from the national emblem on their tunics. Those who had done so already were reckoned to be democrats, the others to be still Nazis, creating further discord. 'You should not order them to do that,' a small screening officer, told him. 'They must decide for themselves.' The visitor who put on an act and according to Borcherdt blew cigarette smoke in his face was possibly Major Kettler, who told him that his attitude was all wrong and he would be replaced as camp leader and posted elsewhere. Re-education, however, made virtually no impression at Crewe Hall. Ten months later 'a training report' said that the camp was 'dominated by the intellectual force of nationalist opportunists'.

There were many camps, many societies, some more Nazi and tribal than others, with different factors making for cohesion or discord, freedom or intimidation. It might be a mistake to emphasise the internal and external tensions too much. A neutral and pacific observer like Pastor Forell found that in the main the POWs were content, sometimes even pleased with their conditions. These might even be embarrassingly better than those experienced by their families. The common German soldier, the exhausted *Landser* who for five years had fought in far more actions than his Allied counterpart, was also a realist. 'What will you do on Sundays after the war, Hans'? Answer: 'Take a bicycle ride round Germany.' This wry joke was current well before the end of the war. But what would he find when he eventually got home? How many wives and girl friends would have remained faithful? How many fathers and mothers be dead or missing? At Colchester round Christmas and at other camps a song was sung by thousands of prisoners. Rudolf Bradatsch does not know where it arose, but says, 'It expresses our thoughts and feelings better perhaps than any writer could have done.' It was sung to the tune of 'Es war einmal ein kleines Bubchen'. The first verse and chorus might be rendered:

> Many years are gone and over since we loved each other so,
> The last words that I wrote you make you think of me I know,
> Your letters follow after but they're lost along the road,
> The enemy has got me and the way to you is long and hard.
>> My life and your love are all that's true I own,
>> Wait then, wait then, for I am coming home.

But home also meant changes impossible even to imagine: Germany reduced to a shrunken and split shadow of her former great self; hatred sown in every neighbouring state; a future level of existence that would be decided by the apparently merciless Great Powers; the beginning of everything again from the bottom. This brought an inner suffering—thousands upon millions of personal crises adding up to a stupendous national trauma. This was the essential starting point of renewal. 'The inability to suffer,' wrote the Russian philosopher Berdyaev, 'is sometimes the worst evil of all.' The ordeal of pain, loss and darkness suffered by countless Germans in 1945 was, in spiritual terms, the necessary condition for the rebirth of a nation.

6

1945: The Gulf Diminishing

The suicide of Hitler on 30 April and the end of the war in Europe
nine days later totally altered the psychological situation of the
prisoners. The Führer's death released those middle-of-the-road
men who still felt bound by their oath, while the capitulation of
all German forces was the ultimate low point from which there
could only be a slow climb into a new reality.

In the camps these events were experienced in a great variety of
ways. Some remember a feeling of 'at last', some a private numb-
ing, others just a confirmation of the inevitable. At Rimini A.E., a
former SS-man, now an active Christian, recalls the monstrous
and pathetic impression of untold helpless men huddled in the
fields, feeling totally abandoned. It gave him a picture of what
Jesus felt when he wept over Jerusalem. At Atterbury in Indiana
Fritz Seufert immediately cut the swastika out of the badge on his
uniform as a 'symbolic act'. 'You would not have dared to do that
a fortnight ago,' a comrade commented. At Hollywood overlooking Belfast Bay the Commandant made the announcement in
a cool, objective way that the prisoners appreciated, but the 2,000
men spent the next three days in gloom, hardly talking to each
other and listening to the joyful celebrations around them. Later
they had a grandstand view of George VI arriving on a battleship
for a victory review. At Norton the regrettable Major J. apparently
had the prisoners and the British staff lined up on the parade
ground opposite each other. Having made the announcement, he
called on the latter to give 'three cheers for victory' as at the end
of a sporting event.[39] Lord Napier's handling of the event has
already been noted. Fritz Pons, a sergeant radio operator shot
down in the big Coventry raid of 1941, recalls how it was in his
camp in Canada. 'All of us were called on parade and the camp
leader announced: "Comrades, your Führer is dead, fallen for the
Fatherland. Long live the Homeland, long live Germany!" There
was a short, rigid silence. "The ceremony is over. Dismiss!" You

could have heard a pin drop, but there wasn't a damp eye to be seen. We returned downcast to our huts. That evening no one mentioned the matter. I wrote home: "With the world's help, they have destroyed Beelzebub [the small devil Hitler]. Now they have the devil himself in the house [Stalin] and will never be rid of him." '

Pastor Gursky was in transit to Kempton Park when the news of Hitler's death reached him. 'Strangely enough, no one seemed strongly affected, perhaps because we were all so exhausted from our time in the Belgian camps. At that moment, all of us, young and old, the Nazis and their secret or open opponents, seemed to me to be one great company of fellow-sufferers.'

Was there more relief that the war was over, or mourning for what had been hoped for and lost? Who can tell? Eighteen-year-old Private Erich Leverkus, the radar technician who surrendered at Erschaffenburg, was in a Liberty ship on 8 May, one day short of Newport News. The entry in his diary was brief and eloquently factual. 'Unconditional Surrender of Germany = end of the war. First bowel motion since being captured five weeks ago.'*

Four hundred miles to the north across the Canadian border at Grande Ligne Camp, Quebec, a Prussian officer uttered perhaps the most telling words spoken on that day of defeat. He was General 'Papa' von Ravenstein. He came from an old Silesian family with a distinguished military record going back to Frederick the Great and he himself had won the highest decorations for bravery in both world wars. A dashing commander of the 21st Panzer Division under Rommel in the desert, he had been captured in November 1941, near Capuzzo. Put on a British destroyer which had then been torpedoed, he had been fished out in the nick of time, after a remarkable incident in which he had shared a plank with a half-drowned English soldier. He tried in vain to give him courage to cling on by saying to him in broken English the Lord's Prayer. This is an indication of another side of von Ravenstein: he used to tell his close friends that he would much rather have studied theology and become a Lutheran pastor, but the strong tradition of his family had diverted him. To a degree that is strange

---

* Leverkus' entry for the next day: 'Arrival Newport. Amazed at American talent for organisation, unimaginably large material resources, and mechanical aids. Bath, delousing, then while still naked interview by young woman reporter'. The Americans never ceased to astonish their German captives, one way or another.

to most English, he combined a religious spirit with a strong belief in the military virtues. This not uncommon Prussian trait went with a social responsibility and a warmth towards other human beings. Men like Ravenstein, liberal conservatives in politics, formed the best of the old Prussia. They despised Hitler, and saw in him the ruin of their country. Scores of them, we now know, were involved in plots to bring him down, many of them paying with their lives for it.

For the average Prussian the words 'Gott' and 'Vaterland', invoked together in song, oath and toast, were not far apart. But for Ravenstein the Nazis had divorced them completely, and so, on that late spring morning at Grande Ligne, after the Canadian Camp Commandant had read the proclamation of the surrender, he followed with a few words. He said: 'My young comrades, I know it is a sad thing for a soldier to have said to him, "You have lost". But let me tell you this: it is better for Germany, better for us, that we have lost, because if we had won we would have lost ourselves.' The effect on his audience, fighting officers from all three services, was profound. Coming from the General they called 'Papa' because of his concern for their good and their welfare, his words carried weight. Leutnant Boettger, captured nearly three years before south of Alamein, and today a colonel in the Bundeswehr, recalls: 'As we walked thoughtfully away, there were those who said he was a traitor. But I and many others will never forget his words as long as we live. With them he gave us a new beginning.'

After 8 May a sombre mood descended on the camps. Singing of the old songs virtually ceased and so did the overt violence. Men were in a state of delayed shock, bowed down, bitter, bewildered. 'A world had collapsed' is the phrase used again and again. Some, like Dieter Hankel of Featherstone Park, the huge officer camp in Northumberland and near the Roman Wall, retired into themselves: 'I was very lonely to start with—no friends. At first I couldn't take the blow that everything I believed in was over, that it was false, so I took refuge in myself. I used to walk alone round and round the camp perimeter for exercise repeating lines from Goethe that I knew, trying to draw the spiritual meaning out of them.

> Thou who from heaven art
> Assuageth every hurt and grief,
> To him whose life is doubly hard
> Doubly thou dost send relief.

Equally appropriate to Hankel and to many more were those less consoling, more searching lines that Goethe makes the blind harpist sing in *Wilhelm Meister's Apprenticeship Years*:

> Who never mingled tears with bread
> Nor sat all through the long night hours
> Distraught with weeping on his bed,
> He knows you not, you heavenly powers.

> You lead us to life's very core
> Load wretches with guilt for what they've done
> Leave them to rue it more and more:
> All guilt is paid for under the sun.

The theological student, Leutnant Wallmann, later to become pastor at the Hatch End camp, was sustained inwardly for months by gratitude that he had survived the war. The more extrovert Herbert Schmitt raked the situation over with his comrades. This twenty-one-year-old U-boat Lieutenant had been First Officer on *U-1105* which surrendered in the Irish Sea on 9 May. The submarine was then handed over to the Royal Navy at Loch Eriboll, and a month later Schmitt too found himself at Featherstone Park. His occasional journal traces the changing mood during the rest of the year.

Early June. Our temper is indescribable: depressed and dejected, expectant and curious, completely insecure yet defiant. Already while at sea it had begun—on 9 May—what has taken up hundreds of hours ever since: self-examination, self-tormenting questions about 'why' and 'wherefore'. Was it really all lies that our Führer told us, everything criminal that they ordered us to do? Were they fools, cowards, criminals, or only men who have submitted to superior force? Were they traitors—or were we—for capitulating?

September. Gradually we have reached the point that we have formed ourselves into small groups and try to work out answers together to the still-unanswered questions. It isn't easy. I am suspicious of those who were 'always in opposition'.

November. The English appear only to be interested in what goes on behind the barbed wire in so far as it concerns good order and hygiene. For the rest, they play the role of the silent observer. They send newspapers and periodicals into the camp, we listen to the BBC, now and then people visit us and talk on political, but not only political, subjects. This is laid on without any propaganda, nor do we have to attend. They are letting things take their course. I believe this is the right way. But when will they let us go home?

No one in authority was even beginning to consider repatriation. The British had strongly disapproved when the French kept the Germans for up to two years after 1919, for, according to the Geneva Convention, prisoners should be returned immediately after the signing of peace. Churchill in fact hurried on repatriation in advance of the Treaty of Versailles. But now there would be not even a peace conference: there was no German Government to make a treaty with. Indeed, the word 'peace' was used very sparingly in 1945; the question was whether and how a weary Europe could recover from so much hatred and destruction. This left the prisoners in a kind of limbo, political as well as psychological. They had time to brood and muse—the officers more so, as they could not be made to work, though they also had more time to develop their own educational and cultural activities. But the other ranks, who were soon mostly out working on the land, on rubble clearing, road repair, drain digging and so on, could feel equally isolated. They may not have been cooped up all day, but total cold-shouldering by the populace month after month could be almost as depressing. There were strict penalties for anyone who spoke to them, other than for work reasons, or who gave them so much as a cigarette or a sandwich.

The authorities were determined, however, that POWs should not be insulated from the recent past of their country, and struck at them hard with the one compulsory act of 're-education'. As a kind of shock therapy, every single prisoner was compelled to sit through a twenty-minute horror film, the audience being held to be partially if indirectly responsible for the horror. The order went out in some areas to have camp guards present at each showing to prevent disorders; the sick and wounded were not to be spared. It was an American film of the liberation of Belsen Concentration Camp, with the visit of the British Parliamentary Delegation spliced in, and was a good deal more grim than that shown to news-reel audiences. By the beginning of August over 200,000 men in 131 camps had seen it.

Hans Freiberger remembers the announcement at Lodge Moor, Sheffield. 'There was to be no speaking, no utterance at all during the performance. That's going to cheer us up, I thought! What sort of horror story are they going to give us now? When I entered the hall there was a deathly hush. At every corner stood a guard with a tommy-gun. I don't recall the content of the film any more. I only have a clear memory of heaps of human skeletons which were supposed to have belonged to concentration inmates from Buchenwald who had been gassed, hung or shot. That was what was put over to us. We were meant to accept this horror without a word and repent it for the rest of our lives. We felt this excessively mean, for at the time we had only the faintest knowledge of such camps.'

At Glen Mills, Oldham, Father Jansen recorded how the film was shown in one of the huge weaving halls, without seats. They had to 'crouch or kneel on the floor with armed guards all around preventing us getting up or speaking to each other. But the effect was to let in a bit of air. The SS themselves (nearly all Waffen-SS and youngsters) were shaken and shocked. It can't be true, many said spontaneously; or it was the result of the final days of the war. I myself heard then of Buchenwald and Belsen for the first time; till then I had only heard of *Konzentrationslager* in Dachau, Papenburg, Oranienburg and Auschwitz. Without exception we were all gripped and stirred up—none of us had conceived the goings-on in the *KZ* thus.' It is an extraordinary sign of the confused perspectives of the time that Father Jansen could add, 'What we couldn't understand was why we all were more guilty than the English, who after all had liberated us much too late from that Hitler.'

Otto Leichner, conditioned by propaganda to believe all films must be propaganda, was like most of his comrades at Lodge Moor a sceptic. The corpses, suggested one who lived near Buchenwald and should know, must have come from the raid on Dresden. Others would say, 'Made in Hollywood'; 'in a typhus ward of an Indian hospital' was a later explanation. Others, more rationally, blamed the extent of the horror to the breakdown of commissariat transport in the last weeks of the Third Reich. The more reflective Hans Freiberger recalls the showing of the film at the Belfast camp: 'It took a whole day for everyone to pass through the cinema hut. We came out of the performance visibly shaken and in silence. We had heard of the concentration camps, and believed they were necessary for the detention of enemies of the State and economic saboteurs. Posters kept saying that the Jews must leave Germany, but it wasn't really explained to us why the Jews were bad, though we knew the Catholic Church was antisemitic and Hitler was a Catholic. Now the truth came out of what had been allowed to happen in remote camps with the help of his faithful SS. We had to grit our teeth, and accept that we were hostages for such crimes, and that we would have to remain prisoners longer than we had reckoned.' Yet how long must it take for facts of such a kind really to sink in? Fritz Pons, who already in 1945 could refer to Hitler as Beelzebub, could write in 1977, 'I needed ten, twenty, thirty years before I could grasp the abomination of the Nazi regime.'

An attempt was made to assess the effects of the film by asking for reports from Commandants. In not a few camps the reaction was remorse and anger. At twelve a manifesto was drawn up expressing disgust at the Nazi regime, though at six they rejected responsibility on behalf of the people. Four camps made a collection for concentration camp victims, and at one a chapel service was held immediately afterwards. At one black camp, where sufficient precautions had not been taken, the film was greeted with laughter and derision, and a notice was put up on a blackboard saying that every decent German should approve the rotting away of so many Jews, Poles and Russians. At hospital camps, like Naburn, near York, where several hundred severely undernourished prisoners from the Channel Isles were being nursed back to health, there was much resentment at the tactlessness and timing of showing the film. But a survey conducted at three 'white', three 'grey' and three 'black' camps, covering 1,000 prisoners altogether, showed that even in the last group 39 per cent thought the film was genuine.

Prompted by these revelations the intrepid parachutist cum intellectual, Colonel von der Heydte,* did not hesitate to enter into a new contest—that of the honour of Germany itself. Writing in the *Wochenpost,* the POW magazine, as a firm Catholic he pointed out that denial, opposition, hatred was the hallmark of National Socialist thought and that the whole of Germany had

* See pages 9 and 50; Freiherr von der Heydte later became Professor of Political Philosophy at Marburg University.

been taught to think in the dichotomy of either-or, of friend or foe. He pleaded that the new guiding principle should be not to fight against, but to work for. 'Our models should not be the master-men, but those who stood up for their beliefs though threatened with destruction, not those who wore the gold-embroidered brown uniforms of the party, but the blue and white striped denims of the *Konzentrationslager*. I feel as deeply ashamed for what has been done as a Roman might have felt 1700 years ago at the persecution of the Christians. I have served with pride under many superiors, but of none am I so proud as of the president of my student union in Munich, a simple Jesuit father who died in Dachau.'

The *Wochenpost* invited comments, and Unteroffizier Franz Püringer told the Colonel to 'come off it'. He had fought under the much-decorated von der Heydte and recalled him taking quite a different line at Döberitz, at Torgau, at Gustrow, where he had urged his men to fight to the last breath 'for our beloved Führer'. 'How many severe sentences of detention did you give my comrades because they failed in their duty? Now that you are sitting with a whole skin as a prisoner-of-war you present yourself as a Christian at the moment when the world knows that millions of people were slaughtered in the *Konzentrationslager*. You are too late.' Von der Heydte answered him with the actual text of what he had said at Gustrow in August 1944. It was a call to the love of one's country as the one force to hold them together. 'If in the coming months the storm floods sweep over us and everything falls apart, let us hold high above the raging waters a flag on which is written one word: Germany.' He was only sorry he had not known the name of Püringer at the time for he, as a reliable anti-Nazi, was such a man as Leutnant Brunnklaus of their regiment was searching out in 1944 for active work against the Party. Further, how could an army fight without penalties for indiscipline? Must a soldier who rejects Nazism be a poor soldier? Here was the nub of the matter. The *Wochenpost* editors' hopes that articles like this could raise the level of debate were premature. Motives, especially of anyone who was an officer, were questioned, sore points aggravated, respect for another's opinion very rare. The 'open forum' was suspended.[40]

Many expected that the *KZ* film would be the prelude to reprisals—indeed, that some had been taken already in the sudden reductions of rations just before war ended. Their ration scale had been, in fact, higher than that of British civilians throughout the war. This was because, by the Geneva Convention, it should be related to that of the home forces of the custodian power. This had been objected to in the Commons as early as 1941, but as long as reciprocity existed because prisoners were held on both sides, no reduction was made. When it was reduced from 3,300 calories a day to 2,000 for those not working,* which was the great majority at the time, the word went round, 'The Tommies are punishing us for the concentration camps.' Lying hungry in their bunks, they took it as a sign of hatred, which was not true. The prime factor was the general world food shortage, which resulted in a fall in rations for the British housewife too.

A copy of the *Geneva Convention on Prisoners of War* was available in all camps. It was a much perused document and was mistakenly thought to have the force of international law. The interests of the prisoners had been in the hands of the Protecting Power, in this case Switzerland, but only as long as hostilities existed. During that time the Swiss Government acted at a diplomatic and political level, with a *status* in international law. When, at the end of the war, the International Red Cross, at the invitation of the British Government, became custodian of the interests of the German prisoners, it had no such status and powers. Britain, without fear of reprisals—but also bearing in mind the likely reprisals in any future war—could conduct its affairs towards them as she saw fit. It was, for instance, against the Convention to house prisoners in tents after the month of November. The International Red Cross pointed out the danger to health of such camps, but it was only by the autumn of 1946 that tents were entirely dispensed with. The British could plead unprecedented pressure, the Germans could accuse them of cynical neglect. Undoubtedly, there was lax administration. Dr Hartwell, Forell's assistant, remembers how he went to one supposedly winterised camp and found abject and pathetic men floundering about in wet, cold mud, with some tents so water-logged they could barely lie down. He reported this at once to the International Red Cross, which immediately informed the War Office. Within two days action had been taken. Hartwell still remembers with emotion how, when he next visited the camp, the men overwhelmed him with their gratitude.

Earlier there had been scenes over priorities in saluting. Major Kurt Schwedersky was at Llanmartin Camp in Wales. 'An English

* Those working received 2,800 calories.

Lieutenant walked by. I was with some younger officers who saluted at once, to which he replied, and then I saluted. He said angrily, "Why didn't you do it earlier?" I said that according to the Convention I was to salute earlier in the case of officers of higher or equal rank, but in this case I was the higher rank, and had acted correctly. "But you have to salute every British officer, don't you?" he said; for which I was to be taken before the Commandant. But I wrote him a letter asking if the Geneva Convention had been altered—and heard no more! People didn't know about these things! These protests were, of course, a way of keeping up morale.' Saluting practices in fact differed from camp to camp until the end. At Llanmartin offenders who were put in the 'cooler' were without light after dark; the Convention stipulates that 'the cells are to be artificially lighted till curfew'. Protests were unavailing. It was strongly argued by some Germans that the attempt to conduct a 're-education' of prisoners-of-war at all was against the Geneva Convention.* Some of these attempts to take the British down, to nail certain acts as inhuman, cynical and vengeful did now and then have a certain substance. But they chiefly filled a need to hit back, to relieve in some measure a guilt complex: they gave an emotional outlet to pent-up feelings of helplessness. A formidable advocate like Dr Geisseler, for all his anger, soon saw the futility of protesting; Schwedersky, an equally sharp lawyer, enjoyed the fun of the game more. But natural grumblers kept up a line on British perfidy and unfairness till the end of the war, and afterwards. Indeed the great majority never weighed in the balance how Germany might have behaved in a total victory, or the totality of what Hitler and the Third Reich had visited upon Europe.

'A heavy, almost grave-like atmosphere fell over the camp— the screeners had arrived,' reports Werner Leichner of the Belfast Holywood Camp. The screening and categorising of prisoners was an important part of Anglo-American policy from the autumn of 1944 onwards. Most, but not quite all, received labels—they were either white, grey or black, usually set down as A, B, or C—with quite a few labelled C-plus, which indicated the maximum identification with the National Socialist group ethos. Parachute-troops,

* Faulk points out that the Geneva Convention simply did not deal with such a possibility, or with a war being fought on ideological grounds.

U-boat crews and SS were, with few exceptions, at first labelled C. Those who were apparently free from Nazi influence, with a positive philosophy of life, became white or A, though not a few did so by singing the right song to their interrogators. There is no parallel in European history to such a selection of prisoners of war, unless one harks back somewhat fancifully to the much more pitiful end to the Sicilian expedition of the Athenians in 413 BC. The survivors were thrown into the quarries at Syracuse and those who did not perish in the terrible conditions were branded as serfs. But Plutarch also tells us that 'discreet and orderly conduct was an advantage to them', while those who could recite a passage of Euripides were set at liberty by their masters and were allowed to return to Athens, where many of them went to the house of the great playwright to thank him personally.

The Anglo-American policies of screening and segregation were, in fact, decided stage by stage and reached pragmatically. Already in Algiers a handful of Germans had been set apart who were willing to help the Allies in radio broadcasts. But screening proper began with the need to separate off all those whose fanatical attitude was preventing the others from being used as labour and was continued with those who later on were preventing re-education. These were the 'blacks'; in the middle were the great majority, the 'greys'; while the 'whites' were those thought worthy of early repatriation to take part in the rebuilding of their homeland, and capable of leading re-education in the camps.

The screening interview might take a minute or two, or much longer. At Devizes Hans Frieburger and his comrades all decided they would enter the screening hut with the 'Heil Hitler' and the Nazi salute. They were all immediately given C-plus, but were astonished that their behaviour did not rouse the least animosity on the part of the interrogators. At the same camp Willi Wolf remembers a screener called Herr Riess who would shout out to those who considered themselves to be Czech, Austrian or Polish to step forward. 'It was shaming to see who did so to save their skins.' His group also decided each to give the Hitler salute, at which Herr Riess would dismiss them immediately with a 'Nazi—Jawohl—'raus!' Occasionally he would enjoy himself by correcting the angle of their salute. 'Arm a little higher—no, lower—once more! 'Raus!' Devizes certainly seems to have been a rough camp. Heinz Ruemmler remembers an eighteen-stone RAF sergeant who treated them worse than any of the Polish guards.

In the early days of coarse screening there was a good deal of bawling out and maybe worse. 'Frankly, there were quite a few sods among the screeners then,' Faulk has said. Dr Leverkus remembers pictures of Belsen being shoved under his nose by an American in Marseilles to get his reaction. To such a question as 'When did you first hear of concentration camps?' the answer was often 'In middle school.' 'What do you mean?' 'In our history lessons. They were in South Africa—set up by the British during the Boer War.'* This could, in fact, be a true if highly provocative answer and an indication of a man's spirited character, not necessarily of his convictions.

Prisoners were not meant to know their grading but they often did. When Leutnant Herbert Schmidt received a first automatic grading as a U-boat lieutenant, he wrote in his diary: 'They have given me C. That means years before I go home. These damned Tommies believe they can read thoughts and uncover opinions. In despair.' The temptation to become overnight a changeling was great when it was assumed that by giving the 'right answers' one might get home earlier. At the same time, there were occasional prisoners who would quietly denounce those who did this, in order to curry favour with the victor. The Nazi system had itself encouraged denunciation as a method of political control and it sometimes happened that its unsavoury practitioners transferred their activities to the new superior power. Interrogators might have to discriminate between those who tried to blacken their

* This episode has been made much of by German historians while English historians have played down the facts. During the last guerilla phase of the Boer War, Boer women and children were collected into concentration camps, where disease became rife. Out of nearly 120,000 some 26,000 died. When their plight was eventually exposed to the world by an Englishwoman, Emily Hobhouse, the government in London was at first evasive, but the Colonial Secretary, Joseph Chamberlain, had become personally convinced and speedily saw that the conditions were reformed. Meantime, the Opposition leader, Campbell-Bannerman, had been speaking in private, then in public of 'methods of barbarism'. This phrase reached the Boers in the field and they were profoundly touched by the action of an enemy statesman who faced jeers and hatred on behalf of their families. Five years later, when Campbell-Bannerman became Prime Minister and offered self-government to the South African colonies, the majority of Boer leaders, and Botha and Smuts especially, had such a feeling of gratitude and trust towards him that they worked sincerely for reconcilliation. (See Ensor, *England 1870–1914*, OUP 1936.)

comrades and those who were really concerned when a bad type was slipping through the screening-net because it had holes in it. Faulk found cases where a crypto-Nazi element dominating a camp denounced actual whites as blacks and got them posted away. Certainly much of the early screening was extremely coarse and many mistakes were made. Indeed, a captured priest, Pastor Jentsch, observed that the whole process of screening 'which, beyond doubt, was necessary, was an awful burden to a sensitive man'. The approach of many officers was that of *vornehme reserviertheit* (honourable detachment) while quite a few other ranks had a joky attitude to the three categories: *Amokraten, Bemokraten and Cemokraten*—the nice implication being that no one at all reached the level of *Demokraten*. But no one could regard screening as quite irrelevant to themselves personally. It gave A-men a virtual certainty of earlier repatriation; a B-man could soon be billetted out with a farmer's family and a C-man could not; a C-plus man appeared to be branded for an indefinite stay. After Colonel Faulk became Field Officer of the re-education programme in May 1945 he brought a great improvement both in the methods and the principle of screening. His rule was: never to be rude, never to shout, never to bully. He personally trained the 'segregation officers' as the screeners were now called and made periodic spot checks to see his principles were being carried out. There were twenty-seven officers in all, whose main job now was to identify prisoners who would co-operate in the re-education programme, 'men capable of initiating new norms and the establishment of a quiet camp'. In Faulk's own definition 'the real white has a positive aim for the future, not merely a revulsion for the old way of life.' The new-style segregation officers based their judgment not on the political views of prisoners; these were barely discussed. It was the attitudes acquired from their family and social background that were significant and in particular their attitude to race and to other groups. Above all, those who were actively hindering the new democratic norms of open discussion and toleration had to be identified, so that, if necessary, they could be segregated off. There is an interesting comparison between this form of screening and that practised in the USA which was based on a man's political record and party membership. The American screeners produced only 0.7 per cent 'whites' and complained that their terms of reference excluded too many good men; in Canada the score was 1 per cent. In Britain, on the new system, the figure

5*

was 10 per cent. Faulk claims that the results his teams achieved
were overwhelmingly confirmed whenever subsequently a man
had to go through a de-nazification tribunal in Germany.*

Commandants were mostly wary of segregation officers. They
were apt to think they themselves knew who were the trouble-
makers better than Faulk's experts who came for a few days from
Bush House. Commandants tended to judge soldierly behaviour
as good and non-Nazi, whereas, observes Faulk, it was frequently
the reverse. He tells of one who trusted a POW with an impressive
military bearing. Thinking him, therefore, a 'decent chap', he
appointed him to an influential post. He was, in fact, a fanatical
Nazi who despised the commandant and stirred up anti-British
feeling by spreading lies about him. The latter curtly dismissed a
warning of his true nature from the screener who interviewed him.
A few weeks later the POW escaped, taking with him the civilian
clothing and valuables of the commandant who was then exposed
to the contempt and scorn of his camp. It was this case that converted the War Office to throwing its weight behind re-education.
In order to be successful it was essential that commandants should
be sympathetic about it and this might require something like their
own re-education. A pamphlet outlining the purpose was prepared largely for their benefit, with a preface recommending that
all commandants do all in their power to help 'in this important
work'.

The tone of a camp was almost always set by the quality and
character of the commandant. Among them were some excellent
and sagacious colonels who were much respected, such as Wilson,
former Chief of Police in Liverpool and Plymouth, and Vickers,
an ex-ranker, and McBain, under all three of whom Herbert
Sulzbach served; the Australian Grondona at Wilton Park; Major
Boughton, the Catholic commandant of the 'theologians' camp at
Norton. The gentlemanly Colonel Darling, who never got the
measure of the Nazis either at Bridgend or at Crewe Hall where he

* By November 1945 there were 208,058 German POWs in Britain
(PID Progress Report No. 10). Of these 19,448 had been screened as
white, 85,380 as grey and 50,205 as black. The remaining 53,025 had
not yet been screened. By August 1948 a total of 37,580 men were
repatriated as white. At the end of 1945 137,000 Italian POWs out of a
total of 162,000 still remained, but were steadily repatriated in 1946,
being replaced by Germans from the USA, Canada and Belgium. (See
pages 170–2.)

succeeded Lord Napier, came more into his own as an inspector of POW camps. At Bridgend where all the generals were collected, Major Topham and his successor, Lieutenant-Colonel Clements, were much liked for their human qualities; of all these officers more will be heard later. Those who, like Vickers and Colonel Selby at Warth Mills, had themselves been POWs in Germany during the First World War often had the surer touch. Commandants might be fatherly or harsh; among them were humorists, martinets, eccentrics and now and then a 'hun-hater'.

Forell in his visitations confronted many types. One told him that he was against his charges learning English as it would assist them to escape. Another said to him, 'All Germans between twelve and sixty should be shot—then we will have peace in the world'; but this bar-generated manner of speech of the peppery English colonel did not deceive Forell and the next morning they had quite a reasonable conversation. The Commandant at Ludlow told Leibholz, who went round the camp lecturing on constitutional issues, 'Hitler was quite right really, only he went too far'. The good professor decided that it was his way of being friendly to him personally as a German. Not a few commandants insisted on a degree of 'bull' in their camps that for the prisoners out-did any Prussianism in their own army. At Moreton-in-the-Marsh the Commandant was called 'Old Woodbine' because he had a wooden leg; he used to slam on charges of twenty-eight days for offences for which in the German army three to seven days would be the most.

Some commandants were appreciated for being strict but fair and even thought of as father figures, but the morale in such places could be below average: the prisoners were still being oppressed from above. The less secure commandants stuck to the letter of regulations, sometimes to an absurd degree. At the camp of one—it was after freedom of movement was allowed—the last bus from the local town arrived back at 10.05 p.m. The rule laid down they must be in by 10.00 p.m.; so he put all those who stayed out beyond then on a charge, until the arrival of Faulk put an end to such stupidity. At Tiverton Major Alan Craycroft, a territorial officer and a member of the BBC singers realised there were some good musicians in his camp and—it was before the war ended—went down to Exeter to rummage through the music shops. He spent some £5 of his own money and came back with, among other things, a copy of Mendelssohn's Violin Concerto. With a formal clicking of heels and a bow he was told with great feeling, 'You do not know, sir, what a delight it is for us to be able to play and hear this music which we have been forbidden for so many years.' Craycroft's successor at Tiverton was Lieutenant-Colonel Oliphant. Later that year he heard that his prisoners wanted to borrow a plough to level off some ground for a football pitch, pulling it themselves. 'That would be barbarism!' he commented, and at once got a bulldozer to do the job. It is said that he thought the world of his prisoners and they of him. Colonel Wild, RAMC, of Northern Command who headed the hospital camp at Naburn near York, is remembered for going out of his way to overcome shortages during the austerity period at the end of 1945.

Probably one in ten of commandants in the end deliberately hindered the re-education programme, another tenth saw the point so completely that they only needed material and support to carry on independently, while the rest co-operated increasingly. But the start was shaky: such was the suspicion of the War Office that those sent to the camps from the POW division of the Foreign Office were instructed to say they were involved in welfare—till Faulk changed this. The operation had also to be conducted in virtual secrecy from the popular press, which Wing Commander Hitch spent much time keeping at bay. 'We have so-called experts who believe in good Germans,' wrote the sardonic John Gordon in the *Sunday Express* in April, having got wind of the affair. 'Being beastly to the Germans' was the mode of the moment. Any official actions which could be interpreted as signifying a soft policy towards the Nazis—and all Germans were Nazis in the popular imagination—might give rise to questions in Parliament, editorials querying the use of public funds, letters to the press from self-appointed watchdogs. Furthermore, re-education was attempted under a name which most of those engaged in it, from Hitch downwards, heartily disliked. The men sent out from Bush House started with another disadvantage: Pastor Forell had been going round the camps for a year and the re-educators were inevitably compared with him and others from the YMCA who gave succour in a neutral spirit without trying to preach or teach.

Nevertheless, the extraordinary and unprecedented project of putting across the elements of the democratic way of life was carried through and applied to some half a million prisoners (including the 100,000 held in North Africa). It was carried through, moreover, on men held captive mainly as a work force who were promised no date of return and who were forbidden to fraternise with the British people. That, in spite of such handicaps, it did have some success was due to two factors: genuine hunger on the part of the prisoners to discover or re-discover an alternative to Nazism, and the human quality and dedication of many of those who carried democratic values to the camps.

At Comrie Camp in Perthshire the season changed. The rounded flanks of Ben Halton and Ben Creog Uchdag turned to a mottled patchwork of white and dun. Then the snow disappeared altogether except in a few high north-facing corries and even there it did not survive the summer. Similarly, the defiance of the prisoners melted as the war ended, in all but a few cases. Sergeant Sulzbach's hard feeling towards them also thawed. In March his view had been, 'These millions of Nazis, partly here in camps, will be a terrible trouble and will try for ages to talk and start revenge.' Now he saw them differently. The super-Nazis were segregated off and sent far north to Watten in Caithness. As the others abandoned their aggressive postures, he could feel himself to be once more among Germans he could recognise and accept as Germans. Strangely enough, further up in the Highlands at this very time, Victor Gollancz, staying at the Nethybridge Hotel with his suitcase full of books, was having his own faith in the basic goodness of humanity repaired.

Meantime, the matter of the lynching of Sergeant Rosterg was being cleared up. The Scotland Yard murder squad had returned in April and arrested twelve men suspected of taking part, among them Senior Cadet Pallm-Koenig, the SS men Goltz, Zuellsdorff, Brueling and Herzig. Their trial in July lasted ten days. The accused were caught off their guard when one of them turned King's evidence, a practice not followed in German law. Also, the atmosphere at Comrie had changed sufficiently for ample witnesses, in the event, to come forward. In the end five men were hanged.

In March Sulzbach had written that the Comrie administration was 'efficient, but a bit too gentlemanly'. Now he found nothing but praise for the urbane and benevolent Colonel Wilson who had once pacified a prison mutiny at Dartmoor without using violence. And Wilson, who called Sulzbach 'Mac' (because he was in Scotland) and had come to admire him as 'one of the finest men I've met', gave every support to his initiatives. At first these were mostly on paper; circulars challenging Nazi ideas, putting out items of interest about the British awy of life. The *KZ* film had to be shown, but for Sulzbach the follow-up was to show the actions of those who had resisted the evils of National Socialism. He sent out the story of the Munich students of the 'White Rose' who had dared to distribute leaflets crying out against the Nazi tyranny and Hitler's harvest of German dead in Russia, and who were caught and executed. 'You believed they were traitors', proclaimed Sulzbach, 'these fighters for freedom, whose names will be recalled for centuries to come with reverence.' He was beginning his own personal and passionate campaign of re-education, or 'demonstrating the truth', which he would maintain for the next three years. The fact that he was a Jew was, of course, an asset. His whole appearance and character were a rebuttal of what the younger prisoners had been brought up to believe was a typical one. In speech and culture this cheerful yet earnest fifty-year-old was as German as could be. Even in his British sergeant's uniform he could, without offence, speak of 'we' and 'us'.

Though Sulzbach was not trained or meant to do any screening, be began practising it unofficially. When Faulk saw the results, he considered that they would be found to be at least as accurate as those achieved by his trained teams. (Sulzbach's essentially intuitive method is described in more detail in Chapter Nine.) A sensitive man, he was guided by his own feeling of another's quality as a human being. He easily saw through a friendly-seeming man who was out for himself; and into the man who was basically sincerely idealistic (like himself) but who had been manipulated by Nazi propaganda. Those who were not blinded by bitterness and anger sensed that their fellow German who had no guile about him only wished them well. Sulzbach's assessments tended to be more favourable than most; a POW marked as C could well be B or at least what he called 'C-redeemable'—men weaned from Nazism because of its collapse and now struggling for a new footing. These latter Sulzbach would quietly remove from the black compound to a white one, where a trusted POW would be asked to take him unobtrusively under his wing, talk to him and report progress, if necessary asking for help. Admittedly, the most defiant element had been sent away to the far north, but Sulzbach reckoned that only four months after defeat a mere 5 per cent of the 1,200 in the main camp were still imbued with Nazi doctrines. Faulk visiting Comrie noted that an amazing transformation had taken place through the combined efforts of Wilson and Sulzbach who 'would be a treasure in any camp'. He also observed a tendency among POWs to regard the sloughing off of Nazism as an end in itself. 'When it is achieved they are keyed up with a new hope and courage. It is at this point that they are able to absorb the tenets of a new philosophy and to be instructed in the democratic way of life. Otherwise, they tend to sink back into apathy and this has happened in quite a few camps.' Faulk defined the 'real white' as 'the man with a positive aim for the future, not only a revulsion from the old way of life.'

It was time, Faulk felt, for the ban on politics in the camp to be lifted and he himself started the ball rolling by giving a talk on basic democracy and the mechanics of the House of Commons. He then set up a formal debate with himself as Speaker. Many were eager to take the floor, and a motion was voted on. When he had gone, such was their zeal for the 'new freedom' that they laid on two debates a week. Sulzbach attended the first on the surprising motion 'That this camp is of the opinion that it is unwise of Britain to send us back to Germany yet'. He enthusiastically reported to Faulk a high level of argument, much trust in the Press and the BBC and in the ability of the Allies to judge the situation, and a winning of the motion.

The change of heart at Comrie by that autumn was spectacular and culminated in a dramatic proof of the new spirit. A psychologist might point out that the switch of loyalty was too fast, that it came from a need to follow a new line as whole-heartedly as the last, or to appease the victor; that it was very much inspired from above. But a way of life had been shattered and Wilson, Sulzbach and Faulk had worked hard to demonstrate the alternative. And there is no doubt of the emotional impact of Armistice Day, 11 November, a date that had deep personal significance for Sulzbach. As a lieutenant in field-grey, he had been the one to announce to his batteries in France the original armistice of 1918: *Von 12 Uhr Mittags an ruhen die Waffen* . . . and the weapons, he had devoutly hoped, would lie still for ever. Now he sent round a circular explaining the spirit of the traditional Armistice Day in Britain and the two minutes silence, and the significance of the poppies which grew so prolifically in Flanders as a symbol. The lines

> In Flanders fields the poppies blow
> Between the crosses row on row . . .

he said, spoke for the sorrow of millions and the yearning for the end of war. This 11th November was to be dedicated by the Allies to the commemoration of all the dead of both World Wars. He therefore hoped that all the Germans in the camp would attend a ceremony on the parade ground to commemorate their own dead, those of the former enemy, the freedom fighters in all countries and the victims of the concentration camps. But they should only come if they were willing to take a vow, a copy of which he sent to every man in the camp:

> Never, never again shall such murder happen in future. It is the last time that we will allow ourselves to be lied to and betrayed. It is not true that we Germans are a superior race: we have no right to believe that we are better than others. We are all equal before Almighty God, whatever race or religion we belong to. We now have realised where arrogance leads to; endless misery has come upon us, and is this not the retribution the Almighty has brought upon us? At this moment we swear to return home as good Europeans and as long as we live to take an active part in the reconciliation of all people and the maintenance of eternal peace, according to the principle of the true, the beautiful, the good.
> Only if that is your own sacred conviction, should you take part in these minutes of silence.

On that day, out of 3,000 men in the Comrie camps, only some 150 stayed in their tents. All the others came to the parade-ground, stood for the two minutes silence, head bowed and cap in hand, and made the vow. It was the proudest moment of his life. There may have been honourable men among those who stayed away, fearing to be captured once more by mass emotion. But surely that day of memory of the past and the yearning for a better future must have marked in many an inner movement of change and renewal.

A month later Sulzbach was posted south, and began to receive the first of thousands (literally) of letters from those whose hearts and minds he had touched.

To: Staff-Sgt. H. Sulzbach   11.12.45
These few lines are sent to accompany you on your journey.
We German POWs find no words to express our thanks for what you have been for us. You looked after us at the most

difficult time and through the generosity of your character gave
us new faith. You left Germany severely outraged, yet you set
out to rescue for Germany any German who showed good will.

We only knew England from the German press, and came to
this country as men humiliated and in despair. You can understand what we expected. It was not words and promises which
quickly made us think differently about the English, but your
person. No Briton could have brought us so close to the people
as you have done. You gave us insight, faith and confidence,
and that greatly helped us when we went out to work among
the English people.

These few words tell what we are losing in your departure.
Should we find ourselves at home again our memories will often
go back to these Scottish hills. You, Staff, will for ever be connected with these thoughts. We cannot and never will forget
you.

In the name of everyone in 'D' Compound.

(Signatures)

7

Island in the Fells

Day after day
You work for liberation.
You sit in your room writing.
Do you want to know how your work really strikes you?
That little chestnut tree in the corner of the yard,
Look, that was a canful of water you carried to it.

Brecht, *Thoughts on the Length of Exile (1945)*
(Written in California)

In 1977, when Shap Wells Hotel in Cumbria was being renovated for the tourist trade, a corner of the old kitchen was deliberately not plastered over. On the wall can still be read the name M. Mörschbäcker, and that in 1943 he built an oven there—the only evidence of one-time German occupation of the capacious hotel. Deriving from the time when fishermen and grouse-shooters were less mobile, it lies tucked into a hollow of the moors below Shap summit, on the railway line to Scotland. A familiar sight used to be the tank-engine running back down the track to Tebay, having banked a heavy express up the steepest main-line gradient in England. Scarcely another habitation can be seen from the handsome three-storied pile built round a courtyard, reminiscent, to one prisoner, of a Karlsbad hotel set in the midst of nowhere. Except in high summer there is the constant sound of Birk Beck rushing down a bouldered stream, across which between 1940 and 1947 a narrow foot-bridge led to the hutments of the British soldiers who lived rougher than the men they guarded. At first, Camp 13, which was its official designation, was used for aircrew shot down over Britain and for prisoners from the battle of the Atlantic. There were several escape attempts but the defences were formidable. A tunnel—the site of the entrance in a corner room then used for music making is still shown—had not made much progress through the craggy soil when it was discovered; but two pilots of KG 27 did bluff their way out and seize a Miles Magister trainer aircraft at Carlisle. At Horsham St Faith in Norfolk they were caught trying to refuel in order to cross the North Sea. After being fêted in the RAF mess, they were duly returned to camp. This was in November 1941. Four years later the Shap prisoners were scarcely even guarded for it had become a special camp for 'white' officers, the only one of its kind.

Suitable candidates were being chosen by screeners in the last winter of the war. In November 1944 at Comrie, which then had an officer compound, it took place largely through a kind of spontaneous self-selection. On the long walks over the moors which they were permitted under guard, kindred spirits discovered each other. They formed small friendship circles which, if they were too blatant and outspoken, could mean danger. Among the hundred in each Nissen hut there might be a handful of democrats sleeping in one corner—but one always kept awake in case of a sudden visitation in the night. An obvious case for political treatment was a stocky Bavarian artist from Seeshaupt who kept a wooden club beside his bunk. This was Karl-Josef Huber who, with his friend Tyroller, had walked through the barrage of spit at Le Havre. Huber was a puzzle to interrogators. How could this vivid, vital and spontaneous man, speaking broad Bavarian, whose art indubitably belonged to the kind denounced as 'degenerate', not only have survived in Nazi Germany but become an officer? He seemed almost too good to be real. 'How would you like one of my paintings in our mess?' he once asked his adjutant. 'Bring one along!' Innocently he did so. 'Mein Gott, you had better keep that hidden away!' Huber was protected by luck and by fellow-officers who liked him; one of them, in fact, arranged for his final posting to be in France instead of to Russia. In England too, without asking favours and in spite of a few brushes with authority, he landed on his feet. He delighted one interrogating officer, called he believes Colonel Butler, a Cambridge don, so much that he said, 'We must do something special with Huber', and he was in fact repatriated in one of the very first groups.

At Le Havre Huber had got to know a singular-looking major who commanded a bicycle liaison unit outside the fortress, a duty most appropriate to a man who was both unaggressive and a good communicator. Bespectacled, extremely tall and thin, narrow-headed like a Borzoi, he was actually a prince of the Swabian nobility—Fürst von Urach. As with all the aristocracy after the July Plot, he had been taken off the staff and barred further promotion. He and the well-bred, cultivated Graf Clemens Podewils gravitated to each other. The latter had been a war-reporter at Stalingrad, had upper-class connections with England, had translated John Keats rather well, and, in the half-light, might have been mistaken for Edward VIII when he was Prince of Wales. These three, all Catholics, formed the nucleus of a South German group.

Pastor Rudolf Halver of the Confessing Church came from Hamburg. In the Belgian camps he had welcomed the breaking down of the usual barriers between padre and men—they were all in the same boat. In Comrie he discovered six theological students and a bath-hut where he began taking services after morning roll-call. At one of these he first saw a most unmilitary and informal young man with a blanket over his shoulders. This was the gifted, artistic Werner Düttmann, son of a Berlin sculptor. He too had a club in his bunk and was keeping as far as possible out of the way of Colonel Mann, ardent Nazi defender of Brest, who was trying to insist that young officers attended the tactics instruction he was carrying out on a sand-tray. Düttmann and Halver became firm friends and linked up with Kurt Lichdi, a pianist and musicologist. The camp administration had provided him with a portable gramophone and records with which he conducted recitals with works such as Handel's *Water Music* and Beethoven's *Ninth Symphony*. The sight of a Nissen hut packed solid with officers standing in total stillness and attention, listening to Beethoven's *Hymn to Joy*, is something Halver will never forget. Lichdi had no piano to play on, so Düttmann, unconsciously imitating what Albert Schweitzer did in the African jungle, got some paper and painted a keyboard on it for him—though Schweitzer's dumb keyboard was in wood. Adolf Fecker, with talent as a composer, naturally joined up with Lichdi. Halver organised evenings of song and poetry, writing out the music on toilet paper. Small, symbolic acts cemented new-found affinities. Halver, the pastor, was asked to hold a service in the larger other ranks section of the camp, for which he needed a pass to enter. As a thankoffering, the cook there presented him with a small piece of bread and cheese, a precious gift in those days. He brought it back and gave it personally as a token of his esteem to von Urach who was emerging as the natural leader of a small, like-minded group of dissidents.

Watchfully at the edge of this group was a former student of

physics at Dresden University, Panzerleutnant Hugo Staudinger
(whom Patton's tank men had asked if he wanted to go back into
his bunker and continue the fight). Extremely bright and thoughtful, he had been active in the Catholic Youth Movement. During
a walk over the mountainside where Huber and Düttmann had
picked up their clubs, he had begun to arm himself against a much
more subtle enemy than the camp bullies. His companion was a
young SS officer who struck him as a decent and honourable person. But from this man Staudinger learned for the first time the
extent of the mass killings in the east. 'It *had* to be done,' he heard,
'however dreadful, so that our future generations can live without
the parasitic race of Jews. Our children will never know of the
horror, but will be able to live better lives because of what we did.'
And with horror Staudinger listened to this revelation of the way
the concept of honour and duty could be used to justify an act
which was understood to be terrible.

That Scottish valley with its moorland flanks was one of many
cauldrons where the values of the Third Reich began to disinte-
grate. 'A wonderful landscape,' Düttmann summed it up, 'but a
dreadful camp. The dramatic thing was the way every standpoint
one took was still false.' People questioned the past, but on a soil
that was still being harrowed it was hardly possible to sow seeds
of the future. Staudinger, however, had his starting point; he
began to ponder deeply on the implications of the morality of
the naked will, on its roots in German philosophy, and how
these roots might be exposed for all to see them for what they
were.

The selection for the 'white' camp at Shap was conducted by a
sympathetic Norwegian captain. He spent an especially long time
with Düttmann, trying to find out whom he would like to go
with him if he went to another camp. As they talked, a knot of
hostile and suspicious officers was waiting outside to grill Düttmann about what had been said. 'Tell them,' the captain said, 'that
we have been talking about Norway and I have been trying to get
information about certain war criminals.' The actual extraction of
the men for Shap—these and others—took place suddenly and
late in the evening—POW transports were almost always at night.
Huber was not with them but found himself in a group of rabid
Nazis probably on their way to a 'black' camp. It could have been
a muddle, though he thinks it might have been to test him out. At
any rate, the first group set up a shout of 'Huber, Huber!' to show

he belonged to them and a sergeant took him across to join his true companions.

When the Comrie group—those named and several others—arrived at Shap in early December they were not unlike a group of actors glad to be taken out of an unsavoury production and given a chance in one more worthy of their talents. Their opening scene was dramatic enough. Every man found a pile not only of blankets but white sheets for his bed. The hotel buzzed with suspicion: what were the British up to? Such privileges must have purpose—they would only be given to collaborators, and this they were not. To slide between sheets might be the slippery way to treachery. Not a few were left folded. If at Comrie they had split off from the main group, now they split among themselves. Most divisive was the use of the Nazi greeting; it had become a symbol of one's opinions, but sometimes inversely. Staudinger, for instance, continued to use it because he did not want to be identified with those who had too quickly turned about. There was yet another division—between the older men who regarded themselves as soldierly Christian patriots and younger radicals who rejected everything that to them smelt of militarism or nationalism and even the contaminated word, *Deutsch*.

It was not long before von Urach stepped into his natural role when the democratic camouflage of the first camp leader was uncovered: he was wanted for enquiries by the Scotland Yard murder squad active at Comrie. The 'Lagerfürst', as Prince Urach became known, was a born mediator and diplomat and, in Halver's words, 'a living bridge into Germany's past'. His prestige was enormously enhanced by his being, supposedly, a rather remote cousin of the British royal family. He wisely never commented on this and allowed the mystery to deepen, so that over thirty years later the totally false belief is current that he received regular food parcels from 'the Queen', which he shared with his nearer friends. Certainly his air of *noblesse oblige* helped his relations with Lieutenant-Colonel Walker, the Commandant, a strong Tory of the hunting-and-shooting breed, who was delighted, indeed flattered, to have a prince as his camp leader and one so able and trustworthy. Quite soon he handed over the weekly room inspections to him; and by the end of the year when among the earliest of the camps the barbed wire began to come down, he was happy also to pass the main security of the camp to his responsibility. Rotas of the younger officers took over the guard duties, to the pleasure of the Tommies, who were not a little resentful that the Germans had better accommodation than they did, better cooks and smoked Players, not Woodbines. For a while, however, the routine searches by the army continued. After one of these Urach was invited by the Commandant to inspect some illegal objects that had been found. Among the things laid out in the Colonel's office were some small finely-ground knives which Urach at once recognised as Huber's wood-carving implements, made out of the hotel cutlery. With a cool nerve and shrewdly judging that the Commandant would not dare say anything, he quietly pocketed them when his back was turned. The Lagerfürst's prestige grew still higher.

His deputy was chosen at an election set up by the British. Each officer nominated had to speak before the whole camp about his private and military career. The choice fell on Hubert Walter, the staunch Catholic who had been interpreter at Lamsdorf and who had had an uncomfortable time at Ascot when his principles forbade him to speak on the BBC against Hitler after he had not dared to speak out at home. The Commandant used to take him along to Penrith to shop for the canteen. The 'korrekt' Walter was amazed at the way the Commandant, puffing his Three Nuns tobacco, disclosed to him, a POW and a foreigner, his hearty dislike of the new Prime Minister, Major Attlee. Others in the executive committee of the camp were Graf Podewils, Leutnant Mueller, an amiable and able judge, Josef Huber and Professor Joachim Ritter. Ritter was the most distinguished figure in the camp. Designated Professor of Philosophy at Kiel University, he was short, rotund, ebullient, with grey-blue eyes and a naturally dominant but affectionate nature. He was immensely well-read, with great intellectual verve, and could hold forth volubly, but never drily, on Dostoievsky and Kierkegaard, Tolstoy and Pascal, Swift and Blake. He had lain low during the Nazi period; now he could make up for mental starvation by rapidly assimilating Aldous Huxley and T. S. Eliot. Just the person to gather young men round him and put them through their paces, he quickly began setting up a wide structure of university-type courses: in philosophy, history, German language and literature, law, theology both Catholic and Protestant, musicology, geography, architecture. English was widely taught, the British camp personnel lending a hand; also French, Spanish, Latin and even Greek and Hebrew, though these last two soon fell away. Examinations were held and in some cases the equivalent of a full university year was officially recognised later—there was at the time, of course, no outside German university body to give support or refer to. The original camp library was increased to 2,000 books by occasional purchases and private loans, but chiefly through the International Book Club's work for student relief and the YMCA. It was through this last that Professor Ritter first met Pastor Forell, whom he would one day think worthy of the Nobel Peace Prize. It was all very purposeful and *deutsch*. There were also general lectures on free themes, poetry readings, a choir and regular recitals by Lichdi and by Fecker, who composed his own works and played the violin. There was an old grand piano, but with a note that did not play, so when it came up it was sung, or someone pushed the clapper up from under the piano—a constant source of comedy. The English dailies and weeklies arrived on time, but the most devoured was the *Schweizerische Weltwoche* from Zürich.

Through 1945 the camp settled down into a rhythmic, privileged existence. The monotony was punctuated with small dramas. A trumpeter used to blow the Last Post at the end of each day, but one evening his bugle was missing. A trick by the Germans was suspected and the camp was searched. It was eventually found in the latrine pit behind the lavatories—thrown there by a young soldier furious at not being demobbed. Podewils used to take his ring off when washing and leave it on the inside window ledge. He went down to breakfast, forgetting to put it on again. On his return it was missing. Who had stolen it—an officer, or a batman? There was a nasty feeling that either could have been guilty, but there was no evidence on which to conduct an investigation. The matter was beginning to be forgotten when someone noticed a glint on the rocks by the beck. The culprit was judged to have been a magpie. There were times when a *Lagerkoller* (barbed-wire fever) struck the camp; general depression reigned and codes of behaviour were broken. Once—unspeakable horror—an officer found that someone had defecated into his bed. The Commandant shook his head—what were his officers coming to! The Lagerfürst could only tell him that it could not have been a real officer—only some labour corps commander.

It was a small enough camp for everyone to be aware of each other: 250 officers, with no fewer than 80 orderlies and kitchen staff. As other ranks received no pay, the officers docked some of

their own to divide among them; they could also take part in the
courses and cultural events. One of the quietly important men in
the camp, Father Schoenen, lived with the other ranks. Absolute
hierarchy of rank in fact quickly fell away; all military decorations
were removed and often badges of rank too. In their place came
two strata, one social, the other intellectual. The former was
inevitable in a camp top-heavy with aristocrats (there was even a
second prince, a von Seyn-Wittgenstein); there were many men
from 'good families' and well-heeled business backgrounds, such
as Preussen-Elektra. The other stratum—one could belong to
both—comprised the Herr Doktors, the academics, school-
teachers, economists and lawyers who had often been administra-
tors in the occupied territories rather than fighting officers.
Beyond this there were the young students making up for lost
time, and freer spirits—architects, artists, musicians. There was a
well-known writer of patriotic books about the First World War,
P. C. Ettinghofer. There were two aristocratic playboys who did
not group with anyone, and a Hauptmann Kiesseling from Vienna
who was psychic, and already at Comrie had been attracted to
Düttmann who, he had decided, had gifts as a medium. There was
a tall, grey-haired gentleman Junker from Silesia who was experi-
encing an ironic reversal of roles: Colonel von Lindeiner-Waldau,
till recently Commandant of the famous Stalagluft III at Sagan.
An admirer of the English, he had been well-liked by the high-
spirited RAF officers there, who were so bent on escaping.
Unknown to them, he and members of his staff had gone to the
limit in trying to improve their welfare. After the mass escape
when forty-seven were caught and shot by the Gestapo, he had
been court-martialled on a trumped-up black marketing charge.
Distinguished-looking and wistful, he was also well liked at Shap,
where he stayed in between visits to the London Cage to help
investigation into the Sagan murders.

One more Shap character must be described: Horst Woetzel,
like Staudinger an interrupted student. Small, stocky, bespectacled,
he was a typical dark Thuringian. He twinkled and laughed easily;
having more thoughts than he could express, he talked in rapid,
jerky sentences. With Düttmann he was inwardly probably the
most liberated person in the camp, the least touched by the Nazi
virus. In Düttmann's case the antidote had come largely through
a liberal family background; in Woetzel's from liberal schoolmasters, two of whom were purged and one of whom had a

Jewish wife. His religion teacher had let him see forbidden books,
and a bookseller friend had allowed him to sit in his back-room
'poison-lab', where in his mid-teens he devoured forbidden
authors like Wassermann, Werfel and the Zweigs. Another crucial
experience was a chance encounter on the Lüneburg Heath at a
time when the Nazi government was keeping its citizens barred
from foreign travel as communist Germany would do later on.
There at the Youth Hostel at Bispingen was an English father and
son; he joined up with them, spent a whole week in their company, talking and singing English songs. This spontaneous
affinity with two English people, with Hitler himself there on the
Heath attending the first great manoeuvres of the new Reichswehr,
was deeply meaningful, and he could not wait to get to Britain.
Now at Shap he was expanding with delight into even a con-
stricted experience of English landscape, people and literature.
There was no more watchful and amused or sociological eye
observing the camp scene. Socially very diffident himself, he kept
his views from all but a very few, protecting his integrity with the
equivalent of the heavy horse-driver's cloak he used to wear and
which came almost to the ground. His most prized possession, he
had obtained it in exchange for cigarettes at camp 18. In years
to come it would also keep him warm during his student days in
Münster.

Urach saw that it would be wise to give Huber a room all to
himself in a remote attic (the plumbing system he found useful for
hiding his illegal tools). Here, for the first time in years, he could
get out his paints, ransomed in Le Havre, and give rein to his
daemon on paper provided by the YMCA or bought for him in
Penrith. When his first paintings descended into the hotel there
was the inevitable uproar of taste, for they were both very modern
and abstract. Urach quietened the ideological storm. Düttmann
too had an atelier-bedroom which he shared with Heiks up in the
old servants' quarters. His creative urge was wider than Huber's.
Not only water-colours and lino-cuts, but also sonnets came from
him with almost too great a facility. As fast as they flowed from
him he was ready to give away his pictures of flowers, the landscape, broken cities and refugees, of the Crucifixion, and again and
again of a mother and child. His élan and inner freedom at first
irked the old guard at Shap. Not a few were suspicious of this
handsome youth with a big head and a sculptor's shoulders, who
was left-wing and so annoyingly relaxed, even frivolous. Did he

not allow Hauptmann Kiessling to go to his room, put a blanket against the window and hold seances, with table-tipping, the business with glasses and all that? But to others he was a golden boy with a great future. 'I could be very lazy at Shap,' he recalls. 'I wasn't involved in the quarrels of the camp. I had seen a great deal that was horrible and evil, but I was no longer in a situation that lay heavy upon me. On the contrary, I was full of hope for a better world, for the reception in England had been amazingly friendly. In comparison with all that had gone before, Shap was a good world.'

Woetzel was greatly amused at and points up the difference between the life-style and room of Düttmann and Heiks, and those of Staudinger, Silberhorn and Wagner, who 'had a plan for each day which they kept to with vigorous punctuality from morning to night. It was for them the obvious way to organise themselves in a confined space, and to get through their heavy study schedule; it also fulfilled their need for a rigid inner discipline. There was never a speck of dust in their room, their trousers were always pressed and their boots polished. When not in use pen, pencil and ruler lay neatly along the squared pattern of their linoleum table covering. None of the three relaxed. When they went out walking, they never strolled, they marched; the walk had a specific function in their lives, as exercise and training. They spoke on definite themes or not at all.' Staudinger had succeeded in obtaining through the YMCA a copy of Gerhard's *Handbook of German History*, a vast standard work, and was memorising large parts of it. And were there not history lectures to fit in from Dr Schroetter: essays and tutorials on Kant and Hobbes with Professor Ritter, whose lectures on the history of philosophy also had to be absorbed; not to mention Emminghaus on Catholic liturgy and Father Schoenen and Pastor Pagel's Catholic-Protestant seminar? And this is to leave out early Mass each morning, held in a small room made into a chapel at the end of an upper corridor. It was conducted by Father Schoenen, a member of the Tekbus fathers, who had been called up as a medical orderly.* 'His coming was a joy to us,' Staudinger says simply. The radiant calmness and humility during this Mass of this still very young priest made a strong impression on Woetzel, as did the whole office conducted

---

* He must have been discovered through the questionnaire that Pastor Forell sent round to all camps in the autumn of 1944, aiming to identify for possible re-distribution all pastors and priests in the camps.

with deep seriousness and dignity. 'The servers were officers not in POW battle-dress but in full uniform, pressed and creased as for parade. But it wasn't the outer aspect that struck me so much as the significance of the movements before the altar made with absolute economy of movement and military precision, as this was the best way they knew of expressing their inner collectedness. The quiet was scarcely broken by the Latin words of the liturgy. As the only Protestant who went regularly, I was touched by an act of worship that had no sermon and did not need to be interpreted by a communicator. It was only the younger officers who came; the asceticism, the feeling of *Klausur* (seclusion) appealed to them—though I did see Ritter there once or twice; Düttmann occasionally and Tyroller.' The more usual religious services, both Lutheran and Catholic, were attended by nearly everyone; Urach also encouraged an ecumenical spirit.

Any self-indulgence was conspicuous: at breakfast it was definitely not done to scoop around with the porridge ladle to get more currants off the bottom. They could never eat their fill, or get drunk or even taste alcohol except on Christmas Day. A continual lenten austerity brought to those who accepted it a certain clarity of mind. So did the wide empty landscape across which they could soon wander for miles and miles, at first accompanied by a bored guard who then would sit on a knoll watching his charges at a distance and even, towards the end of the camp, give over his rifle to be carried for him. The therapy of nature worked strongly on many of them. Twice they saw the full cycle of the bracken: the shoots spring up bright green through the compost, myriad bishops' mitres become a forest of six-foot fans quivering in the summer breezes, then sink back to cover the winter landscape with a tawny pelt that the snow would help to rot. They noticed these things and wrote about them. In the second season they could sometimes cut bracken for the farmers, get to know them, and earn some pocket money. There was the endlessly interesting sight of sheep-dogs working the sheep. The moor, the long stone walls, the peat rills and the beck, were the habitat of much bird life: robins and tit-mice in the copse beside the hotel, curlews continually wheeling over the moor, the occasional heron; the alarm call of the wren, and the frequent grouse catapulting into their straight low trajectory when disturbed. The city-bred learned to tell apart the expansive melody of the mistle-thrush and the short musical figure of the common thrush. Some Junkers, who had maybe lost their own estates for ever, thought how they could improve this too bald landscape and leave their mark on it for posterity. They evolved a plan for planting a strip of spruce and the Commandant gave the go-ahead. They began digging the drainage trenches, but a local trade union intervened and stopped work which should be paid properly and given to local men.

The Commandant, every inch the country gentleman in colonel's uniform, gave them a talk about fox-hunting and shooting and the habits of local birds and beasts. They were delighted —they met the real man beneath the authority figure. 'Here,' wrote Podewils warmly in the Shap magazine, 'was a person with heart. No one can appreciate this so well as the prisoner, who possesses an unerring scent for what is genuine and human.'

The most distinguished contribution to *Arbeit im Aufbau* and probably to any camp magazine anywhere came from Joachim Ritter. It was a study of T. S. Eliot,[41] the discovery of whom greatly moved him. In the *Four Quartets* especially he found many indications of how to achieve a true recovery of inner values and at the same time a powerful corrective to dangerous tendencies in German romanticism. 'We have become accustomed', he wrote, 'for the poetic so to transform the nature of things that . . . they are ready to become the vehicle of our feelings and dispositions, and to express our love, our longing, our pain. Eliot's sobriety and severity put us on our guard against this. "You must go by a way where there is no ecstasy." ' The task of poetry, Ritter goes on, interpreting Eliot, 'is to praise, but also to bind us to the permanent condition of life'.

> We, content at the last
> If our temporal reversion nourish
> (not too far from the yew-tree)
> the life of significant soil.

The appeal of Camp 13 to its inmates, or to many of them, was a combination of the austere and romantic. Podewils used to be fond of a poem defining the ideal officer which included the line *Ein Hauch von Mönche und von Kavalier* (a touch of monk, a touch of cavalier). On returning home to Bavaria he tried to summarise the experience in an article he wrote for *Merkur*.[42] 'What united us all in that wild landscape straight out of Ossian or, on halcyon days, of rare peace and clarity, has proved more lasting than I dared to hope. I do not wish to compare it with the ties that bound us in the war itself. In our case there was another factor of our inner and outer condition to add: the essential, unexpressed core of our enforced community life was its monastic stamp. From within ourselves we tried to measure up to what had been compelled upon us and so to transform the obligatory into self-discipline and thus into freedom . . . We succeeded at least in one thing: in spite of the friction and irritability that inevitably arose from our close uninterrupted life in common, our efforts at self-control did lead in the end to an almost easy compatibility.'

To heighten this theme Podewils never mentioned guards or the British or the outside world. It is as though they did not exist. Ehrhart Kaestner does exactly the same thing for a whole book in his now classic *Zeltbuch in Tumilad* about a German POW camp in Egypt. In fact, visitors played an important, even a dramatic part in the life of the camp. Each newcomer had to pass a test—the crossing of some twenty-five yards of gravel between the gate and the front door. His arrival at the guard-house having been noted, fifty pairs of eyes were at the windows ready to bore into him and register the signal he gave off: age, size, carriage, angle of head, clothes, and so on. Quick general assumptions were made on the spot, each watcher adding his personal embellishment. Then a cloak of uncertainty would fall until Urach, who had his room by the front door, had greeted the visitor and word spread as to what he was like. Pastor Forell, for instance, caused great excitement by turning up one day with some Red Cross nurses. The local Catholic priest, long hoped for, at last arrived but acutely disappointed his co-religionists when they showed him the equipment for the Mass which they had fashioned themselves; it was made of tin, he said, and therefore against regulations. A tall fair young man arrived more than once with his Dalmatian dog which put out, of course, a very strong signal. He was Philip Rossiter, a segregation officer; affable, well-bred and intelligent, he spoke his perfect German with an English accent. He was a part Jew from Bavaria and before the significance of this was properly appreciated had been an eager member of the Hitler Youth. In 1934 when on holiday in England he decided to stay on; taking his cousins' name, he finished his education in Kent and at Oxford. In 1939, adventurous and energetic, he joined the Foreign Legion as *volontaire pour durée de la guerre* and escaped from it at the fall of France. Toughened by this experience—his university of life he calls it—urbane and very anglophile, he worked for the Foreign Office and found himself in 1945 as one of Faulk's team of so-called Training Advisers and also as an occasional screener as well as lecturer on English literature. Some POWs related to him at once; others resented the ease with which he could see through the veil they tried to throw across their early enthusiasm for Hitler; and many guessed that this pipe-smoking *Engländer* wearing his Oxford college tie wasn't quite what he appeared. Indeed, today Philip Rosenthal—for that was his real name—believes that Philip Rossiter made a mistake in pretending to be the Englishman he almost felt he was at that time.*

A more formidable visitor than 'the man with the Dalmatian' was Professor King—another compulsory cover name. An extremely big man with abundant energy and brains, he stirred up strong feelings, curiosity, and intense discussion wherever he went and obviously enjoyed doing this. A man with a mission, he resolutely refused to accept that a German officer was a gentleman just because he was an officer, which put not a few commandants immediately against him. He had strong, well-grounded views on recent German history on which he had lectured at Oxford. At any officer camp his main contention was bound to rouse the maximum resentment. It was that German militarism was as much the enemy as Nazism; the Nationalist Party of the press baron Hugenberg, he held, had a special responsibility for bringing Hitler to power, as it hoped to use him to smash Weimar democracy and the Trade Union movement. This old ruling establishment, the 'Hugenbergs' (Koeppler used the term generically) had to go because they were basically anti-democratic, and there could be no sound new Germany unless they were powerless.

At Featherstone Park, the largest officer camp, he had called an open-air meeting. He was in his element—the 'Hugenbergs' were there in force before him—and he needled them relentlessly in his extraordinarily penetrating and powerful voice. He drew them out until, in the words of Dieter Frankel, 'the older officers went on the barricades. Everything they said he contradicted and the provocation escalated. We younger ones held back while our seniors took him on. We were pretty certain, talking it over afterwards, that in spite of his English accent he wasn't English because of some of his phrases. We came to the conclusion he was sounding us out, discovering whose opinions warranted their

* For his subsequent career see below, page 385.

being kept a watch on. Next time he comes, we thought, keep your mouth shut, or you'll be posted to a black camp, or stay an extra year. We discussed Professor King feverishly for days, and everyone was against him for stirring us up. But afterwards I thought how clever to penetrate under our skins like that and get us discussing matters we had avoided so far. He wanted to hear from us officers what got us keyed up. He succeeded magnificently!'

Professor King inevitably turned up at Shap and confronted another all-officer audience, except this time there was scarcely a professional soldier among them. 'That night,' says Huber dramatically, 'no one slept,' and early the next morning the Lagerfürst sent for the small fearless Bavarian as the only man who could confront the formidable King without being dominated by him. He was due to talk to the young officers that morning. 'We must do something,' said von Urach, 'or the camp will no longer be in my control.' Three of them, Urach, Müller and Huber, cornered the visitor in the well in the middle of the hotel and, sitting on the stairs, challenged what they felt was his wholesale condemnation of everything in Nazi Germany. King had been shown some of Huber's paintings. 'A painter like you couldn't make a living in Hitler's Germany!' 'On the contrary, we did manage to make ends meet. No one locked me up. Even people in the Party helped us.' King would not accept the implications of this and the conversation became heated, the other two gradually edging away from them on the stairs. 'Imagine a circus director,' said Huber; 'he has some lions in a cage and a trainer, a keeper, someone to feed the lions, and so on. They are all members of the Party; so one fine day he just sacks them. A few days later the lions won't be prowling around. They won't even get up in the morning because no one has fed them. Is that sensible? If the director is going to wait till he finds staff who are not Nazis but "white" he may have to wait a long time! He should leave the old ones to do the job until someone else can be found. Your wholesale solution is a typical Nazi one!' The visitor was having no more of this and got up. He had a list of German personnel in the camp and Huber saw him underline his name with three red lines. Two hours later he left the camp without giving another talk.

This is the story as told by Huber himself. Its victim recalls nothing of it and vigorously denies the possibility of the red underlinings. All he remembers from Shap is Urach's courtesy, and his belief that some of the young officers had ears for his views. In this he was certainly right, and perhaps the wary Urach knew it. At any rate the 'professor' was expecting to be back at Oxford in the autumn, his lectures on medieval history having been announced. But an entirely different fate was, unknown to him, in store. Who was this imposing man with H.K. mono-grammed on his handkerchief? Certainly not Professor King, the prisoners knew. Obviously a refugee and a German, for all the slight English accent with which he spoke; and at least partly Jewish. One rumour, quite false, was that he had been a journalist on the *Vossische Zeitung*. Professor King was, in fact, a Berliner who had obtained a scholarship to Oxford from Kiel University in 1933 and had stayed on in Britain. Forty-five years later he would receive a knighthood for his life work in international rela-tions, as the pioneer of a new form of discussion centre which started as a 'camp university' for German POWs. Sir Heinz Koeppler, CBE, and his creation, Wilton Park, will have a chapter to themselves later in this book.

This is the place, perhaps, for another of Huber's stories which is harder still to confirm. There was, of course, sexual frustration at Shap, but probably less than in most monasteries. For one thing, solitude even *à deux* was very difficult in such crowding. There were occasional homosexual friendships certainly, but if they became too intense one of the parties could be posted to another camp, which happened once or twice. One officer with a decided kink was discovered to be slipping out at night and climb-ing up drain-pipes to look hopefully into the bedrooms of the nearest cottages. This voyeur was also posted away. Huber's story is about an Oberleutnant Hell, a likeable Prussian of the Pomeran-ian type, who at Le Havre had a French mistress who was very attached to him. When she discovered where he was she managed to get herself over to England and made friends with the driver of the banking engine on the Shap run. He used to conceal her in his cabin and on the solo run back from Shap Summit stopped by the camp to let her climb down. A few hours later he picked her up again, she in the meantime having slipped through the trees and walked into the camp to meet her lover. Urach was, of course, perfectly aware of it all. The tale was told to Huber after he had left by a Leutnant Geigenberger who has since died. Geigenberger himself apparently had a liaison with a local farmer's daughter where he worked. Possessing an international driving licence, he

6

borrowed a car and took her for a drive. But he was stopped, by chance, by the police and posted away.*

Norman Roffey and Geoffrey Forrest ran the gauntlet of eyes for the first time in June 1945. (They were last met in Chapter III as RAF interrogators at Latimer House.) They had now joined the team of re-educators under Cyrus Brooks, who sent them up to Shap to see what was being done by the Germans there and how they could best be helped. They preferred to think that they were actually welfare officers, as they were told to call themselves. The Lagerfürst greeted them with his usual aplomb and courtesy. Unknown to them, he at once assessed their types and, for the re-screening interviews they were to conduct, arranged that each man saw the one he seemed more akin to. Roffey, a small thin man, a former schoolmaster, spoke perfect German and had an excellent and intuitive mind. He at once took to von Urach. 'I was intrigued by the trace of a Habsburg nose and by the grand manner, totally without pomposity, in which he conducted the affairs of the camp. He was also, I felt, more interested in the re-discovery of God than the re-discovery of democracy.' The younger, physically vigorous Forrest, who had seen active service, got on particularly well with the junior officers, and clicked with Woetzel and Düttmann especially. 'We saw everyone for ten minutes or a quarter of an hour and, at the end, made notes for a little career and character sketch and a grading anything from A plus to B minus. We were mild and friendly, they opened up and we had to sit in judgment on them, put a ticket on each—that was the job. Sometimes the barriers fell right down and there was a human encounter, and then it was a pleasure, even rather moving. Of course, at a camp like Shap we hardly had to look out for wolves in sheep's clothing, though I'm sure some opportunists got an A or B-plus they didn't merit at all.'

The receiving end was different. In Woetzel's words: 'There was always the factor that performance might affect repatriation, but the essential thing was that one was being listened to, not just as a POW in uniform or a man guilty of the war, but by another man trying to understand you. However small, these contacts helped end that dreadful feeling of isolation.'

* When the author recounted the first story to a French girl in Berlin in 1976, she said with enthusiasm and admiration: 'Yes, a French girl would be capable of that!'

The cultural and educational life at Shap was so healthy that Roffey and Forrest had only to encourage it. Their relaxed and approving presence had an effect far beyond their knowledge and beyond anything they tried to do. In June 1946 Ritter wrote to Forrest in English from his home near Bremen—he was one of the earliest repatriates.

Dear Sir,

Perhaps you will be astonished to receive a letter from me; but I have to thank you and Mr Roffey so much and there is now the occasion to do so without any ambiguity. You helped us to go our own way. That is more than perhaps you will imagine. What may expect the prisoner behind the fence? How imminent are the dangers of illusion or opportunism or of the indifference which seems to belong to a life without reality! Before you and Mr Roffey visited our camp, I had often but a small hope to maintain and keep going this kind of life we had tried to form in Shap, because we understood that the possibility of a spiritual renewal and rediscovery may be the very chance for a prisoner: *redire ad senetipsum et ad initeriorem veritatem*, to find the foundation where you can build upon the cornerstone of inner truth. Dreamer's hotel? Perhaps, from a so-called practical point of view; now after my repatriation when I examine the question, what has been gained as well as what has been lost, I see that I have grown richer and that I have reached this continuity without which one cannot begin after such long years of trouble and darkness.

What had Roffey and Forrest done beyond the screening interviews? They had tried to bring the Commandant more behind the prisoner's own efforts. They had entered sympathetically into personal problems, writing letters to try to find relatives. Forrest even helped one officer to divorce his much-loved young wife; she was at home in Austria, well-looked after by relatives, but, having married a German, in danger of expulsion and with nowhere to go in Germany. (There were not a few such temporary *divorces de convenance*.) They had sought out or lent books—Forrest brought in some forty of his own which were put in cardboard or brown paper and returned in perfect condition eighteen months later; he had no idea till eight years later how much the detective stories he lent Colonel von Lindeiner, the Sagan Commandant, had soothed his troubled mind. They replied to the gracious, rather formal, little speeches that Germans like to make to their guests. They listened to concerts and lectures. When Major Reitmeier gave a long and dry talk about the history of Anglo-American relations, Forrest rose at the end and told how these had once been saved from disaster by a German, the Prince Consort. His last political act as he lay dying in 1861 had been to redraft a dispatch of Lord Palmerston that could have brought Britain to the brink of war with America. Afterwards, Reitmeier astonished him by the vehemence with which he said privately, 'It is shameful how we Germans don't bring in human touches like that.'

The lecturers who came from Bush House were supplemented by local men of substance such as Captain Liddell Hart, who lived thirty miles away on Lake Windermere, and John Trevelyan, Director of Education for Westmorland. They both came twice to take part in Brains Trusts. The former's first visit caused some embarrassment at Bush House as Liddell Hart had staying with him Christopher Buckley, War Correspondent of the *Daily Telegraph*. It was agreed that he could come too, provided the visit was strictly off the record and not a word reported. They both got into conversation with Podewils who had some interesting observations about the war in Russia and Normandy. 'Do you know,' he said, 'that the name of the village near which Field Marshal Rommel was strafed by the RAF and badly injured was called St Foix de Montgomery?' This little nugget proved too much of a temptation to Buckley and it appeared in the Peterborough column of his paper, with the addition that it had been picked up at a POW camp where German officers were being 'rehabilitated'. Bush House buzzed with annoyance. It was only two months after the war ended and the whole re-education operation had to be kept out of the press; and here it was being mentioned in terms objectionable to both sides involved. Buckley received a letter from Roffey to make even a journalist blush.

Podewils' own monastic seclusion was broken not only by his name appearing in the press, but by a day visit, specially allowed, to the stately home of the local MP, a friend of his youth— William Fletcher-Vane.* Urach went with him. There were outings to the Lake District for a few. Perhaps understandably the Lagerfürst and the 'old guard' looked askance at Koeppler's 'POW University' at Wilton Park, though both Düttmann and

* Later Lord Inglewood, and Chairman of the Anglo–German Society (1978).

Woetzel went there later—but not before both had another diversion. A group were going down to London to take part in some tests on POW attitudes being conducted by a team of American psychologists. 'Would you like to join them?' Forrest asked Woetzel, who was much tickled by the idea. 'Will you let me know my score?' They were put up in a camp which, after Shap, was rather prison-like. 'It was very interesting. The whole expedition caused the most acute anxiety. Most of us thought it was an inquisition into our very soul. Of course, I knew that when I saw the word "blood" on the sheet, I mustn't react with the word "soil", or I would be in the soup. Most of the others were very intelligent but didn't understand this. They got into a dreadful stew about what they had written on the giant questionnaire. Major Reitmeier, with a fantastically high IQ and a very decent man, came back a nervous wreck.' Woetzel did extremely well.

Forrest was at the Colchester camp one evening for a performance of *The Captain of Koepenick*, sitting between two Air Force generals who were wearing their dress uniform epaulettes. They did their best to laugh at Zückmayer's immortal lampoon of Prussian militarism. The tailor who pretends to be a captain was played by a very anti-Nazi private who had waited for twelve years to have this tilt at the German mania for obedience. Then on the stage at the end appeared Düttmann who had painted the scenery. 'What are you doing here?' 'Please send me back to Shap! I said something foolish when we were rescreened.' Düttmann was indeed soon back at Shap, doing an affectionate lampoon of Hugo Staudinger for his birthday—as a knight in shining armour leading the troops of the Pope into action. 'He was concerned for my soul, and it was my way of showing I did not want that.'

Politically, Shap already had something of the flavour of Adenauer's Germany to come. The spirit of the *Restauration* determined the general atmosphere. This was well analysed in some reflections that Woetzel wrote at Forrest's instigation for their mutual interest.[43] He points up the sharp contrast between those who were already adults before the Hitler period and the younger generation brought up under the Nazis, with a constant shifting or nervous hovering of the thirty to forty age group between the two. For the former group 'everything is tradition and convention, social attitude and obligation, rooted sense of status ... They give lectures and write clever articles, but one feels that they are concerned with showing what they used to be like and would like to be again. We discuss things, but hardly ever openly and honestly; too often the gong for the evening service is the signal for the end of an embarrassingly cramped pretence of a debate. It was a twenty-four-year-old who wrote in our magazine the article on collective guilt. Another young man is going to write about reconciliation. Why not one of the older ones? Their basic rule is "Not to Lose Face", no matter what the cost. My generation no longer expects help or stimulus from them. There is much to explain their attitudes. Some have led a miserable existence, almost all had their lives shattered and knocked about. Most of them are faced with the ruins of ideas and a way of life which they at first thought National Socialism would provide the means to bring about. Much the same is true of the younger ones! But as to us, all that is said about the young generation of Germany is true in part. . . . The mass of our youth is retarded in maturity, capacity and knowledge. On the other hand, it is way beyond its years in an experience of life that has unfortunately mostly been pretty grim and very materialistic. But I maintain that many of us still have a balanced hopefulness, and a good-will, and that we are serious and open-minded. By ourselves we don't know where to look, and—it may not be a bad thing—we take refuge in scholarly study, in trying to catch up with the knowledge we have missed. . . . I believe in the good in us. It is there! It isn't all just daemonic hopeless fate. But the process of healing needs time, lots of time. Time, time and more time, that's the most essential factor. There must be no attempt to speed up the search for our real selves, or influence it, or push it along from outside.'

There was time to think at Shap Wells, time to think constructively, time to dream, doubt and despair. The passing trains became for many a symbol of freedom, a reminder of what they were lacking, a shuttle weaving their imagination with the outer world. The sound at night especially drew thoughts far into the distance and into the past. The trains brought mail from home, or failed to. A batch of letters could send the camp into an almost silent, corporate rumination, the absence of a letter being almost as potent to the feelings as one received. Trains would take them home one day, but no one knew when. Trains took the visitors, the screeners and lecturers back to their enviable unknown lives which they never spoke about. But Major Forrest did reveal part of his after a compassionate leave in the French Alps. In October

1945 he went to visit a French girl he had remembered all through the war and had wondered if he might marry. She had been in the Resistance, had been caught, tortured and sent to Ravensbrück Concentration Camp. Rescued by the Swedes, she was now recuperating in a sanatorium. Forrest spent three days with her, just when she was taking her first walks in the crisp mountain air, and returned devastated by hearing her experiences. In a London underground lift people at rush hour were jamming up tight against each other. 'Like Belsen,' someone said, half humorously. A meaningless cliché already, he thought, raging at the obscenity.

Next day he had to go up to Shap. It was not his job to lecture and the Belsen film had already been there. But did they really *know*? He took it on himself to convey something of what he had heard first hand. His theme was announced through Urach and some fifty or sixty came to hear him speak of the women at Ravensbrück in their flimsy striped dresses supplied by the Red Cross, driven out before dawn to work in fields swept by a bitter north wind; of the vile food and terrible hunger pangs; and, worst of all, how they would return through the streets, scarcely appearing like human beings, while the population looked at them with scorn and hatred, or just turned away. The women might call out, 'We're politicals!', anxious to sense that somewhere outside the unending hell was another human being. But no response, ever. Worse still, the children were not prevented from running beside the straggling column with its makeshift stretchers carrying dead or dying, jeering and even throwing stones. As one woman was hit, she cried out, 'But he looks so like my own angel-faced little brother!' It was a strange sensation for Forrest standing there filled with his strong personal emotion, looking at German officers, sitting comfortably but tight inside themselves, hearing but not wanting to hear about these horrors. Aware somehow of their thoughts he found himself throwing out a bridge to them. 'Could it have happened elsewhere, in other countries? Yes, I think so, if humanity were seen to be reduced to that level.' He hopes, but does not remember if he did so, that he added 'and if the witnesses of those horrors had been reduced by tyranny to such insensitivity'. As the audience, after murmured thanks, rose silently to disperse, two of them came up to Forrest and thanked him specially for the last remark that did not point a finger uniquely at the German people. He realised that it was what they most needed to hear just then.

The reality of the immediate past was not wanted in large doses. Only a few wished to try to enter and understand it and these were the younger men. 'There was often a rather hot-house, Magic Mountain atmosphere at Shap,' remembers Düttmann. 'We could be rather silly, too.' Staudinger, with his purposeful self-discipline, was less affected by it: he worked with concepts and principles. Woetzel, on the other hand, was someone for whom pain and joy were woven fine, and the past was part of the present.

A January evening, 1946

The seventh number of the camp magazine, *Arbeit im Aufbau*, will soon be published, and articles are wanted. Woetzel sits in his small three-man room. In the grate is an open fire, burning wood collected on the moor—just in time, for it has snowed. It is quiet in the hotel, boots since supper have ceased clattering along the bare corridors. From outside comes the perpetual sound of the rushing brook, which now makes a curly black ribbon across the white moor. He writes rapidly, reliving with passionate empathy an experience of just a year ago, a journey on leave from Vienna to Hanover in the last winter of the war:

At Halle the waiting room is a huge dark barrel, without windows, indescribably crammed with people. Refugees upon refugees and soldiers. They hang off the chairs, often two on one, lay their heads on the tables. Most stare dully at nothing. The air, palpable, stinking and grey-blue, weighs down on the cowering mass. The big counter at the end of the hall is visible as if through a veil of mist. Remorselessly, roughly and cursing, the waiters hurry and stumble between the tables. The total sight is so oppressive that only slowly can I take it in, separating out single images—groups pressed tightly together like grapes hanging against each other. I can pick out no faces, no features, no individual beings; it is as though they had ceased to exist as persons, but belong to a strange new kind of being.

Among the refugees is scarcely one man: females of all ages with many children and infants, which makes them only more helpless and shocking. There are many soldiers, but they are on the other side, on the opposite bank. They don't belong to each other and no bridge can unite them. The refugee group sits or stands with the salvaged remains of their possessions, women and children squatting and cowering on their cases and bundles.

Yet the soldiers have by far the most chairs, have occupied most of the tables. Here and there one or two talk with a girl, but in general the two sides do not look at each other, as though unaware of each other's presence. Only very seldom does anyone in uniform speak to the many children; the little figures trot about forlorn, turn from one table to another with questing eyes, begging for attention, and when no one has a good word for them, slinking still sadder away . . .

Near me sits a youngish woman with a three-year-old boy, who strikes me with his unnatural calm. Sometimes she talks to him, at which he answers seriously and softly like an elderly person at peace within himself. I notice he has very inflamed eyes, out of which he can scarcely see. He must have much pain, but his almost radiant calm transcends his physical state. . . . She tells me how she has left a small Silesian town on foot, with her child and carrying two cases. She has had no news of her husband for months, and is now on her way to relatives in Hanover. Her words, which she puts sparingly, haltingly together, shatter the peace like little stones on the clear mirror surface of water. The child's eyes begin to inflame again, irritated by the saturated air. We must go and find a doctor. There can be no further journey for her tonight . . .

Woetzel's style begins to falter. It is hard work fishing up from the unconscious so many minute particulars. Yes, the doctor giving his diagnosis; he can still see his tired lustreless eyes and trembling hands: without treatment the child will lose his sight. Did they ever reach the clinic, he wonders; what happened then? The bombing had gone on and on . . . his own wife safe now, thank God, but her letters are too brave to be truthful. Another hard winter. Official statements are saying that reports of starvation are exaggerated, which probably means the opposite. . . . The article has to be finished. He stares into the low flickering fire in the grate and more characters crystallize out of memory.

. . . a tall, peasant woman with a bony, uncannily staring face, her youngest child in a sling on her back, two tethered to her hands and half dragged along, and two more in the tow of a Red Cross sister. With her bulging skirt falling in folds to her ankles as though carved in wood, she is out of the Middle Ages. A lady of over seventy escaping from Breslau sits stiff and up-

6*

right, occasionally taking a lorgnette from her muff to survey the scene, her luggage scarcely anything beyond a huge badly-wrapped parcel containing, she tells me, portraits of her son killed in the First World War and her dead husband, a high civil servant . . . But now a surprise—the gloom of the cavernous waiting-room is being dispelled by a one-armed soldier. He is ceaselessly on the go, helping, running errands, listening to the complaints of the old, fetching drinks, playing with the children, teasing the young girls, scaring those glued to their chairs out of their moroseness: laughing, joking, patient, selfless, a veritable character from a folk tale . . .

Woetzel writes on and on, rapidly, feelingly, 5,000 words of not quite forgotten prose. He too brings energy and caring to the forlorn scene: his homeland while chaos could still be held in check. The journey ends. He reaches Hanover at last, pauses, relives the moment, and finds a final image to bind the whole experience together.

I leave the station and walk through the quiet familiar streets I have not seen for so long. The night is cold and clear. Away on the horizon search-lights flit across the sky. Whenever they stay still they resemble long bandages over a dark wound.

Woetzel takes the article to Düttmann, who at once sees how he can illustrate it with a new version of his mother and child theme. Speedily, surely, he begins to cut into a handy piece of linoleum. Somewhere else in the hotel Fecker is writing some reflections on modern music, and Podewils translating Eliot's *La Figlia che piange*; Dr Gutkess is exploring 'Shakespeare the Unknown' and Dr Helmuth Conradi, gifted architect, having calculated that more than ten million new homes are needed in Germany, is working out in detail the three stages from emergency to permanent construction. Staudinger, thinking harder and deeper than anyone in the camp, is roughing out his own reflections on 'Re-education':

All that is negative in these past years does not have its origins but only its consequences in the totalitarian state. A matter not of the form in which a man unfolds but the nature of his being . . . The great question: does the individual have a final personal responsibility for his own life? If so, he must acknowledge the personal responsibility of others for their lives . . . Need for foundation of firm order of reciprocal rights that cannot be

altered through arbitrary acts or the fickleness of the majority.
No over-enthusiasm or too much haste, or programmes for the
next hundred years. Coming together to solve the problems of
the day. Pius XII's advice: become involved in politics. . . .

Ideas, phrases, keystone formulations; first steps in the life work
of the future Professor Hugo Staudinger, building up in articles,
lectures, seminar papers, books, a new foundation for the
pluralistic state.

The wind blusters against the hotel. The guard stamps his feet
on the gravel. The night mail from Scotland picks up speed as it
passes the lights of the island on the fells. 'What are those Germans
in there cooking up now?' the driver wonders, 'probably another
war . . .'

There were many worse places to be eating the bread of exile.

8

Groundswell to Christmas

In his autobiography, the poet Pablo Neruda describes how as a small boy he came across a hole in the fence in the backyard of their house at Temuco in Chile. Suddenly a hand appeared through the hole and left behind a small wooden sheep that had lost its wheels. He went and fetched one of his own precious possessions, a pine cone, put it in the same place, and went off with the sheep. He never saw the hand again. This experience had a fundamental influence on Neruda's life as a poet. 'To feel', he wrote elsewhere, 'the love of people whom we love is a fire that feeds our life. But to feel the affection that comes from those unknown to us, who are watching over our sleep and solitude, over our dangers and our weakness—that is something still greater and more beautiful because it widens out the boundaries of our being, and unites all living things. That exchange brought home to me for the first time a very precious idea: that all humanity is somehow together. . . . .'[44]

At Frydenberg on the eastern ridge of Oslo there also used to take place an exchange of gifts between two unknowns—children[45] and prisoners of war. Their camp was separated from the road by a deep ditch below a high barbed-wire fence. When the ditch was dry, children on their way to school used to walk along it, and now and then after playing about and waiting till the guard with his Alsatian was far away they would push their sandwich-pack under the fence. They did this although food was very short at the time and they often had nothing at all to take to school in the morning. On their way home they would find waiting for them a little cock or a snake beautifully made out of wood and sometimes brightly painted. The snakes were cleverly made in sections that undulated as you pushed them along the table, and the cocks had tail feathers that sprang up in the form of wood-shavings. These emaciated prisoners were not Germans—that was inconceivable; they were Russians.

Germans did make toys for children, at Crewe Hall, for instance, before Christmas 1944. The present Lord Napier, then a schoolboy, remembers well visiting his father and being shown a hut in which many beautiful and ingenious toys were laid out. They were to be distributed locally when a War Office instruction came forbidding this. Whether it was considered to be 'having relations with the enemy', or whether, as quite often later, local toy shops or manufacturers objected that such a distribution would cause loss of trade, is uncertain. All the toys were burnt and Lord Napier was bitter and angry about it. People in Uxbridge remember a lone German POW—it could have been the following year—who walked through some streets with a sack of toys on his back, left one on each doorstep, knocked and moved on before he could be spoken to.

Unlike the Russians in Norway, German prisoners at first excited almost no sympathy with the public. To such children who saw them they were probably 'baddies' who deserved to be shut away behind wire. Out in Germany Montgomery, now Military Governor, rescinded within two months the regulations which forbade soldiers to play with or speak to German children: they were doing it already. Three months later he raised the whole question of non-fraternisation in the Control Commission, and it was agreed to scrap an unworkable policy in all zones. There remained only rules against soldiers being billeted with German families, and against them actually marrying German girls. But in Britain, as has been mentioned, fraternisation was not allowed for a long nineteen months. The order was very necessary at first, for the safety of the prisoners themselves. It is the responsibility of the holding power to protect its captives from public hostility, and the mood of 1945 could have led to ugly incidents. Secondly, the cold shoulder was the best way of showing all Germans who had fought for Hitler detestation for what had been done in the name of their country. And, since the prisoners were segregated and under discipline, apartheid was not difficult to enforce. But it was the attitude of children that could hurt most. In the autumn of 1945 a young woman walking with a friend through some forestry land in Pembrokeshire came across a labour-gang of lightly supervised prisoners of war. A few words were exchanged and as they walked on a man ran after them calling, 'Tell the children of England we are not all bad. We are sad we cannot speak to them.'

It needed time for a population to switch from wishing the

Germans ill because they were enemies and Nazis (a word which Churchill made sound almost like 'nasties') to wishing them well because they were men. The slogan 'the only good German is a dead German' could not be reversed in a day. But all over the country there were those who, from the beginning, would not accept restriction on their natural feelings of compassion. They were often women who, seeing another mother's son lonely and miserable and far from home, felt a need to make contact, if only silently. 'Stand back there!' shouted the military police on a platform at Snow Hill Station, Birmingham. Red-caps were everywhere as the train drew in to an unscheduled stop. Annie Abbott noticed to her surprise that it was full of prisoners. She was a small, dark woman with large brown eyes and with an inner intensity not uncommon among people from the Hebrides. Germans were leaning out of windows and one of them fixed his eyes on her. 'He had,' she said afterwards, 'the eyes of an Oberammergau Christ, full of despair.' She smiled at him, trying to give him hope, their burning mutual look lasting till the train left. Marion Fox had been Warden of a Quaker rest-home in Germany between the wars, was over eighty, and lived with her crippled sister in a Georgian mansion in the centre of Wellington, Shropshire. Each Sunday morning a party of prisoners used to march past her house on the way to Mass; so she decided to stand at her window when they were coming. At first no one noticed, then one man who quickly averted his eyes. Next week he was looking for her, and soon the whole squad made a point of looking up at 'the wonderful old lady with the beautiful smile'. Hans Seuffert remembers how near the camp at Ravenscourt Park a woman used to stand outside and they gave her an 'Eyes right' as they marched by. They heard that she had a son who had been a POW and had spoken up for their early release. Greeting their *Müttchen* became a ritual to start the day's work with. Frances Marie Thacker, a Quaker, recalls: 'I was in a country lane picking blackberries. Leaning against a gate was a middle-aged man with a kind and patient face. I nodded to him and picked some more blackberries, whereupon he stood to attention and said he was a prisoner of war out on parole. My German was poor but he had a little English vocabulary and we were soon telling each other that war should be unnecessary and was a vile thing.' Petite Marion Edmundson, yet another Quaker, lived in a small cottage near Boltby on the edge of the North Yorkshire moors, half a mile from anyone.

Long a widow, she had brought up four children, and now preferred a solitary life with her dog, the sheep, the grouse and the
heather. White-haired and petite, she was strictly teetotal and her
fare very frugal. She was game for any adventure, full of humour
and without fear. When asked what she would do if German
parachutists landed, she said, 'I expect they would want coffee,
but I have only got tea.' When a small hostel was opened not far
away for trusted prisoners who were working on the land, she of
course wanted to make contact with them. The young corporal in
charge allowed this, but said, 'Mind you are never found here
when the Major makes his rounds.' 'What's this?' said this gentleman angrily one day. He had spotted a vase of flowers Marion had
left in the mess, but his anger subsided when he learned the old
lady's age. The men used to drop into her cottage when they
wished, for a chat and a cup of tea. They would carry her paraffin
and provisions across the moor to the cottage, cut and stack logs
'in the Bavarian manner', listen to her wireless, show their family
snaps. At Christmas her relatives came and a high time was had
by young and old.

Edith Tritton's life was decided for her when she met Clarence
Tritton in 1919 at a rehabilitation centre for conscientious objec-
tors during the First World War. With many like him he had been
harshly treated, and his witness for peace deeply moved the young
Edith who came from an upper class Sussex family. She found
herself in complete harmony with his spirit and they married, to
the dismay of her family, for by occupation he was a gardener.
They made a remarkable pair of Christians dedicated to social
work and good actions. In the summer of 1945, when they were
living at Ringmer near Lewes, Clarence Tritton discovered a gang
of German prisoners working in a field. One of them said 'Feuer,
feuer' urgently; they wanted to make a fire to heat up some coffee.
Clarence Tritton responded and this was the beginning of a long
and illegal befriending which the Trittons engaged in for the next
year and more. Edith, a fluent German speaker, listened to the
prisoners' stories, wrote to *The Times*, made contact with the relatives by roundabout ways, started up an underground letter service with the aid of British contacts in Germany, Sweden and
America. As Christmas approached the Trittons got permission
to send a Christmas tree and a projector to the local hostel at
Halland; one of the guard sergeants went round collecting for the
prisoners. 'There was a knock on our door. Six foot of bristling

annoyance made itself felt before a word was spoken. "Madam, I am sorry, but I cannot allow your Christmas plans to materialize. Under no circumstances." It was Colonel Ponsford, the new commandant at Haywards Heath who was responsible for the local hostels. "May I remind you," he went on, "that the only people allowed to speak to prisoners are farmers, and then only in connection with their work." "But surely," I said, "Christmas is a time when, if only for the sake of re-education, it would be good to relax the rules." "I am not of your opinion," said the Colonel firmly. "If any of these men are caught breaking the regulations—and they will be caught—they will be severely dealt with." '

The commandant had a problem, for he was a soldier and had his orders. Here and there the ban on communication was being defied. In Scotland two teachers had been imprisoned for walking into a camp and just chatting to the inmates. Fines were being imposed on nurses for taking letters in and out of camps. Surreptitious sexual encounters had to be prevented. Colonel Ponsford also knew that public opinion was not on the Trittons' side; they were, in fact, being cold-shouldered by their neighbours in Ringmer because of what they were doing. But they were not daunted and went on behaving according to their nature. They managed to get at least the Christmas tree, candles, and some small gifts into the camp; when a local farmer no longer dared give his prisoners a supplement to their meagre lunch ration, they took these men a meal once a week, carrying it surreptitiously in an innocent shopping bag and leaving it in a cart shed; and on dark evenings there were cups of cocoa waiting in their garage. When in the summer of 1946 Clarence Tritton became an official YMCA visitor, with Edith going along as interpreter, their activities were on a firmer basis. But John Barwick had to write from the YMCA warning him to watch his step, as there had been a complaint (presumably from Colonel Ponsford) about his behaviour; as, for instance, when he got Fenner Brockway, the Labour pacifist and politician, to intervene about the inadequate heating in the camp. One day Dr Bell came to Rodmell. The men crowded round, pouring out their complaints to the Bishop and, as a result, they were allowed on Saturdays to Lewes football ground where there were happy encounters with spectators they had come across at work. Later on the Trittons, who had helped Rudolf Bing, the Glyndebourne Opera producer, at the time of his internment, were able to take twenty-five prisoners to watch rehearsals at the famous opera house. But this is to move ahead too fast.

The conflict between authority and those who desired to help unfortunates took place frequently. But, if the Trittons were intentional rule-breakers, the Quakers were not, or only rarely. In the summer of 1942 two members of the Society of Friends were summonsed for sending food into the camps. They asked whether the hearing should be used to demonstrate against what the Society had been condemning in its public statements as the 'un-Christian non-fraternisation order'. The answer from Friends House was a firm 'No', for it is against the tradition of Quakers to confront the law deliberately. Their attitude to war has long been respected. If they have a unique place among peace-makers, it is because among all religious groups they have had the clearest and most united attitude towards the destructiveness of conflict. Their pacifism has always been constructive. They have been the first to bind up the wounds of war even while it is in progress, and to send out aid or teams of relief workers to ravaged areas afterwards: in Finland after the Crimean War, in France in 1871, all across Europe in 1919–23 and again in 1945–50, as well as among prisoners of war on both sides from 1940 onwards. It began with the visiting of the camps and the sending in of musical instruments, books, seeds. The Berlin Polizeipräsidium, while accusing the handful of German Quakers of being 'deficient in state-mindedness', allowed them to do the same thing; the postal services actually delivered the parcels free, and even at first collected them from the Berlin Quaker Office.[46] (Later on German Friends concentrated on prisoners who were less well cared for than the British, such as Poles and Serbs.) This aid was on a tiny scale relative to the needs, but it was allowed even in Hitler's wartime Reich because of the memory of the *Quakerspeisung*—chiefly soup-kitchens—in starving cities of Germany in 1919–20. This tradition of aid was carried on by six relief teams in Germany alone in 1945. They were able also in the earliest days to make their own conditions about fraternisation, for how could true relief be given if the warmth of human friendship were forbidden? And perhaps there was something deeper still. When during the Napoleonic Wars a small number of Norwegian and Danish prisoners were held in a hulk off Chatham, they were deeply impressed by a copy of Barclay's *Apology* in Danish. They got in touch with some

English Friends who visited them. They could not converse together intelligibly, but 'by signs, in love and friendship, they understood a little of each other's feelings'. This meeting 'in the spirit' was the beginning of the Quaker Movement in Scandinavia. Now and then, perhaps, something similar happened with the 130 Friends who regularly went to the camps, 70 of them being registered as official YMCA visitors.

Richard Ullmann, a gifted Central European convert to Quakerism, once observed that what Friends attributed to the guiding of the holy spirit was often just the English genius for compromise. If Friends generally avoid being thought 'holy', it is because they try always to be realistic and practical; and they have behind them three centuries of experience in reconciliation and social work. They do not expect quick results and like to speak of 'sowing seeds for the future'. So when a Quaker MP approached the Prime Minister as early as 1945 about ending the ban on fraternisation, he did not hope for action at once. By the following spring Meetings for Sufferings* expressed concern about the treatment of prisoners 'as an inferior type of human being', and this led to a statement being issued to the press deploring the continued detention of prisoners of war and urging that a time limit be set for their release. This received little national publicity, though it was reported in forty local newspapers. In June the Prime Minister was again approached. In July *The Friend* published a letter from a twenty-year-old German who did not want to be identified. 'We do not wish,' he wrote, 'for presents or material help. All we seek is that we may be allowed to live as human beings with humans . . . We do not ask for charity or sentimentality; just one kind word helps far more. So desolate and apathetic have we grown that a mere "Good day" or nod delights us. I have met good people here who have proved to me that an understanding between our two nations is possible. But, unhappily, no one can befriend us without coming into contact with the law.'

The views of the Quakers were, in fact, not far from those of two men in Bush House. Wing-Commander Hitch, Director of the Re-education Section of the Foreign Office, did not visit the camps and had no German. But he was a humane man and early in 1946

* The historic name of the central committee which meets every month with representatives from all over the country to consider issues in which the Society of Friends might take action or express a concern.

his instinct told him that the ban on fraternisation could be ended. He also believed that the time had come to put an end to screening, which caused so much uneasiness and ill-feeling. Colonel Faulk thoroughly agreed with the first proposal. From his observation of the POWs in the camps and at work, he was certain that they would not abuse freedom to mix with the public; indeed, it was more and more absurd to continue the re-education of men who were isolated from the people around them. He was sure, too, that once the ice was broken the British public would respond to the prisoners' longing for contact. He and Hitch repeatedly urged this on the War Office without effect. Faulk, however, insisted that screening must go on as it was the only way in which the progress of re-education could be measured through recording the numbers upgraded from black to grey and from grey to white.

1946 was the high point of the attempt to reach the hearts and minds of the Germans. Bush House was sending more literature into the camps, supplementing that donated by the YMCA; information rooms were set up and radios provided—in February all control of listening was removed; discussion groups proliferated, as did camp magazines, virtually without censorship. In January the so-called Training Centre at Wilton Park had opened under the remarkable Dr Heinz Koeppler and was providing six-week courses for selected prisoners under university conditions. Birger Forell's brain child, the special camp at Norton for theologians and teachers, had started the previous August and, mainly under the auspices of the YMCA, had settled down; in June a special re-educational camp for mainly 'black' youth was begun.* Under that unusual pair, Lieutenant-Colonel Vickers and Captain Sulzbach, the compound for 4,000 officers at Featherstone Park was being transformed into a unique 'camp of confidence'. From Bush House more and more speakers on a wider variety of subjects were going out to the camps and hostels. Under René Halkett, head of the lecture section, their number increased to over 200. Halkett was a gifted German, with partly Scottish ancestry, a much travelled writer and artist, who had once been a member of the stage workshop at the *Bauhaus*. He was not a refugee, but had broken right away from his aristocratic background and left Germany several years before Hitler came to power. After living in Spain he decided to come to England,

* See below, chapters 11, 13 and 14.

which he regarded as his natural home. He called his highly praised book about the land which had rejected him *The Dear Monster*. A brilliant broadcaster, he had unwittingly found himself serving the black propaganda machine which he greatly regretted. Now he had a task much more to his taste. He saw clearly how foolish it was to concentrate on direct propaganda for democracy and so reduced the proportion of lectures on politics and recent history in favour of general subjects. In fact, it was not the subject that mattered so much, nor the academic or pedagogic qualities of the speakers, as 'their ability to instil free and tolerant thinking and discussion into their audiences'. During 1946 172 new titles were added to the 42 of the previous year, some of which were dropped.

How much a fresh wind was necessary was evident when in June Halkett went to the hostel at Barnley near Sheffield to see how one of his lecturers, a Mr Lachmann, on 'What Weimar tried to do', was received. When he did not turn up the men insisted that Halkett take over the lecture instead, which he declined. Thereupon, the following conversation ensued (he jotted down the essence at the time):

'You will know, Mr Halkett, the government's opinion on what Weimar tried to do as well as Herr Lachmann.'

'But I have no idea if the government has any particular opinion and I have no idea of what the lecturer intended to say.'

'But you are the head of the lecture section. You must have told your lecturers what to say, and you must have been told by your government what to tell them.'

'The only directive I give to my lecturers is not to spout theory at you, but to stick to their own private experience and views.'

'But that means that two lecturers might contradict one another.'

'All the better.'

'What is the point then of sending lecturers to the camps?'

'Perhaps in order to show that the government does not interfere with private opinions, and also to show what things are like on our side.'*

* A similar exchange took place when Alfons Rosenberg, another lecturer, was told by a POW, 'You say you work for the BBC. If you believe we believe what you say, you are mistaken.' Rosenberg

René Halkett ended by just answering general questions. Apart from applying this indirect approach to putting across democracy, he enjoyed discovering the rich variety of human beings caught up into the Wehrmacht and then captured by the British. 'I found one old man with white hair busy cobbling shoes in a tiny room which was nicely painted in light green, and with geraniums in the window. He was a perfect picture. "What on earth are you doing here?" I asked him. "Oh, I'm a parachutist," he answered. I thought he was joking. But really he was one of those people who were scraped up at the end of the war and incorporated into a grounded parachute regiment. He was made to march a dreadful long way and the only thing that he complained of was that he wasn't issued with army boots. But now he could cobble again and was quite happy!' At one camp Halkett might find a Nazi director of studies, an officious ex-*Kulturreferent* from Hanover; another, where there had been no re-education, was marvellously organised with an astonishing range of activities: a maker of artificial limbs running a course on his profession, an exhibition of models of cheap emergency houses (*Behilfsheime*) comparable with but more practical than *Bauhaus* design standards, and a remarkable performance of a shortened *Faust* during which the commandant nudged him, pointing to the realistic hose worn by the actors and whispered 'Everything's scrounged of course— that's British army underwear dyed in cocoa.' Next time he went he saw an Ophelia who could hardly have been better and who had once driven a tank. At another camp the Commandant asked him in for a drink. 'I was surprised to find a German private having one too—because he had just escaped. He had been asked to mend the sergeant's motor-bike and after doing so couldn't resist riding off on it. When it ran out of petrol he rang up the camp and reported where he was. Now he was back, everyone was delighted and he was being given a drink.' Halkett's happy months at Bush House in charge of lecturers came to a sad end in November soon after he returned from a visit to the general's camp at Bridgend.* Although there was a certain falling off in the management side of re-education due to demobilisation, the best work was certainly

---

answered, 'We do not want you to take in everything the radio tells you. If you had had this critical attitude during the past fifteen years, neither you nor I would be in this hall.'
* See page 351.

done in 1946—in spite of the prisoners being both publicly
ostracised still and kept in the dark as to the length of their captivity. There was yet another hostile factor which PWD had not
reckoned with.

Private Erich Leverkus, now twenty years old, had spent a year
in Virginia when in the spring of 1946 he was told to prepare for
return to Europe.

We saw the words REPATRIATION CAMP FRANKFURT-AM-MAIN
painted on the boxes with all our personal papers in them. We
crossed the Atlantic in a troopship. When we arrived at Liverpool a train was waiting for us and we understood that we
would go as far as Dover and cross over to Calais. The train
stopped at Sheffield and we were loaded into buses. None of
those with me knew anything of English geography, and when
we had climbed a little someone called out, 'The sea, the sea!'
It was only a valley filled with mist. We never came to the coast,
but to a most unpleasant camp, Lodge Moor. We were driven
through the gates like a herd of cattle, some guards using canes
on us. A few days later we heard that we were likely to be kept
there for an indefinite time, and at least another two years. This
filled us with anger, but chiefly with the Americans for deceiv-
ing us. . . . My time in Lodge Moor was traumatic. I had saved
up a kit-bag full of cigarettes, enough to buy a house in Germany then, but lying there in the rain I smoked them all away.
With the despair and uncertainty quite a few of us went crazy—
out of ninety men in our hut there were two mental cases. Since
those days I have always had a touch of agoraphobia.

Paul Seufert, whose POW adventures had begun at the Battle
of the Bulge, came back across the Atlantic in a comfortable
American troopship with good food and entertainment each night.
'We could hardly sleep for thinking what home would be like'.
They also docked at Liverpool, and word flew round that they
'had been handed over to the Tommies. Suddenly only British
officers and soldiers with fixed bayonets were to be seen; the
Americans had disappeared. Next day at Woolaton Park we were
put into fresh units, filed in the usual way, medically inspected and
interrogated. Each of us got a new number. It was like being made
prisoner a second time.'

The arrival of the 'Americans', as they came to be known—

127,000 of them—had a generally negative, even disastrous effect on the morale of many camps. How far the US authorities both across the Atlantic and in Britain set out to deceive is uncertain, but it was an obvious ploy to get the men to go quietly. The prisoners, for their part, were also determined to believe they were on their way home. Their whole being was focused on the one thought. At Atterbury in Indiana Seufert recalls that when some apparently knew the truth they were put on a charge as rumour mongers by their own camp leaders. On the face of it, it was tempting to the Americans to put TO EUROPE on their baggage; it wasn't untrue, except that to any German it must mean the continent of Europe. In fact, a transport or two did deposit men destined for Britain at Antwerp. When they were first sent to join their wretched comrades in nearby camps there was anger and bitterness (see page 31). But the spirit of the shiploads landed at Cherbourg was quite different. It had been announced the previous autumn that 300,000 men would be required for reparations labour in France; they did not expect good treatment and they knew that their own government had used 'serf' labour from France during the war, and they endured it.

It should be added that bringing the 'Americans' to Britain was at first not planned. At the end of 1945 the severe manpower shortage had to be met somehow and Lord Montgomery proposed to draw on the 225,000 who were still held in camps in Germany, which he was wanting to dissolve. The Ministry of Labour, however, proposed the alternative solution of bringing over men held 'on the UK account' in the USA, the only doubts being that no prior selection for labour would be possible and the POWs would have been spoiled by the higher ration scale in America.

Many of the 'Americans' had been captured in North Africa when the war was not yet being lost and none of them had actually experienced the abject last months with their homeland invaded. This made for a more defiant morale. At Carburton they marched in giving the Nazi salute. At Langdon Hills in April 1946 they managed to hoist a swastika on Hitler's birthday, but without impressing the majority in the camp. Time and again at this period Forell found a hardened atmosphere, even a turning back towards National Socialism; when he spoke on how things were in Germany, all they wished to know was the date of their repatriation. At Canonbridge he had his most negative reception ever. When the Studentenleiter thanked him for his address not a single man applauded. At Comrie, where suddenly three out of the four thousand were 'Americans', it was discovered that the Protestant padre actually still felt himself bound by his oath to Hitler. At Peterborough, where a considerable religious revival had developed, fanatics from Canada tried to suppress it.

The 'Canadians'—34,000 of them—were different from the 'Americans'. In the first place, they were not deceived about where they were going; in the second, some camps in Canada had been early subject to sub-terror control and were more Nazi generally than Germany itself. (It might be argued that they were not so much Nazi as patriotic and nationalistic.) They also contained the longest held captives—from 1940, from the Battle of the Atlantic and from the Desert War. At the same time, there was a limited re-education among the officers which led to a change of heart among about 600, some of whom had to be segregated to protect them from fanatics. Their conversion was attributed to contact with Canadians and reading the writings of Dorothy Thompson. Fritz Pons was one of these but, like Erich Leverkus in America, he felt chiefly and lastingly influenced by the bigness of the country and the generosity of the Canadian character.

The general effect of this influx was depressive, especially when it swamped a camp. For some months at least they tended to be cynical or apathetic; and a large proportion formed a heavy lump in the POW world which was never leavened, and they eventually carried their anger home. But there were a great number who rose above circumstances, read, studied, made music, joined in activities, and eventually made friends with British families. Seufert did this. He was quickly caught up in 'frequent lecture and discussion evenings, in which outside speakers took part. Many of the younger men learned for the first time in their lives to form an opinion of their own and stand up for it.' Moschallski, captured in Tunis, took the transit in his stride. He holds that in spite of their often defiant mood there had been no more real Nazis in the American camps than elsewhere. It is true that they would march out with Prussian discipline, in parade formations and singing, to the cinema, and that the demoralised prisoners from Normandy were soon caught up in this, but it had two purposes. 'It was to impress the families of our guards and the civilians who used to assemble each week to see the show we put on. It was also a way of combatting a creeping loss of self-respect. It still puzzles me to know what that had to do with Nazism.' In England Moschallski and his companions had, in fact, a sharp fall in living standards. In America the 80 cents he earned a day could buy him 120 cigarettes, sixteen candy-bars or eight bottles of Budweiser beer. In England on pay day—they earned from three-farthings to a penny halfpenny an hour—they would buy slab-cake, sweets and cocoa-powder to enhance their porridge; and they got three cigarettes a day. But there was a compensation: they saw that the British in their calm way were also enduring severe shortages. 'The Tommies were almost in the same boat as us . . . Also the American way of life, often proclaimed with a big mouth, seemed rather superficial. The correct and pragmatic Briton is nearer to the German.'

As they were moved about, unaware of why and sometimes even where, the POW were a part of a huge shuttle of servicemen. Millions of Allied troops were being repatriated. Shipping was so short that most of the 100,000 Germans held in the Middle East could not be moved at all till 1948. 1946 saw the repatriation of the Italians from Britain, and then the 22,165 Austrians; and also the dubious 'Operation Fox' in which 'surrendered enemy personnel' in Germany were brought to Britain as a POW labour force, along with 80,000 in the Belgian camps. All had then to be distributed where the agricultural or industrial needs were greatest. At the same time, the War Office was under pressure because of the demobilisation of British troops and the needs of the army occupying Germany to reduce the guards available in the camps. This where possible led to prisoners themselves taking over these duties—which was also good for their morale, as few things were in 1946. But if they felt they were in the hands of a vast impersonal organisation this was not entirely so. For some time Pastor Forell, Dr Hartwell and their allies in the Chaplains' Department had been pressing for earlier repatriation not only on the grounds of sickness—which was logical as a prisoner could not then work—but also on compassionate grounds. Hartwell, visiting one camp, was told of a man in despair because of the dreadful news he had received from his wife. 'The Russians had entered his home in Berlin intending to rape their two daughters. To save them she offered herself. You would have expected the man to feel for his wife; instead, he wanted to divorce her. We had a long talk in which I tried to persuade him to have compassion for her. But he cried out, "How can I? I am behind barbed wire!" I promised to do something for him. I rang up Charles Cranfield at the War

Office, and he was on his way home within three days.' In all no fewer than 19,761 prisoners were repatriated out of order because of the situation in their families. But this operation did not start in earnest till February the following year.

The Reverend Charles Cranfield was one of the youngest Non-conformist Chaplains in the army. As a student of twenty-three he had sat in Basle at the feet of the great theologian, Karl Barth, and spoke fluent German. He was in Algeria in 1943 when German prisoners began to come in, captured by the First Army. At once he felt a pastoral responsibility towards them, and towards the men he thought were his brother chaplains on the other side. When with the Royal Tank Regiment he had always at service prayed for German as well as British soldiers in battle, and no one had ever objected in that often chivalrous theatre of war. Both the Chaplain General, The Reverend F. Llewellyn Hughes, and his deputy, The Reverend A. B. M. Hewson, had the imagination and vision to give unfailing support to Cranfield in his concern. This led to him being given, as soon as war ended, an assignment in the POW camps in Italy to identify German pastors and priests called up into the fighting services, to arrange for the repatriation of some and the redistribution of others. From this he was summoned home to a similar roving commission in the camps in Britain, where he arrived in October 1945. By then he had seen a great deal of war and its chaotic aftermath, with the victor all too easily treating the vanquished as if he were not a human being at all. 'I was once present at the handing over in Algeria of a batch of German prisoners to the Americans. They were all severely wounded—legless, or worse—yet a section with tommy-guns at the ready was there to take them over.'[47] Cranfield came home after first visiting southern Germany. Here, owing to careless liaison, many SEP (Surrendered Enemy Personnel) were arriving as they thought for demobilisation, but instead were being sent straight off to France in labour battalions. Here in the American zone he observed the posture of the victors at its worst, lording it over a cowed population. 'They were forgetting that the purpose of human justice', he wrote at the time, 'was to preserve and restore orderly and decent life, and not to take the place of God's justice.'[48] In their ignorance of Europe, the Americans were making crass mistakes over de-nazification, being severe on the small fry Nazis but often letting the clever and dangerous ones go scot free. He saw Germans starving beside American camps with a gross superfluity of food, and the flourishing of a mammoth black market. His Christian conscience was appalled.

Having made valuable personal contact with churchmen in South Germany, Cranfield returned home to the special post created for him. During eight months he made the rounds of the camps—it was an astonishing individual effort—visiting over 130, some of them two and three times.[49] He met the Protestant chaplains, discussed their needs, assessed their effectiveness and, in spite of his youth, acted as a *pastor pastorum*, listening to troubles, and counselling and supporting weary, often dispirited, men. He was continuing and supporting the work of Forell and of Hartwell of the YMCA who had so long borne the heat and burden of the day. Like them he had a strong sense of a 'living church behind the wire'. He wrote three pamphlets which were distributed through the British Council of Churches all over Britain, designed to show how local clergy could help their German counterparts. 'For,' wrote Cranfield, 'an important part of the Evangelical Church of Germany and a major part of its youth is now in the prisoner of war camps in this country. We need to think of it in terms of a diocese embracing all Great Britain, with 179 pastors ministering to 288 main congregations along with their attached hostels . . . Fellowship established between the camp congregation and a local British congregation can have far-reaching effects both here and in the Evangelical Church in Germany.'

'Being able to speak German did not matter,' Cranfield added, 'for a handshake can mean a tremendous lot to a man behind barbed wire.' During 1946 churches, chapels and Meeting Houses were the one type of place where fraternisation was allowed. Many a vicar was grateful when a whole aisle filled up with POW battle-dress for a much more rousing rendering than his diminished congregation could achieve. And much was the surprise of prisoners on one occasion to find in the Anglican hymn book that 'Glorious things of Thee are spoken' was sung to the tune of 'Deutschland, Deutschland, über alles', which they could not resist singing instead, and lustily at that. At Wells, Moschalski was soon attending the Catholic church unescorted with fifteen or twenty others and making the first of many English contacts with stumbling words and surreptitiously passed cigarettes. The Quaker Meeting House at Jordans was a convenient place where a girl could meet a young prisoner from the 'college' at Wilton Park without breaking the law. When a prisoner sat at the organ of St Alkmund's, Shrewsbury, the vicar, The Reverend Sidney Austerberry, heard the notes swell out joyously into a glorious sound. But it was one in the eye for the regular organist who had been insisting to his dubious vicar that the organ needed rebuilding. At Wybunbury prisoners from Crewe Hall would troop into the church on Sunday filling both the aisles, but the aged vicar simply did not involve them in the service at all. His temporary replacement, a young man who had been a chaplain in Australia, The Reverend Geoffrey Hadden immediately, with the aid of a German interpreter, introduced the creed and the Lord's Prayer in both languages, and a little later asked the Germans not only to join in the hymn singing but to bring a hymn of their own. 'It was somewhat thrilling to hear the comparative thunder of the German voices, after the customary tentative Anglican whispers.' But by no means all the parishioners agreed with him; the war was barely a year past. At Quorn in Leicestershire, Cranfield noted in his report, the parish council refused the use of the church to prisoners, although the local commandant, the vicar and the bishop were in favour. But the clergy of Sussex and Surrey, he found, had excelled in making contact, and the Bishop of Rochester was full of initiative. In Scotland work for prisoners was generally well in advance of south of the border, because of first-class co-operation between Dr Golzen of the YMCA and the Assistant Chaplain General of Scottish Command. During all this work Cranfield supported numerous of his German brother priests. He was also the eyes and ears of the British Council of Churches in the camps. In June he wrote, on request, a long memorandum for the Bishop of Sheffield, Dr Hunter, who was due to raise the whole question of prisoners of war in the House of Lords. He was asked what evidence there was for decline in morale, its reasons, and what points should be put to the government. Cranfield reported a widespread loss of hope and interest:

> They say sometimes that even a criminal is told the exact length of his sentence, but they who were only doing their duty as soldiers were not told. There was worse and worse news from home, the strain of separation from wives, with news of hunger and broken marriages. Why could not prisoners be allowed to send money home—or parcels? It was only the sick who were

sent home as unfit for work. By keeping them so long we were making democracy stink in their nostrils, and forcing them to look more and more elsewhere for hope. The undermining of family life in Germany was bad for our own self-interest. Could not young men in Germany, who would be liable for call-up, be sent to Britain in place of older men?

On 11 July the Lords debated what was the duty of the government towards the German prisoners of war. For one and a half hours, late on a hot summer afternoon, the civilised and Christian conscience of Britain was heard. Bishop Hunter of Sheffield, stimulated perhaps by having the most unhappy officer-camp in Britain, Lodge Moor, on his doorstep, echoed the gist of Cranfield's report and the moral unease that the government—and a Labour government at that—should treat men as 'so much material for a labour pool'. The saintly Edward Woods, Bishop of Lichfield, wished to see young Nazi prisoners sent to harvest camps with picked young Englishmen and women. That would be in accordance with 'our whole English tradition of care for the oppressed, of care for the personality, of fair play, and for the decencies for which we all believe we have been fighting this war.' He was followed by the elderly Liberal statesman, Lord Samuel, who questioned the right of Britain in international law to take reparations from a defeated nation in the form of compulsory human labour. The Under-Secretary for War, Lord Nathan, made a bland speech for the government, followed by a very long-winded but proper hint from Lord Manvers at what might have been German policy to prisoners had they won. The Bishop of Chichester then took up Lord Samuel's point by awkwardly comparing present British policy with what the Nazis had done in France after 1940—transporting serf labour into Germany. He put his finger on a crucial fact when he said it was extraordinarily short-sighted of the government to allow user departments—the Ministries of Agriculture and Labour—to have so much control over the retention of POW labour.

That autumn the reviving German press, when calling for the return of prisoners, did not fail to point out that the Nuremberg judgment made the deportation of forced labour a crime. Albert Speer had, indeed, accepted that he had been rightly sentenced for this: incarcerated in Spandau he wrote in March 1947 with that dispassionate moral logic which is such a remarkable aspect of his secret diary, 'Despite all the mistakes of the Nuremberg Trial this is a step in the direction of re-civilisation. And, if my twenty years imprisonment could help the German prisoners of war to get home only one month earlier, it would be justified'.

In Britain, however, even the serious press scarcely reported the House of Lords debate and Dr Bell's words not at all. Eden's 'turbulent priest' had no longer any news value. When Geoffrey Forrest, by then a civilian, had visited him in Chichester a few days before the debate, he had remarked wistfully, 'It's no longer any use attaching my name to a cause to do with Germans.' It might be asked, in any case, what political weight there could be in the predictable views of bishops in the decorous forum of the Lords. Cranfield saw the matter differently: it was the best way of bringing the issue into the open at last; the facts, as they became known, would more and more speak for themselves. But would the government listen? In the same forum Lord Vansittart still aired his views, still acceptable to many.

What was the Catholic participation in this movement for re-conciliation and compassion? In his report for Bishop Hunter, Charles Cranfield wrote that 'the British RC clergy have been miles ahead of the British Protestant clergy in making contact with POW priests and helping them. Catholic commandants, too, tended to be more diligent in seeing that they got what they needed; and the Pope's appeal for the repatriation of prisoners has been excellent RC propaganda value.' Was this, in fact, the situation or did Cranfield's remarks display something of the rivalry of the time as well as a desire to instil action? If Anglican and other clergy were, in fact, laggard, they did not long remain so, partly owing to Cranfield's own efforts. Certainly Catholic concern was more from the grass-roots, for the hierarchy at that time was ultra conservative. The Papal Delegate, Monsignor Godfrey, in whose province prisoners of war naturally fell, was a stiffly formal and cautious man, and besides, his post was more diplomatic than religious. Already in 1944 Pastor Forell, hoping for his co-operation in welfare work in the camps, obtained an audience after much difficulty but found the Monsignor 'only moderately interested; he will "weigh the matter over", but seemingly won't do much. I will have to use my "involvement technique" on him.' But the two men were quite incompatible and he got no response. It was still at the time a sin for a Catholic to attend a Protestant service, and working with non-Catholic bodies was severely frowned on. There was spontaneous co-operation between Catholic priests and Lutheran pastors in the camps themselves, especially in times of need and genuine distress. But Cranfield noted at Shalstone Camp in Bucks, 'The local RC monastery has lent a harmonium but the Protestants may not use it!' But if Monsignor Godfrey was a defender of positions, incapable of advancing on to new ground, this was made up for at the other end of the scale by local parish priests and the remarkable Miss Foss.

Mary Foss was the young woman who heard the heart-rending cry 'Tell the children of England that we are not all bad!' She had been working at the convent at Alton as a domestic, but had had to stay at home to look after her invalid mother. Mrs Foss strongly approved of what the Nazis had done for Germany and said so, and, as a result, in the big round up of 1940 had been detained for a while under the 18B Regulation. Her daughter did not take over her political views, but did inherit a warm heart and the habit of speaking her mind. She also believed in action. 'One could, of course, throw a packet of cigarettes into a lorry full of prisoners, but personal efforts like that are misunderstood. For me the war was over, and it was time to make friends. I read in *Picture Post* a letter which said that three things needed to be eradicated: bugs, leprosy and Germans. I was infuriated, and wrote a letter to the *Catholic Herald* saying that this was just the sort of thing that we had been fighting against. My letter was answered by that live wire, Michele Hunter, who was at that time trying to start a Guild of San Leonardo—he is the patron saint of prisoners—but for Italians. I suggested it should be broadened to include Germans, and at a meeting held in the house of Lady Clare Annesley I was elected general and German secretary of what we called the Prisoners-of-War Assistance Society, with my mother as treasurer. I wrote to inform the *Catholic Herald*, the editor felt like us and made our effort front-page news, and the whole thing snowballed.'

Mary Foss had done three things: she had sensed a human need for help, discovered a concern to give it, and opened a channel along which it could flow. The Fosses worked until mid-1947 from a one-roomed thatched cottage at Alton.

I often felt we were given more than our own strength to do

what we did. My mother, whose heart condition suddenly
vanished, used to sit up in bed typing while I dealt with the
correspondence on the table. And there were two cats. The local
convent didn't at all approve of what we were doing. We never
appealed for money but put our own savings into the enterprise, about £50. The first day there were twenty letters, some
containing money, from 2/6d to a few pounds. We did it all on
the shortest possible shoe-string, but enough money always
came in—once we were sent £100. My brother said, 'You must
get some big names on your notepaper.' So we wrote around
explaining our objects. Dr McGrath, the Archbishop of Cardiff,
agreed to have his name printed; so did Lord Lindsay, Father
Gerald Vann and Middleton Murry, and, of course, the Society
of Friends and the Peace Pledge Union. We were not at all
exclusively Catholic but 'Christian-based'. Later we got two
German Cardinals and Dr Hunter, Bishop of Sheffield, and
Richard Stokes. It needed a bit of nerve really, seeing how small
we were! We asked people to do what they could within the law
to show prisoners that there were people who cared for them.
In the first place this meant being a general information service,
helping them to make contact with their relatives, sending
rosaries and books into the camps, alerting parish priests to
camps where they could hold a Sunday Mass, till a prisoner
priest could be organised to serve a whole area.

There was one great difficulty: communicating with the prisoners at all meant breaking the law, as the War Office did not
recognise the Society, but regarded it as a 'private person'. 'The
trouble is', wrote Bernhart Harnick to Mary Foss from a camp in
Staffordshire, 'that your parcel with the rosaries arrived and I got
it in an illegal way. Nobody knows it. They are looking for the
parcel because they saw your letter, but they will not find it. . . .
If you write to me, or send a parcel, please take the address of
Father O'Connor, Ballance St., Uttoxeter.'
Many a Catholic priest up and down the country must have
positively enjoyed aiding and abetting Mary Foss in her unlawful
contact-making. Her simple service was to identify caring people
and put them in touch with prisoners and their families. She conducted her campaign for peace in the pages of a large ledger which
after two years contained some 700 names. It was ruled with seven
columns across a double page:

NAME	NUMBER	CAMP ADDRESS	CONTACT	CONTACT'S ADDRESS	HOME ADDRESS	REMARKS

The fourth column contained the names of those who volunteered to help; they were usually allotted according to nearness to a camp. The last column indicated the service needed which, during most of 1946, still had to be rendered illegally and secretly. After fraternisation there still remained certain restrictions on prisoners' correspondence, but the whole operation was much easier, especially as regards the parcel sending, which became part of a huge charitable effort, largely inspired by Victor Gollancz through the movement 'Save Europe Now'. The ledger was written in a variety of hands, for two or three prisoners gave clerical help. Here are some typical entries in the REMARKS column:

> Captured Africa, hints of suicide—wants to be visited, family at home in difficulties—mother needs insulin injections—classified wrongly as fanatical anti-Nazi, ill—help in any way (often) —wife displaced from Silesia living in small dark room, Catholic, 3 children—family in distress adopted by J. Kelly.

The ledger contains the names of two generals and one field-marshal. Among the 'contacts' two occur again and again: Mrs M. Bladsbrough for Glen Mills and Bessie Midgley—a Quaker of whom much will be heard later—in connection with the Youth Camp at Saffron Walden. Another extremely active supporter was Edward Freaney. An Irishman and a devout Catholic, as a miner he was exempted from call-up. He joined the Prisoner of War Aid Society and appealed often for food, clothes and medicine. In his house in Yorkshire he had first Italians, learning their language, and then Germans. Sometimes after a hard shift underground he would cycle eighteen miles to Selby to deliver a kit bag full of gifts.

Who can say if all the cases who appealed to Mary Foss were genuine, that someone here and there did not spin a tale to a soft heart? This certainly happened when repatriation began to be allowed on compassionate grounds. But what did it matter in the scale of human misery and loneliness that was being lessened?

Among the warring and warred-over nations of Europe only Britain was not overwhelmed by problems of reconstruction and national revival. It alone had the capacity and potential good-will to take the lead in sending relief and aiding the restoration of

7

the shattered continent; (the conscience of the Americans was much slower to be aroused after victory). Already in September 1945 Victor Gollancz, renewed after his holiday in Scotland, had founded the movement 'Save Europe Now'. Its aim was both to channel this good-will into practical actions and to act as a spur to the government. Gradually, as the anti-German feeling subsided, it was realised that in the mammoth destruction and dislocation of Europe the German people were perhaps the worst sufferers, even if deservedly; furthermore, they were burdened with an unparalleled refugee problem. More and more people understood that the first victims of the Nazis had been on home ground. Early on a cartoon by Low in the *Evening Standard* showed some cowed pathetic people emerging from a concentration camp. A figure representing world opinion says, 'The whole German people should be wiped out for this.' One of the survivors says, 'Don't forget some of *us* are German, friend.' The true state of Germany began to emerge in reports of *The Times* and *Manchester Guardian* correspondents. Lord Beveridge travelled there to see for himself and in his booklet, 'An Urgent Message from Germany' he showed how far below the truth were the Control Commission's statistics on deaths from starvation. Gollancz, in order to arouse public awareness, wrote another impassioned book, *In Darkest Germany*, in which he exposed the 'ethics of starvation'. He questioned the figures on which government statements had been based and argued that there were not 10,000 cases of hunger oedema in the British zone but ten times that number. Over the next year or two he kept up a constant campaign in press and radio for a more just treatment of Germany. Thus, in 1946 a change of heart took place from motives that were Christian or humanitarian or—for the politically minded—from a fear that West Germany could become a seedbed for the spread of communism as far as the Rhine. It was, of course, a minority feeling but it gave rise to a developing groundswell that began to disturb the flat sea of indifference towards the former enemy. The prisoners of war sensed it with an 'At last!'

Only five days after the Lords' debate a public meeting took place at Central Hall, Westminster. It was organised from the office of 'Save Europe Now' in Henrietta Street, the house of Gollancz's publishing firm. In the chair was 'the conscience of the Labour Party' Richard Stokes MP; other prominent speakers were Pastor Forell and Gollancz himself. They had first met a year before in Scotland when the Swede was one of those who helped to restore Gollancz's faith in Germany. Others included Professor Courvoissier* from Geneva, the Berlin correspondent of the *Manchester Guardian* and Reginald Paget, the Labour MP and KC who would later defend Field-Marshal Manstein at his trial—he said it was an infringement of human liberty not to allow prisoners to send parcels home. The Reverend Henry Carter discussed the degeneration of family life in Germany with many fathers away. The Quaker John Fletcher pointed at the TUC for accepting a situation where POWs were employed as degraded labour. The feeling against non-fraternisation was strong and unanimous— Clarence Tritton spoke up for openly defying the rule. But the meeting was by no means single-minded. Two refugees wanted Nazis and anti-Nazis treated differently; a Methodist warned those present not to forget what the Germans had done and that they must be converted before they went home.

Forell's diary reports some reactions to the Central Hall meeting. Courvoissier thought it too soft on the Germans—'but then he sees everything through French–Swiss spectacles'. Officials of the British Council of Churches were dubious about the whole value of the occasion, Craig, the General Secretary, being 'in the highest degree British' and even against lifting non-fraternisation. The Foreign Office were somewhat suspicious of Forell because of his long time in Berlin; at the War Office he was told politely that, as a guest in this country, he had gone too far by speaking critically of government policy on a public platform. Indeed Forell's drive and lack of sympathy with well-meaning bureaucrats who nevertheless felt it their duty to keep the brakes on could, in the view of Cranfield, sometimes be counter-productive.

Meanwhile, the serious press was speaking up for the German prisoners, criticising the government for shilly-shallying. The Minister of State, Philip Noel Baker, on 29 July conceded in Parliament that 'the prisoners have a right to know, within a measurable future, what lies ahead.' All very well, said the Tories, but why didn't he tell them? More and more letters in the press demanded that a definite decision be taken. At the beginning of August the *Times* parliamentary correspondent wrote sharply, 'An energetic Cabinet would take the matter in its stride no matter how much it was beset by other problems', and pointed up his

* Representative of the Ecumenical Chaplaincy Service for POWs.

argument with a scene in Central London he had witnessed the previous day: 'Two German prisoners were sweeping the Duke of York Steps. Each was wearing his dingy uniform with the white PW lettering on either trouser. They did their sweeping like automata—robots. It was early afternoon and the Important were passing down the steps, having lunched at their Pall Mall and St James's Street Clubs. For all the notice the sweepers took of them the Important might have been as dust. And they really were important—generals, admirals and civil servants, don't you know. The sweepers never raised their heads. Mechanically, lifelessly they swept, heads bent, faces hidden . . . To the honour of many of the Important let it be said that they involuntarily averted their eyes. And Cabinet Ministers would no doubt have done as much. But they, at least, are in a position to do so much more.'

The next event in the rising swell of public opinion was on 21 August, a memorial sponsored by 'Save Europe Now' appealing to the Prime Minister in the name of common humanity to draw up a scheme for repatriation and announce it as soon as possible. The 875 signatories included three Roman Catholic Archbishops, 55 Anglican Bishops and other church leaders, 118 MPs, 76 members of the Royal Society, a large number of heads of colleges and schools, as well as men and women prominent in public life and the arts. (The absence of the two Anglican Archbishops as well as of Cardinal Griffin and Monsignor Godfrey rather spoiled the unanimity of the Christian voice.)

Here in a nearly unique way the conscience of Christian and liberal-minded Britain was addressing itself to a Socialist government. The Prime Minister immediately ordered a review by all the government departments concerned of the whole POW situation in Britain. The response on repatriation was quick, on fraternisation slow—and on the possibility of changing the working status there was never any statement at all. In October the rate of sending prisoners home was stepped up from 2,000 to 15,000 a month, with a schedule that stretched out till the end of 1948, the 'whites' and the sick being released by quotas, and generally the first to go,* and then in order of length of captivity. The following month the general public was allowed to send food parcels to prisoners' families through the agency of 'Save Europe Now'. But as late as 29 November the Minister of War, to the obvious displeasure of the Commons, was saying that the ban on fraternisation was not

* In all 37,580 men were sent home as 'whites', 46,310 as sick.

to be relaxed. Then suddenly, just in time for Christmas, came the announcement on 12 December that the prisoners could visit private homes, walk within five miles of their camp, take rides in private cars, accept small gifts such as cigarettes and tobacco. They could stay out till ten o'clock; they could not use public transport or go to pubs, restaurants or the cinema, but they could play football against British teams. Amorous fraternisation was forbidden. The response of the public and the relief to the prisoners was overwhelming.

Why did it take so long? Would the policy of a Conservative government have been different? Certainly Churchill's famous motto 'In victory magnanimity, in peace goodwill' does suggest that he would have acted in a different manner to Attlee. In 1919 he had castigated Clemenceau for wanting to 'keep German slaves' and also speeded up the repatriation of German POWs on practical grounds: they were costing £90,000 a day to keep and could be sent home on the very same trains that were bringing British soldiers back from the Rhine.[50] Churchill's attitude a quarter of a century later as Leader of the Opposition is hard to discover. He may well have discussed the matter in one of his lunches with Victor Gollancz, but he never put down a parliamentary question on the subject, nor made a responsible statement. The harrying in the Commons came less from the Conservatives than from the Labour back benches and especially from Richard Stokes. It was, in fact, probably widely known that the government was in a cleft stick and had little room to manoeuvre. The crux of the matter was that in 1946 one quarter of the work force on the land was POW labour; so when the Ministry of Agriculture began to work out the norms for the following year up to the harvest, it saw that a rapid release of prisoners must be resisted, however much it might be desirable from the human point of view. The 100,000 displaced persons who were to come over in 1947 from the refugee camps in Germany were only part of the equation with repatriation. The Bishop of Chichester was right: the user departments were calling the tune. There was another factor: the first true Labour government in Britain was determined to put through a great deal of new and complicated socialist legislation; it also had to clear up the mess of war and to begin to dismantle the British Empire. The POW issue had a low priority, and a big inter-departmental feasibility study for a new policy was not on.

But why did Attlee's government hold on to non-fraternisation so long? Could it be that government in general after long years at war had not become used again to responding to intelligent public opinion, especially when the popular Socialist organ the *Daily Mirror* was not pro-prisoner? The Cabinet discussion on 4 September which authorised speedier repatriation was largely in response to the memorial of 'Save Europe Now'. The grounds were political and included the hope of influencing the first local elections in Germany which were about to take place. The need for an increase to the trifling pay of POW in order to increase production was also mentioned but not given. Bevin, the Foreign Minister, preoccupied with Four Power issues in Germany, tended to see them simply as a work force.* The War Office went on seeing them as soldiers who, they feared, would no longer behave as such if they mixed too freely with the population.

The issue of 'slave labour'—an emotive expression that was freely used—went on troubling consciences till the Germans went home. In February 1947 the government announced that repatriation could not be accelerated for economic reasons and especially because of the needs of that year's harvest. At this, Liddell Hart, meeting Richard Crossman (not then a Cabinet Minister, but aware of the thoughts in Whitehall), protested that it was a most immoral line and strange for a Labour government. Crossman said that the country simply could not afford to let them go. 'Then why not allow them to be repatriated,' asked Liddell Hart, 'and return as free labour?' Crossman said it was not possible because of Trades Union objections. The farmers preferred having them to workers of any other nationality as they worked better, but it would raise any amount of trouble with our own workers if they were paid a competitive wage.[51]

It is tempting, but probably unfair, to call this an early example of the way Trades Unions can dictate policies which negate the broad humanitarian base of the Socialist movement. But it was too soon after the war to let such considerations rule; few ordinary people are far-sighted idealists. In any case, the atmosphere in

* (See Faulk, op. cit. 649.) But at the Moscow Conference in April 1947 it was Bevin who secured the signing of an agreement that all POWs from France and Russia as well as the United Kingdom should be repatriated by the end of 1948. (The Russians, in the event, kept many POWs much longer while the British returned all theirs five months before the deadline.) In a letter to the author (29.11.77) Lord Bullock writes, 'This was the one positive achievement of this sterile year.'

Britain was far in advance of that in formerly occupied Europe. When Woodbrooke, the Quaker College at Selly Oak, Birmingham, began at once to invite German prisoners, they had to stop doing so as visitors from Holland refused to sit at the same table as men of the *Wehrmacht*.

Perhaps in the end a rough political justice was achieved on a scale parallel to the damage that Nazi Germany caused to other peoples. America kept its prisoners working and fed them well for fourteen months after the war; Britain kept them reasonably well for up to thirty-nine months; France and Belgium rather longer but under much harsher conditions; while the prisoners in Russia suffered appallingly, worked like real slaves, and most never came back.

That Christmas of 1946 brought a dramatic breakthrough of human feeling. All over the country invitations poured into the camps. On Christmas and Boxing Day there were queues of cars outside many sentried gates, waiting to take home an unknown guest, oddly signed for in the army manner as 'one live body'. (The sensitive Bishop Woods, when he heard an escort use this formula, was very annoyed and announced he would ask a question about this practice in the House of Lords.) For the first time in years Germans sat down with a family, with women and children. The villagers at Walderslade near Chatham had earlier protested at the building of a camp for German POWs, and later had tried without success to have the names of girls published who— illegally of course—had fraternised. Now they sent over two hundred invitations up to camp. At Woodborough in Nottinghamshire The Reverend Charles Harrington wrote to his parishioners asking them to invite a POW from Wollaton camp to their homes. Many were in favour, though quite a few were against. At the vicarage itself where four were guests at Christmas dinner, a father of five broke down and sobbed when he saw the white tablecloth and was almost too overcome to eat. At Peterborough two thousand POWs filled the great Gothic nave of the Cathedral and heard a message from the Bishop which ended with the words *Wir heissen Euch hoffen* (we bid you hope). Ruth Fisher recalls that at Mattishall in Norfolk 'we had some Italian prisoners with us, my sister was feeding her first baby and we were listening to King George VI on the radio. My mother looked up and saw Johann's face looking in at the window, full of sadness and yearning. We asked him and his companion inside. It was a wonderful Christmas and the beginning of a friendship which has lasted for over thirty years. Johann could not trace his wife and two little girls and wanted to stay in England, but my mother persuaded him, miserable though he was, to go home and try to find them, which he eventually did.'

At Hatch End in Middlesex the camp chaplain. Pastor Wallmann, remembers how 'some 500 out of 800 were invited to families that Christmas and those who had no invitations were simply hauled in from the streets although it was against regulations. All returned with touching tales to tell, and for weeks there were happy faces in the camp. I have told this story again and again lest it be forgotten. It was this overwhelming hospitality and goodness of heart from rich and poor alike that showed us what we really could learn from being in England.'

In halls and huts, in churches and private houses, there was carol-singing of unusual significance. At Wells Hans Georg Moschallski sat at the organ at the end of Mass while his comrades sang carols, and no one left the church. Under a Christmas tree and by candlelight reconciliation again and again was discovered in the singing by both sides of 'Silent Night'. At Low Cowling in Yorkshire they talk about it to this day. At Scunthorpe the local members of the congregation stayed behind at a joint service on Christmas Day in the chancel and sang it in German, many being overcome with emotion. At March in Cambridgeshire, The Reverend Robert Neill before Christmas took a hand-organ on a cart and a party of young people carol-singing into the local POW camp. They had a tremendous and touching reception. The Germans next gave a concert in the church on a Sunday morning which delighted the whole congregation and led to their doing the same at other churches in the neighbourhood. At the bleak camp near Croydon Aerodrome the silence following the singing by 200 men of 'Silent Night' was so profound for Albert Steel 'that one could almost hear the flicker of the candles. That was a precious moment in which we felt the presence of God, and the men thought of their families waiting for their return home.'

Affecting, tearful scenes marked for many at this time the real end of the war and the beginning of person-to-person peace. At Kingsthorpe, Northampton, the Baptist Minister The Reverend William Reece, who spoke German well, arranged for junior school children to paint and decorate cards with 'Fröhliche

Weinachten' on them. One was given to each of the 133 men who came from Boughton Camp to the Christmas service which he read and preached in both languages. There was a children's choir and his nine-year-old daughter had learned 'Stille Nacht' by heart. 'She sang,' he recalls, 'as though inspired. It was one of the most touching experiences of my life. But there were so many tears, I felt it was almost cruel. After this we were invited to a party which the camp gave to war-stricken children from Northampton, which the Mayor also attended. I tried to avoid sentimentality and said that the wounds of five years of war could not be healed by the singing of a few carols. But a start towards reconciliation could now be made.'

But what touched guests most at that 1946 Christmas was that German refugees too asked them into their homes, including Jews. Richard Koch, a Berlin lawyer, and his wife Eva had emigrated from Berlin in 1939 and settled in Nottingham where they became attenders at the Quaker Meeting. Five prisoners were invited to the Meeting House for the Christmas party. Eva Koch remembers how 'an elder came up to us. "These are our German friends from Wollaton. I am sure you would be delighted to act as interpreter." I was far from delighted, but when I saw an older man sitting and watching the games with tears in his eyes, I went and sat beside him. He could hardly speak and was very near a breakdown. He told me his son, aged sixteen, had been killed on the Russian front and his elder daughter during a bombing raid, and his wife had fled first to Silesia then back to Berlin in front of the advancing Russians. He sat for most of the evening with a two-year-old boy on his knees and could not take his eyes from the child. He became our first regular visitor. It was incomprehensible to him afterwards that we acted as we did. But my husband had himself been a POW of the British from 1917 to 1919, and later on in Sachsenhausen Concentration Camp, and then as an internee in the Isle of Man. He was much more understanding and eager to befriend these boys at the beginning than I. But after a while it was easy: we ourselves had been stranded and hopeless not long before, and here were disillusioned, insecure young men kept in captivity, bombarded with news from the Nuremberg Trials and the atrocities committed in the concentration camps. They needed a home to come to and friends to talk to and we were glad to be able to provide that.'

The lifting of the ban on fraternisation may have come late,

7*

but it was the one factor that made 1947 tolerable for many POWs, along with the fact that each one now knew the date of his repatriation. By no means all, indeed only a minority, managed to have significant human contacts outside the camps, but for those who did the discovery of the British people was a touching and lasting experience. It set a seal on the most intimate episode in the history of Anglo-German relations and was the beginning of many enduring friendships.

9

Camp of Confidence

A people enjoying a living tradition expressed in daily practice and example have no need to fear deliberate indoctrination, nor need they be ordered by fear and compulsion.

The Featherstone Park POW Camp, unlike the blood-curdling barbed wire and floodlit compounds so fashionable among 'new' regimes and apparently so essential to their fragile self-respect—this English camp healed and encouraged the human heart and spirit. Instead of wounding and destroying life, instead of awakening hate and intolerance, it furthered and generated the only basic principle of mankind's survival—that is, mutual respect and mutual trust.

Yehudi Menuhin[52]

Camp 18 was at Featherstone Park, near Haltwhistle, and lay on the Tyne just south of Hadrian's Wall and halfway between the east and west coast. The Americans for whom the camp had originally been erected called the place Death Valley because of its, to them, unfriendly remoteness. When they had gone, Italian POWs came in first, then Germans who were shocked to find themselves taking part in the wholesale destruction of abandoned American equipment; the local press was shocked too.[53] Field dynamos, typewriters, teleprinters, repair kits and spare parts and even thousands of ration packs were rendered useless or burned. During 1945 the camp became exclusively for officers, with some 580 other ranks acting as orderlies. There was one compound for these and three others, all separated from each other by a 'death line' where over 3,000 officers though not yet screened were divided roughly into 'whites', 'greys' and 'blacks'—the SS, U-boat men and paratroopers all being automatically in the black compound. The Nissen huts were crowded up closely and for exercise the prisoners were taken on route marches with armed guards at the front, rear and at the sides. Ill-feeling was rife: if the officer taking the roll-call offered a cigarette to the German in charge and he accepted it, that man was regarded as a semi-traitor. Woetzel, who was there for a while, says: 'There was tremendous tension. The camp leadership was Nazi and militarist in the worst way. Extracts from newspapers were read out, censored heavily; when a lieutenant-colonel of the paratroops protested he was court martialled.' But when the war ended, a new mood entered. 'In that first summer,' Dieter Hankel remembers, 'we used to lie idle in the huts; discipline got lax and the top brass tried to keep us together with regulations about uniform, but that made matters worse.' Ideologies fell down like a house of cards. There was a parting of the ways between those who wanted to work for the future and those who endlessly mulled over the past. Small study circles had already begun with almost no books, and only toilet paper to make notes on. Architects got together and made up elementary courses; they had no literature and as soon as some paper was available they drew from memory the great buildings of Europe. The Commandant, it seems, was an amiable gentleman-officer, not much more. The Red Cross made some adverse comments on the camp and it was decided to replace him with Lieutenant-Colonel Vickers.

It was an inspired appointment. Vickers was *not* a gentleman, having risen through the ranks in the First World War. If his rather ruthless, braggart nature could offend the typical British officer, it did not the German, who saw in him a red-faced, big-hearted, outsize character. Many commandants had no idea how to treat German officer prisoners; either they lacked firmness and insight, or they tried to keep them under because they were 'Huns'. Vickers felt no doubts; he saw them as soldiers and respected them as men. Pastor Gursky remembers his words one day at roll-call. 'Gentlemen! In the First World War I was in a German prisoner of war camp and was treated as a gentleman. I will therefore treat you in the same way.' Following the example of his old camp commandant at Lahr in Baden, he said he would be on their side if they gave their word of honour valid day and night not to try to escape. Vickers could see that, the war being over, what his Germans needed was to be trusted, to feel less hemmed in and to have ways of relieving their cramped feelings and muscles. The different compounds were opened to each other and later the watch towers were sent crashing down, the thick rolls of barbed wire removed and in their place came a token wire three feet high 'to keep the cows out'. Next, the guard company of Poles from the Anders Army were not needed; a *Wachkompanie* of Leutnants and Oberleutnants was formed to take over most of their duties. Vickers was all for the maximum outside contact for his POWs. His passionate outburst to Pastor Forell in May 1946 has already been noted: he felt so strongly about the continued restrictive policy towards prisoners a year after the war that he was prepared to put his career at stake in an attempt to change matters. The Germans had no idea of this but they greatly respected his frank, open nature. Already by the autumn of 1945 a convoy of trucks left the camp early each morning filled with officers going to outside jobs. It was the beginning of an extraordinary volunteer labour scheme that the prisoners entered into with zest: in one period of thirteen months no fewer than a million man-hours of work would be given to the neighbourhood by 850 men, for the sake of distraction, keeping fit, doing their bit for reconciliation; by bringing in the harvest, some liked to think, they were indirectly relieving the food shortage in Germany. No one was more delighted than Vickers' successor Colonel McBain when next year the 'farm labourers' asked the Rector of Hexham if they could take part in the harvest festival. (It could be that the instigator was, in fact, Pastor Martin Niemoeller who was on a visit to Featherstone Park.) On 17 November coaches brought a thousand prisoners to Hexham Abbey. The aisles were crowded and the doors locked, there being room for only 400 local people inside. The service was conducted by a Lutheran naval chaplain, the sermon preached in German by the vicar of St George's, Jesmond, and the organ was played by Heinz Goettsche of Lübeck. A large orchestra, conducted by Heinz Wakter of the Saarbrücken Opera, sat in candlelight at music stands made in the camp and played Schubert, with the baritone Hans Heim singing solos from Mendelssohn's oratorio *Saint Paul*.

In January 1946 Peter Hehn, one of the *Prominenten* in the camp, wrote in his diary: 'A new I.O. has arrived ... Sulzbach impresses me a lot. More artist than officer. We talked about Wiechert, the Bonhoeffer Circle, the political work in the camp. I believe that not only a gentleman has come among us but a human being.' The sending of Herbert Sulzbach to Camp 18 by Faulk was a second inspired appointment. As we have seen, he had won his spurs at Comrie and had now been promoted from Staff Sergeant to Captain. He worked on exactly the same principle as Vickers: trust.

To the prisoners, as they got to know about him, he was a phenomenon: a Jewish refugee who had lost relatives in Hitler's holocaust, yet was full of goodwill towards them; a former German officer who was as proud of his King George's commission as he had been of the Kaiser's, yet hardly a turncoat; a man whose very presence in the camp could both make men regret their Nazi past and face the future with hope. His former commandant, Colonel Wilson, had just supported his application to become a British citizen, calling him 'a man of the highest ideals, humane, and one of the most conscientious men I have ever met.' Strangely, it was just when the Home Office was vetting his naturalisation papers that he was rediscovering his German roots. At Comrie he had been with other ranks and only made contact with individuals; at Featherstone Park he had come back among his own. Once again he was with familiar people, among men who were after all recognisable and decent Germans, the kind who might have been his fellow officers in 1914–18, even though most may have caught the Nazi infection—a highly curable disease in his view.

Sulzbach got on extremely well with Vickers. But they had a problem. The German senior officer, a Luftwaffe colonel who had long been the chief camp spokesman, was a 'Yes-man', not up to the job; and his deputy, Korvetten-Kapitän Oesten, Sulzbach did not at all consider to be one of his 'splendid fellows'. They were totally opposite types. Jürgen Oesten was a thirty-two-year-old U-boat ace and had a *Ritterkreuz* for sinking over 100,000 tons of Allied shipping. His great days had been in convoy hunting and then, once sonared by the escorting destroyers, evading the kill, move by silent move, under the Atlantic. It was a grim but exhilarating game of chess that could last for days and at which he had proved master. Being still at sea in *U-861* at the end of the war, he had surrendered his boat at Londonderry on being told that along with others who did this the crews would not be regarded as POWs but as 'surrendered enemy personnel' with early repatriation.

This promise from the Royal Navy was not allowed to be honoured, because automatically, whether Nazi or not, all U-boat officers came under the category of 'militarists, war criminals and security suspects' and as such were barred by Allied agreement. Also, any proscribed list ranked above the political grading. Most other ranks so captured were sent home quite soon.

Oesten, as though highly dangerous, was moved about accompanied by three armed guards. But, a born survivor, he did not harbour grievances and as a born man-manager, he quickly asserted his force of character and ability at Featherstone Park. He was, however, not widely popular. He tended to bear rather heavily on the younger naval men and, though he came later to appreciate Sulzbach's goodness of heart and readiness to help, he was not behind the new spirit that was being created in the camp. He had adjusted his own life successfully, but was a stranger to the ferment of inner change in others.

Another German camp spokesman had, therefore, to be found from outside, and in May 1946 Faulk asked Sulzbach to travel to the generals' camp at Bridgend in South Wales to interview Ferdinand Heim. Heim was a dark, lean, keen-faced Swabian and an unusually cultivated man for a general; he had the unique distinction of having been thrown into Torgau prison by Hitler after Stalingrad for disobedience: refusing to lead demoralised Hungarian and Rumanian troops on a sacrificial counter-attack, he had been made the scapegoat for their weakness. Soon after the war ended he had not hesitated to enter the fray in print, writing an article in the official POW newspaper, *Die Wochenpost*, on the question of the future of Germany. Under a quotation from Kant, 'A state is power and freedom and law; barbarism is force without freedom and without law', he asked readers to examine the difference between the German authoritarian state and the Anglo-Saxon democracy of the people. In the same way as Freiherr von der Heydte a month later, he was trying to raise the level of debate to one of fundamental principles. But the same thing happened: the response was personal abuse. Readers questioned the right of any general to lecture readers on freedom, especially in Heim's case, as in 1944 he had patriotically returned to take command of the defence of Boulogne (where, unlike at Le Havre, both sides agreed on the evacuation of civilians during the siege).

Sulzbach convinced Heim that he had a role at Featherstone Park. The two men took to each other at once, soon dropping all formality and calling each other by their surnames. Professor Courvoissier of Geneva, reported of the general: 'C'est un homme remarquable par sa largeur des vues, sa sureté de jugement, son absence de préjugés et sa sérénité'. Every morning Heim met Sulzbach to discuss the needs of the camp which Sulzbach thought of rather as a township of 4,000 souls, with himself town clerk to

Vickers' mayor. There were other officers, like the excellent Oxford-educated Major Grove and NCOs such as the much-liked Sergeant Woodcock. But it was the trio Vickers–Sulzbach–Heim that created a spirit at Featherstone Park unparalleled elsewhere. The 'Camp of Confidence' became a reality, wondered at by other visitors from abroad like Frederick Biri of the International Red Cross, Pastor Niemoeller who later wrote of Sulzbach's 'great humanity and Christian charity', Bishop Lilje of Hanover, the conductor Hans Schmitt-Isserstedt—who came from Hamburg Radio to record the choir and orchestra; Richard Stokes, known to POWs as 'our MP' and many others. Sulzbach, in his eagerness to prove that a camp for German officers could be full of decent men turning their backs on Nazism, kept his secretaries busy copying out the evidence to send out far and wide: to Victor Gollancz and Captain Liddell Hart, to John Hynd, Minister for German affairs and his successor Lord Pakenham. Never fearing to be importunate, while still at Comrie he was dispatching his missives even to Lord Vansittart who used to reply in a courteous, careful Foreign Office manner, 'I am glad you are maintaining your cautious optimism.'

Optimism was always Sulzbach's strong suit and it was hardly cautious. He exuded a faith both in human beings and in the recovery of the real Germany. Pinned up on the wall by his desk was his favourite quotation from Goethe: *Edel sei der Mensch, hilfreich und gut* (Noble let man be, helpful and good). Here in his private room in the intelligence officer's hut he interviewed all those who came into the camp or who asked to see him. From colonels past sixty to boys of barely twenty, they would wait outside trying to keep calm and dignified, sometimes absurdly so, discreetly eyed by the eleven officer typists and confidential clerks who helped Sulzbach in his manifold work. They would find themselves before the very opposite of the cool, trained interrogators they usually met, a very human man who might hurry into the main office looking frantically for a lost file, or checking that a bet had been placed for him by telephone on a horse he had picked. Sulzbach was an amateur in the true sense of the word: he loved his work and did it in a caring way for its own sake. Interpreter officers were not responsible for screening—this was a task for trained, visiting specialists—but on his own initiative he did a spot grading on all those he interviewed. In September 1946 when the shortage of screeners was acute his results were accepted officially. By May 1947 when screening finished and before he had covered the whole camp, he had put down 388 as A, 913 as B and 26 as C.

His approach was very personal. It was as though he had his own dowsing technique into a person's true feelings, into his quality as a human being. He wrote down his brief impression and assessment in a brown alphabetical ledger. His positive adjectives are most often *genuine, decent, frank, modest, sincere, pleasant*. A man is very often *a good type*, or *an excellent type*. The obverse and much rarer is *not frank, not pleasant, not genuine*. Everyone is seen as going through, or as being caapble of going through, an inner modification process. On Leutnant R.S. he writes: '*Seen by P. and D. believed very bad . . . can be cured, yet very cynical and arrogant.*' Total condemnation is rare and again this is on feeling rather than a man's record. Only once does he put down that he had to shout at a man and there is a single case of someone who is *slimy and crying*. One of the three compound leaders *seems decent, but a bit too polite*; another is an *awful creeper*; a third *behaved badly with the driver of the bus*. A Naval Commander *according to letter of English woman saved life of French lady. Later report: double crosser*. A U-boat commander, *captured Singapore 5.9.45, interrogated by Japs, very fine chap*.

Every man who confronted him Sulzbach judged against his ideal standard of a gentleman and an officer. But he was also looking for some latent quality that might have been suppressed or muddied by Nazi doctrines. This is particularly evident with the Waffen-SS and even with the Allgemeine-SS, who were seen in the same unbiassed way. *Allg. SS 1933–45, Nazi, interesting mixture with good German qualities, may become OK*. An SS-Captain since 1937 *seems not bad at all*; but a comrade of his is *opaque, Volksdeutsch, not frank, yet in a pitiable state*. One of the young lieutenants who was in an Ordensburg from 1937 to 1939* is *very shy, yet frank, decent, learned his lesson*.

Many of Sulzbach's brief notes indicate personal tragedies and redemptive deeds. Lt. W: *urgent case, mother died (hunger tuberculosis) his son (he never saw) died, father ill, wife on the way to desert him. Very nice and modest*. Capt. N: *customs official; excellent letter re his*

---

* The Ordensburgen, or Napola-Schools, were colleges for selected boys with a high IQ, good Aryan appearance and leadership qualities. They were given a wide, first-class education that had elements of both Eton and the Jesuits. Its pupils were to be the ruling intelligentsia of the future.

deed for the French in 1942. Modest first class man. Naval Captain M:
*See letter from Lt. Col. Hicks from Athens, March '46, excellent be-
haviour praised by the Greeks in Patras. Decent type.* Paymaster D: *44,
party member 1937, SA. Nov. 33 as student teacher, sister imprisoned
for listening to BBC, he helped her at the Gestapo. Seems OK. Lost wife
and child by bombs in Dortmund.* Rittmeister Dr. S: *See M's declaration
on oath: condemned to death by fellow POWs in Canada, 100 per cent anti-
Nazi.* There is a Dr. G. who *joined the party in 1933. Seems OK,
saved Jewess in Antwerp—see letter.*

Sulzbach confesses that he sometimes graded young men higher
than they deserved. He also revised earlier gradings, by no means
always upwards. He was rarely hard on the old Prussian officer
class, looking at its more decent rather than its chauvinist characteristics. More than one of his contemporaries was a *good old chap.*
Certain qualities upset him as with a lieutenant who was *not too nice*
(*cat-lover!*). His reaction when someone tried to bribe him is
characteristic. Faulk tells the story of a prisoner whose sister was
married to an English film tycoon. This man came to see Vickers
whom he talked into allowing him to lay on a party in the camp.
Faulk happened to be there and enjoyed food he had not seen for
years. There was even a floor-show provided by the light entertainers of the camp. Then the brother-in-law approached Sulzbach
suggesting that he might be willing, for a sum of money, to re-
grade his relative to A so that he could be released earlier. Sulzbach at once reported this to Faulk who said, 'Lead him on, and
when it comes to the moment of his handing over the money,
we'll have a couple of plain-clothes men in the next room.'
Sulzbach recoiled in horror from the proposal. Faulk's comment
is 'In order to understand Herbert, you must see him as someone
who would feel soiled by contact with such a man. He has to have
a kindly humanity around him to be fully alive.' It goes without
saying that there were those who thought Sulzbach's approach too
simplistic, who related more easily to more sophisticated screeners
like Rossiter or Dr Otto John, who were less of a walking rebuke.
But none had his charisma with a certain kind of German, nor his
compassion and awareness.

Sulzbach was always hard—he had a right to be—on self-pity.
When the wife of a POW wrote to him complaining that the fate
of the Germans was that of leaves being driven before the autumn
wind, he wrote back, 'Like all Germans you suddenly see misery
all around and you are full of self-pity. But where was your pity

with the hundreds and thousands and millions that from 1
September 1939 onwards were driven across Europe, after Hitler
and his criminals had loosed their armies over innocent lands?
Where was your disgust at the millions of slaughtered civilians?
. . . You speak of things that are primitive and inhuman. What
happened before was inhuman, and what Germany has to suffer is
the consequence of the inhumanity of her Führer, whom you
yourself voted for.'

Sometimes Sulzbach over-reacted. After the two Admirals
Räder and Dönitz were given heavy sentences at Nuremberg, the
naval POWs wanted to send in a petition on their behalf. Sulzbach
took this almost as a personal insult. 'With this petition,' he wrote,
'you exhibit all the old arrogance. Only a few days ago I told some
press men that there are only 5 per cent Nazis in this camp. You
are undermining my faith in you. Do you want this camp which
has won a good reputation suddenly to come into ill-repute again?
. . . And let me ask you one thing more: when, between 1933 and
1945, did any of you put in a petition where it was really needed—
for the victims of the *Konzentrationslager*? . . . It would have been
a risk to do it, and here there is no risk.' Sulzbach was acting like
a hurt parent, bitterly disappointed that his children have not lived
up to his expectations. Later he saw that he had been over-
anxious about the reputation of his camp and unfair to officers
who still regarded the two admirals as their commanders-in-chief
to whom they owed a certain loyalty. But it was possible to let
him down without offending him, if done in the right style. One
evening an officer was due to go to London District Cage. The
two guards detailed to accompany him there waited in vain for
him to turn up. Late that night Sultzbach found a note on his bed:

I am most terribly sorry to have to break my word, but I do not
want to go to London for interrogation, as I might have a conflict of conscience. I hate having to make difficulties for you in
particular, who have done so much for our welfare. Please forgive me. I give you my word of honour never to do anything
against England; I will work only for understanding between
our two countries. Forgive me again. With best wishes for your
future work.

The officer was never found. It was rumoured that friends put him
on a ship from Newcastle to Norway. Sulzbach was oddly proud
of him and wished him luck in his heart.

The youth of the camp were often drawn to Sulzbach as a new non-authoritarian father figure. One such was Herbert Schmitt, the young submariner who kept a journal.* He found the uncertainly about repatriation almost unbearable:

> Waiting for it grinds the nerves to the limit, lies like a coat of mail round the heart that prevents feelings and sensation coming in or out. The process of clarification has begun, is fermenting and working. It was so incredibly depressing to suspect and then in the end to know that even ideals could turn into clay, appear hollow and empty when the hammer of fate struck. In this heap of debris I stood and with me nearly the whole youth of the camp, and had to fight through to something more valid. There were plenty of those who thought themselves competent to help us along into the next thing, but one knew their past. They can't help, however much they may try to. Their wanting to do so is too transparent. . . . The force of youth unused becomes distorted, consumes itself in lifeless polemics while it is bitterly needed at home. . . . Don't overestimate our power to wait and endure.

Schmitt went to work in the office of General Heim, but this did not relieve his inner feelings. Heim was a strong and lively character who knew a lot. He could give, again and again, a talk which electrified most of the camp on 'How Stalingrad happened —a look behind the scenes'. He could show up Hitler pulling Germany down into chaos around him; and the fact that he had returned to serve him at Boulogne was understood by the older men as not running away when the house was on fire. But it was not quite good enough for the more radical young, like Dieter Hankel, for whom Heim was a *Respektperson*, and no more. He was not someone who held up a way into the future—or he could hardly have held the camp together. But Sulzbach was. In that summer Schmitt had his first conversation with him:

> I had practically given up hope of getting home. I had come round to believing and feeling ashamed and guilty of the horrors of Auschwitz, Bergen-Belsen, etc; I felt that the world would never forgive the Germans and that our personal futures were very bleak. I told Sulzbach my feelings. He listened attentively and sympathetically and eventually he began comforting me

* See page 116.

with words like these. 'Do not lose hope. Germany didn't only produce *Konzentrationslager*; it produced great composers, philosophers, poets, artists, who have given much to the world. One day there will be a united Europe and Britain and Germany will be members.' He then reminded me of the inscription over the main entrance to the [bombed-out] Frankfurt Opera House: *Dem Wahren, Schönen, Guten* (To the True, the Beautiful, the Good). This, he said, should be my motto. I have tried ever since to live by it, and whenever I pass the ruin of the Opera House, which happens quite frequently, I think of Herbert Sulzbach, the man who made me an anglophile and whose name in my family has become a household word for tolerance, democracy, courage.

Dieter Hankel first got to know Sulzbach when he came into his hut and said, 'I notice that you haven't sent out any letters yet.' 'I haven't an address to send them to,' he replied; 'My parents are bombed out.' Sulzbach immediately sent a repatriated prisoner back with the relevant information, contact was re-established with an aunt and so with his home.

In 1974 a group of boys attending a Colony Holiday Camp at Featherstone were taking down an old stone wall. They came across a bottle with a message in it, written in both English and German. The English text read:

This wall was built by POW officers in March-April 1946. They did it for their professional training and to obtain practical dexterities, always thinking of their country devastated by Allied bombs, the reconstruction of which henceforth will be the task of their lives. Once returned to their well-loved homesteads they will be at work with more carefulness as here.

Unfortunately moisture had got into the bottle and parts of the German text, which was in red ink, had become blurred.[54] So had the four signatures but not their designations, which showed them to be a fighter pilot and officers of the infantry, the U-Boat arm and the Waffen-SS. Their message for posterity might, however, give a false idea of the work ethos at Camp 18. Activity was the order of the day. The number of other ranks was greatly reduced, so that officers could entirely take over the seven kitchens and also most of the tailoring, hair-cutting and cobbling, learning the trade first and usually getting certificates of proficiency. When Colonel

Vickers sent round a circular asking for trained bakers, it was thought that they were for repatriation. But no; shortly afterwards, a strangely-shaped hut was erected opposite the sick quarters on the main street, huge ovens arrived and it became one of the sights of the camp to look through the windows at the rows of gleaming bodies stripped to the waist, their arms deep in tubs of dough. The 150 officer-bakers, working three shifts, were among the most looked-to men in Featherstone Park. Not only did they produce marvellous white bread for all camps for miles around, but also, for the consideration of a few cigarettes, rolls, buns, biscuits for their friends and even, if one provided the ingredients, rather fine cakes and tarts. Nor did they fail to produce statistics: 2,465,588 loaves weighing 4,405,935 lbs were baked, made up out of 22,436 sacks of flour each weighing 140 lbs, 420 sacks of yeast weighing 112 lbs, 2,177 seven-pound bags of yeast, 141 forty-five-pound tins of emulsion, fuelled by 277 tons of coke.

If *Deutsche Ordnung* reigned, it was less and less military. No badges of rank were worn, though on Sunday the old uniforms might come out without decorations. A procession was indeed seen one day advancing to the little bridge across the Tyne, which received numerous orders won in the service of the Third Reich. Legend had it that not long afterwards a local fisherman caught a pike wearing a ribbon and a Knight's Cross. The many in-workers, carpenters, tailors, builders, gardeners, could not however enjoy the extra cigarettes, cups of tea and conversations with farmers that the out-workers enjoyed. From the beginning these volunteers were delighted with the warmth of their welcome, while more than one small farmer was surprised to find he was given not only willing hands but a cattle or forestry expert. The young lawyer, Baron von Aufsess, became the popular hard-working gardener for the Bell family at the The Fox and Hounds. Professor Kurt Sandig who, as at Crewe, continued as a lecturer in business studies and a study leader, went home a healthier man with a certificate that he had 'worked from 1.10.45 to 13.9.46 on drainage without payment'. Another formula on one all-important piece of paper was that someone had 'volunteered whilst in England to work for the public good'. Very popular were the three outlying hostels at Catton, Colwell and Rayless where a total of 200 prisoners lived through the week in small comfortable rooms, with only a sergeant and two privates in charge. When in 1947 the hostels were handed over to the Baltic DPs from Europe, many farmers tried to keep on their German officers, but almost always in vain.

Camp 18's reputation for possessing specialist talent spread far. Oesten recalls how they would be rung up with an SOS to tackle an emergency job at a pit or a power station. 'Once a farmer had lost his water-supply and asked whether we had a diviner. I found we have five who claimed the art! I took two or three to the farm and one of them criss-crossed the area for a while with his hazel-rod, said "Dig here," and sure enough there was plentyof water.' Oesten, who found a role travelling round assessing jobs available and matching them with the work force, boarded out himself for a while with the archaeologist, Eric Birley, and his wife who lived just under Hadrian's Wall. 'I drove his cars, fed her turkeys and generally made myself useful. I called myself his "prisoner of peace" '. The Professor's application of archaeological techniques to intelligence work intrigued and even awed the Germans. Largely on the basis of his knowledge of the organisation of the Roman army which he had gained through contact with German scholars, Birley had made himself the chief expert on the battle order of the Wehrmacht. 'I knew the German mind,' he would say, 'and it was much easier to piece together tiny pieces of information which were contemporary.' In the summer of 1946 when he retired he invited twenty officers to form a fully academic seminar. They were all either historians or classicists, with the later Professor Kleemann, holder of the Chair of Pre-history at Bonn, as his senior student. He had groups working on local inscriptions, the history of the Wall, Roman building techniques, British settlements and his own pet project, the 'terra sigillata'. In addition, an archaeologist from Newcastle led a POW team in the excavation of the first Roman bridge over the Tyne; others took a brief part in digs or visited sites; a vet in the camp collected and identified all animal bones discovered. As ever the way to many a German's heart was to give him an occupation to his detail-loving mind.

Once fraternisation was allowed, outings were organised in many directions by Lieutenant Howard, British Entertainment Officer at Featherstone Park. During the summer of 1947 eighty coaches took 2,500 POWs to the Lake District. They also went to bathe at Dumfries and Whitley Bay; they went in parties to Durham and Newcastle, Carlisle, Barnard Castle and even Edinburgh.

In one period of ten months 330 coaches were hired with 10,500 places for an average trip of sixty miles. They could pay, of course, and refreshments and museum tickets were part of the package. That this was done at a time when the basic petrol ration was still tight raised some local eyebrows, but it was a War Office matter and paid enormous dividends in goodwill. 'Wearing just bathing trunks we could feel real civilians again, but as we charged into the cold water also rather like barbarians compared to the gentlemanly English with rolled up trouser-legs paddling gingerly in the shallows.' Just to hear the roar of city traffic around one after so many years could be thrilling, as could sitting in the Café Lockard in Gateshead served by gentle hands. There might even be an opportunity to put an Englishman firmly in his place. A soldier on leave from Germany is overheard boasting, 'Just for a cigarette or two I could always get a Fräulein.' The POW standing nearby keeps his cool. Taking a packet of Players out of his pocket, he says, 'In this country you get a packet of cigarettes as a present', and gives it to him. Countering this, Kurt Schwederski can say, 'Only in England would the following happen. Two POWs are waiting at the head of the queue for a bus. When it arrives, the conductor calls out, "Two only". The two prisoners —I was one of them—are let on; the rest wait for the next bus.'

But the chief reality of the situation, as in every camp, is still constriction and the long wait. Angry, lost, depressed people amble down the camp 'street' or stare vacantly at the ground. The barbed wire has gone but traces of the fever are everywhere. 'You have stolen my piece of bread,' one colonel says to another. 'You did not wash this morning,' is the reply—both in deadly earnest. Reality is the Nissen hut with its forty or so double bunks, four chairs and two tables; the driving wind and rain of autumn and winter. Reality is clothes getting wet and smelling mouldy, the hut-fug analysed by Herbert Schmitt into its component parts: straw-mattress, coal-gas, cured fish, drying washing, body sweat —the same as U-Boat fug, only you cease to smell it. On one of the three stoves that send clouds of white vapour into the grey afternoon a favourite brew is steaming: camp coffee, cocoa and oxo cubes. Jam jars tied up with string to catch the drops where the roof is leaking. Someone is playing the game of rumours and is waiting for the result. He has put one into circulation to see how quickly and in what form it will come back to him: he will work out on a graph the speed of circulation related to credibility.

Schmitt approves of rumours as 'part of our daily nourishment, as the froth on one's cup of bitterness'. But sometimes the only thing is to get right away. 'You grab a walking stick, make the two obligatory rounds of the sports field, then cut loose through the gates and over the Tyne. Only you don't lose thousands of men so easily. At last there's not a soul to be seen! A great surge of joy! A few paces further and then a sign: OUT OF BOUNDS. The more you are allowed back the smaller freedoms, the more you miss freedom itself.'

Featherstone Park was also a huge adult education centre, with its law school and language school, numerous vocational and cultural courses and political study groups. The organisation of the curricula was ably undertaken by a Mecklenburg Junker, Colonel von Viebahn. A guards officer and airman from the First World War, he was inevitably known as the *Kulturpapst* (Culture-pope) and himself taught Russian history. There was a hut in the south compound where, except for certain times, only English was spoken. In another hut those taking *Abitur* (the equivalent of 'A' level) lived along with their tutors. In all some hundred passed it. The facilities by means of a regular news-sheet and correction of written work were extended to 120 other rank camps, the examination being standardised and later accepted in Germany. The YMCA and the International Red Cross were indispensable suppliers of writing materials and books. The library with 5,500 volumes was perhaps not large for the size of the camp—Shap Wells have five times as many books per prisoner—but officers had the money to buy their own, which they did in thousands; there was eventually a book shop in the camp and a bindery.

There was an admirable and unique twelve-page monthly newspaper, *Zeit am Tyne*. The editor was the young Rolf von Bargen, later of *Die Zeit*, who once a week took the text and mock-up down to Catherall & Co, the Hexham printers; passing through Sulzbach's hands, the paper never had a word censored. Of its circulation of 2,500 copies only a thousand were sold in the camp. It had its own cuttings archive, for the outer world entered the camp through no fewer than 1,230 regular subscriptions to newspapers and magazines from *The Times* to the *Baseler Nachrichten*, from *Technical Engineering* and *The Dancing Times* to *Men Only*. A Gallup-Poll set-up was cut short by more rapid repatriation. Sporting fixtures took numerous teams away to other camps. The football eleven played twenty-two matches against British teams, and on the Durham Ice Rink a scratch ice hockey squad in a notably good-humoured game lost 1–3 to the Durham Hornets. Parties were taken to see local government at work and the organisation of elections, the Town Clerk of Newcastle being especially co-operative. The list of activities might be extended but it is already an indication of the unique character of Camp 18.

Every self-respecting POW camp of any size had a stage—Featherstone Park had four. There was a marionette theatre built up from scratch without a single professional puppeteer. There was a stage for operetta and light entertainment. There were two rival playhouses, the *Theater der Zeit* and the *Theater am Tyne*. The original acting core had been first at Bridgend, the camp of the mass escape, and was sent to Carburton where it was 'blacked' during Faulk's dramatic confrontation with the Nazi bullies. One part then went to Crewe Hall and further built up its talent; another part went to Worksop. But most of them came together again in 1946 at Featherstone Park, including their 'house dramatist', K. O. Hermanns, who had already written two pieces. In the space of some two years the two groups put on 319 performances of forty-two different plays, the most popular being *Charlie's Aunt* with twenty-four showings, followed by *Pygmalion* with twenty. Seven Shakespeare plays were shown—*Troilus and Cressida* most often at sixteen times. Three fresh pieces by Hermanns were seen in all thirty-eight times. A culminating achievement was the presentation at Christmas 1947 of *Hamlet* and *Othello* simultaneously on the two stages—something, remarked *Die Zeit am Tyne*, hardly to be dared by competing stages in a German city. In the same period the versatile Philip Rossiter, visiting Camp 18 as a Training Adviser, was giving a well-received lecture on 'Shakespeare the Man'. The hundred or so who were involved found it almost a way of life and one that brought many privileges, like outings to other camps where they performed. British supporters and friends of the stage provided some materials and costumes, but most of what was needed, from thrones to liqueur glasses, was laboriously constructed from materials in the camp: tins, sacks, cardboard, packing cases, blankets. Uniforms could be converted into a variety of attire. Several men found they were adept at playing female parts. among them Herbert Schmitt who says, 'Never once was I the subject of innuendos or smutty talk'. The stage fever at Featherstone Park was far more under control than at Colchester, an other ranks camp, where there was even a bit of transvestism. But Colchester was also more adventurous in its repertoire, putting on *The Captain of Koepenick* as early as the autumn of 1945. The great satire on the absurdity and cruelty of Prussian bureaucracy and militarism was apparently considered for Featherstone Park, but not played because of the problem of the women's parts—or was the will somewhat lacking in that very conservative setting?

The steady change of heart at Camp 18 was remarkable and there was no looking back. In 1945 the main feeling had been one of despair stiffened with defiance. In the second year the average prisoner had regained self-respect and was looking at the world around him; by the third there was a positive sense of the future. In the latter part of 1946 Pastor Forell made one of his always welcome visits and during a talk he gave he was asked. 'Herr Pastor, what is going to happen to those of us who have lost our homes in the East? What can we go back to?' Forell answered by asking another question. 'Which of you know of any *Munas* in the west— that might be one answer.' *Munas* were the huge ammunition depots of the Wehrmacht usually located in remote forest areas.

One of the officers spoke up. 'There's one in the Minden-Bielefeld area. As far as I know it was never bombed. It's not only on the railway but is directly on the Mittelland Canal. A huge place. Scores of good solid buildings.'

'What is it called?'

'Espelkamp.'

This name was to be uppermost in Forell's mind for the rest of his life: as a vision, a hard-fought enterprise and a new town. The British never knew about Espelkamp till they got there, so cleverly had the munition dump been camouflaged from the air and kept secret. In December of that same year Forell was able to inspect the site. He found one lonely guard living there with his dog in an area of four square kilometres with 160 buildings, mostly substantial ones, with fifteen miles of good roads. Over the main road was a camp overcrowded with refugees who could not live in the *Muna* which was doomed. The previous summer its complete contents, including poison-gas shells which fortunately had never been called for, had been dumped in the sea. This was prior to the intended blowing-up of the place in keeping with agreed Four Power policy that in disarming Germany all such installations should be destroyed. Indeed Espelkamp would have been blown up in 1947 if the military governor, the admirable General Bishop,* had not used delaying tactics.[55] He had already listened to various schemes for its development, but it was Forell's that he gave his backing to, basically the same one as had been born at Featherstone Park. For it was Forell's observations of the achievements, with the minimum of resources, of German POWs in Britain that first convinced him of the tremendous power of recovery latent in the German people—a power that was not yet evident in Germany itself in those first years of Allied occupation.

The inner stirring at Camp 18 was first evident as elsewhere in the thronged religious services of 1945. But they were not conducted by any of the fifteen pastors who were officers; these were banned from acting as priests until screened. Two chaplains came over from the other ranks' compound to do so.† Some eight of the pastors published a message deploring and expressing contrition for the horrors of the *KZ*; it did not go down well. At first the services were thronged, but then as everywhere declined. Dieter Hankel was probably typical in regarding them less as a religious experience than as a way of feeling closer to the *Heimat*. Only Forell, whenever he came, and Hans Lilje, soon to be Bishop of Hanover, seem to have been able, in the Quaker phrase, to 'speak to the condition of' the prisoners.

Almost all the officer pastors were posted away to other camps or to refresher training. Cranfield, making his survey for the British Council of Churches, found the naval chaplain in charge inadequate to his responsibility and rather weak. When Pastor Niemoeller came to speak on the theme of Christian responsibility and war guilt he was actually booed, in spite (or perhaps because) of his fame as First World War U-boat ace and subsequent opponent of Hitler. When in the following year Pastor Werner Jentsch, successor to Forell in his YMCA post, visited the camp, he had to wait three days to gather a group of officers together to speak to them—and this although as a Luftwaffe chaplain he had visited General Heim in the Moabit prison. He considered in fact that keen young Christian laymen in the YMCA were in a better

---

* Espelkamp, today a town of 26,000 inhabitants, has a *General Bishop Strasse*, as well as its *Birger Forell Realschule*.
† Hardly any Catholic chaplains were officers, but the great majority of Protestant ones were. Larger numbers of Protestant pastors as well as RC priests when called up served in medical units as 'protected personnel'.

position to spread the Gospel than any of the pastors. There was one such group which Jentsch linked up to a home branch in Erlangen. As usual the local YMCA offered much undiscriminating hospitality.

If Featherstone Park was weaker on the religious side than many camps, this was made up for by the wealth of political and cultural stimulation and also by the great variation in persons and in beliefs. At one extreme was Leutnant Fritz Broger whom Sulzbach noted down as *son of the working class poet, Karl Broger, the most intelligent anti-Nazi in the camp, modest, refuses to speak to SS as his father was in Dachau.* At the other extreme were some of those very SS who under Sulzbach's influence were themselves going through a deep crisis.* General Heim had to repeat several times his lecture on 'How Stalingrad Happened—a Glimpse behind the Scenes' in which he exposed a callous indifference to human life and a streak of madness in Hitler. The up-and-coming Student of Christ Church, Hugh Trevor-Roper, made a three-day visit in which he spoke on 'The End of an Ideology'. Afterwards his audience ordered four hundred copies of his book *The Last Days of Hitler.* Dr Fritz Borinski came up to give a series of lectures on adult education, religious socialism, the Youth Movement and 'The Crisis in Democracy', each session being packed out. This sincere and clear-minded refugee never preached or talked down to audiences; he threw out to them responsibility not only for implementing the ideal they believed in but also preserving its integrity. This was a particularly good line with former Nazis who had followed Hitler uncritically, believing that he had a programme of genuine social reform and who now felt betrayed.[56] Another catalyst of change, but a bitter one, was the regular bulletins on the Nuremberg Trials, for many of the older generation in particular were angered and affronted by the verdicts. Colonel Borcherdt remembered how the announcements were made on the radio: 'Death by hanging', followed by the announcement 'Here is some light music'. 'It's true what they say,' he added, 'It's here in England we have become National Socialists.' There were probably not a few Borcherdts at Featherstone Park, and many protecting themselves from too much exposure to the past. The volunteers for outside work were often transported in five-hundredweight covered trucks open at the rear. The exhaust fumes curled up into the nostrils of those at the back, so the trucks

* See below Chapter 13.

got the name *Gaskammer* (gas-chambers). Was this obscenity a sign of closed minds, or just normal black humour ?* At this stage even the open-minded resisted taking in the horrendous facts of the 'Final Solution'. The lawyer, Kurt Schwedersky, obtained a book in Russian by Wajni Grossmann called *The Hell of Treblinka*. 'I thought: how can anyone have invented such fiendish fantasy? Many years later, as a judge investigating war crimes, I was given a whole file on the Treblinka Commandant. It was all absolutely true, but in 1947 I had been too shocked to believe it.'

Those with light spirits were a boon to the whole camp. There was a group of young Roman Catholics who used to go to Mass in Haltwhistle where Father Cunningham had his church and priest's house. Never did he have so many willing and grown-up altar boys, so many repairers to his house, so many gardeners. One officer, Norbert Pohl, who later became a pastor, volunteered to repair his organ. When it was dismantled he could not put it together again. 'But,' writes Pohl's friend, Theo Palka, 'Father Cunningham was an understanding priest. Not for nothing had he christened his dog 'Whisky'. But it was terrible for us as whenever he called him our mouths used to water. When we could not put the organ together we made him a peace offering: we would paper his bathroom for him, which he accepted. But he was not without other problems. One day he had to speak sternly to one of his altar boys. For he had observed how one afternoon a parishioner, Old Mary, was walking round the churchyard hitting her chest with a brick. "What are you doing that for?" the priest asked her. "Oh, father, but that was the penance you gave me when I went into the confession box this morning." ' He had no doubt where the culprit came from.

Colonel Vickers' *obiter dicta* delighted the camp. Oesten was in his office when a local lady rang to protest against a certain habit of the POWs. Apparently it frequently happened that the out-work volunteers had watery porridge before they made a rush to catch their truck, or bus. When it stopped, they relieved themselves on the side of the road, whoever was about. Vickers ex-

---

* An example of 'black' folk humour at the other extreme could be found recently (1975) at the Kibbutz Nir-am Askelow near Gaza. Here there was a large-scale Israeli poultry enterprise. The chickens which died in the course of nature were disposed of in an incinerator over which was written the word 'Ausschwitz'.

plained to Oesten the lady's shocked reaction with his hand on the mouthpiece. Taking it off, he addressed her: 'I am very sorry Madam; I cannot do anything about it. It is an old German custom!'

The landscape of the South Tyne, The Roman Wall to the North which bisected the permitted walking area, the crinkled, grey waters of the river itself flowing rapidly by the camp, the flat, narrow valley studded with oaks, the castellated manor house on the edge of the perimeter—all these left an indelible impression. Anticipating a romantic nostalgia for the place where so many spent a not insignificant and not wasted portion of their lives, Norbert Pohl wrote, lightly but with feeling, his *Last Tyne-Time Ode*, which might be translated thus:

> This is the Lord's Day
> and it could be too,
> but I am miles away
> O Tyne, from you.
> Then leave these banks
> to silence every night
> and the misty pale moonlight;
> let the serried ranks
> of Nissen huts
> fill up with constant rain like water butts;
> let your daughters do without
> the attentions of moping
> prisoners who lounge about
> you hoping.
> Then, O Tyne,
> there'll be a time
> when you'll receive my boundless thanks
> and love for one so fair—
> from over there!
> The further that we part
> the more you'll have my heart,
> and sweeter far the song
> of rushing waters no one looks upon
> when we are gone,
> O Tyne,
> life-long memory of mine.

By the autumn of 1946 Colonel Vickers had gone. He had been

chosen for the toughest of commandants' jobs at Sandbostel near
Bremen, which was crowded with disaffected internees and SS-
officers. He was succeeded by Lieutenant-Colonel Herbert
MacBain of the Durham Light Infantry, another capable and good-
hearted officer who came up from a large working camp at Ripon.
He continued the policy of trust with a slightly different emphasis;
to him Featherstone Park was to be 'a Christian democratic village'. He called himself 'Colonel Hope' and established extremely
warm personal relations with Heim. After breaking into the local
and then national press at the time of the Harvest Festival at
Hexham Abbey, it was quite often in the news. A local correspondent of the *Manchester Guardian* wrote in May 1947: 'I would
never have believed that prisoners could create such a happy and
vital community; everyone seemed to be looking forward to the
future to the prospect of a new life in Germany, not backwards to
past injustices and failures.'[57]

MacBain later on used to say that his year at Featherstone Park
was the most useful of his life. He liked taking tea with his fellow
colonels on the German side—there were some 150 of them, many
of whom lived in a separate hostel in the nearby village of
Penmiller. One of them recalls him expressing the popular view
that it was the Russians who were the enemy, and also that he did
not hold with the segregation of men into categories. When the
'repatriarchs', as they were called, left for home from Haltwhistle
Station he was there to shake those he knew by the hand. These
last observations, however, may refer to his successor for the last
nine months, Lieutenant-Colonel 'Bottles' Bartlett, a mellow man
of whom Sulzbach, glad that he left the running of the camp to
Heim and himself, said in fun that he did at least know that his
prisoners were not Italian now!

The working relation between these two grew into friendship.
They were of the same age and could reminisce together about the
First World War and their childhood before it. Sulzbach, con-
templating his chance of a life-time, could scarcely connect the
spoilt, ambitionless son of Emil Sulzbach with the British captain
in happy partnership with a German general. But surely the chief
reason for his great sense of purpose and energy at Featherstone
Park was the fact that his life had come full circle. What might be
called the Sulzbach effect—Schwederski invented the affectionate
word *Sulzbachheit*—had its roots in an unclouded childhood, in his
patriotic pride as an artillery officer in Flanders and in the optimis-

tic *Kultur* world of Frankfurt at the time when he was growing up. Moreover, there was a certain childlike quality that he had retained all his life, a quality that in relationships can—in the words of the historian, Herbert Butterfield—'dissolve the crust over human nature, soften the thick hide and open up the gateway to more hopeful things'.[58] This is exactly what Sulzbach was not seldom able to achieve, with SS men too. When first faced with fanatical Nazis in the mass he lost his faith for a while. When he discovered that the basic German decencies and virtues (and sentimentality) had survived, great was his joy. He could give out, in addition, what he had learned from England and his belief in a united Europe. But what he chiefly communicated was his own revived faith in his country. There was nothing a German wished to hear more than that in those years of defeat and shame. Since his message came from the rejected Jew it was all the more compelling. When asked for his own explanation of the effect he had, he gives one so simple that few believe it, or else mistake his attitude for modesty. He says again and again to and of former prisoners at Featherstone Park: '*You* showed me the way back'. Some years after the war he wrote to Waffen-SS Captain Herbert Christiansen, 'I do remember our conversations and perhaps I am as grateful to you as you are to me. We both achieved something together, perhaps.' Sulzbach is not unlike an actor who follows the gracious custom of applauding back at his audience at the end of a performance: it has been a shared experience, and each has given something and is absolutely necessary to the other. For his own fulfilment Sulzbach needed the officers of Camp 18 as much as they needed him.

Comparison of Featherstone Park with Camp 186 at Llanmartin, the other big concentration of officers, is instructive. The type of prisoner was hardly different but by all accounts the latter was as stiff and earnest as the former was relaxed and happy. Llanmartin, situated near Newport in South Wales, was converted from an other ranks' camp in August 1946, taking over officers from Crewe Hall and Llanover Hall near Abergavenny when these two camps closed, and from Lodge Moor. There were very few 'whites' and many 'Americans' and 'Canadians'. The intake from Crewe Hall included Lord Napier's able and urbane interpreter, Dr Kurt Blohm, and the lawyer and intelligence officer who became a baker, Dr Günther Geisseler. In the nearly two years of its

8

existence Llanmartin developed its own community spirit. It had a very active English teaching staff and press group under Blohm who edited an excellent and unique magazine in English called *The Onlooker*. Llanmartin also had the best of the camp libraries as well as a broken-down book-bindery which was made to operate efficiently with the aid of such *ersatz* materials as the scrapings of the porridge pots for sizing.* There was a talented theatre group which produced lively reviews, a controversial play of its own called *The Patriot* and like Featherstone Park an excellent *Troilus and Cressida* in which the Greeks' breast-plates were made up from milk-bottle tops. There were many concerts, music cum poetry evenings, besides the usual vocational and educational courses and visits to local institutions.

Yet Llanmartin stands out awkwardly in Bush House reports, especially in the last one in March 1948. The training advisers had been asked to estimate attitudes in different camps under six headings: hatred, dislike, mistrust, suspended judgments and liking. (This was long after the 'whites' had gone home and only five months before every prisoner had been repatriated.) The assessment for Llanmartin was 100 per cent mistrust towards the British authorities. The chief cause was the Commandant, Colonel D, a martinet respected by no one. Various rumours circulated about his past. Kurt Schwederski, an amiable man, felt he had many complexes and resentments. His management of the camp made the work of his officers hard, though Captain Carnie and Captain Peter Walker were liked—the former being given the nick-name of 'Zenzi', a Bavarian girl's name, because he wore a kilt. Sulzbach could not have worked under such a man and instead of a General Heim there was a nondescript camp spokesman.

Relationships with the local Welsh, however, left nothing to be desired. 'I never met' says Geisseler, 'with anything but great friendliness when, for instance, I went to a religious service, often movingly so. It was much more the ordinary people, those not well off, who were most able to open their feelings to us. But everything that came from Bush House or smelt of re-education

* The library was made up of an original consignment from the P/W Division, the libraries from Lodge Moor and Llanover Park (which also sent the bindery), purchases by officers and volumes sent by repatriates and also gifts from Switzerland and Sweden. 2,500 volumes were light literature. The whole thing seems to have been run in a most professional manner by Siegfried Bandelow.

was suspect.* Refugee lecturers were disparaged for not being true Germans or patronised for 'overcoming a resistance in themselves for associating with us at all and carrying through something they believed in. Our honour as Germans and the attempts to convince us of the superiority of the British way of life could not succeed with the primitive means used.' Certainly few men at Llanmartin would have been impressed by the visit in July 1947 of the last 'Director of Re-education', a central European intellectual and a weak man who tried to be on the prisoners' side. He was no match, as Faulk would have been, for A. Weber, the former member of Goebbels' Propaganda Ministry who following that visit composed a special number of *Die Aussprache* on 'Re-education', which was regarded as a totally wrong-headed attempt to cure the prisoners of an illness which they did not suffer from. (They could only conceive it as a kind of political schooling practised by the Nazis.) They had themselves, wrote Weber complacently, been through a hard school of suffering through loss of home, family and property, and had no use for empty theories such as, for example, the well-meaning Swiss lecturers provided.* Even Stalin was quoted to prove that Germany was not responsible for the war which arose 'as the inevitable result of the world economic and political forces on the basis of monopoly capitalism.' Nazi apologists often used such arguments at this time.

The Llanmartin officers did, in fact, find a way back of their own from the Nazi disaster. It came unforeseen through the back door, owed nothing to the British and could even, another writer in *Die Aussprache* admitted, be called a kind of re-education. It was the discovery, through their cultural studies and performances, including a whole *Kultur* week in September 1947, that the German contribution to European civilisation was great, essential and something to be proud of. Germans basically were, or could be, *good Europeans*. Thus, the versatile Dr Blohm in *The Onlooker* wrote an article on the Anglo-Saxon myth of Beowulf, side by side with one on 'The United States of Europe' which proposed a federal solution to the ills of the continent. But even as they took up this theme of 'Europe' which would be a *leitmotiv* of the new Germany, the Llanmartin officers baulked at the urgent political issue: how to create an alternative to the authoritarian

* In 1947 the Swiss government offered to send up to 200 lecturers to help in the re-education programme. The arrangements were made by Hitch but they came too late to be really effective. (Faulk to the author.)

state. British policy was to encourage them to do so, but this made them suspicious of the official British to a man. The Featherstone Park spirit was quite different. In that Camp of Confidence, an atmosphere of trust and co-operation having been created, the cultural and the democratic solutions went ahead side by side, reinforcing each other.

PART TWO

Cosi disse il mio duca, ed io con lui
velgemmo i nostri passi ad una scala
e tosto ch'io al primo grado fui,

senti' mi presso quasi un mover d'ala
e ventarmi nel viso, e dir: *'Beati
pacifici*, che son senza ira mala.'

Thus spoke my Guide, and I with him did turn our footsteps
to a stairway, and, as soon as I was on the first step,
near me I felt as 'twere the stroke of a wing, and my
face fanned, and heard one say: *'Beati pacifici*, who are
without evil wrath.'

Il Purgatorio, Canto XVII

Towards the end of 1916 Hardy was enabled to visit the camp of
German prisoners of war near Dorchester. 'He came home,' says
Mrs Hardy, 'very moved by the experience, and glad that he had
gone, although he went most unwillingly.' Quickly making contact with the captives, treating them as individuals, he continued
to show them practical kindness which, the same authority tells
us, resulted in similar kindness being shown to British prisoners
in a similar camp in Germany.

from *Thomas Hardy* by Edmund Blunden

Sometimes I feel as tired after a day's brain work as I felt after my
usual day work before, but it gives me a lot more satisfaction and
happiness. We get new outlooks, state our view, but we don't get
it presented like a meal, only to listen and say 'that's the new
belief—democracy'. No, no, we have to work hard and turn it
over in our minds and become bearers of that ideal that will lead
the life between nations to a happier future, and to have more
understanding for each other, to be more tolerant when we should
be more tolerant and to have a firm attitude against ideas that have
proved the greatest disaster, especially for our own country.

Letter written in English to Norman and Evelyn Cox
from Wilton Park, 9 July 1947, by Paul B.

10

The Twilight of the Generals I

The German officer corps believed in trying to maintain dignity till the end. They hoped that the time-honoured usages of war would allow them to surrender in honourable manner. If the old protocol of handing over a sword could not be followed, at least a certain chivalry might be observed. It was often far different, especially towards the end. Hans Bender has written a telling story of the last days in East Prussia.[59] A German general with his army disintegrating around him orders his batman to get out his best uniform and all his medals. Absurdly he sits in his dug-out waiting with his adjutant for the Russians to arrive. They do so in the form of a Red Army major and another officer who reel heavily down the steps. The major hardly notices the general. All he is interested in is the bottle of Schnapps on the table and the elegant cut glass to drink it out of. With contempt he points out how miserably small the glasses are.

But, to begin with, the courtesies were observed. The first German general to be captured was Major General Hans Friemel on 10 May 1940 in Holland. Three air landings were made at dawn that day on airfields near The Hague, it being hoped to seize Queen Wilhelmina in her country residence to prevent her fleeing with her family to Britain. But she had already moved to safety. The operation failed in two of the zones and Friemel was captured. It was not for another eighteen months that he had a companion of his own rank who turned out to be the remarkable Hans von Ravenstein, Commander of the 21st Panzer Division. His capture at Sidi Rezegh on 29 November 1941 and rescue from the sea a week later have already been described.* Fitted out temporarily with a British general's uniform, he was taken to the Abbassia Barracks on the edge of Cairo where he was held under guard. There was something about this Silesian aristocrat, who had been page to Kaiser Wilhelm II during the visit of Edward VII to

* See above page 114.

Berlin in 1909, that commanded attention, though many did not see beneath his snobbish-seeming air. At Christmas he received presents from English officers and a book inscribed 'From an enemy with respect'. He was visited by the Papal Legate to Egypt and Palestine and escorted to GHQ to meet General Auchinleck who shook him warmly by the hand and said, 'You and your division have fought with chivalry'. But from 3 January onwards Ravenstein's circumstances changed. On that day he was taken by two friendly officers sight-seeing to the Pyramids; when he returned he found he had another Afrika Korps Major-General as a companion. This was Artur Schmitt who had headed the German administrative staff in the fortress of Bardia, held mainly by Italians and overrun in the 'Crusader' Offensive. They immediately exchanged news—into concealed microphones which had almost certainly been installed during the trip to the Pyramids. Afterwards they were more cautious but, in any case, they had little to say to each other. Schmitt, a Bavarian who had joined the Reichswehr from the Police, was a dyed-in-the-wool Nazi. Six years later instead of being released he would be sent to the Civilian Internment Centre at Neuengamme as a security suspect.[60] The day after his arrival at Abbassia Ravenstein noted in his diary: 'General Schmitt is registering strong objections to our treatment.' The following day he himself had a bad attack of migraine. The tension between them continued, though on 6 March he was still trying to appreciate the 'decent, soldierly, unflinching traits' of Schmitt's character. 'The greatest wisdom in life,' he added, 'lies in being able to cope with the most diverse personalities and circumstances, just as others have to put up with me.' Ravenstein did *not* tell Schmitt that when he heard that his opponent at Sidi Rezegh, General Jock Campbell, had won the VC, he wrote him a personal letter of congratulation.

In March the two generals, along with over a thousand German prisoners from the Middle East, were transported in the liner *Pasteur* to South Africa. During the voyage a plot was hatched to seize the ship and sail it to Singapore which had recently fallen, Ravenstein as the senior officer giving his approval. When the well-planned operation was nipped in the bud, he took personal responsibility and went through some anxious moments when reprisals were considered, and then dropped. After spending most of April in Pietermaritzburg the two generals were shipped via New York to Canada in the *Queen Elizabeth*. Here at Bowmanville they came together with General Friemel, the three of them remaining here and in other Canadian camps till 1946.

In November during the Battle of Alamein a still more important general fell into British hands when his tank was disabled during a reconnaissance. This was Ritter von Thoma, acting commander of the Afrika Korps, whom General Montgomery at once invited to dine in his mess. They went over the moves of battle in an amicable manner and next morning, on taking leave of his host, von Thoma made a little speech of thanks: he had not believed such chivalrous treatment was possible and he would let his friends in Germany know of it. He ended by asking his vanquisher to visit him on his estate after the war.[61] Sections of the British press took a poor view of such fraternisation, but Churchill, who had visited the Commander of the 8th Army at his desert HQ two months before, brushed the objections aside. 'Poor von Thoma!' he quipped in the House of Commons, 'I too have dined with Montgomery.'

Six months later a quarter of a million Germans and Italians capitulated in roughly equal numbers at Tunis. It has been put about that General Alexander gave a dinner to the German general staff, while ordinary soldiers were put on a charge for fraternisation. This is not true. Alexander did entertain Field Marshal von Arnim in his tent, but comments in his memoirs that he failed to extend any compliments on the way the Germans had fought, and indeed regretted that he had not been more chivalrous towards him. The Allied Commander-in-Chief, General Eisenhower, refused even to meet von Arnim or to receive his sword in surrender —an earnest of American attitudes later in Europe. The time-honoured European usages of war were not to be followed with soldiers of an evil regime.

Among the Italians who surrendered at Tunis was Marshal Messe with seventeen generals and two admirals. It was decided to give them special treatment. Colonel Grondona, Commandant at Wilton Park, was ordered to make two floors of his officers' mess in the White House at Wilton Park available for them as high security quarters. Having the right connections, he quickly obtained from Windsor Castle the searchlight equipment last used at the coronation of George VI. He was instructed by the War Office not to shake hands with Messe, and to expect a film-camera team. But when the small, affable Marshal advanced towards him with hand outstretched, Grondona, an Australian of

8

great courtesy, could not refuse it, nor the warm hand-clasp of
each member of his staff. (This was, of course, cut from the news-
reel pictures.) Later, while hammering was still going on above,
he escorted Messe up the broad marble staircase to the well-
appointed bedroom just vacated by himself. The Italian expostu-
lated when he saw three sappers cheerfully fixing stout barbed
wire frames to the bay windows overlooking what had been the
finest private croquet lawn in England. His ADC and interpreter
tried to keep up with his voluble protests. 'The Marshal has not
the intention of trying to escape—it would be absurd! And is not
England an island?' Grondona asked him if he would give his
parole d'honneur. No, his King's Regulations forbade it. An informal *modus vivendi* was amicably found, all the special security
measures were dispensed with and Messe, his staff and the two
admirals settled down for the next six months to a rather pleasant
existence. They could play croquet or tennis with two ball-boy
Italian POWs always provided. Messe had arrived not only with
cigars and liqueur in his baggage, but with £1,000 in £5 Bank of
England notes, his staff with rather less each. It was allowed back
to them in a weekly allowance. Grondona gave his own staff, who
still used the ground floor of the White House, special instructions
on their behaviour. All conversations on the lawn and the terrace
were to be carried on in a low tone. The first reason was security,
the second 'courteous consideration for people who are at a
disadvantage . . . undertones evidencing obvious caution should
be avoided'.[62] When Mussolini was overthrown in July the
Italians were all delighted, and sent home by the end of the year
in order to co-operate with the Allies.

Meanwhile, the German generals from North Africa were
twenty-five miles away at Cockfosters, leading a more constrained
but not disagreeable life. They were given occasional outings to
London to keep them sweet. Von Thoma was the most keen to
get back to normal life, and spent a large portion of his POW pay
collecting art-books.[63] No attempt was made to get non-Nazi
generals to broadcast on the BBC or to use them politically, as the
Russians did. But von Thoma in the final winter was co-operative
enough to try to persuade the German command in the Channel
Isles to surrender. The idea was that he would speak personally
through a loud hailer from a boat near the shore. But the conditions were rough, von Thoma became very seasick and the plan
was abandoned.[64] Meanwhile, unknown to himself, this likeable

and talkative Bavarian had, with von Crüwell and others, been of considerable value to the British. He would greet each new arrival warmly, ask for the latest news about old friends and discuss their performance. What the senior officers at Cockfosters did not know, or preferred not to know, was that their rooms were bugged. 'Mother' was always listening. From scraps of conversation whole dossiers could be built up on generals and their ways in all theatres of war. It was a question of von Thoma to a newcomer in 1944 that put the British intelligence back on the lost trail of the German rocket weapons.[65]

An edited transcription of the bugging from Cockfosters was like a fascinating daily gossip column for the interrogation staffs there and at Wilton Park and Latimer. The arrival of the kidnapped General Kreipe provided his colleagues with a theme for banter. Seized near his villa at Heraklion and bundled for twenty-two days across the Cretan mountains, this pastor's son with a frosty smile, as his abductor Patrick Leigh-Fermor saw him, did not entirely enjoy the teasing of his peers, from which he was saved by being sent off to Canada. During the Normandy campaign, the club of Wehrmacht generals steadily enlarged and, with it, the work of the listening ears. In the endless churning over of possible reasons of the defeat, one of the new arrivals threw out the remark: 'The years of occupation made us soft. If you ask me, it was the big double beds of France that did for us.'[66]

Victors like to have scenes of surrender recorded for posterity. The Prussians took care to have war artists with them in France in 1870 and the episode when Bismarck rides to meet the humiliated Napoleon III at Sedan is captured in a memorable painting. The September mist, the gleaming black charger of the Iron Chancellor, the stationary coach of the Emperor and the disconsolate group of Frenchmen encapsulate one of the breaking points of history. So does the picture of the glum Germans signing the 1918 armistice in Maréchal Foch's railway-carriage in the Forest of Compiègne; and, only twenty-two years later the same railway carriage in the same place with Hitler caught by a film man gleefully enjoying his reverse triumph.*

The scene photographed inside the HQ caravan of General Mark Clark at Florence on 4 May 1945 has a very different quality.

* The manic quality of Hitler's strut, as seen in some historical documentaries, was achieved by tampering with the original frames.

With the Stars and Stripes behind him the American Commander-in-Chief, spruce in full dress uniform, is handing a folded document, the instrument of surrender, to a German whose face is barely seen and who is wearing an old belted combat jacket.[67] (The general's cocker spaniel, we are told, has just nipped at the stranger's trousers.) As their eyes meet, the American's searching gaze seems to be telling him that this gaunt, haggard figure, speaking cultured English, is not the kind of man he expected. He was, indeed, a most unlikely soldier of Hitler: General Fridolin von Senger und Etterlin, one-time Rhodes Scholar and member of St John's College, Oxford. A staunch Catholic and former cavalry officer, von Senger had been full of moral scruples about serving a repugnant regime. He had commanded a Division that tried to relieve Stalingrad, but when ten months later he defended Cassino with brilliant tenacity he regarded it as a personal tragedy because it 'would reduce the Allies' chances of asserting themselves at least as much as the Russians'. At the evacuation of Corsica he had thrown into the waste-paper basket an order from Himmler that all hostages were to be shot. As Commander of Bologna he had forbidden the installation of brothels (they encouraged indiscipline and were mainly of use only to supply troops), and reopened the opera, to which hundreds of troops were sent each night from their billets. On the subject of love of country and evil in the Third Reich, he liked to recall the saying of an old Jewish friend that it is 'a higher form of patriotism to feel ashamed of one's people if there is cause to do so'. The deep dilemma of his situation he resolved by submitting it to daily prayer, and by being as honourable a member of his profession as he could.

When SS-General Karl Wolf had deceived Hitler in negotiating a separate surrender for the German armies in North Italy, it was this man he sent to arrange the practical details. Von Senger was no stranger to the role, for in June 1940 he had been bearer of the armistice terms to the French when they surrendered. Now, after a hazardous journey along Lake Garda during which American soldiers protected him from Italian partisans, he arrived at Verona. Here at the Hotel Colomba d'Oro he was met by the liaison officer, Major John Profumo, and sent on by air to Florence. He was very aware what the Allied officers must feel towards him. 'I had to respect them as opponents,' he writes in his memoirs, 'whereas they could see in me only a representative of the Hitler regime. How could they know that this scene evoked in me little of the bitterness that they themselves felt? For me it marked the end of twelve years of spiritual servitude as well as a very personal turning-point in life, whatever my eventual fate might be. . . . The long, narrow face of the Allied C-in-C [General Mark Clark] with the wide open intelligent eyes of the soldier made a very sympathetic impression on me. This impression was strengthened in the course of the afternoon when, in a long discussion alone with him, I spoke about the technical difficulties of the surrender.'

Among the commanders on both sides in the Second World War there were few more noble spirits than Fridolin von Senger und Etterlin, who faced the vicissitudes of life under the ancient motto *Nec metus nec spes*—Neither fear nor hope.

The capitulations in Northern Europe were delayed by the German hope, after Hitler's suicide, that, given time, more troops could move westward and be saved from surrendering to the Russians, and more refugees come across the zonal demarcation line. Montgomery stage-managed the first approach at his tactical HQ on the Lüneburg Heath with characteristic showmanship. When Admiral Friedenburg and his negotiating team arrived, he kept them waiting under the Union Jack beside his caravan and then emerged demanding 'Who are these men? What do they want?' The stolid and grim mood of the Germans was only broken during their solitary lunch when Friedenburg wept and his staff kept silent. Afterwards Montgomery, while showing a certain flexibility about accepting surrenders from the East, threatened to reopen the offensive if the surrender was not made at once. Next day, Friedenburg returned with the authorisation of the new Führer, Admiral Doenitz, to sign. Montgomery laid on 'a trestle table covered with an army blanket, an ink-pot and an ordinary pen you could buy in a shop for tuppence. The Germans were clearly nervous and one of them took out a cigarette. I looked at him and he put it away.' A similar scene, at once grander and still more tense, took place three days later on 7 May at the HQ of General Eisenhower at Rheims. Friedenburg was this time joined by Field Marshals Keitel and Jodl. After Jodl had signed the final instrument of surrender on all remaining fronts, he asked to speak. 'The German people' he said, 'and the German armed forces are, for better or worse, delivered into the victors' hands; both have achieved and suffered more, perhaps, than any other people in the world. In this hour I can only hope that the victor will treat them with generosity.' These complacent words were spoken into a stony silence. Three days later, a similar act of surrender took place in Berlin, when Keitel afterwards accepted the Russians' invitation to be present at a celebration banquet at Karlshorst with caviar and champagne. Albert Speer in his memoirs comments on his 'lack of feeling and dignity': he should have just satisfied his hunger, but refused the wine.

None of the three empowered to sign these final documents lived for long. Jodl and Keitel were executed as major war criminals after the first Nuremberg trial. The emotional and broken Admiral Friedenburg committed suicide on 22 May just as the entire High Command and the Doenitz Government were being taken into captivity. He was thus spared the scenes at Flensburg which Churchill himself regretted: the harassing arrest by troops highly respected in Germany—the 7th Armoured Division—of men with whom till then the British and Americans had been treating, with rigorous searching and confiscation of valuables. Even the pockets of Friedenburg's corpse were plundered, for which an apology was made. The chief reason for the harsh body searching was fear of suicides. It was known that leading Nazis all carried cyanide tablets on the person, of the kind that Himmler was to use when discovered next day. Albert Speer, though disgusted by it, understood the reason; and also a possible reason for another scene that Churchill deplored, the making of the whole Doenitz Government stand in a long row for a considerable time with their hands raised: it was for the news-reel cameras. The whole operation may also have been designed to show the Russians, who were thought to be setting up a puppet government in East Germany, that the Western Allies had no intention of doing this themselves. The main party was then flown to Luxembourg. Their reception there by a double cordon of American soldiers with tommy-guns at the ready reminded Speer of the end of a gangster film with a round-up of the criminals. Six days later the Wehrmacht's master of defensive fighting in the East, Colonel-General Gotthard Heinrici, was picked up in the home of the Burgomaster of Horup. He had been away in Flensburg when some men of the Monmouthshires came to fetch him. Returning, he found that his clothes, valuables and a wallet containing 4,000 useless Reichsmarks, recently and hopefully cashed in Berlin, had been stolen. He was given five minutes to get ready.

Two years later this very correct East Prussian was still writing affidavits hoping to get satisfaction for his loss from honourable opponents. The old German officer caste did not want to know how much times had changed.[68]

It was about this time that Paymaster Karl Hildebrand, a peaceable chartered accountant in uniform, looked across the barbed wire at Jabbecke POW camp into the next compound. He saw a line of some thirty of his generals, including Field Marshal von Busch, in their under-pants, each carrying a towel. A British sergeant was leading them to the bath-house. The good *Zahlmeister* could not help feeling a certain sardonic satisfaction at the pay-off: it was *their* total war, they had lost it and now they had totally lost face. Jabbecke was probably the scene of General Heinrici's private story[69] about generals being deliberately humiliated by being made to eat like animals out of their mess-tins. For it was in this camp that the order went out that no one was to possess knives and forks, as they were potentially aggressive weapons. Hildebrand points out that old soldiers would get round this, but that generals used to bellowing orders at the officers' mess would not have any cutlery stowed away and might have had to make do with tins till issued with a set. It was probably all due to a muddle and a strong inclination to see insult where none was intended.

During May, 127 of the officers of general's rank who surrendered in the West were routed through to Britain, 105 from the Wehrmacht, 13 from the Luftwaffe and 9 admirals. The most important of these found themselves at Wilton Park. Colonel Grondona completed the security measures in the White House, not used for the Italians. When the taciturn sixty-nine-year-old Field Marshal von Rundstedt was shown to the best bedroom, he appeared not to notice the barbed wire at the bay windows. The searchlights were turned on at night and an extra acre had been enclosed with double barbed wire and two sentry-towers with machine-guns. If the Germans found these precautions absurdly excessive, they made no protest and walked stiffly round their cage for an hour each morning and afternoon. When Professor R. V. Jones, master at 'the most secret war', came to conduct some technical post mortems and asked for a certain general to interrogate, he was reminded of going up to a trout tank in a restaurant and saying, 'I'll have this one.'![70]

Most of the generals were living on a gridiron of bitter, rankling thoughts as they mulled over the causes of the disaster to their country and their profession. The great General Staff, born in Prussia two hundred years before, and a power in Europe almost ever since, had been progressively ignored, purged and humiliated by Hitler and was no more. Von Rundstedt, tense, angry, but with the outward manners of a *grand seigneur*, was the epitome of all that had been overthrown. But the public and the private von Rundstedt were different. When the Führer, at the height of his triumph at the fall of France, had in a Napoleonic mood created nine Field Marshals in a single day, he had given each a large sum of money so that they could live more grandly. Rundstedt put his in the bank, never touched it, and referred to it in his family as his *Saugeld* (dirt-money).[71] He had held himself together with his sense of duty, his Lutheran faith and his professionalism—and increasingly with alcohol. During the last year he would give his crisp, masterly orders at the beginning of the day and then lapse into steady drinking.

Von Rundstedt's relationship with Hitler, the bane of his existence, was unique. He could look back on scores of meetings, he alone in deference to his age and prestige being allowed a chair in the Führer's presence. To the Wehrmacht he was *der General*, utterly dependable and master of his craft. Four times he had tried to resign, either because Hitler had dishonoured his colleagues or ignored his advice. Twice Hitler had accepted his resignation—at the invasion of Austria in 1938 and during the purge of 1942—but he had banked on his intuition that the Field Marshal would never bring himself to break an oath of loyalty and could always be manipulated through his patriotism and professional pride. Rundstedt had sat on the fence. He had been, it is true, privy to a plot to kill Hitler in 1942,[72] but two years later was still there after the 20th July, untarnished by any evidence of intrigue or resistance: he would be the very man, Hitler saw, to preside over the Court of Honour by which the army would purge itself of its treacherous elements. So Rundstedt had begun the final phase of his military career by delivering some of the bravest men of the Wehrmacht to the torturers and hangmen of the Gestapo. (This was done on the basis of extracts from Gestapo files without even producing the officers or giving them an opportunity to defend themselves.) Rundstedt saw the Nazi salute replace the military salute throughout the armed forces. Still mesmerised by the authority of his hated leader and convincing himself it was his patriotic duty, he gave his name to and took command of the last forlorn offensive in the Ardennes, during which all officers visiting Hitler had not only to be disarmed and thoroughly searched but to walk down a double line of SS men. There had been another act of manipulation by Hitler he did not yet know about. In October 1944 he heard that he was to represent the Führer and deliver the oration at the state funeral for the national hero, Rommel. The news of the Field-Marshal's death from the wounds he received in Normandy when he was thought to be recovering affected Rundstedt deeply. He proposed that Keitel would be a more appropriate person, but word came back, 'The Führer lays particular importance on you personally doing it'. He went with a heavy heart. The text of the oration, full of patriotic and Nazi clichés, was placed on the lectern a few moments before he had to read it. But the whole scene was a vile lie. Neither von Rundstedt nor almost anyone else at Ulm that day had the faintest notion that Rommel had been forced by Hitler to take poison because a dying conspirator had whispered his name in connection with the *Attentat*. The truth was known to Rommel's widow and their son Manfred, who divulged it after the war. Rundstedt did not hear of it till he reached his next POW camp, Grizedale Hall. But the humiliation of captivity was only the latest and not the greatest nor the last for several of the highest German commanders.

At Wilton Park at least two generals became ill. Von Thoma was removed to hospital (he later had his leg amputated), and on 17 July Field Marshal von Busch died in his bed from a heart attack. The War Office instructed that his body was to be removed to Aldershot for burial and that Grondona could lay on reasonably appropriate military honours, which he did. An RSM of the Guards put some men through the ceremonial drill and next day the body of von Busch was carried down two lines of troops with heads bowed and reversed arms. Another party slow-marched ahead of the hearse and the dead soldier's colleagues, and presented arms at the perimeter gate as the coffin was driven away. Rundstedt afterwards congratulated Grondona on the excellence of the drill.

The following morning, the Commandant accompanied him and the eight most senior generals to a secret interment at Aldershot. By War Office orders the blinds in the coach were drawn.

As they approached Windsor Grondona allowed them to be raised sufficiently for the Germans to see the Castle, but not to be seen themselves. Rundstedt, who revealed to Grondona that the last time he had seen Windsor Castle was as an official German representative at the Coronation of George VI, then amazed him by asking if there would be a firing party from the Brigade of Guards at the funeral. Grondona, who knew what was in store for them, allowed his charges a fascinated glimpse of the Eton boys and of the deer in Windsor Great Park and had the blinds lowered again. Forty minutes later the coach linked up with a simple hearse bearing the remains of von Busch. Soon they were driving over a rough surface and arrived at what looked like an open field—the cemetery's reserve ground. As the party debussed half a dozen rather scruffy and astonished German prisoners of war were galvanised to attention. At a word of command and thoroughly scared by the august company they bore the coffin to the grave they had just dug. The chaplain on duty went through the burial service in English, turned his back and walked off. Rundstedt raised his baton for the last time as all present gave a final salute to the dead Field Marshal. They then moved over to the coach which had been moved conveniently close to a temporary hessian-screened latrine.

The atmosphere on the way back was frigid in the extreme. That evening von Rundstedt asked Grondona to come and see him. He poured him a whisky and, speaking with unaccustomed emotion, asked why he and his colleagues had been subjected to a bitter experience none of them would ever forget. Grondona replied that, as commandant, he had no comment to make, but speaking 'off the record' and man to man, asked von Rundstedt if he had seen the pictures of the concentration camps and whether he understood the detestation of all things German that had consequently spread over the country. The War Office did not believe that the dead man was personally involved, but had von Rundstedt noticed, when at the cemetery, the solitary figure of a policeman in the distance to keep the public and press-men away? Did he not understand that questions would have been asked in the House of Commons, had there been more than a simple ceremony. Pale and tense, Rundstedt put his head down and his face in his hands. 'We do realise what you say, and have the utmost shame. But I give you my word of honour as a soldier that the revelations concerning the concentration camps have appalled the Wehrmacht even more than the people of Britain.' Grondona had several more private conversations with von Rundstedt, whose dignity never relaxed and who never tried to vindicate himself. His private purgatory was to continue and even increase during the remaining seven years of his life.

After a while security became less tight. The generals could watch cricket on the Beaconsfield ground which is adjacent to Wilton Park, their curiosity in the game being matched by the spectators' own curiosity in them. Rations, as with all prisoners of war, had been reduced, and General Dittmar, no Nazi and the much respected commentator of the High Command, led a party who made an allotment into a successful vegetable garden. Now and then they would send their compliments and baskets of produce to the British officers' mess. General Gerd Bassange, the short, thick-set and happily extrovert Württemberger, got permission to set up bird-scarers in an adjacent somewhat derelict cherry-orchard. Senior sapper of the Wehrmacht, he was provided with wire, a soldering iron and, using anything from tobacco tins to petrol cans, erected an array of ingenious contrivances—such as windmills which caused pebble-filled tins to rotate and sound like a rattle. Using wood, trouser buttons and turkey feathers, he constructed and suspended on wires between the trees a more fearsome-looking predator than any hawk. As the heavy crop of cherries ripened, he set up his inventions at strategic points throughout the orchard, making tactical changes of his scarers from day to day, or even hour to hour. The birds went off to other orchards less well defended, but, as can happen in war, the general's technological inventiveness was exploited by a new enemy—the grey squirrels. His tintinnabulations, noted the friendly Grondona, seemed to act less as a deterrent than a magnet to the invaders and he could do little to stop their day and night raiding.

Grizedale Hall—now demolished—was an ungainly building in limestone and slate in the forest between Lake Windermere and Coniston Water. Something of a businessman's folly, it had harboured senior German prisoners of war in the First World War. At the beginning of the Second World War captured Luftwaffe officers were confined there. (The celebrated von Werra made one of his bold escapes from Grizedale—local people still talk about it forty years later.) For a time in 1942 it was the temporary home of

fifty French officers who surrendered at the invasion of Mada-
gascar but refused to go over to de Gaulle. They had a semi-
privileged status and were allowed to walk around and about and
used to make friends with the local population. It is hard to think
that this gloomy grey pile, to which hutments were added, was
ever a happy place. It certainly was not during the spring and
summer of 1945 when it gradually filled up with captive generals.

Five miles away lived a man for whom their arrival was a great
and ironic piece of good fortune: Captain Basil Liddell Hart. As
an early theorist of the so-called *Blitzkrieg* he had watched his
ideas neglected at home and developed by the enemies of his
country. And here on his doorstep were not only leading practitioners of the tank tactics he had visualised twenty years before
but many other possible candidates for historical interrogation.
He had news of the first arrivals from the press and an eye-
witness account from a Canadian WREN visitor who travelled on
the same train to Windermere Station. Some eleven generals, he
noted, 'were made to haul their own trunks from the train to the
station yard and then packed into a single truck which had come
to meet them. A bad piece of manners and a sad contrast to the
tradition of the British Army as well as to the courtesies observed
in the field by both sides'. Liddell Hart was eager to have
access to the generals but he had to go warily. From his years as
the powerful military correspondent of *The Times* and his period
as personal adviser to the War Minister, Hore-Belisha, he had
friends in high places, but also enemies. He had come out as a
critic of Churchill's conduct of the war, during nearly all of which
he had been out in the cold, little consulted. Another difficulty was
the non-fraternisation rule. But through a family connection with
a member of the re-education section of PWD he obtained permission to visit Grizedale with this kind of activity in mind, it
being tacitly accepted that he would also be collecting material for
his future history of the war.

For the generals the presence of Liddell Hart was a boon and a
boost to their morale, all the more so, perhaps, as his first visit on
9 July came the day after one from 'Professor King'. During a
period of half a year his high 1937 Rolls Royce could be seen nos-
ing its way between the stone walls of the narrow Lakeland lanes
up to Grizedale. No one was more welcome there than this tall,
eminent and courteous visitor. On his visits to Shap Wells Horst
Woetzel noted how he would lean just a little towards his audi-

ence, itself a gesture of wishing to communicate. With his elegant clothes, pince-nez and a thin balding head dominated by a domed forehead, he gave an impression at once formidable and kindly. Most important, he could talk to the generals about their own craft: they had the chance to explain themselves, at least as soldiers, before the bar of history. They could relive their campaigns. Field Marshal Ewald von Kleist, a small flinty Prussian and Commander of the First Panzer Army, could once more bend over a map to explain his great unopposed swanning manoeuvres from the Don basin across the Kuban Steppe, the oil wells nearly in his grasp and the gleaming peaks of the Caucasus just ahead. On the highest of them a Swastika flag would be raised, a thousand miles inside the Russian frontier, with Stalingrad far behind on his left flank. Replacements were beginning to lag, but no hint of the danger to come. All that was three years ago now, but every manoeuvre was pigeon-holed in his mind. The later aspect of Kleist's career which would lead to his long sentence as a war criminal was of no interest to the expert listener across the table.

Liddell Hart visited Grizedale Hall sixteen times, conducting his historical interrogations with the aid of the interpreter, Captain Kingsford, who was delighted with such an interesting assignment. His substitute, when he was away, was General Bechtolsheim, whom Liddell Hart had known before the war as military attaché. In November when the contents of the former German Embassy came up for auction it was typical of Liddell Hart that he became involved by request in trying to save certain of Bechtolsheim's family heirlooms which were in danger of being sold. On five occasions, recorded because he claimed the usual three guinea fee, Liddell Hart justified his 're-education' role by holding a 'brains trust' on current political opinion.

He almost never set down feelings in his diary, but on 26 October he jotted, 'We almost fell on each other's necks!': he had met General Dittmar 'one of the few men I respect in any country for the objectivity of his commentaries under great difficulties'. Liddell Hart, likewise practised in putting across unpopular truth, and Dittmar, the remarkably independent Wehrmacht commentator throughout the war, became firm friends. Hearing that one of the Nuremberg defendants, Hans Fritsche, head of radio propaganda, was in secret agreement with Dittmar's frank broadcasts, Liddell Hart at once communicated this information to Hartley Shawcross, the chief British Prosecutor, who offered to pass on Dittmar's evidence to Fritsche's German counsel. It must have helped towards Fritsche's acquittal. Other generals Liddell Hart became acquainted with were Blumentritt, von Thoma, Manteuffel, Eberbach, Rohricht, Student, Heinrici, von Tippelskirsch, von Siewart, Elfeldt, Rear-Admiral Engel and, of course, von Kleist and von Rundstedt. Two other Field Marshals brought to Britain that Liddell Hart particularly wanted to meet were von Brauschitsch and Manstein, but they were never sent to Grizedale. Others, including General Halder who as prisoner of the Gestapo was so nearly executed at the end of the war, were collected into an American camp at Allersdorf near Nuremberg, in order to write historical papers.

Liddell Hart's overall impression of these men as a body was that 'few resembled the typical picture of an iron Prussian soldier. Rundstedt came nearest it, but in his case the impression was off-set by his natural courtesy and light touch of humour. In contrast to him were a number of aggressive young generals, blustering and boorish, who owed their rise to Nazi favour. But the majority were of a different type to both, and by no means a dominating one. Many would have looked in their natural place at any conference of bank managers or civil engineers'.

The prisoners at Grizedale had no idea of their ultimate fate, nor that the government was far from any decision about it. The press was kept away, though a *Daily Express* man snooped around and reported sarcastically that the generals had white sheets and spent the days sun-bathing. In fact, most of them were in an acute state of depression. It was a restless camp, with many coming and going, especially to and from the London District Cage, where the preliminary examinations of possible war-crimes witnesses were taking place. The War Diary for 11 September records: *War Criminal 967240 O/Gruppenführer Berger sent to LDC.* This SS-General, who was head of the Hauptamt of the SS, did not return.* There were signs of barbed-wire fever, but tensions eased when they were allowed to go for walks on parole: the gloomy forest of Grizedale, dispiriting to most Englishmen, might have been in the Harz Mountains. Nevertheless, the Commandant, Lieutenant Colonel Morton, was concerned. He rang up John Trevelyan, Education Officer for Westmorland, to say that he was worried about the state of mind of some of the prisoners and

---

* He was condemned in 1949 by an American Tribunal to twenty-five years imprisonment, but released in 1952.

feared suicides. Could he not come and talk to them about the outer world? Trevelyan, a genial, outgoing man, remembers being ushered into a large room in which eighty or ninety men were sitting in ordered rows with senior ranks in front. In that eruptive way that both alarms and flatters an Englishman, they sprang up and clicked to attention and waited till he motioned them to sit down. He was impressed to find that if he spoke slowly and clearly in English they preferred him to do without an interpreter. He talked about what kind of world might be created out of the mess of war and, twice more, was asked to return.

On the third occasion a small group had asked to discuss 'Expediency versus Morality', a theme which went to the heart of their personal problems in the Third Reich. Colonel Faulk was there at the time and he asked if he could attend. At first, he just listened. Trevelyan tried to create what he felt was a frank and happy atmosphere. The German need for 'living-space' was brought up but someone quickly quashed it as a red herring; questions of personal loyalty were raised; Admiral Erich Voss, an engineer, appeared particularly sensitive and intelligent about the main issues. Faulk listened impatiently. To him this approach was misplaced and ignorant, mere tea-party talk; Trevelyan was accepting their credentials all too easily. He could contain himself no longer. Had they really no alternative to going along with Hitler because of their own traditions of service and loyalty? There was also another factor: ambition and the hope of promotion in their profession.* At this, one of the generals burst out, *'Sprechen Sie unsere Ehre ab?'*—Do you deny us our honour? *'Jawohl'*, answered Faulk. Trevelyan was extremely annoyed, said he could not approve the turn the discussion had taken, and the group broke up unhappily.

Faulk had no regrets. It might be quite right to treat them as individuals, but he saw them as men who had known what they were doing all along and why, and therefore responsible for the

---

* Cf. the hard judgment of the German generals by Wheeler-Bennett: 'Technically able and physically courageous, they yet lacked moral courage and, in the main, were wholly wanting in spiritual resistance and intellectual independence. The majority were out to make their social and material careers in the most material sense. Marshal's batons and knight's crosses, gifts, estates and building permits silenced the pangs of consciences as may, from time to time, have assailed them. They were not disposed to overthrow Hitler while he had those honours in his gift.' (Wheeler-Bennett: op. cit., p. 536.)

consequences. His conviction that men over forty could not change and that they were not worth including in the re-educational programme was only strengthened.

Rundstedt—it was a special favour obtained from Montgomery —had his only son with him at Grizedale. Major Dr Hans Gerd Rundstedt, whom his father affectionately called the black sheep of the family, was very unlike him; at the University of Freiburg he had so disapproved of the students' duelling corps that he had set up an umbrella as his personal symbol.[73] An archivist by profession, for two years this gentle, likeable man had nevertheless been the Field-Marshal's aide, and at Grizedale was very popular, quietly leavening the atmosphere in his position as librarian. The Rundstedts had a small room with a view. On his second visit Trevelyan was asked to come earlier so that the old man could meet him personally. To his amusement, Colonel Morton, who always used to refer to 'My Huns' or 'My Boches', took him to the door of his prisoner and at once became a different man. He stood to attention and said deferentially, 'Mr Trevelyan to see you, sir.' Years later, when John Trevelyan had become official censor to the Film Board, he was reminded of his reception when he saw the film *Judgment at Nuremberg*. Burt Lancaster as the German judge displayed, he felt, the same sort of dignity as Rundstedt. 'Do you not feel very cut off?', said Trevelyan. 'Yes, I often do,' answered his host, taking him to his small window, 'but on a clear day I can see from here a little patch of sea, and this makes me feel I am not entirely cut off.'

Inwardly, however, Rundstedt was almost entirely isolated. He never unburdened himself. Neither now, nor later to his family, did he ever reveal his inmost thoughts and feelings about Hitler and the Third Reich. His stern Lutheran faith upheld him, but the strain of such powerful repression had to break some time. One day he was seen bashing the barbed wire violently with his stick, a sentry pointing a gun at him and ordering him to stop. Could it have been when he had read in a newspaper the true story of Rommel's death, or the effect of sheer nervous exhaustion after sleepless nights from sciatica? There was no solace in alcohol at Grizedale, as there had been, to a limited extent, at Wilton Park. Or was it simply that no person could keep up such a stoical front of dignity all the time? The visits of Liddell Hart were important to him, for he liked England; having once had an English nanny, he had unconsciously picked up certain English ways, besides learning the rudiments of the language. His almost spontaneous relationship with the courteous and thoughtful Liddell Hart broke down part of his Teutonic crustiness; in his isolation and frequent despair it was one of the most real things in his life. After they had been talking in the interrogation hut outside the wire, the historian would stand beside the gate to let the older man go first. 'No, Captain, you go first!' Rundstedt would say, 'this is my house!' Liddell Hart noticed that the Field Marshal only had a thin palliasse to lie on. Something clearly could be done about this. On 29 November he wrote to Captain Kingsford: 'Have you been able to get a mattress for von Rundstedt from the hospital? If not, I could lend him a mattress from one of our beds. I would like to ease the pain from his leg so that he can get some sleep.' The Rolls Royce duly arrived with its unusual cargo. But when the very correct Colonel Morton, who had been on leave at the time, arrived back, he at once became nervous and annoyed at this breach of King's Regulations. Every military establishment had a list of equipment allowed, and it was strictly forbidden to extend it from a civilian source; the nearest Military Hospital should have obliged. Official letters buzzed back and forth from the War Office, which, a friend of the Liddell Harts told them, had to open a file marked 'Rundstedt's Mattress'.

Liddell Hart was specially asked to come to Grizedale on 12 December, which was Rundstedt's seventieth birthday. There was a small party in his room and a birthday cake and a presentation of a water-colour of Grizedale Hall by the Camp spokesman, General Heinrici, which was later given to the historian by Rundstedt's family 'as a memento of their meetings and as a mark of friendship'. Kathleen Liddell Hart sent up the last chrysanthemums from her garden and the Field Marshal asked the doctor for some aspirins to keep them alive longer. The stay of the generals at Grizedale Hall, however, was not to be prolonged. Early in the New Year they were moved *en bloc* to Bridgend in South Wales.

The relationship of the German generals and Liddell Hart was a special one. If his visits were balm to their self-respect, they were also the best possible grist to his historical mill. Did he judge them correctly? Did they ever try to mislead him? Faulk tells of a curious incident while he was addressing them on 28 December. A message announcing a visit from Liddell Hart next day was brought in, and Faulk asked them if they wished this, at which several senior generals rose and went into a huddle. They discussed whom he would be seeing and agreed on what line they should take—possibly about Hitler—and went back to their places. Faulk who had acute hearing and understood German perfectly felt he should report what he had heard by phone to Liddell Hart who at once invited him for tea. The historian, who had recently heard from Sulzbach that Faulk was a 'marvellous man', received him courteously but completely refused to accept his story. From this, Faulk concluded that Liddell Hart believed in both an elitist and chivalrous form of society in which a general must automatically be an 'officer and a gentleman'. Faulk mistook the man, but not totally. Liddell Hart had a notably courteous, human-to-human approach to everyone—milkman, schoolboy or Prime Minister. He treated the German generals with the direct personal curiosity he showed to everyone. But this kindly side was balanced by another, as shown in two contrasting portraits by Eric Kennington, one benevolent, the other hard. His curiosity had a cool, gimlet quality which made him perhaps the shrewdest living judge of the military mind. Also, as a commentator for five years, he had been trying to live inside the heads of the enemy General Staff, and it was unlikely that, if they tried to put any gloss on history, he was deceived. Certainly, he was more interested in their craft than in their politics; he observed, also, that 'many of them have a passion for preciseness about facts, although their conclusions may be like froth on beer'; and that 'they were essentially technicians, intent on their professional job, with little idea of things outside it. It is easy to see how Hitler hoodwinked and handled them, and found them good instruments up to a point.' He criticised their 'blind eye' but doubted whether generals in other countries would have done more to overthrow a regime such as Hitler's, instancing the numerous generals on the Allied side he had met who deplored the 'barbarism' of mass-bombing, yet never made public or official protest on that score. Liddell Hart noted, too, a tendency to self-pity among the generals, though not with Manstein and Rundstedt. What Faulk sensed but did not quite put his finger on was Liddell Hart's own tendency as a liberal rationalist not to probe too deeply into the shadow side of Nazi Germany. René Halkett, who knew him well, makes the shrewd comment that 'Liddell Hart's attitude was radically chivalrous, his mind sober and analytical. Nazi ideology just did not fit into his concepts. His pursuit of truth coincided with his pursuit of justice. He would, therefore, give the benefit of the doubt to the defendant.'

The generals left on 9 January 1946 and for the last time local people witnessed the scene at Windermere Station that many, besides Liddell Hart, deplored: the transit of high-ranking officers, several of whom walked with sticks, carrying their own baggage between lorry and train, no German batmen being provided and their escorts being forbidden to help them. Courtesies could only be in private. Captain Kingsford rang at once to tell Liddell Hart how everything had gone, reporting that Rundstedt had been the first on parade, though the oldest and most infirm. Next day a lorry returned the mattress. Liddell Hart intended to continue visiting the generals in South Wales but he was now *persona non grata* both at Bush House and at the War Office. The affair of the mattress had alerted the latter to his excessive fraternisation and in February his War Office pass was cancelled. A little later some articles in the *Sunday Dispatch* based on his conversations at Grizedale were regarded by Wing Commander Hitch as a breach of a tacit agreement. All publicity with regard to the generals was embarrassing. The official policy was to keep them in purdah until their fate was decided. Liddell Hart had had the cheek to lift the veil for a moment.

11

Koeppler's College

When the parliament of the newly founded German Reich was
constructed in Berlin after 1870 the inscription on the front of the
building read *Dem Deutschen Volke*, that is, 'To the German people'
—given by a magnanimous ruler. It is not the way democracies
arise.[74]

Heinz Koeppler

By that autumn of 1945, when the Wehrmacht generals had gone
from Camp 300 at Wilton Park, it was ready for its second transformation—into a residential centre for selected prisoners-of-war.
Grondona, who stayed on as Commandant, sent out one of his
whimsical circulars to those remaining from the original staff. The
old Wilton Park was to die on 7 November and be reborn next
day. Certain structural alterations had to be made.

> The *raison d'être* of the new baby is to re-educate groups of 300
> Jerries in the way they should go. Courses will last varying
> periods, after which the victims will return to their Fatherland
> —all white or, should one say, all red, white and blue! Instruc-
> tion will be imparted by a staff under an Oxford don. . . . We've
> met only a couple of the long-haired section of the new estab-
> lishment as yet, but they seem God-fearing folk and bid fair to
> being good mixers in the time-honoured fashion. . . . Struc-
> turally, the guts will be torn out of the original offices—
> partitions will be ripped down to make large rooms on the
> north side of the grille; all barbed wire, compounds and iron-
> bars are going west. . . . The Jerries will provide their own
> police . . .

Wilton Park had been earmarked for this purpose a year before
by Wing Commander Hitch, who acted smartly when he heard
that the premises would be free soon after the war ended. The idea
was that the re-educational programme could only be completed
with a special 'training centre' for chosen POWs where in an

adult education setting they could study the theory and practice of democracy intensively. The Principal had obviously to be an Englishman and would probably have been Faulk, did he not have a still large job on his hands. The choice fell on Wing Commander Roffey, who had been a schoolmaster and was later to prove an excellent civil servant. During the summer he began looking round for tutors and lecturers and preparing a modest syllabus with the political and cultural side equally balanced. He was going to be particularly careful to see that the bugging equipment was removed. Then an embarrassed Hitch sent for him and said that, by a high level decision, the then head of the lecture section at Bush House, Dr Heinz Koeppler, had been appointed in his place. He personally had many misgivings—and so did Faulk—but could do nothing about it. Hitch feared that the ambitious Koeppler, with his many good connections, would make Wilton Park into a 'show place'; he was also much too German and too domineering in his whole way of doing things.

Koeppler had spent most of the war with the Political Warfare Executive, under Sir Robert Bruce Lockhart—with Richard Crossman and Ritchie Calder among his colleagues—rising to be Assistant Director of the German Region. In 1943, in response to Churchill's request for creative ideas about post-war Germany, he had written a memorandum advocating the setting up of a centre in England to which Germans in public life might come to discuss mutual problems in an intellectually invigorating atmosphere. This proposal lay dormant for two years till Sir Ivone Kirkpatrick sent for Koeppler and told him that his scheme was premature but could well be adapted to those Germans who were compulsorily in Britain anyway—the prisoners of war; and Koeppler himself, with his background and mental energy, was the obvious man to launch and direct the enterprise. Though committed to giving a course of lectures on mediaeval history at Oxford that autumn he was appointed Warden of Wilton Park.

Predictably, however, he had an often stormy passage, if not in the same way as he had had in the persona of Professor King at Featherstone Park and Shap Wells. But, like a handful of other refugees from Central Europe who carved out highly successful careers in Britain, the future Sir Heinz Koeppler was well armoured against rejection. He had the force of character to create his own milieu around him; his vision and the keenness of his intelligence attracted others similarly endowed.

He was born in 1912 at Wollstein in a corner of Prussia returned to Poland at the Treaty of Versailles. His well-to-do father, whose prosperity derived from his being an expert in the potato, resettled his family in Berlin. Heinz, intellectually very bright, went to the Friedrich Wilhelm University, then to Heidelberg, and finally to Christian Albert House at Kiel University. His experience of this last institution, at the time unique in Germany, was undoubtedly one of the threads which went into the creation of Wilton Park. Founded by a wealthy Swede called Bergmann, it was a small élite hall of residence where one third of the students had to be from abroad and all with the calibre of a future professor. Bergmann's conception was that the insular German mind could benefit from both a Spartan setting and a lateral mixing. The young Koeppler, rubbing together with his German and foreign contemporaries and very much a political animal, was elected student president of Christian Albert House. This enabled him to get the pick of scholarships abroad available to its scholars—one at Magdalen College, Oxford.

It was in the autumn of 1933 that the twenty-one-year-old Koeppler, conspicuous with his great height and multi-buttoned German overcoat, had his first shy taste of a way of life that he would increasingly adopt as his own. He tracked down with equal eagerness the more subtle English idioms and the background to the Holy Roman Emperor, Frederick I, whose life he hoped to write. He was taken up by that paragon of liberal humanists, Gilbert Murray, Regius Professor of Greek and befriender of many a promising young man. From Gilbert Murray, he says in an interesting phrase, he learnt a lot about 'the stage-craft of the good'. When the Nazi government blocked the export of currency, Mary Murray and Arthur Gillett, an Oxford Quaker, guaranteed his bank balance so he could stay on after obtaining his Ph.D. His Master of Arts and his British citizenship were then speeded up so that he could be appointed, though only twenty-five, as a junior lecturer. But mediaeval history compelled his attention much less than the root causes of what was happening in Germany. About this, however, he found most of Oxford to be woefully, almost wilfully, ignorant, in spite of 'lamentably well-meant efforts to improve Anglo-German understanding'. Professors and students were invited on visits but they 'were introduced to the mysteries of the game of cricket; they were taken down to the Thames to admire the picturesque if highly insanitary boat-houses; they were shown the glorious architecture and the generous hospitality of Oxford colleges. But Oxford refused resolutely to discuss the things that mattered. For, to have discussed political issues would have been awkward and might have led to lost tempers, which to avoid has ever been one of the glories of *homo Oxoniensis*. Looking back on this period, it is clear to me that I learned from it how not to enlarge international understanding.'[74]

The Wilton Park formula which Koeppler developed over the years was essentially a solution to the dilemma implied here: how to discuss acute international differences frankly and without tempers being lost. Put briefly, the answer lay in creating a milieu that was friendly, not too formal, and allowed time for contenders to get to know both each other and the issues at stake; also the mixture of those attending should be wide enough to stimulate lateral thinking on a broad number of topics.

The staff that Dr Koeppler collected round himself had two main elements, German refugees and the British. The chief of the former and, so to speak, the second father of Wilton Park was Waldemar von Knöringen, whose activities with prisoners of war first in North Africa and then in Ascot Park have already been described.* In 1945 he was still generally known by his cover name 'Captain Holt' and he was still in charge of the team of POWs who were working for the BBC. The difficulty was that he had every intention of returning to take up his political life in Bavaria as soon as possible. However, his idealism and attractive persuasive personality were available to Koeppler at least for the early stages. Knöringen approached Dr Fritz Borinski, a North German who had been travelling round the camps exploring ways of preparing politically competent POWs for their return home. Borinski, who had deliberately kept himself free from political entanglements in Britain, was at first reluctant, fearing to compromise himself at the last moment. But Knöringen said, 'I intend to return home soon. Do you think I will compromise myself at Wilton Park?' Borinski's doubts were stilled and the two joined forces. They proposed that a special section staffed by refugees should be set up under the name *Aufbau* (lit. 'building up'). This was accepted and able intelligence sergeants like Reichenbach and the English-born historian Godfrey Scheele as well as three former Ascot prisoners were brought in. The work of the section was

* See page 48.

divided into three classes: political adult education, literature and the arts, and the press.

The second element balancing the refugee one were the dozen or so British tutors, including George Roundell Greene, till recently a POW himself, Alex Glasfurd of the old Wilton Park staff, Ken Morgan, gentlest of the London District Cage interrogators. They were more numerous than, though not so high-powered as, the refugee element; together they made Wilton Park a unique Anglo-German institution. By introducing the Oxford tutor system as well as seminars, Koeppler ensured that each student in a group of fifteen or twenty had a personal link with someone who was aware of him as an individual. He also encouraged the staff when they could to wear academic gowns, even in some cases over a military uniform. His own motivation, Koeppler has said, came from both 'a real sense of pity for young men who had no part in the shaping of the world they lived in and an enlightened self-interest for the West.' The aims of Wilton Park at the outset were defined as 'to make the students more effective leaders in the study and discussion programmes being conducted on a large scale in the prison camps from which they came, and to increase their capacity when repatriated to help lead public opinion in post-war Germany in the direction of responsible individualism and democracy.' The means were chiefly teaching German history since 1871, the practice and principles of democracy, and the projection of Britain, with POWs themselves giving lectures on suggested themes.

Camp 300 reopened under its new management on 12 January 1946 with exactly 300 students. The first course had been hastily assembled from the camps near London. Preference was given to those whose homes were in the British zone of Germany and also to the younger one of two applicants if otherwise equal. Another instruction was that a solid trade union man, though with only elementary education, was to be preferred to a boring and pompous university professor. (It was a constant complaint and regret that not enough students from working-class backgrounds were selected.) When they arrived they were gratified to find beds and sheets, not bunks; they were served at table and had no dishwashing afterwards. There were no distinctions of rank at all, each being addressed as Herr So-and-So and asked to address each other in the same way. This coming together on equal terms of officers and other ranks, till then separated, was immensely impor-

tant; the former, well in the minority, were made to realise how
often men of intellect and character had not been commissioned
either because of their political views or because they frankly preferred not to join the officer class. The food was at least adequate
—the rations being equivalent to those in a work camp. There
was a large selection of German language newspapers, as well as
all the English ones. The library was excellent and included Nazi
literature. Dieter Hankel from Featherstone Park was thrilled to
see *Mein Kampf* side by side with a work of Churchill—unaware
that it had been thus cunningly arranged by Koeppler himself—
and the twenty volumes of Brockhaus together with its equivalent,
the full Oxford English Dictionary. Besides the distinguished
evening speakers there were films. What did it matter if *Bismarck*
and *Jew Süss* were played again and again? The sixty strong *Aufbau*
group, handpicked at the beginning of each course, was responsible for a wall newspaper every other day, the *Wilton-Schau*, and
for *Die Brücke*, the magazine with a wide circulation that was
issued at the end of each course.

'To Beaconsfield and Wilton Park College. Koeppler very hos-
pitable, tired and triumphant with justification.' So Geoffrey
Forrest, now a civilian, wrote in his diary for 13 February when
the first course was still running. The Principal had much to con-
tend with still. Not surprisingly he and Grondona did not hit it
off. When at the outset Koeppler began to assert himself with his
usual force the Commandant dug his heels in. There was an
awkward official confrontation, after which their areas of authority were precisely defined. (Grondona would always welcome the
prisoner-students with a little speech, never failing to mention
what excellent settlers the Germans had made in New South
Wales, and that he had served in the First World War under its
outstanding Commonwealth Commander General Monash, whose
parents came from Germany and *who was a Jew*.) Koeppler distanced himself from the beginning as far as he could from Hitch
and Bush House. He disliked the official term 'Training Centre'*
and the whole 're-education' concept, which to his mind betrayed
a British sense of superiority. On the pedigree of the word 're-
education' he once said, in his colourful, pungent style, that it was
'born of Arrogance, out of Ignorance, and such a horse never won
a race.' But he had, of course, to use the machinery of re-education

* It was little used except in official documents.

9

as a channel for providing students. There was a minor battle between him and Faulk about the subsequent grading of Wilton Park students—who fortunately were themselves quite unaffected by the pin-pricks and back-stage conflicts that went on. They also had no idea that they were helping to pioneer a new form of adult education.

The impact of a mass of prisoners, average age about twenty-seven, stiff-faced still, POW patch on their backs, could be potent, and in different ways. On the evening before the first course opened Koeppler walked round the camp uneasily, remembering previous hostility, wondering if the experiment would succeed. Together with his administrative assistant, Captain Griffiths, he came to the reading room which was packed with new arrivals. They were so uncertain of their reception that Griffiths said, 'There is only one exit, sir, but I have got my revolver.' It was not a joke. When Dr Hans Walz, a visiting lecturer and former *Dozent* at Heidelberg, saw the mass audience before him in the elephant hut that was used as a lecture hall, he felt a mixture of affection and fear. 'Those poor devils, I thought, defeated and wretched. At the same time I had an irrational sense that they were capable of seizing and torturing me. Seeing their uniforms gave me goose-flesh. Yet they were harmless and friendly, even smiling at me.' The urbane Harold Nicolson, ex-diplomat, ex-MP, man of letters, wrote in his weekly column in the *Spectator*: 'It was dark when I arrived and in the light of the hurricane lamp that guided me along the cinder path I saw the rain-drops glistening upon the barbed wire. When I entered the large hut I detected that smell which is the smell of prisoners all over the world from Opocno to Wormwood Scrubs. Three hundred faces stared at me . . . that were uniform only in the fact that they wore the grey mask of unhappiness that captivity brings.'[76] Nicolson was impressed by the uninhibited way that for an hour and a half after his talk his audience asked questions, in spite of the presence of both Grondona and Koeppler. But he must have imagined the barbed wire, which had been removed inside the camp; and their 'unhappy faces' may well have been glazed with concentration or the strain of trying to understand English—consecutive translations were often long delayed; or it could have been sheer weariness, for it was near the end of the first course and there had been long days of study and little let-up. There was also a current of suspicion abroad in the early period. Few people realised that when Gron-

dona gave instructions for the 'guts to be ripped out' that this
implied the removal of the secret microphones and recording
system. Koeppler had no idea of that side of Camp 300 during the
war years; the War Office, it seems, assumed the FO would tell
him and the FO assumed he knew already. He only discovered the
truth when one of the students said, 'Don't you know, sir, what
this place was once used for?' Some Germans who had been there
before believed they were still being bugged and had spread the
word around.

Wilton Park did, in fact, soon become just the 'show place' that
Hitch had feared, not least because of the galaxy of distinguished
men and women from public and academic life that Koeppler was
able to attract as visiting lecturers: Bertrand Russell, Lord
Lindsay, Lord Beveridge, Lord Soulbury, Philip Noel-Baker,
Harold Macmillan, Quintin Hogg (on whose platform Koeppler
had sat in the famous post-Munich bye-election at Oxford),
Richard Crossman, Kingsley Martin, A. J. P. Taylor, Jennie Lee,
Lady Rhondda, Lady Astor (who came over from nearby Cliveden
and told her Churchill stories), Barbara Ward, Lord Pakenham,
W. R. Matthews (Dean of St Paul's), Herbert Read, Harold
Nicolson, Sir Robert Birley, Bishop Bell and Bishop Hunter—the
last six all serving later as members of the Wilton Park Academic
Council. Lord Lindsay, Master of Balliol, came over every week
from Oxford in 1947 to conduct a seminar. Koeppler could also
call on the cream of the lecturers he had recently supervised at
Bush House—like Professor Leibholz, Dr Demuth, Dr Burmeister,
Dr Redlich and Dr Bernhard Menne, former editor of the socialist
Vorwärts, a brilliant and emotive speaker who once got entangled
with U-boat Commander Oesten about certain facts. But the great
success on the staff was a man without any academic qualifications
at all. After the first course Waldemar von Knöringen returned
home where he soon became leader of the Bavarian Socialist
Party. His place was taken by a versatile Sudentenland refugee
with whom he had worked in the *Neubeginn* movement—Werner
Lauermann. He had learnt printing in Dresden and was a model of
the self-educated artisan and trade unionist with his feet on the
ground. With only a primary education, he had amassed an
enormous amount of general knowledge. Naturally modest and
with a rare combination of humanity and political talent, because
of his background he was full of self-doubt, and Borinski often

had to persuade him how good he was. For, with his great ability, his gift for languages and empathy for others, he was the most sought-after of the tutors, the best of translators of visiting speakers, the most loved member of the staff. Prisoners often congregated in his home in nearby Jordans, a village founded in 1919 by the Quakers with whom, incidentally, Lauermann, humanist though he was, felt a passing affinity.

Koeppler had gathered a remarkable team and showed his own considerable 'stage-craft' in holding it together. His general aim was to offer the prisoner-students a great variety of viewpoints, all valid, and ask them to choose for themselves. He especially delighted in presenting a double bill of two new MPs, one Conservative, the other Labour, doing battle together—Julian Amery and Denis Healey—who then demonstrated that they were the best of personal friends. The three tutors, Glasfurd, the keen Socialist, Greene, the Liberal, and Gibson, the die-hard Tory, also set to at each other relentlessly but with good nature. From the third course onwards two classes were held in English only. Koeppler himself used to take the 'youth class'—those with the least political background. When some POWs started a whispering campaign about Lauermann's background, he got Greene to write an article for *Die Brücke* on the patriotism of refugees, and another one called *Das Recht Unrecht zu haben*—The right to be wrong. Greene was a special asset to Wilton Park, because if any POW began to bleat about his length of captivity, he could say, 'I was one for five years and it is because I was that I am here.' He was also, as Leutnant Bierhaus put it, 'young enough to know we wanted to be foolish sometimes'. Koeppler himself was not at all displeased when one course decided to send up the mock election with which each six weeks ended. Word was passed around that it would be fun for the Communists to do outrageously well in the poll. In fact they piled up 58 per cent of the vote, to the general merriment. The mock elections had, in fact, by then outlived their purpose and ceased. This sign of not being grimly earnest about politics was all to the good. Horst Woetzel found working on political models for the future of Germany could lead to caucus-making so strong that party discipline was almost being applied. If you moved a point or two towards the other side you lacked character or were considered a traitor.

A tradition also grew up, much encouraged by Koeppler, of a knockabout puppet cabaret which ended each course and poked fun at the establishment, sharply yet affectionately. The man who began it was discovered at Featherstone Park. He was Willi Brundert,* an old friend from youth movement days of Borinski, who soon made him his assistant. Among many other gifts being clever at puppets, Brundert put Wilton Park into a *Kasperlspiel*;† the arch devil was Warden Koeppler and his sergeant interpreters the lesser devils.

In 1946 newly emergent Germans of the post-Nazi world began to be invited to Britain. They included several famous churchmen: Cardinal Frings of Cologne, Hans Lilje of Hanover, Pastor Niemoeller and Bishop Dibelius of Berlin. None of these spoke at Wilton Park. At the time there was a feeling in certain circles in the British Zone—a sign of the in-bred nature of life there—that only those who shared in the life-struggle to recovery could really help reconstruction; Wilton Park, therefore, was irrelevant. However, the education ministers of Hamburg and Hanover, Adolf Grimme and Heinrich Landahlm, did come over in the summer of 1946 and speak at Wilton Park, as did Kurt Schumacher in the autumn, a most dramatic occasion. Schumacher, an official guest of the Labour Party, was the leading Social Democrat to survive the Third Reich and the natural leader of the reformed SPD. To Koeppler he was 'the man who had been right all the time'. Eight of the twelve Hitler years he had spent in Dachau, Buchenwald and Neuengamme. In May 1945 Faulk had seen him in the remains of his house in Hanover when he was recuperating and re-orientating himself. 'It was sad, sad, sad how a decent man like that was burnt up inside. He was fifty-two but looked at least sixty-five. On top of everything he was still anti-British from the First World War when he lost his arm. In his bitterness he almost drove me away from his house and all I could do was to leave all the cigarettes I had behind.' Meantime Schumacher, having picked up the political reins, had made a plea for not loading the young

---

* Brundert, one of the earlier repatriates, returned in July 1946 to the Soviet Zone where he became Professor of Economic Law at Magdeburg with a high post in the Ministry of Economics. Three years later he was made the centre-piece of a spy trial, the *Dessauer Prozess*, being lambasted as a British agent trained in the 'Spy School Wilton Park'.[77] He was amnestied after eight years in prison and came across to West Germany, becoming State Secretary in Wiesbaden and Lord Mayor of Frankfurt. He died in 1970 of a liver disease contracted in prison.

† *Kasper* is the German equivalent of Mr Punch, though less crude and violent.

generation with guilt for the Nazis and the war. He also frankly criticised Allied policies and was potentially the first post-war German Chancellor. Tall, bowed, hollow-cheeked, and 'as thin as a ration card', he came to Wilton Park in October. 'Just to see this man from the past,' recalls Horst Woetzel, 'was an extraordinary experience. With bad sight and bad teeth which made it hard to articulate, he came in on someone's arm, which naturally aroused sympathy among us. But the harsh provocative tone of his voice shocked me—it was almost like Hitler's. Not a single passage did he put over soberly.' For the tutor, George Greene, 'he was a disappointment, though we all loved him. I felt humble towards a man who had been through so much.' But Borinski felt the matter of his speech was sound and new for German socialism—that the Marxist, humanist and Christian approaches were all three legitimate and must be recognised. Koeppler was not surprised at his bitterness as 'we saw it as a German trait at that time'. In his cottage afterwards the Social Democrat leader slumped into a chair, the sweat pouring from his face. Afterwards, a question was asked in the Commons about what he had said, and received a bland reply. The French Government, angry at his speeches in Germany, made an official protest at his being asked to Britain at all.

Much further to the left were the 'politicals' from 999 Penal Battalion who arrived from Egypt that same autumn and almost caused Koeppler, for the only time, to have a riot on his hands. Conspicuous among them was Wolfgang Abendroth, who had been in the Communist opposition in Frankfurt up to 1933, two KP functionaries, and several left-wing socialists. With all the fervour of their KZ background they protested at the presence of officers on the course who must, in their view, have been Nazis. Koeppler mollified them by pointing out that the Wilton Park policy was to pick the widest possible mix of future citizens of Germany who—and this was the point—would have to live together one day. Abendroth was in Borinski's press class and exercised considerable sway on some younger students, including both Woetzel and Düttmann who had come down from Shap together, joined the *Aufbau* section and had stayed on as 'veterans' to the next course. Woetzel remembers Abendroth's big thin, stooping body, his ascetic, immensely lively and intellectual face, and his personal, almost Christian kindness. They were both fascinated to hear for the first time well-grounded Marxist theory from a man who had really suffered for his opinions and could unfold the whole history of Communism in the twenties lucidly and dramatically before them. According to Woetzel, Abendroth with the force of his faith and personality simply took over the press section. He also took up old political links. On one occasion, being very short-sighted, he got Düttmann to help him through a broken section of the perimeter wire in a corner of the park. He had to get out unseen on to the London road where a car was waiting to take him to a secret assignation with certain very left members of the Labour Party. Koeppler had a vague idea that such things happened—but not of what Woetzel heard late one evening when Abendroth took him to the hut where the 999 men lived. They had lit a stove and, sitting round it, their faces burnished by its glow, they were singing softly and with great inner devotion their hymn of faith, the Internationale.

Long before fraternisation was allowed, prisoners were meeting local people and were also taken on all-day outings to London or Oxford, three at a time, but selected by size; for Koeppler had organised from his staff—and at a time when clothing coupons were still required—three civilian suits, large, medium and small. Grondona, though he would probably have approved, was not told, out of tact. The sudden impact of freedom and normality could be an intoxicating experience. When Forrest wished to take Woetzel out he had to do it in secret with the willing aid of Lauermann who lent him clothes. They had a full day seeing the great sights of London, with lunch at Schmidts. Long after, Woetzel, quoting Auden, remembered this break-out day: 'the galleries were crowded, Eros was back in place and, after the nightmare of the dark when all the dogs of Europe barked, I was back in the light again.'

But this was nothing to the excitement of Düttmann's freedoms. The arts being encouraged at Wilton Park Woetzel used to see him in the corner of a hut dashing off his gay water-colours of 'foxgloves and daisies and boats at a pier, the same again and again, and giving them away in the most charming manner'. One day—it was well before fraternisation was allowed—a visitor from Jordans, Betty Jenkin, was walking through the camp. Herself an artist, she saw him and invited him to visit her house. A little later she gave an exhibition there of his more serious work and no fewer than three famous men came to see it—the poet Walter de la Mare, the critic Herbert Read and the sculptor Henry Moore.

Moore was so struck with Düttmann that he invited him to London to see his art and inscribed for him a copy of his 'Shelter Sketchbook'. Years later they met again when Moore was having his works cast in a Berlin foundry; Düttmann, by then the leading German architect of the revived city, obtained a Reclining Figure to place outside his Academy of Arts. Nor did Koeppler fail to notice the brilliant blond artist and he was often in the group of POWs whom the Principal used to have round in the evening to yarn with and sing songs to a guitar in his cottage. He even took him on a visit to Richard Crossman in Oxford; and he still has two of his paintings.

The local environment was itself a benevolent influence. Moments of peace and personal encounter might dispel the hurtful tangle of the past as much as the most enlightened political education. They could walk in the large oak-studded park or up through the beeches of Crutches Wood to Jordans Village—for them mercifully, because of the Quakers, without the forbidden territory of a pub—to watch cricket on the Green or take tea with the Coopers or the Witzes, or for Sunday supper with the Edmonds who received in return a new stone wall. They might sit in silence with the worshippers in the Friends Meeting House where one snowy Sunday prisoners outnumbered the local worshippers. At Crippetts, Commander Grandjean, whose U-boat had been sunk in the Thames in the first year of the war, broke down when he met Mrs Plant: he had not spoken to a woman for seven years.

Discipline was anything but strict. Church parties to Beaconsfield were trusted on their own. But when an SS officer, saying he was a Catholic, joined the walk to St Theresa's he absconded, took his own private walk and reappeared only later in the day. 'He should be severely punished,' was the opinion of the camp, but to the general surprise nothing happened to him. There were socials to attend in Beaconsfield, arranged by the Christian Council and the Fellowship of Reconciliation; and the gentler types might call with the padre, Pastor Siebert, on the deaf and blind author, Miss le Pla, champion of underdogs, who sent a parcel to a student's brother who had written that he was too hungry to work. The most relaxed times were probably had at the Jenkin house. Here Erich Huhle came with wire-cutters pretending he had used them to cut his way out of Wilton Park; here Schley who claimed to have been Rommel's chauffeur, got the use of the family's old

Morris which he drove with great exuberance on the London road.

Grondona's very human side inspired the affection of one of his personal clerks, Hans Freibusch, who glued together a matchbox-holder out of dock-stems and inscribed it 'Made in Sing-Sing'. But nothing gave Grondona (who was no mean staff officer) so much satisfaction as what he could do for Corporal Herbert Krause, a young man arrived at Wilton Park from a hostel in Cumberland and found to have leukaemia. He was put in Amersham Hospital and was not expected to live long. His mother who lived in Hamburg had lost both her husband and other son in the war. 'Why can't she be flown over?' asked Mrs Grondona. In 1947 this was a tall order, but the War Office gave permission for the Commandant to go ahead on his own. It happened he was about to inspect the fifty British personnel in the camp; he told them about Herbert Krause and immediately—it was pay-day—half the air fare from Hamburg was produced, £27. He then assembled the 400 German students and staff, told them what the Tommies had done and immediately they collected £40 from their meagre pay of 6/- a week. Meanwhile the Salvation Army in Hamburg was locating Frau Krause and getting her a civilian travel permit, Jean Grubb, a hospital almoner, arranging for a Methodist family to put her up and the Soldiers', Sailors' and Air Force Families Association tracing the boy's girl friend in Carlisle. The mother was met next afternoon by the Grondonas and taken at once to the hospital. Screens were put round the bed. In the tense silence of the ward the amazed boy's frail voice was heard, 'Ach, Mutti, träume ich?' (Am I dreaming?) Next day the girl friend arrived. A dramatic improvement in his condition continued and he was sent home by hospital ship. In Hamburg he recovered sufficiently to take up civilian employment. Grondona wrote up the story for the *Evening News* which syndicated it round the world in a series entitled 'Did This Really Happen?' Sadly Herbert Krause's remission from leukaemia did not last and he died within a year.[78]

In January 1947 twenty-five civilians from Germany joined in at Wilton Park—officials, journalists, educationalists, trade union men. It was bitterly cold. Bread rationing had been introduced for the first time in English history, as Attlee diverted 50,000 tons of grain to Germany (even this was only half of what

9*

was needed). The visitors from Germany were so hungry that they had to be prevented from over-eating. A student from Camp 18, however, writing afterwards in *Zeit am Tyne*, was amazed at how starved and shut-in their minds were and asked himself who had been the free men, who the prisoners. For most of them the world began in 1945; therefore everything wrong in Germany was due to the occupation. Some too had come expecting to be able to fill their pockets with chocolate, or believing that butter had vanished from Germany because it was on the London market; they had no idea that coal and cigarettes were short. Some (such was the legacy of the Nazi era) wanted to know if the *Manchester Guardian* they had been reading was not a propaganda edition especially printed for Germany. Yet they also brought news of how in a small way, especially in education, life was really beginning again at the grassroots.*

Four courses later women came over too. The bureaucrats at the War Office were absurdly worried about their safety, imagining that the sex-starved POWs would at once fall upon them. Grondona had to send out instructions about conduct and set up separate dining and sitting rooms for them; but within a week the arrangements were all ignored and no one minded. The reporter of *Der Neue Weg*, the Youth Camp paper, listed their names like a litany: Lisel, Gerda, Ursula, Gretel, Hildegard, Frieda, Ilse, Lotte, Elizabeth, Hilda. The ten, who stood up excellently to being scrutinised like some re-discovered species, included two Landtag members, a university lecturer, a pastor, a Trade Union secretary, a Communist Party official, a radio journalist and two housewives. For the three hundred prisoners it was deeply moving to hear from their lips the saga of how they had carried on undaunted and so often had taken the lead in getting things done.

The feed-back from Wilton Park into the camps is hard to judge. Faulk's training advisers reported a mainly good effect with most returning POWs enthusiastic. Depressed anti-Nazis, often in isolation, had a real taste of the democracy they believed in and 'felt human again'. Those who really got the message passed it on, provided they had the character to do so, sometimes starting do-it-yourself courses in free politics in the old or fresh camps and hostels. Largeish parties came down from Featherstone Park.

* At this time too the future President Heuss, then leader of the Württemberg Liberals, paid a visit to Wilton Park on his way to an international conference of Liberals at Oxford.

Hankel and his group on return got dirty looks which meant, 'You know it all, do you?' to which they countered, 'Let's talk about it, shall we?' But in thirty months only about one per cent of POWs —some 3,600—were able to go to Wilton Park and from those who did not get the chance to go or rejected it a completely travestied picture spread around. It was a 'dream factory', and 'academy for cronies of the British', a 'school for super-democrats' or 'an open-Sesame for repatriation', an equivalent of the *Napola* Schools. Another attitude is evinced by Bernhard Harms, a man of culture: 'One could have applied to go to Wilton Park, but most of us preferred to work and work as much as possible on the side and spend the proceeds on sending parcels to our starving relatives in Germany.' There were complaints about Wiltoners being insufferable, like a general at Bridgend who wore a rag tie and open shirt and put his feet on the table. 'Oh him!' a visitor was told. 'He's just back from Wilton Park; he is *demokratisiert*. He knows all the answers.' Another negative factor was the fear, justified as we saw, that those returning to the Soviet Zone could suffer for having been at Wilton Park. Up in Camp 177 at Bury Father Jansen knew no better than to jot down: 'Wilton Park, a Socialist indoctrination camp. They operate with such success that, for example, a Junker of the purest water like Egbert von Tirpitz (grandson of the Grand Admiral), who just before he left translated for me into German a papal encyclical for use in my lectures, came back after six or eight weeks as the complete Socialist agitator.' Von Tirpitz was simply an able and open-minded young man who had the sense to take advantage of what was offered in Wilton Park. Fortunately there were many such.

The post-Restauration Bundesrepublik of Willi Brandt and Helmut Schmidt has one of its roots in Wilton Park, some of its leading men having attended either as a POW or later courses or conferences there. Schmidt himself, who came to know Koeppler well, paid tribute, when Minister of Defence, to its seminal influence, adding: 'Almost a whole generation of German politicians defined their concept of and attitude towards Britain and the British on the basis of impressions they received at Wilton Park. . . . It might have been a ruse of history that a historian such as Heinz Koeppler was called upon to work at Wilton Park, just in the nick of time—or was it rather the artful historian who realised that his time had come to write a few letters in the book of history?'[79] Schmidt was speaking more specifically of the Wilton Park when it had been moved to Steyning and the Dutch, French, Scandinavian, Italian and other European nationalities began attending. It then had such a strong life of its own that when, for reasons of economy, in 1956 the Foreign Office which had paid the bills since 1948 (£36,000 a year) decided to close it, it refused to die. Powerful support came not only from Britain but from German Wiltoners who were prepared to raise money to keep it going, as were the Swiss, for it was largely at Wilton Park that the appallingly bad post-war German–Swiss relations were repaired. The British Government relented and by the seventies Koeppler's formula for informal lateral meetings between persons of influence in different fields had proved sufficiently strong for a similar annual course to be held in Wisconsin by the American Friends of Wilton Park.

Koeppler's achievement is now an historic one, marked by his knighthood in 1977, the year of his retirement. But thirty years before, his vision and his adamant dedication to it were not so easily appreciated. His vital Anglo-German presence, itself a bridge between the two nations, was by no means always acceptable to prisoners of war who tended anyway to have a complex about refugees. His political background, as Borinski points out, was bound to cause a certain distrust. Commander Oesten was not alone in wondering whether he was not just an opportunist. Koeppler also raised a smile by having at once an honest German accent and a great zest for all things English—in which, says Ken Morgan, 'he was more papal than the Pope'. At the same time his well-defended personality was not easily penetrable. To Düttmann who saw a lot of him he remained 'a rather opaque character'. To Woetzel he was 'a bit loud, but spoke marvellous German'. To Dieter Hankel he was 'always *ein Stimulanz*, a man of intellect we did not laugh at even though we criticised him'. It was political animals like himself who perhaps appreciated him most. Willi Bründert found it quite amazing that only eight months after the war ended 'Heinz Koeppler gave us the chance to be partners and by his encouragement and humanity won our respect, esteem and very often real affection'. George Greene, so loyal a man that he does not recall how, if one of the plots against Koeppler had succeeded, he would have been asked to take his place, had liked him since Oxford days. 'The blessed thing about Heinz was that he encouraged each one of us to "do our own thing". He would say something outrageous; afterwards I would say to myself, "By God, he was right," but wonder if his method might not be counter-productive. But one knew that behind that often bland exterior a great deal of long-range thinking went on.' Borinski saw his intelligence as essentially a pragmatic one; he was able to appraise power factors coolly and flexibly and knew how to use them realistically. This enabled him to carry through the Wilton Park concept into another era against much opposition.

The Reichstag building in Koeppler's home city has been done up to look like new. The grandiloquent inscription 'To the German People' stands out as boldly as it did a hundred years ago. Koeppler as much as anyone has taught that the reverse is true; that the power which assures the liberty of a people can only arise from the people and that it rests on responsible individuals in all walks of life. For the 'ruse of history' that Helmut Schmidt spoke of had had a rich surprise. It had decreed that it needed a man who started out with many of the characteristics of the overbearing German male to create an institution dedicated to intelligent tolerance; and that a man whose great ability, drive and charm arose from his doubly strong inheritance as both Prussian and Jew should develop an ideal milieu in which political freedoms could be put to the test and grow.

12

Christian Responses

These crimes are the deeds of Germans for the results of which we too have to accept responsibility. For, as God visits the iniquities of the fathers upon the children unto the third and fourth generation, so he lays the guilt upon the whole nation for what its rulers have done or commanded. Many pages of the Bible teach us this lesson. Therefore let us bow under God's judgment not accusing others, but beginning with ourselves turn whole-heartedly to Him who can transform the severest punishment into a blessing. It is because we believe in the God of this transformation that we are not despondent, not in despair.

From a letter by Pastor Friederich von Bodelschwingh written on Trinity Sunday 1945

In the national disaster of 1945 there was only one body in Germany ready and prepared to face the situation—the Christian churches. They alone had largely intact organisation as well as a natural function of aiding the distressed; and they possessed a teaching capable of comprehending the magnitude of the disaster. Dozens of well-known texts from the Bible were appropriate to the state of the nation: 'They have sown the wind and shall reap the whirlwind'; 'Out of the deep I cry unto thee O Lord, and thou hearest me'; 'It is good for me that I have fallen in trouble, that I may learn Thy statutes'. Since political activity was, for the time being, suspended, prominent churchmen emerged as the first natural leaders of the people under the occupying powers—respected names like the newly elevated cardinals, Galen of Münster and Frings of Cologne; Bishop Wurm of Stuttgart and Hans Lilje of Hanover; and Bishop Dibelius and Pastor Niemoeller both of Berlin. Most of these soon made their mark by mild opposition to the Allies and by speaking up against the abuses of military government.

If the Catholic church in Germany and Austria remained nearly solid under the Nazis, the Lutherans had been both strengthened by persecution and weakened through the large numbers of clergy who veered with the Nazi wind, or even joined the Nazified 'German Christians'. A purge of the more blatant weaker brethren was undertaken at once with much heart searching as to how much could be forgiven of those who repented. Repentance was also during 1945 a great and dividing national issue. Pastor Bodelschwingh's letter three weeks after total defeat can be seen as the attempt by a deeply feeling Christian to measure up to the extent of the cataclysm that had befallen his country, which to not a few came like an act of divine justice. It had been foreseen, feared and even wished for. Dietrich Bonhoeffer, martyr of modern Christian existential faith, was asked in 1941 what he was praying for. 'For the defeat of my country, for I believe it is the only way my country can pay for all the suffering it has caused in the world.' A strong Christian like General von Ravenstein could tell the assembled officers at Grande Ligne that defeat was better than victory for Germany. Certainly shame was felt by many in 1945 for what had been done in their country's name. But could and should such personal feeling be transformed into a call for national repentance and common guilt?

Guilt is always a loaded issue and one that easily boomerangs. Memory of the 'sole guilt' clauses that were fastened on Germany at the Treaty of Versailles was one source of resistance to such an admission; another was blind patriotism. Millions had fallen for Nazi exploitation of the ideal—a basically un-English one though always quoted in English—of 'my country right or wrong'; there was a confusion also, which the Allies never clarified, between collective responsibility—a political concept, for the Germans had willed Hitler to power—and collective guilt, which implied the moral condemnation of a nation. The ironic thing was that those who were most able, because they were Christians, to accept such guilt were not those responsible for the black name of their country. Thus, when the combined Protestant Churches came together at Stuttgart in October to seek inspiration for a new beginning, they made an historic declaration on behalf of the German people before a notable delegation from the World Council of Churches: 'We know ourselves to be one with our people in a great company of suffering and a great solidarity of guilt. With great pain do we say: through us endless suffering has been brought to many people.' The declaration was in no way a political manifesto, but much more a pious resolution. It was an attempt to purge the past, a moment of renewal and hope for what might be achieved through prayer and Christian fellowship, and also an attempt to clarify relations then being restored with Christian bodies abroad. It was broadcast, however, to the world as 'Protestant Church acknowledges German war guilt'. But on behalf of whom?—that was the question. Certainly not of all its members, still less of the millions who had fought in the Wehrmacht. (The Catholic Church in Germany on the whole kept outside this issue and made no such declaration.)

In all POW camps men flocked to religious services in the second half of 1945. Chaplains rejoiced to see such eager congregations. The usual barriers were down and it appeared to many to be the opportunity of their lives. 'It was a tremendously deep time for us pastors,' remembers Rudolf Halver. 'We were happy that with only a Bible in our hands we could really reach these young men who had been so knocked about and were so confused. The different confessions came together and we hoped that this would continue when we got home. But that was a spiritual dream.' To Pastor Jentsch, captured in Italy, they 'were all comrades, Christians and non-Christians alike: all poor, defeated, hungry and deprived of freedom. When the men streamed into the quickly-built chapels many confused the rising curve of attendance with a religious revival. But it was not different in 1933 which people thought to be a positive upsurge. Now mass religiosity is seen in negative terms, for we understand the close relation between shock and intoxication.' A sobering statement, but many did come to Christianity because of 1945 or became stronger Christians.

It would be a mistake to view the whole harrowing and quickening of the human spirit that took place behind barbed wire after defeat only in a Christian context. It has been said that the very experience, often a long one, of being a prisoner in the Second World War was parallel for Germans in its spiritual effect to that of being in the trenches during the First World War. In each case it brought a deepening of private experience, and inner change. In neither case did people easily speak about it afterwards.

A month after the British and Americans entered Berlin Dr Stewart Herman, American Lutheran minister in Berlin till 1942, returned there and was soon being welcomed at a meeting of the Federal Council of the Confessing Church in Dahlem. In front of him he saw 'shrunken frames—ill-clad from broken shoes to ragged collars much too large for scrawny necks—and sunken cheeks under eyes doubly haunted by the memory of brethren murdered by the Gestapo and the vision of the Cross that would not let them go. They looked better a few months later'. Compared to theirs, the situation of the chaplains in the prison camps was easy. Most of them had been combatant troops, either as officers or other ranks, and had been protected from hardship and persecution. But such were the demands on them that by the spring of 1946 they too were in due need of succour.* Charles Cranfield, having been round most of the camps, found many splendid men and summed up his general impression of close on two hundred Lutheran pastors as 'all very tired, mentally and spiritually and often physically. Some of the best of them are most weary because they have worked themselves to the limit. One such is the excellent chaplain at 17 (Lodge Moor), Pastor Ahlbory, though I hear that he went back from the refresher course at 174 tremendously refreshed. Many are in their "state" for lack of spiritual and mental stimulus. One has to remember that the great majority have not been padres during the war, but have had to serve as combatants, and so are out of practice. Those who were officers have to learn not to be still officers, and those who were ORs have to learn not to be ORs! And the strictness of German discipline makes this all the harder.'

The 'refresher course at 174' was available at Norton in Nottinghamshire. This camp was the brain-child of Forell who had proposed as early as the autumn of 1944 to the War Office that a special camp should be started for theological students, new or interrupted ones, coupled with a *pedagogisches Seminar*, a teacher-training unit at which men could take their *Abitur* (the equivalent of the British 'A' levels). The former would give indispensable support to Christian ministry in the camps, and both would be financed and supervised through John Barwick, the American secretary in Britain of the World Alliance of YMCAs. The War Office were thoroughly co-operative. For some ten months Forell and his assistant, the Reverend Dr Hartwell, worked to prepare the ground. The latter travelled round collecting books. The widow of an East Anglian vicar gave him her husband's valuable theological library and he was allowed to comb the library at his old college—Mansfield College in Oxford—for theological books in German. The Bishop of Chichester provided a large number

* See page 175.

and the Ecumenical Council of the Chaplaincy Service to prisoners of war at Geneva eventually sent sixty-six cases of books. But the library was the least of the problems. Not surprisingly, no single professor of theology could be found in the camps; so the teaching staff had to be chosen from among the existing chaplains and academics.

Not without reason screeners were suspicious of the past political loyalties of several of the Wehrmacht padres, a large number of whom had thanked God for Hitler from the pulpit.* Cyrus Brooks, the 'father of re-education', when collating screening reports on a list of proposed staff made up by Forell, struck off all but two names. Those excluded included Pastor Bodelschwingh, Dr Damrath, a short, thick-set and able Prussian who had the possibly suspicious looking rank of *Wehrmachtsoberpfarrer*, and, to his great surprise, the distinguished theologian, Dr D. G. Friedrich. Forell at once went to beard Brooks whom he describes as 'a kind of police chief for our work who had to prevent us doing anything foolish'. He found him sympathetic. Various misunderstandings were smoothed out and his list was eventually approved, apart from Friedrich. Nevertheless, John Barwick felt the atmosphere was so unfavourable that he wondered whether the Norton project should be allowed to go forward at all. But Forell, who always emphasized to recruits that Norton would be a place of trial, had much more faith in its future and performed the opening ceremony on 8 August, preaching a sermon on the text, 'The truth shall make you free'. Part of Forell's confidence lay in the remarkable Commandant, Major Jack Boughton, who had been hand-picked by the War Office from his reputation as a 'kindly disciplinarian' when in charge of Italian prisoners.

For more than a year the Nortoners were as worried as all POWs because no date of repatriation was given. But early in 1946 Faulk made a typical visit in which he allowed everyone to get their grumbles and complaints off their chest. Damrath reported that, although Faulk could not answer all questions, a frank, friendly and sincere statement from a man in authority made a big and good impression. The many pastors on a refresher course went back to their camps 'ready to help their fellow POWs to bear cheerfully what cannot be easy.' But there were other and deeper tensions. Existing German accounts of Norton only hint

* By July 1947 67 per cent of chaplains screened were reckoned to be 'A's, though this was a higher proportion than for any other profession.

at the heart-searchings and even mutual suspicion that existed, at least early on. The theological courses were set in a liturgical framework of study and worship, so that, outwardly, all might go smoothly. But not only did barbed wire, as ever, act as an enlarging mirror for minor defects, as Forell observed; there was also much hiding of the past. 'Many of them,' in Hartwell's view, 'were more officer than pastor. Many had bad consciences. They inhibited personal feelings of repentance by saying, "We fought for the Fatherland." ' A sympathetic listener, Hartwell sustained not a few troubled men through a spiritual crisis. One such in another camp where a refresher course was being held asked to see him.

'There is something I want to confess.'

'There is no need to confess,' Hartwell said. 'I am here to help.'

The man then told his story. He had been a pastor in peace time but, having violent feelings against the Jews, had resigned, and taken an active post with the Party, and when war broke out had joined up. Trying to put all this behind him he had come forward as a camp chaplain. Now he wanted to get it off his conscience. Hartwell listened in silence; then heard him say, 'Why do you, who were persecuted by the Nazis, help us POWs?'

'I am a Christian. It is my duty to do so . . . but I am not interested in your past.'

'But can you forgive me?'

'It is not for me to forgive, but God. If you really repent sincerely, He will forgive you.'

'Will you allow me to take part in the communion service you are taking tomorrow?'

'Certainly.'

This man later wanted to be reinstated as a pastor in his own city but the church authorities, being aware of his past record, refused. In despair, he wrote to Hartwell who sent a letter saying that he had experienced a complete re-conversion. 'Reinstate him —he will be a good pastor.' And so it turned out. But he was never able to bring his past out into the open among his comrades and colleagues, nor has he to this day.

Outer conditions at Norton were excellent. The prisoners had the same rations as a work-camp; indeed, as regards food, clothing and heating they were better off than students at any German university at the time. If coal ran out, wood could be brought in on the quiet from the park. Nevertheless in the first months Barwick's fears seemed justified. A representative of a group of officers came to see Major Boughton to ask whether they could have sheets and pillow-cases. The Commandant said, 'Oh, do they! If they want that they can leave tomorrow. Do they want to know the time of the next train? You are all students here!' Some of the officers also wished to have batmen, as they had had in previous camps. This too was turned down. The camp spokesman made out a rota of duties for keeping the camp clean, which was not accepted as it interfered with their studies. When he threw the responsibility back to the students, the camp quickly became so filthy that the Commandant had to take firm steps. By November problems of discipline and morale had become so acute that Barwick had to ask for help from the Re-education Section at Bush House. A training adviser, sent down by Faulk, reported that the root of the trouble was a deep unwillingness to face the inner stresses that existed. 'Whereas the camp inmates,' he wrote, 'acknowledge democratic ideals outwardly, most of them are strongly nationalistic, even if unconsciously so.... They may have turned away from militarism, but not towards anything positive. ... The academics feel they are a race apart and look down on the British other ranks. Another mistake is that they work far too intensively, so that the Commandant had to intervene and order a midday interval. This is, in part, a defence against facing the past and a way of maintaining a sense of superiority.... Another factor is that the YMCA as an international body is reluctant to be active in any political way and afraid of appearing to be involved in disciplinary problems.'[80] The recommended solution was for Norton to be integrated into the re-education programme, if in a restricted way, and also the introduction of screening. Both these things happened in February 1946.

There was another factor which the report did not deal with— a purely spiritual one. This was the very nature of Lutheran piety and inwardness, that *Innerlichkeit* which over the centuries has been a hall-mark of German protestantism. It came to the fore in a controversy over *Der Monatsbrief*, the excellently presented YMCA sponsored monthly journal with a circulation of 3,000, which was sent out to all the camps. Its object was to bring Christian doctrine and comfort to its readers and restore the broken links with home, family and nation. Wolfgang Theopold, the first editor, mixed Bible passages, homilies, poems, stories—

some in dialect—a garnering of traditional piety and wholesome wisdom mostly of a pastoral kind, all presented in a setting of the Church calendar. Repentance was dealt with in the personal terms of inner change and making amends. It contained nothing controversial and lay rather uneasily on a borderline between renewal and nostalgia. In April 1946 John Barwick wrote to Damrath enclosing a searching criticism of the paper which had come through the Bishop of Chichester and Bush House. The *Monatsbrief*, suggested Barwick, was in danger of being escapist and of falling into the old neo-romantic tendencies. It did not reflect present needs enough, nor current religious thought. On the other hand, the YMCA would never accept any kind of political interference in religious matters.

Here in a mild form was the challenge that the next generation would make to the whole course of German recovery and which Marxists and progressives were already making: it was an attempt to avoid the truths of contemporary history. At the psychological level this German inwardness could be a shield held up against reality, a way of not looking closely at the shadow side of human nature. But the Christians at Norton were not explorers, hardly even existentialists. Their theme was *'Traditio-Krisis-Renovatio'*.* Quiet meditation, hard study and an unadventurous convalescence seemed best after the tremendous spiritual shock the nation had undergone. It was through the far more searching experiences of the POW camps in Russia that the Lutheran Church would receive its chief challenge and injection of strength.

That the inherent problems of Norton were almost entirely overcome was due above all to the Commandant. Major Boughton, a Londoner in his mid-fifties, was a staunch Catholic and indeed later became an Oblate Father of the Benedictine Order. Having no family he dedicated himself utterly to his work; he never took a day off and leave only twice in two years. On his motivation, he says simply, 'It was a great opportunity'. Having been in the Indian Army at the end of the First World War, he had then entered the furniture business, returning in 1940 at first to a desk job in the Army until he was sent in charge of Italian POWs. His voice, which thirty years later in his mid-eighties was as clear as a bell, had something of the clipped tang of Field Marshal Montgomery, but was much more benign. 'I always' he said 'made

* The title of the booklet that the last head of the theological school, Dr Ernst Dammann, wrote about Norton thirty years later.

the same speech when taking over a camp: If you behave yourselves, you'll get all I can give you. If you misbehave yourselves,
again you'll get all I can give you—and some! They knew who I
was. I took over Norton from a very crabby major, an "illegitimate", and we crossed swords more than once. I told him I
wanted the stores checked. He said, "If you want that, I'll be here
a week." I told him he had to be out at eleven o'clock that morning. An unpleasant man—a common thief at one period.'

Boughton discovered a motto for Norton: *Fide non armis*,
Through Faith, Not Weapons, and had it put up over the gate.
He also ended all saluting, instituting a brief bow instead, which
he acknowledged with a movement of the arm. On his birthday
musicians and singers would greet him with a trumpet fanfare and
a motet. The POWs knew that he would always stand up for them.
Father Lotz, the Catholic chaplain at nearby Carburton, whose life
had been in danger from the fanatical Nazis in March 1945, used
to be sent to local camps. He told Major Boughton that the driver
of his pick-up always put him in at the back, which meant that
when he was fasting he felt faint from the fumes. An order went
out that the driver was to be driven in the back of his own vehicle
for a while, after which Father Lotz always had a seat beside him.

'You are pro-German,' someone once said to the commandant
accusingly. 'You could not have made a bigger mistake,' he replied. 'I am pro-humanity.' He could not bear glumness and
decided early on to do something about Dr Damrath's dour
Prussian expression. 'I remember seeing him coming down the
hill in his peaked cap. "Good morning!" I said. He said, "Good
morning, sir!" I said, "How the devil must be laughing at you!"
"Why, sir?" "You look so bloody miserable on your way to
heaven. I can afford to laugh on my way to hell!" He never met
me again without a smile.' The Nortoners did not always know
when their Commandant was pulling their legs or, indeed, what
his humour meant. He recalls how 'we always used to say that
Germans take kindness for weakness; so I said to them one day,
joking about their own slogan, "If you want strength from me it
won't be strength through joy!" One of them came up afterwards
and said I had upset them—they never took my kindness for weakness. Of course, I had spies round the camp—there were plenty of
people only too glad to get hold of my ears; only I had to sort out
the creepers and those that played fast ones. That's the art of
being a commandant.'

Boughton did his best to get local people involved in Norton. The church at Cuckney at first refused to welcome POWs, then relented and sent an apology. In the end the Norton Germans received as much hospitality in the neighbourhood as any camp did. Boughton arranged for the football team to play a Notts Forest eleven and kicked off himself. At Christmas time the Duchess of Portland came over with her daughters from Welbeck Abbey and, after the British army custom, helped serve the POWs at table. The Portland estate was adjacent and contained some attractive lakes which, being outside the wire, were a sore temptation to the POWs as Major Boughton found out.

One hot summer day one of the schoolmasters I knew came and told me—or rather I had to wheedle it out of him—a guilty secret. 'I was out in the lake last night, sir, having a swim.' 'Anyone else there?' 'Yes.' 'That's disobeying orders,' I said, 'Don't do it again—and if you can, tell the others not to do it—or they'll be in trouble.' Well, the same thing was reported to me by one of my junior officers, so I had to act. I sent for the heads of the camps—the padres, Basil Wilke the headmaster, the doctor, and so forth—and said, 'You know I'm like a panther. I have had some experience of panthers—they won't touch you until you touch them.' And I said, 'You've touched me. I understand there are some people getting out of this camp to swim. If you do, you'll be shot outside the barbed wire by one of my officers. Now you can go.' A bit later Basil came to me and said, 'Did you say six people got outside the camp to swim?' 'I mentioned no number.' 'If, sir, you'd like to step out of the office—all the men who bathed in the lake are on the road lined up and they will own up to you personally.' 'No,' I said, 'I don't want to see them. I might see faces that I had respect for. And I shall have none for them if I see them now.' But I was also very amused and said to Basil, 'Really, your behaviour is worthy of an English public-school!'

Wolfgang Kaftan, the gifted and very anglophile puppet-master at Norton, describes an occasion when Major Boughton had to reprimand the whole camp: 'He made the facts of the situation plain and then probably intended to add something moralising, but stopped and said simply, "No, I will leave it at that." That sentence made a fundamental impression on me. He did not offend anyone but made us feel ashamed. . . . It was an educational master-

piece which impressed me as a teacher deeply.' At such times
Major Boughton had the camp in the palm of his hand. Indeed by
June 1946, a year after opening, Norton had been so transformed
by his occasionally stern paternalism that for Forell it was 'the
brightest spot in his life'. The Commandant in turn spoke of
Forell as 'the double bass in the orchestra—he always struck the
deepest note.'

After Boughton's death a number of albums were found among
his effects, containing photographs, water-colours, testimonials
and verses presented to him on his birthday and other occasions,
evincing the esteem in which he was held. Nearly all are written
in English, but one document in bold illuminated gothic script is
in German, perhaps because English words can hardly convey,
and would perhaps falsify, the very German sentiments:

DEED OF FATHERSHIP (*Vaterschaft*)

Herewith is acknowledged to the Commandant of Camp 174,
Herr Major Boughton, fathership over 468 children and gratitude expressed for his faithful fulfilment of his father's duties.
Cuckney   The Children of the Camp 174
3 February 1947

At first sight such sentiments may appear mawkish, a sign of
that *Schwärmerei*, or eager naïveté in some Germans that is easy to
exploit. But that would be wrong. It was usual, for instance, for a
company sergeant major to be called '*Die Mutter der Kompagnie*'.
The document is a 'serious joke', given point by the fact that the
word *Vaterschaft* is most used in connection with alimony cases.
It is a touching testament of affection for a good man, who in the
long isolation of the prisoners from their families was more than
a father figure to them.

'I want one of the students removed,' said Damrath to Boughton
one day. 'He has started burning candles.' The Lutherans were
always on the look-out for creeping Romanism. It had been
originally intended to have a Catholic seminary at Norton as well,
but typically Monsignor Godfrey vetoed this. 'The Nuncio,'
according to Boughton, 'was dead nuts against us because we
were supported by the YMCA.' Those intended to be priests were
sent to a small special unit at Colchester.* Against this the YMCA,

* Its teething troubles, with political tensions between instructors and
students, appear to have been worse than those at Norton.

being non-denominational, was happy to equip the Catholic chapel at Norton. When John Barwick was told that it needed altar cloths—an expensive item—he said at once, 'Charge them up to us.' The Catholic presence at Norton became, in fact, quite strong and included an outstanding young Benedictine, Father Wahler, who came from a camp in Canada with a whole case full of vestments he had been given there. He, like the other priests, soon called Boughton 'Jack', though only privately. On one occasion he took over for tea to the Trappist monastery at Colville a party including Boughton's friend, Ferrenbacher (the German Abbot of Buckfast), a choir, and Otto Spar, the outstanding Norton organist. The monks were given dispensation to speak and there was a moving, highly-charged atmosphere. Their organ was played as never before and, at parting, the Colville Abbot—Boughton has never forgotten—asked for one more song, and listened with tears in his eyes.

The big events at Norton were the visits of distinguished churchmen, for the Catholics that of Cardinal Frings of Cologne. He had recently hit the headlines when he preached in the undamaged part of his famous cathedral a sermon in which he said that citizens who were cold and starving were justified in stealing coal—something which, in practice, the military government was turning a blind eye to. He came to Britain very conscious that he was a spokesman for his people and a Cardinal—for whom, however, there was no travelling category. His permit, therefore, bore the rank of Field Marshal. On board ship he protested that there had been a mistake, and that he was a 'Prince of the Church'. At this, the British corporal who was mustering the passengers gave the German some advice. 'If I were you, sir, I'd forget about being a Prince of the Church. That doesn't cut any ice. Just be a Field Marshal—you'll get top treatment.'[81] Cardinal Frings came to Norton with the Bishop of Nottingham to find that Boughton had laid on a pontifical High Mass in the Catholic chapel. Twenty-five POW priests on retreat attended, as did the Anglican vicar who had lent carpets and his best church furniture for the occasion, everything, in fact, except the vestments. 'It was a great success,' says Boughton. 'The press was there, but the Cardinal was very tired.' After visiting some other camps, Frings, preaching in Westminster Cathedral and obviously referring to Norton, said he had been with prisoners of war who were 'in a golden cage—but it was a cage, nevertheless'. He wanted to see the men home.

The Times and other papers reported the words 'golden cage' without qualification. There was much resentment at this in many camps. Up at Warth Mills, Bury, an embarrassed and blinkered Father Jansen was at pains to explain to angry comrades that the Cardinal could not be referring to their camp and rather oddly assumed that he had used the words 'diplomatically, in order not to make their situation worse.'

For the Protestants at Norton the first high point was the visit of Hans Lilje, soon to be installed as bishop in the ruins of the historic Marktkirche in Hanover. A pungent and stirring preacher with a stocky, almost pugnacious physique, he had spent the last period of the Third Reich in prison. Gursky describes how the dining hall was packed and the prisoners sat in total stillness to hear him preach on the text of St Paul's words to his shipmates when they were expecting to be wrecked: 'Wherefore, sirs, be of good cheer.' It was the most inspiring and gripping existential sermon Gursky had ever heard, for it arose directly out of the situation they were all in. This occasion was a complete contrast to the more dramatic visit later in the year 1946 of Martin Niemoeller. Famous U-boat commander of the First World War, he had from his pulpit at Dahlem in Berlin become an outspoken critic of the Nazis and though never harshly treated had spent eight years all told in different *KZ*. He was one of the framers of the Stuttgart Declaration on Germany's guilt for acts committed by the Nazis. His name was so prominent outside Germany that during the war he was suggested (by Adam von Trott) as a possible Chancellor, if Hitler were overthrown, to create confidence abroad.

For the first week of Niemoeller's tour of POW camps Pastor Forell acted as his 'adjutant and travel marshal'. 'It was,' he wrote to his wife, 'very strenuous but one of the most rewarding tasks that came my way. At a camp near Chichester with full hall and overflow, there was such tension that one was aware of it physically. At Luton Airport he gave a sobering picture of the inner and outer chaos in Germany and spoke in a fatherly and brotherly way on the guilt issue. . . . Coming to Norton he held a wide-ranging conference in which he kept on at the non-Germans present—I was sadistic enough to enjoy it!—confronting them with the difficulty of making plans for the church or for reconstruction as long as people can think only of hunger and the victors cannot agree on how to provide jobs and food. John Barwick sat there quite confused by his pessimism, pale and nervous at the likely reaction of POWs.' Later on in his diary Forell, glad that the turbulent days as Niemöller's companion were over, says that he was frequently misunderstood, and also that many of his utterances were ill-judged. 'It was sobering, but it could have been a great deal more human.' Not surprisingly the famous pastor's reception at officers' camps was generally hostile; at Featherstone Park, as mentioned, he was actually booed.

At Norton most tensions gradually passed away. Damrath stayed little more than a year, being posted home early to join the *Kanzlei* of the Confessional Church. Superintendent Schnuis headed the theological school for a while till Dr Friedrich, cleared by screening, arrived at the end of the year and was elected in his place.* By all accounts a remarkable community spirit developed, scholarly, hard working and liturgically based. The academic level was raised and distinguished lecturers came from abroad. The most notable was the Swede, Professor Nygren, soon to be Bishop of Lund and President of the World Lutheran Federation; he stayed three weeks lecturing mainly on the Epistle to the Romans, that key-work for German Protestant apologetics because it concerns the right relation of the Christian to the State. There were visits of inspection from America and Germany and also from France where a year later at Montpellier a rather similar, larger POW seminary was set up. There was no difficulty in having Catholics and Protestants together: the Papal Nuncio at that time in France was Cardinal Roncalli, the future Pope John XXIII.

A separate section of Norton was devoted to teacher training and those taking *Abitur*, and later on Pastor Werner Jentsch, Forell's successor in his post at the YMCA, introduced a course for youth leaders, attended by seventy-two POWs, a third of them Catholics. This secular part of the camp was called in the traditional German manner 'Hell', while the theologians lived in 'Heaven' and—it was at least Gursky's impression—rather looked down on their more radical confrères. There was an awkward episode when some of the 999 'politicals', parked at Norton for a while pending repatriation, made the same sort of representations as they had at Wilton Park. A few of them believed that the theological school was being run by ex-Nazis and militarists and

* Later Professor of Theology at Kiel University and editor of Kittel's famous *Dictionary of the New Testament*.

even tried to convince the authorities that this was so. There was at least one former SS officer, Leutnant Kurt Bergmann from Featherstone Park, grateful to be at Norton;[82] he was later joined by SS members of the former Rimini Choir which travelled out from the camp. There was the already mentioned Otto Spar, who not only raised the Norton choir to an excellent level but drew an increased flock to Cuckney Church by his organ playing. The camp was also the base of Wolfgang Kaplan's remarkable puppet theatre, the fame of which spread far and wide. There was in fact a rare mix of interesting Germans at Norton, not the least being Dr Ernst Dammann. He had been a missionary in East Africa in the thirties when it was felt advisable for Germans officially abroad to join the Party as a test of their Germanness. He had done so and become a Group Leader. He put this down on a POW form and was sent as a C-plus to the North of Scotland. Forell is said to have rescued him from there and he became the last head of the theological school which finally closed in June 1948. It was hoped—and plans for it were quite advanced—that the whole school with its library should be reconstituted in Germany when Kloster Moellenbeck near Rinteln was made available for this purpose. But the scheme failed, apparently because of 'bureaucratic difficulties'. But its alumni have carried its achievements into many corners of the German world and beyond and, like those who were at Featherstone Park, sometimes meet together to remind themselves of old times.

Major Boughton suggests that the ecumenical spirit at Norton did not go much beyond friendly leg-pulling. But across the country there was a good deal of Christian fellowship between denominations and more than a touch of the *una sancta* spirit that deep down unites all Christians. Nevertheless, most Lutherans found it not easy to make a close entente with any of the British churches. The Anglicans seemed halfway to Rome, the Presbyterians were Calvinist and the other nonconformists too different —except the Methodists. Pastor Gursky was shocked and hurt when reading the English press at the time of the four hundredth anniversary of Luther's death in 1947. The doctrines of the founder of his church were put down as largely responsible for the political passivity of the German people; a trail of influence was even detected from Luther that led through Frederick the Great to Hitler. The only article that appeased Gursky was in a Methodist journal—not surprisingly perhaps, for it was directly from a moment of insight received from Luther's *Preface to the Epistle to the Romans* that John Wesley was inspired to make his great reform.

For the Norton Lutherans what mattered most was communion —in the Christian sense and with the homeland. Hans Nükles, a talented young theological student and graphic artist, found a striking emblem for this: a bold cross inside a strong circle and across the upright a young man is handing to an unknown prisoner the *Brot der Heimat*. A taste of this bread is to be had in a letter that Wolfgang Theopold wrote back to Norton in the summer of 1947:

From one of your advance party
Like a mother that has grown old in sorrow the *Heimat* has greatly changed. As it did during the war a great burden lies on the heart of all women and girls. They must do man's work in the farm and fields, in factory, office and shop, and must bring up your children, your brothers and sisters to be useful people, with no father's hand to help. It seems to me that the women have become harder in the face and not only because they go to work in men's clothes. Yet inside them a heart beats that longs to lay down their heavy fate, so that they may love and be loved once more. Feminine virtue is cheap. Like flies drawn to the light many fall just for pleasure and are burned. When you return you must bring them a great understanding, forgiveness, chivalry, and a sincere love to your girls and wives. It often seems to me that many have behaved so thoughtlessly because their true love is never matched. Your girls make no great demands on life, for they know better than you can, who have still to find your feet here, that expectations must be kept low. Most of them want to be brave and good and are ready to go with you through thick and thin if only they can feel that the man they give their trust to is reliable. What a great task for you, you men! Together with such a woman whom you love and who can love you back, however poor you are and though you have lost your hearth and home, you will not be a released prisoner, but a homecomer, even if you return to a part of the Fatherland that is strange to you. There have been no better moments for me than when such a couple, he a prisoner of war, she a refugee, come and ask me to marry them, and they sit on the traditional sofa under the lamp-light and the three of us talk

about their marriage and their plans. For the marriage will be a different one from what you older ones recall: no feast or finery, but he in his everyday jacket, she in a borrowed gown. But when both of them, in spite of all the uncertainty they are faced with, have made their solemn vows and then knelt at the altar to ask for blessing, then has a fresh life blossomed amid the desolate rubble of our time.[83]

On 25 February 1947 some fifteen German Lutheran pastors, chaplains from the surrounding camps, were sitting in the historic St Alkmund's room in Shrewsbury, eagerly writing. They had been asked to put their feelings on paper about not being allowed to return home along with their repatriation group. It was War Office policy, agreed by the Germans, to hold them back for the sake of morale and cohesion in the camps. In the case of married men, some already prisoners for years, it meant great self-sacrifice and often an intolerable burden upon their wives and home parishes. 'I have never seen such intent writing in silence, even in an exam,' says Archdeacon Sydney D. Austerberry, then vicar of St Alkmund's with a special liaison position to POW camps. 'I can still recall the atmosphere of that conference; it was like an old boys' reunion. One of them was married to the daughter of Field Marshal von Witzleben who was hanged for his part in the 1944 plot, and his description of what the SS did to him as he lay in his bed was very vivid.'

The situation of most chaplains by this time was extremely depressing. There were no fewer than 1,400 POW units, including hostels, to be ministered to as far as possible and less than 276 pastors, curates and lay readers (in August 1946) to do it. They were isolated from each other—no post was allowed between camps. Their congregations had dwindled steadily since 1945 and most of the alert prisoners were preferring to spend Sundays with English friends. With the 'whites', usually though not always the most positive element, now at home, in the majority of camps a more and more disgruntled element was left behind. The only solution seemed to be for 'exchange pastors' to come over from Germany. Niemöeller the previous November had promised to send ten at once, but none had come. Dr Hartwell worked long and hard to bring over seventy-five, to which the German Church Council agreed, but the scheme never really worked. Only twenty-six ever arrived and none before the very end of 1947; they were nearly all used in transit camps to prepare POWs for the shock of homecoming. The Reverend B. S. Johnstone, Cranfield's successor as staff adviser chaplain to the P/W Directorate at the War Office, felt it was not fair on humane grounds to keep chaplains longer against their will, but when the exchange system broke down he had reluctantly to revoke plans to start sending more home for fear of thinning down the pastoral care in the camps too far. When they did return many were shadows of their true selves.

Everything in the way of fraternal meetings with each other and with British colleagues that could be arranged was, therefore, vital. The Bishops of St Albans and Rochester had already been forward in doing this when in August 1946 Cranfield set up the first proper pastor's conference at Brockenhurst Camp, attended by twenty-three camp chaplains from all over Southern Command. The system of conferences, retreats and refresher courses was from now on extended to help all the Protestant chaplains who could make use of it to carry their heavy burdens. The Catholic chaplains, being unmarried, had one less problem, and also had the opportunity for retreat in seminaries. In his four-year Odyssey in the camps Father Josef Jansen went to three retreats, two with the Jesuits at Rainhill near Liverpool, the third at Hadzor near Droitwich. He found the first occasion which involved silence and spiritual exercises not appropriate to his weary and isolated state. Information on the Catholic side is, however, scanty, but it seems that because the Apostolic Delegate was, as we have seen, slow in taking initiative, the fate of prisoner priests was very chancy and left to local awareness of need. *The Universe* on 22 November 1946 published a letter from six 'disgusted and indignant' lay Catholics from Liverpool who had met a prisoner who turned out to be a priest. His clothes were old and dishevelled: a faded green battle-dress top and an ancient pair of grey flannel trousers. He had to minister to several wide-ranging camps and had just walked six miles, not being allowed to use public transport. 'We are sure that the people of England would not tolerate this kind of thing if they knew it existed.'

But all over the country local clergy and theological colleges and lay Christians did see a need and responded to it, sometimes having to be prompted from above, as by Cranfield's booklets, sometimes from below, as by Mary Foss's remarkable solo effort, and very often spontaneously. Margaret Owen, German-speaking

wife of the Vicar of Walton-on-the-Naze, was asked by some
Quaker camp visitors to go with them into the hostel at Beau-
mont. She made a little speech to them from the stage in their
common hut. Could she and the Vicar help in any way? Yes, they
needed above all something to read and lights in their huts. So
she collected candles and magazines for them and made other useful purchases. Later they came to the vicarage on Sundays. Soon
there was a monthly service for POWs at Walton Church and a
social afterwards. The vicar appealed from the pulpit and the local
baker, a POW in the First World War, provided all the rolls
needed and a farmer made a similar offer of milk. These services
and socials were kept up for eighteen months. The Reverend
Charles Owen sometimes himself preached in German. Pastor
Gursky over at the main camp at Halstead heard enthusiastic
reports of the Owens and joined in, being allowed to take a truck
full of men each time with him. These afternoon services, jointly
held in English and German, and the garden parties afterwards
were, he wrote, the most enjoyable of his activities at the time.
The lesson was often read by an emigrated German Jew, a Dr
Meyer, who was usually there in a wheel chair, having come from
Frinton where he lived. A Rabbi's son from Hanover, he had become a Lutheran and was a living example of how anti-Semitism
can be combatted. Many POWs looked up to him as a father, as a
marvellous example of a man who overcame the difficulties of
exile and illness in a positive way.* The Owens also organised a
Sunday *Packkreis*, a parcel-sending circle, which they kept up for
another decade, even after they moved to the Channel Isles in
1950. This service went exclusively to former prisoners in East
Germany where the need was greatest, and for a while Margaret
Owen actually made a journey to visit these families each year,
even selling furniture to be able to do so. The Owens in turn
inspired Pastor Gursky and his wife, as soon as he returned home,
to start up their own parcel service to needy Christians in the
East, as a thank-offering for returning safe and sound. Most of
the addresses they obtained from the Red Cross or Church
organisations, and 'with the cellar of our house sometimes re-
sembling a warehouse, we carried on for nearly twenty years.'
   Another way was to introduce POWs to joint worship and even

---

* Dr Meyer returned home to Hanover in 1949 where Bishop Lilje
found him an administrative post in the Innere Mission, but he died
after a few years.

pilgrimages. Maurice Brunsden* was then in the RAF and an Anglican lay reader. He found himself at Shipham, the American Air Base in Norfolk which the RAF took over, including a well-equipped chapel. There were 500 British and 500 Germans on the base and he would sometimes get over 800 of them to take part in ecumenical services. Several times he took a coach-load of Germans, some as pilgrims, to the Anglican Shrine of Our Lady at Walsingham and many who had lost touch with religion were reconciled to their faith again. The POWs on the Air Station at Nettleton in Lincolnshire asked the local vicar, the Reverend I. T. Wilson, for his 'priestly services' which he gladly gave, at first in a chapel hut. Can they not come to my church?, he asked, and they did so, at first under armed guard, till he objected; then they were allowed to walk to church unescorted. 'The services were inspiring, with a Moravian Brother, Fritz Stahl, from the Black Forest acting as organist and occasional preacher, and Berthold Stocker, a poet who composed and read religious verses to the typical choral singing of their home church. It was a time of small acts of mutual aid. The Vicar might be teaching advanced Latin to an interrupted student, while his garden was being done. Like so many vicars' wives, Mrs Wilson 'would always conjure up some miraculous meal', the local farmers being lavish in their gifts of food. Indeed the Wilsons recall those days as the happiest in their ministry. Another couple at Barningham Vicarage, Norfolk, also called Wilson, had enough glebe land with goats, hens and rabbits always to provide meals for POW guests. The vicar's widow remembers how her husband followed the custom he had learned in little Lutheran churches of all saying the Lord's Prayer standing at the end of the service, while the bell was tolled inviting those within earshot to join in if they wished. Then he himself led the Germans in the same prayer. The atmosphere, Mrs Wilson recalls, was 'electric'.

At a Harvest Festival service in Bristol Cathedral in 1947 attended by hundreds of POWs the Bishop said: 'Our gratitude is mixed with misgivings for we remember that you too have farms and fields. As the months lengthen into years we can understand something about what you must be feeling about those harvests at home which you might be helping to reap. I assure you that some

* Thirty years later Canon Brunsden was in charge of the Heidelberg (black) parish in Cape Province.

of us have a very uneasy conscience about this!'[84] It was a change for Germans to hear that some English felt guilty towards them, but conscience was hardly the motive for most of the innumerable acts of peace that ordinary people, acting according to their nature, performed. If Reg Shepherd, just home from a prison camp in Malaya, gave gramophone recitals to Germans in their captivity and later took them on lightning tours of London; if a Rotarian in Hitchin with his lungs badly gassed in the First World War became a great collector of clothing for parcel sending and lent a POW a suit of his own to take him to an out-of-bounds restaurant; if the Donahues of Harlech persuaded local farmers to give rationed articles for parcels in exchange for extra work done; and the Doherties, Desforges and Ecclestones of Sheffield adopted families of POWs and got others to do the same—these acts were less prompted by conscience than by a practical and sensitive response to human need. Thousands without initiative themselves were only too grateful to be organised to do their share. Margaret Horwill, the Quaker to whom the town of Dudley in Worcestershire owes several thriving community centres, both opened her home in Barnett Lane to POWs and got five hundred families to give them hospitality at Christmas 1947 (She regards the work she did of this nature as the most important of her life.) On a still larger scale the Baptist Central Committee organised links between two hundred and fifty churches in the Baptist Union with the same number of churches in the four zones of Germany, which involved sending over food, clothing and books.

Occasionally careful planning and spontaneous good-heartedness went hand-in-hand, as when the village of Beetham on the edge of the Lake District set out to achieve reconciliation through 'integration'. The vicar there was the Reverend Alexander Macleod Murray, a rare spirit whom Father Jansen was drawn to much more than to the local Catholic clergy. Tall, scholarly, and high-church with an outgoing loving nature, he had also a shrewd knowledge of a man's world; he bore the scars of the Kut campaign of 1915 and till recently had been chaplain to the Royal Tank Corps Depot at Warcop. Arriving at Beetham in January 1946 and discovering that Camp 104 at Bela River was within his parish, he simply regarded its inmates as his parishioners. He put it to the existing ones that here were cast-down and ostracised people living in their midst, prisoners of war as many British had been. Let Beetham become for them a 'little sanctuary', he said.

As soon as regulations permitted and indeed long before, people responded. With young Mrs Murray playing her full part, the vicarage became a centre where Germans brought their loneliness and private troubles, or even their problems with their Commandant. When some prisoners told the vicar of a schoolteacher they knew in Germany who, though a good man and no Nazi, had been unjustly dismissed, he asked for a dossier on him which he sent to the local MP, William Fletcher Vane. He, in turn, passed it on to Lord Pakenham, then Minister for German Affairs. With astonishing speed the case was reviewed, the teacher reinstated and his denouncers exposed. The vicar put a large box in the church to receive gifts, chiefly clothing and food, and Beetham for a time became probably the greatest parcel-sending centre for its size in England. When furniture was required for a quiet room in the camp, a three-ton truck was soon taking in two dozen old easy chairs and a settee. Later a billiard table was sent up. The beautiful church with its unique rose trellis walk to the south door was used for several joint services in two languages and for memorable concerts (among the Germans was a violinist once selected to play in Westminster Abbey at the 1936 Coronation). There was community singing, music-making in private houses, and the occasional discussion group. So swiftly did this spirit of reconciliation get going that for Christmas 1946 members of the Bela River Camp secretly prepared a surprise gift to the parish—a full set of carved and painted crib figures, with a dedication which read:

We GERMAN PRISONERS OF WAR from Bela River Camp are giving this Stable and figures of the Nativity story, which have been made by BRUNO BAUMANN and his assistant GABRIEL FABIAN as a gift to the Parish of Beetham.

By doing so we will express our gratefulness for having been able to realize the real spirit of Christian brotherhood, which has been proved to us by the rev. A. MACLEOD MURRAY and the congregation of BEETHAM.

We are praying with you to the CHILD OF BETHLEHEM.
On behalf of the Camp
Christmas 1946
B. Baumann—Artist   Werner Janicke—Camp Leader
Erich Schmidt—Camp Padre

Thirty years later Canon MacLeod Murray, as he goes up the

stairs of his Georgian house beside Lake Windermere, passes more work by Bruno Baumann. He was a shy Latvian, rather apart from the others in the Christian group at Bela River. 'It was,' the Canon believes, 'in order to pierce the shadow of his despondency that he began carving that crucifix over a metre high. He was an accountant by profession and had never had an art lesson in his life, yet with a broken kitchen knife he made that figure of Christ looking upwards, perhaps at the moment of asking why he had been forsaken. When the camp was dissolved in 1948 he and Paster Erich Schmidt, to my astonishment, insisted that I should have it.'

Canon Murray is himself the first to pay tribute to the caring and diligence of the camp chaplains he knew in encouraging their comrades to bear up and prepare themselves for home-coming and better days. One of these was Father Josef Jansen who was sent up to Bela River as an easier camp after collapsing with the strain of his ministry at Glen Mills and later at Warth Mills, Bury. He was disappointed to find that the local Catholics had a diaspora mentality and his fellow-priests anything but welcoming; one of them, indeed, warned him against Macleod Murray who, Jansen records, 'welcomed me with friendship and love'. He travelled the area as far afield as Kendal where a convent of Irish nuns did his clerical washing and to Barrow-in-Furness where some U-boat specialists were working with the Royal Navy.

One might add here, perhaps, that the now more relaxed Jansen's last posting was to Toft Hall, Knutsford, a camp containing some thirty nationalities, all segregated from each other and many of them on the list of potential war criminals. 'Here,' he writes, 'there was more piety and religious feeling than anywhere else, for these people were in deep trouble. The most religious were the Belgians and then the Czechs. I could be particularly useful to those who wanted to get testimonials from their local pastors and priests.'

Jansen's memoir for Bela River gives a striking account of Dr Margaret Rosenberg, 'the Angel of the Lake District Camps'. Canon Murray remembers her as a dark, shortish Jewess in her late thirties, with a powerful, sometimes overpowering personality, fearing neither man nor beast. Jansen writes that:

> . . . she would suddenly appear among the POWs working in the quarries or on drainage or in their farm billets, greeting

them with '*Grüss Gott*, brother!' in the Austrian manner. 'Is there anything I can get for you?' She would note down little items from mending wool to pipes and tobacco, purses and pocket knives, and even medicines, and within a week or a fortnight she would be back with everything as ordered, to be paid for if possible, but not necessarily so. She lived on Lake Windermere, at Ambleside, or possibly Bowness, where a hotel manageress had befriended her, earning her keep and extra money by washing glasses in the bar. Every day she would be on her bike, 'shopping and carrying', doing sixty or even a hundred miles a day. The English guards, even before fraternisation was allowed, never put difficulties in her way. Only Major S., Commandant at Bela River, could not abide her and refused access to his camp after an incident in which she boxed his ears. . . . Her family had fled to Colombia but she had stayed on in England, having an account to settle with Hitler, choosing like Victor Gollancz to do so by repaying inhumanity by being human, by returning evil with good.

Though she was a doctor of law at Vienna the POWs called her Sister Margaret, or even 'Iron Margaret'. Rumour had it that she had been engaged to a Viennese SS officer who after helping her family to escape had for such a dereliction of duty been hung in Dachau. But she never answered questions about this. When she left to join her family early in 1948, the POWs of the surrounding camps gave her a party in Carnforth railway station. The strength of her feeling for the country which had cast her out can be seen in the farewell letter which she wrote to her 'comrades and dear friends', expressing gratitude that she 'had been able to give back, as far as was in my power, what Germany gave to me so abundantly'. She had spent the last Christmas visiting Featherstone Park and a letter she wrote from Bogotá in March to Father Jansen gives a late, vivid glimpse of that unique camp:

> How thankful I was and am that Camp 18 has so much to offer and does it in a way that both lifts the heart and delights. There were vespers on Christmas Eve; the chaplain's sermon said nothing but the fir-tree decorations, Advent wreaths and candles said a lot, and still more the 'Our Father' which rang

* A place in Upper Austria where in 1625, after an uprising had been crushed, captured peasants had to throw a dice in pairs as to who was to be executed, an occasion accompanied by fervent prayer from all involved.

out as though on the *Haushamerfeld*.* On Christmas Day they
did the *Christmas Oratorio*. . . . The artistic performance suffered through repatriation, but that made it almost more lovely
as with the fewer voices the instrumentation came over more
clearly, and one thought of the men who, by now, were at
home. *As You Like It* was lovely too, but best of all was the
fact that everyone in the camp had contributed to make it what
it was; that, in spite of some thinking differently, behaviour
never degenerated into arrogance; and that they had known
how to make 18 into a *'Deutschland am Tyne'*.

13

The Waffen-SS: Glimpses of Their Fate

I must admit—and about this I have no illusions—that, as a former member of the Waffen-SS, I can only expect hatred and rejection; and, beyond this, since I was involved in certain events, though without my actually doing anything or knowing about it, I realise I am regarded as a specially unpleasant former enemy and as a nasty type—even though God knows I have never been and have always striven not to be either. When I was confronted by all this, suddenly and fiercely, at my interrogation at LDC I was brought completely to the edge of despair . . .

> *SS-Major Emil Reinhard Stürzbecher in a letter to Captain Sulzbach from Friday Bridge Camp, Wisbech, March 30th, 1948*

The presence of Waffen-SS in POW cages and camps was an uneasy, and not infrequently, threatening one. They were part of the Wehrmacht, yet not part of it; indeed, it was decided at Nuremberg that they were, in effect, 'a private army of the Nazi state', a judgment which they bitterly resent to this day. They were easy to identify by the runic SS on their collar, and by the slightly different cut of their uniforms which on active service was not black, as is generally thought, but grey-green with black facings. They also wore the national emblem, the eagle with a swastika in its claws, in a different place. '*Vogel hier gut, Vogel hier nicht gut,*' a Belgian said to Paymaster Hildebrand, indicating the left breast where the Wehrmacht wore it, then the left arm where the SS wore it. But if they tried to hide who they were, as sometimes happened, they could easily be unmasked by a glance inside the upper left arm. Following American practice in the First World War every SS man's blood-group was tattooed on to him instead of being stamped on to his identity disc.* This was the 'blood-mark' that

---

* This was in fact discontinued near the end of the war when the

hundreds of thousands of surviving SS men still have and will carry to the grave. In Russia a batch of prisoners on occasions were ordered to strip off their shirts and raise their arms; those with the tattoo were hauled out of the ranks and beaten up before their comrades. In the camps there was a good deal of talk about how to get rid of it. In the Eutin collecting area there was a German who specialised in making a sham wound in the appropriate place to hide it. But this could arouse suspicion, as could even a large mole. The present author has seen two SS men strip off their shirts for him in a Kent kitchen and raise their arms. On one the tattoo was clearly visible, on the other the trace of an amateur attempt at removal. It is told that in one or two American holding camps in South Germany men actually had the left arm amputated high up, for the wildest rumours prevailed, such as that all SS would be castrated or sent on slave labour for twenty years.

The reputation of the Waffen-SS stemmed from both their prowess in the field and the atrocities they had committed. In the West there was the murder in 1940 during the retreat to Dunkirk of some seventy men of the Royal Warwicks by the *Leibstandarte* Division; then in 1944 the wiping out of the population of Oradur in a reprisal action by the Division *Das Reich*; and in the Ardennes Battle the slaughter, again by the *Leibstandarte*, of seventy-one American prisoners at Malmedy. As a result, a feeling of revenge ran through the American army. It nearly accounted for Werner Kuwertz of the *Leibstandarte* who, on capture, was put up against a wall. 'The strange thing was that I was already as if dead, completely at peace with myself, before they would have shot. But an officer stopped it.' Kuwertz was then taken back some miles for some pretty rough interrogation on the details of the latest tank.

In the frantic closing stages of the war in Germany itself the SS sometimes spread terror with their draconian methods of whipping up final resistance. As POWs, while the war was still on, they often took the lead in the brutal actions against defeatists or dissidents, as at Comrie and Warth Mills. Such behaviour virtually ended with the war itself, as they could no longer defend such actions as meting out justice to defeatists. Also the most militant bullies were removed to special camps. But they could still ter-

---

availability of blood-plasma in first aid dressing stations made it unnecessary to know a man's blood-group.

rorise their own comrades who saw what they had been involved
in and renounced their loyalty. Geoffrey Forrest was long haunted
by the look of a Waffen-SS cadet who turned up briefly at Shap
Wells. He was the perfect Germanic type the SS loved to enlist,
ardent and fresh-faced—a physical counterpart of Werner Düttmann. He was in a state of highly nervous shock, having been
beaten up by his comrades, and had asked for asylum. Shap
buzzed with discussion of his case; he did not qualify to stay and
was sent on to a safe camp.

As prisoners, the Waffen-SS were sometimes extremely frightened men, as Father Jansen found in Brussels, but they tried to
keep up, by whatever means, their 'esprit de corps'. They had the
most to lose and so the greatest need to maintain their group
identity. At Featherstone Park, according to Schwederski, they
alone held their heads high in that summer of 1945; Oesten speaks
of them as 'a band of brothers, as they were trained to be'. Elmar
Tremmel recalls that in the grimmest times at the dreadful
Overisje Camp they were the steadiest element. His compound
leader there, an SS cadet of the *Leibstandarte*, had had his arm shot
off and might have been sent home, but opted to stay with his
men. Even those who hated the guts of the SS admired him.

Why did young men enter the SS? In his classic study Hoehne
has written that it was 'because it satisfied two innate yearnings
peculiar to the German, a yearning to belong to a military community promising fame, security and the glitter of martial exercise; and the yearning to form part of a secret elite, an all-powerful
secret society.' And how attractive the SS could seem both to
adventurous spirits and to opportunists! 'They were the wild
boys,' one intelligent and extremely physical POW told the
author, 'the buccaneers. They were, as the saying went, "hard as
iron, tough as leather, swift as greyhounds". I had rather a disturbed childhood and longed to join something really glorious—
and the SS seemed to be to a boy like some elite Roman legion.'
The SS could boast the physical qualifications of a British guardsman, a Spartan training harder than that of the Wehrmacht, a
uniform of a sharper cut, an elegant rococo hilt to their swords.
Aryan pedigrees were vital and in the case of officers researched to
three generations. Whether in marriage or not, their sex drive was
thought vital for the future of the Reich, provided the partner,
married or not, was also 'of good race'. Commissions had to be

won from the ranks, which made for an easier and informal relationship between officers and men. In barracks they did not turn the key in the lockers to show they trusted each other. In Nazi establishment circles they had considerable cachet. The SS could both attract and repel an old East Prussian family, one member becoming an SS-Colonel, another being executed as a member of the resistance. A powerful industrialist might like to see a younger son in the SS as an insurance in case they became the ruling caste. Two extremes met in the SS: the dreamer who had been educated at an exclusive public school like Salem and carried Shakespeare, Rilke and Stefan George in his baggage; and the sadists and bullies from broken homes. Both needed to work out their fantasies of power and glory or to compensate for their own inner self-doubt. Walter Kuwertz tells that he was in some minor trouble as a teenager with the police and joining up was given him as a way out. His friend, Otto Erxleben, says that being an ardent Nazi from his youth onwards meant being a Socialist, so the elitist political principles of the SS were a denial of all he believed in. A genuine military elite like the paratroopers looked down on the SS for its arrogant apartheid. What few SS realised was the nature of their bond of service. For their motto bound them with a double knot both to the Führer and to Himmler, the *Reichsführer-SS*. It drew on the mediaeval concept of *Treue* or unquestioning loyalty and service to the liege lord, and on the at once noble and primitive concept of *Ehre*, meaning personal honour and glory. The two words combined into *Meine Ehre heisst Treue* were stamped on to every SS man's belt. But the nature of the service to be rendered and the will to be obeyed were left entirely open. They were thus recklessly committed to serving a cause with unlimited aims of domination and superiority.

In their arrogance the SS were also becoming a culturally deprived section of the German people. Horst Woetzel discovered this on the last day of 1941 near Kaluna when he went to liaise with a Waffen-SS artillery regiment which his own unit was due to relieve. Woetzel was one of 800,000 Germans who at the beginning of December had stood poised to take Moscow. The Red Army had launched its great counter-stroke with fresh troops and the Wehrmacht had pulled back with 150,000 casualties, their first defeat of the war. Woetzel in the desperate retreat from Tula had helped pull the guns, for the horses could not grip in the freezing mud. And it was half-freezing that he reached the group of houses where the SS had installed themselves. It was late afternoon and, to his astonishment, he found a deep silence everywhere, not only in the snow-bound landscape but even in the SS lines. For the SS were motorised while his own regiment was usually full of bustle and noise because they had horses. Waiting in this unaccustomed quiet, he found lying on a table a Waffen-SS *Heimatbrief*—a monthly circular sent to all units from the Homeland. It could not be a Christmas number because the SS rejected Christmas, but the editor had taken as a seasonal text an old fairy tale:

> In a cottage there lived a grandfather with his son and his wife and their young son. As he grew old his habits at meal times became so messy that the couple decided that he could not sit at table with them any more. So when meal time came they sent him out of sight behind the stove, giving him no crockery but just a wooden plate to eat off and a wooden spoon. Family meal times were different now; their son became rather silent. After a little they noticed that he had taken a knife and was making something out of wood. 'What is it?' they asked, delighted that he was being so constructive. 'It's a wooden bowl and spoon.' 'Why are you making them?' 'For you, so that you can have them when you are old and have to go into the corner!' At this the parents suddenly realised what they had done and, full of remorse, had the grandfather back at table with them. The family circle was complete again.

The moral of this tale, said the editor, was that when a man had worked hard and done his duty for his country and his family, he should not be left out in the cold but decently treated. Woetzel was amazed at the intellectual brutality of the brief comment. The true meaning and depth of the story was consciously avoided: the unity of family life, the clear vision of children, the need for compassion for the elderly who should be accepted as they are even though ugly and messy, the sense in which we all belong to each other—all this deep content of the story was totally omitted. 'Subtly, subliminally, the SS were being guided away, deprived of all that was most precious in our cultural heritage.'

The Waffen-SS* at this time won many battle honours. They

---

* It should be made clear that the author is writing of the Waffen-SS which came into being late in 1940. The controversy whether they can be regarded as a separate arm from the Allgemeine-SS which provided the KZ guards and liquidation commandos is barely relevant to the

had pushed through the advance on Moscow to within sight of the glittering towers of the Kremlin and when the tide had turned they had borne the brunt of the Soviet counter-attack. More and more was expected of them. To the anger of the Army they were given first use of the new Tiger tank and leading roles in much of the subsequent fighting, suffering casualties accordingly. It was these sacrificial actions that later on the Waffen-SS recalled in the POW camps and have done to this day, as a vindication of their honour and as a cover for their association, directly or indirectly, with shameful deeds. As time wore on the Waffen-SS grew and grew, but was less of a volunteer force and less of an elite. Not only had the huge losses in Russia to be made good, but as Hitler increasingly lost confidence in the Wehrmacht generals and feared for his own security and that of his Reich, the more he had to turn to the SS. For the scheming mind of Himmler they were to be the means for his ultimately taking over supreme power. Thus the number of the Waffen-SS divisions doubled each year of the war till there were no fewer than thirty-eight divisions in 1944— 910,000 men. Whole age groups of police had already been drafted across to the Waffen-SS. Press gangs snapped up spare man- power; for instance, at the Tempelhof Airport in Berlin they appeared without warning and picked out the civilians who were the right physical size and type.[85] But this was in the last two years or so. Before that—and the Stalingrad disaster was the watershed —the Waffen-SS had recruited without much difficulty for a great 'anti-Bolshevik Crusade'. There were many genuine adherents, as well as opportunists, from France, Belgium, Holland, Norway, Denmark, Latvia, Hungary and Croatia. There were Turks, Indians and even a handful of British in the SS. Men from dis- gruntled minorities of the Soviet Union—Cossacks, Tartars, Armenians, Azerbaijanis—had the wretched distinction of forming two SS divisions at the end of the war, being used for much dirty business in the Balkans.

---

theme of this book. It suffices to say that although operationally under the High Command of the Wehrmacht, administratively the SS was one body under Himmler and wore the same uniform and that, of the original divisions which formed the Waffen-SS, the Totenkopf was largely made up of cadres from the *KZ*. In this way, writes Hoehne, the Waffen-SS were 'injected with the poison of a barbarous attitude to prisoners learned over the years'.

But the largest influx was *volksdeutsch** from the racial minorities in Jugoslavia, Rumania, Poland, the Baltic States and Alsace. Those who were Jugoslav citizens were given the chance of joining the hated Hungarian army—which fought on the German side —or the Waffen-SS, with a bonus of German citizenship for their families. Those in Rumania were subjected to a huge recruiting campaign with bands and festivals, for where else than among nearly a million Transylvanian Germans was such a reservoir of pure racial stock—having survived as a German outpost and enclave for eight hundred years? The SS were empowered to enlist men both direct and from German-speaking troops already called up into the Rumanian army, who were all too willing to be transferred under German command. There were many thousands like Michael Zeck who found themselves being broken in at the SS barracks in Breslau, washing a staircase with a tooth-brush and a glass of water, or at 2 a.m. on a freezing night, '*Aufstehn*! *Sofort am Paradeplatz*!' There they would be drilled in their nightshirts till, '*Zurück in die Barracke*!', where they would find their bedding, clothes, everything hurled into the four corners of their dormitory. 'How we longed,' says Michael Zeck, 'for a miracle to transport us back to our farms in Siebenbürgen!'

The SS have entered the mythology of mid-twentieth century man. Their image is of the cruel, efficient servants of a ruthless power. They are for ever associated with the *Konzentrationslager* and the death camps in Eastern Europe. There is a place in the mind where they meet Tolkien's faceless 'black riders', a sense of whose all but invisible presence chills with terror. Not only were they dealers of death but they were masters at it, the inspiration of Paul Celan's haunting lines.

Der Tod ist ein Meister aus Deutschland sein Auge ist blau;
er trifft dich mit bleierner Kugel er trifft dich genau.
(Death is a Master from Germany his eye is blue;
he hits you with leaden bullet his aim is true.)[86]

But the SS myth is a dangerous one. It feeds a romantic attraction to the dark, destructive side of life. It can be a focus for the paranoid imagination of a disturbed mind. The next generation, without having experienced the reality, is easily fascinated by the

* Of the estimated 910,000 in the Waffen-SS in 1944, 400,000 were from the Reich (Germany and Austria), 310,000 Volksdeutsche, and 200,000 foreign volunteers. (Ploetz)

dream of power that lay behind the SS ethos. This is the very
thing that unregenerate servants of that power like to see happening, for it enhances them and gives them a continuing role in
history. The SS myth also freezes the course of events at the
end of the war. Today there are hundreds of thousands of Waffen-
SS still alive, some old men, none under fifty. In 1945 most of
them, justice having been done to what their organisation stood
for, had most of their lives before them. Moreover, and this is the
main point, the vast majority of them had been nothing other than
hard-fighting soldiers. Would they be able to find the way back
into decent ordinary life? For they were haunted by their past. In
an eloquent passage at the end of his book Hoehne writes:

> In the wooden huts and on the parade grounds of the Allied
> POW camps a great debate began—it is not finished yet—the
> debate of the disillusioned and the defeated, the defiant and the
> retrospective, the ashamed and the broken. They were tortured
> by a sense of sin and guilt. Many were unable to still the nagging
> question: how had it come to pass that with enthusiasm and
> self-surrender young men had turned into unthinking instru-
> ments of force, into slaves to a perverted notion of loyalty and
> honour which made every member of the SS a morally defence-
> less executive functionary of the Führer's will?

In Britain the Waffen-SS were never segregated as such, nor
treated differently from other POWs. It was the whole organisation that was proscribed at Nuremberg, not its individual members. Contrary to their belief, they were never put down automatically as 'recalcitrant' by the British—this was a term used only
by the Americans. In Germany, however, huge numbers of
Waffen-SS who were rounded up at the end of the war came into
the category of SEP (Surrendered Enemy Personnel) and were
interned in special camps on security grounds. They were 'security
suspects' and not released with other SEPs. They were held year
by year, pending investigation. Some escaped to live under cover
—in Germany or abroad, perhaps in the French Foreign Legion.
A few got an almost immediate release, like two vets from
Bremen who had been conscripted into the SS and could prove
that in their house they had sheltered a Jew.[87] But the 20,000 who
came to Britain went through the ordinary mill, and only those
who actively hampered re-education or were otherwise trouble-
some or had a dubious record were sent to 'black' camps. Not a

few were on a list of possible war-criminals or were required as witnesses. These found themselves at the London District Cage.

The unsavoury reputation among POWs of the London Cage has already been discussed. This large Kensington mansion in 'Millionaires' Walk' became when war ended the official 'War Crimes Interrogation Unit'. (It was also for reasons of convenience a staging post for the movements of higher officers.) By 1945 the building was even more tatty and seedy, the brusque bawling of the corporals and sergeants undiminished. Tough customers were treated toughly. If a man came in with a 'Heil Hitler' he was spoken to in a manner he could understand. Major Kettler's big act now had more genuine feeling in it. '*Jetzt sind Sie der Amboss*', he would shout, '*und ich der Hammer.*' (You're the anvil now, and I'm the hammer!) He would point to his insignia. '*Sehen Sie has— Sicherheitsdienst*' (Intelligence Corps). Strong men quailed before him. The bluffed threat of handing a man over to the Russians if he didn't 'sing' was still used with occasional success. Many of the cells were unheated in winter, laundry facilities poor, and harass- ment not infrequent. One SS Colonel did not appreciate the grim humour of the guard who searched his room at night for nails in the wall. 'Don't hang yourself here—that's for later.'

Some extremely unpleasant individuals were sent to LDC, like the senior Gestapo officials involved in the murder of the forty-seven RAF officers who escaped from *Stalagluft* III. Among the interrogators were refugees who had plenty of motive to break the rules in order to bring the SS to book. But all, says one reliable member of Colonel Scotland's staff, kept this code: no physical touching of a prisoner. It might be that a particularly recalcitrant suspect was ordered to clean the stairs with a tooth-brush to re- mind him of his own training, or bootlaces and belt would be removed to strike at his dignity—as well as to prevent suicide. But such treatment, says the same witness, could be the pre- liminaries to the creation of an 'acceptable relationship which could sometimes be described as mutual respect'. Some of the SS are prepared to acknowledge that their handling at LDC was *korrekt*, others who had been used to a gentlemanly politeness at previous interrogations reacted sourly and still do whenever the London Cage is mentioned. Major Biri of the International Red Cross took a poor view of it; it was solely a War Office affair, the P/W division of the Foreign Office having no part in it.

The techniques used at LDC had been developed over the years but they did not work in the case which Colonel Scotland had most had his heart in: the murder of the Royal Warwicks in 1940 by members of the *Leibstandarte* at Wormhoudt. Grenades were thrown into a barn full of prisoners and those who tried to get out were mercilessly shot down. A handful of eyewitnesses survived, British and Belgian; and Scotland had a big dossier of evidence. But at the time Sepp Dietrich, Commander of the Division, had bound an oath of silence on all involved either as perpetrators or as witnesses. It was so tight a seal that a case was never brought and Scotland admitted defeat.[88] But there could be no seal on conscience. The inner debate that went on in the heart of many an SS man is nowhere better illustrated than in the words quoted at the head of this chapter. The writer, SS-Major Stürzbecher, spent some time at LDC before being sent on to Camp 18. Here he found a sympathetic listener to his troubles in Captain Sulzbach to whom he wrote a long letter of gratitude some months later. It is worth quoting further:

You will have received many letters, dear Herr Captain, from repatriated former POWs, but from among those who passed through your sphere of influence scarcely one from a man who was so inwardly tormented and hopeless about the future as I was. . . . Almost everyone who went through Camp 18 thinks back to that time with a deep thankfulness and respect and regard for your personality and, believe me, beyond this every former member of the Waffen-SS that I know speaks of you with a decided feeling of downright shame, for we all felt that in your manner and your real understanding for the personal tragedy that so many of us underwent with the fall of the Third Reich you showed the majority of us the right way of self-examination and changing ourselves round for a new beginning.

Herr Captain, I once clung to the ideas of Nazism and, because of my narrow education and horizon, I believed that they were the only good ones and even the summit of human knowledge; then slowly and surely—long before the end of the war, believe me—I began to understand that my ideas were nonsense. Then came the end with the cowardly exit of the idols I had once worshipped. I had lost everything a man can lose, apart from his miserable life. As a Silesian I had lost my beautiful homeland, a happy parental hearth, my profession and all my possessions, as well as belief in God and mankind. And, on top of this, was the great question mark: why did it have to be *me* who joined the SS; and why did I have to survive? Beyond this, why did I have to belong to that wretched battalion in 1940? If there is a hell of the mind on this earth, I have been through it.

As to my fate in coming to Great Britain at all, there is something tragic, almost ironic, about it. As a boy and a student it was always my unfulfilled wish to see England and now I have landed here. . . . With your help I had the fortune to be also at Wilton Park where I could gain a deeper insight into the connection between past and present. I am firmly convinced that it is only through overcoming this past and finding a way to each other beyond all ideologies and frontiers that we in the West can maintain the values of our culture, religion and intellectual traditions which give meaning to life in a truly human society. . . . The only practical way to reach these goals is through the lives and actions of people such as we have come to know here in England, of a Victor Gollancz and of you, respected Captain. . . . I would like to express also for my own self deep and sincere thanks, and beg you not to think what I have written is in any way importunating or opportunist. What will happen to me here I do not know, though I expect it will be something unpleasant, perhaps another visit to LDC, but with firm belief in God's grace and power and in justice on earth I will strive to walk my way ahead erect.

Sulzbach never heard from, or of, Emil Reinhart Stürzbecher again. But another SS officer, Herbert Christiansen, who expressed similar sentiments to him, became a personal friend. This man, tall, swarthy, eagle-nosed and imposing even for a member of the *Leibstandarte*, was thirty-three-years-old when taken prisoner at Schwerin. He had come through many tough battles but few tests of endurance had been greater than at Overisje in the winter of 1945–6.* 'Tents with only ground-sheets,' he tells with military precision, 'two blankets each, up to twelve degrees of frost, no stoves, starvation rations. The oldest of us did not come through. It was no good trying to escape.' They were totally defiant and the British left them alone. He has never forgotten the indignity of being paraded with other SS and made to exchange his tunic for a battle-dress top with a patch on the back, and given what he calls

* See page 31.

a 'certificate of dismissal from the Wehrmacht'. The disgrace hurt him deeply.

In February 1946 Christiansen and five other members of the *Leibstandarte* were called for by Colonel Scotland for questioning. 'At Dover there was a special announcement over the ship's loud-speaker: *Attention please! No one is to leave the ship before the German war criminals!* You can imagine our feelings. At the London District Cage we were treated correctly and asked questions about certain misdeeds in Belgium for which some men were tried and punished by the British, and rightly so. But our physical condition was so poor that they soon sent us up to Featherstone Park.' Here they were put at once into sick quarters. Next, on 25 February, before their scarecrow figures had begun to fill out, they had to report to Sulzbach. As he was on the phone when the SS man entered, Sulzbach pushed a newspaper extract across the table towards him. Christiansen glanced at the headline: MILLIONS OF JEWS MURDERED BY THE SS. When Sulzbach had finished speaking, he pushed the piece of paper back to him. 'I don't wish to see it. I don't know anything about that sort of thing.' At this Sulzbach dismissed him and wrote down, 'Liar—C plus' in his ledger. He had the other five in one by one; against SS-Major H. Koke he wrote 'Seems not bad' and against SS-Sergeant E. Oddey 'Not too bad'—without a grading in either case. Two hours later Sluzbach sent for Christiansen again, looked at him closely and said, 'Your comrades have been telling me about Belgium. It's terrible, I can't understand how it happened.' They had a long talk. 'I gradually realised' says Christiansen, 'that here at last was someone who looked upon me as a human being, who cared about my condition. Our trousers were in tatters, our underwear non-existent from that time in Belgium, and he at once saw that we had new things.' After the formidable-looking Christiansen had gone, Sulzbach crossed out the word 'Liar' but left in C-plus.

The Swiss Major Biri, of the Red Cross, happened to be there at the time. Sulzbach knew he would welcome information about conditions in camps which inspections did not always reveal and sent Christiansen to him. Whether or not his evidence was used, the situation at Overisje about this time greatly improved. More significantly, twenty years later when a letter in *Der Freiwilliger** accused the Allies of war crimes in the Belgian camps, Christiansen

* *Der Freiwilliger*, lit. The Volunteer, is the monthly magazine of The Old Comrades Aid Society for Members of the former Waffen-SS.

wrote a reply. He told of his first experience with Sulzbach and
Major Biri and pointed out the tremendous strain on the Allies of
having to handle such a flood of POWs. It was a courageous line
to find in that paper.

Soon Sulzbach was noting down a change in Christiansen, who,
however, remained lonely and broody, pulled down by the depressive company of his fellow SS. He wanted to join a work party
and get away from the camp but they told him it was undignified,
collaborationist and unworthy of an SS officer. But he broke the
taboo and soon felt better, especially after an incident with a
civilian when waiting to be taken back to the camp. 'He caught
my eye—he wasn't allowed to speak to me—then nodded meaningfully at the wall behind me. I turned round and saw in a hole a
packet of cigarettes. When I turned back again the man had gone.
You can have no idea what that act meant to me when I was still
so full of despair.'

Christiansen stayed on at Camp 18 till repatriated in June 1948.
Sulzbach remained a beacon light in his life. They exchanged the
letters quoted in Chapter Nine and are friends to this day. The
one-time SS captain has been a faithful attender at all Featherstone
Park reunions and comes with his grandson, who is as tall but
gentler than he was, and adheres to the YMCA. Christiansen's
way back has been bitter and hard. With great difficulty he has
made a go of a small business. Loyalty to his oldest comrades
means a great deal to him, but he refuses to attend the annual
Whitsun gatherings of the *Leibstandarte*, preferring to meet his
surviving comrades in a more personal way. No longer concerned
with the restriction of full pension rights for the Waffen-SS,
his great hope is that their honour as fighting men will one
day be fully vindicated. The wound in his soul is far from healed.

A.E. was a young Rumanian German in the Prinz Eugen Division of the Waffen-SS.[89] He was captured at the end of the war
and held along with other SS, police units, paratroops and a few
midget submarine men under strict guard and the hardest conditions in the Grottaglie Camp near Taranto. 'Now you'll know
what it was like in a *KZ*,' they were told. 'It was here,' writes
A.E. 'that my inner change began. There was not only a chance to
grapple with and overcome the old ideas about *Deutschtum*
(Germanism); it was much more that during a time of expected
retribution there arose in me a belief in God, in his power and his

people. Little by little I became free of the idols of the free-thinkers—I experienced Christian humanity and kindness. . . . I could use the time to look into myself with endless tent discussion, occasional talks with the camp chaplain (a member of my unit!),* taking part in many educational activities. The urge to make up for lost time was immense. It was a precious chance to learn and unlearn.'

Sent to Rimini after a year, A.E. at once started on an education course and joined the Rimini German Male Choir under Heribert Bertel. It had been started by the YMCA† and was mostly made up from SS and other so-called recalcitrant POWs. A.E. writes movingly of how membership of this choir was a way back for stigmatised men into the human community and of the 'effect of coming into contact with sacred texts, taking part in acts of worship and church concerts, singing to the wards of military hospitals, discovering how music could be the bearer of the Word and mediator between human beings—all this was a living reality. Most of them were serious people, and, like me, thankful to be still alive. It was as though God had made a pledge with us which we had to live up to.' A year later A.E. found himself at Llanmartin Camp near Newport in South Wales. In Italy they had not been allowed to work, but now they were, and this brought a new meaning to their lives. 'Many of us were very young and had not been trained for anything. I became a road cleaner and forest worker. It gave me back self-confidence to find that I could be useful to society. It was a time of healing. In the camp itself I met many educated men I could learn from. Returning, so to speak, to school I attended every lecture I could. At Llanmartin German "war criminals" were befriended by Welsh families and local communities, the Baptists fetching us each week to shower us with goodness. It made an enormous impression on me when I was accepted into one of their families, a kindness that I have never forgotten and which makes me want to do the same to others in similar circumstances. The English churches showed us the mean-

---

* He had been a theological student, then joined the SS and had now rediscovered his faith.
† This was an achievement of Pastor Werner Jentsch, himself a member of the YMCA and then a prisoner. Already mentioned, he was repatriated early and he became the first German ex-POW to be sent on a post abroad when he came to Britain on behalf of the International YMCA in 1947, to be Forell's successor.

ing of Matthew XXV.* I have seldom since come across such genuine community-based love as in that summer and winter of 1947.'

At the end of that year A.E. was transferred to Norton where Pastor Jentsch had arranged for the Rimini choir to be reconstituted, still under Heribert Bertel, but much smaller and more professional—its twelve members now included opera singers and a former member of both the Aachen Cathedral and the St Thomas Choir in Leipzig. They fulfilled an intense programme, giving no fewer than 122 concerts, mainly of sacred music, between Christmas and the end of April, in camps and officers' messes, churches and church halls and YMCA centres from the South of England up to Scotland. 'Every member of the choir,' says A.E., 'was aware of a "missionary" dimension in what they did, and that they were contributing to reconciliation with former enemies. Everywhere we made contact with mayors of towns, with officers, with ordinary folk—acquaintanceships that led sometimes to parcels being sent to their relatives at home. These were not lost years.'

There is no typical SS man, but there must have been many similar cases of crisis and attempted inner change, successful and unsuccessful. But they are hard to discover, for few are prepared to expose their past. It is notable indeed that in the voluminous German anti-Nazi literature there are virtually no striking contributions from former SS bearing witness to what they were caught up in and their revolt against it. This applies even to those who became Christian. Is it a matter of pride, or honour, or perhaps that the German is reluctant to beat his breast in public? Is it due to a need to forget a bitter past in order to be able to build a better future? Werner Jentsch, today a Professor of Theology and a leading churchman, has another and interesting explanation, derived from his long experience of the YMCA. 'Conversion,' he writes, 'is a matter of silence, particularly among males in their twenties.' And he adds that in such cases 'there is a chastity of experience which needs to be respected.' Pastor Gursky, too, has heard the confessions of many former SS, including some of those who came home years later after first finding their way incognito into the French Foreign Legion. He emphasizes the need for the utmost spiritual tolerance towards the past of such men. But

* I was a stranger, and ye took me in. I was sick, and ye visited me; I was in prison, and ye came unto me.

probably the great majority of those who needed such help from priest or psychiatrist never found it, or even sought it. Happy the man who found an alternative in the love of a good woman. But for the others repression of the intolerable was inevitable. The quietly efficient manager of a Düsseldorf insurance firm, much liked and respected by his employees, was not an isolated case. When he committed suicide, they knew he had once been an SS-officer and understood.

At the opposite end are the SS who cling tenaciously to their past, their rights and their martial glory. They belong to their Old Comrades Associations, are watched by the media and put across an inflexible version of the past with all the old techniques of Nazi propaganda. In between there is another large group who have made a sophisticated adjustment to the new Germany and often hold good jobs in industry and commerce. In so far as they are critical of the past, it is more in the spirit of '*c'était pire qu'un crime, c'était une faute.*'

One day in July 1947 the War Office signalled to Camp 18 that a party of two hundred officers would arrive, eight of whom were not to be housed in the huts but in the cells. Among these were two Austrian Gestapo men and a colonel, Günter d'Alquen. His distinctive Huguenot name was familiar to Sulzbach as the well-known chief editor of *Das Schwarze Korps*, the SS weekly. When he had inserted a large black-rimmed death notice for Czechoslovakia after Hitler marched against Prague—a typical piece of Nazi wit —Sulzbach, in Basel at the time, had written a disgusted letter (anonymously because his sister was still in Berlin) to this man whom he now saw on the platform of Haltwhistle Station. He was amazed; here was no bully type, but an urbane, rather stylish officer. That night in the cells—the only brick structure in the camp—Sulzbach began by giving him a piece of his mind, but changed his tone when he realised that he was faced not with a fanatic but a man with manners and a certain culture.

D'Alquen was 'good-looking, bien soigné and a good conversationalist';[90] to Hoehne he was 'one of the most versatile brains in the SS.' Son of an Essen wool manufacturer, he had given up his university studies to become a journalist, at which he was cut off by his father. 'I was against the old bourgeois values,' he told Otto John who talked to him at Featherstone Park. 'University life, the old *Studentenkorps*—that was all bloody nonsense. The old generation were in the way. I went to work for a small paper with a half-Jewish editor—he taught me all I ever learned about making a paper.' D'Alquen then joined the *Völkischer Beobachter*, the main party organ. Here he was so disgusted by the sterility of Nazi journalism that he had the effrontery to suggest that in order to stop the Nazi state hardening its arteries, the *Völkischer Beobachter* should offer constructive opposition to government policies. Such dangerous ideas brought dismissal, but soon he was on the *Schwarze Korps* which he eventually raised to a circulation of 750,000. It was written in a crisp pungent German and edited with a socially sophisticated, often brutal panache that lived up to its motto: *Auf Hieb und Stich*—With cut and thrust. In the same spirit he had created a thrustful team of SS war reporters. In 1943 he had personally persuaded his chief, Himmler, to give up the official SS propaganda line that the Slavs were *Untermenschen*, made absurd by the quality of both Russian courage and tanks. He had then become deeply involved in persuading a million Russians to fight for Germany and was a friend of the tragic General Vlassov.

The end of the war saw d'Alquen in Italy in Camp 209 at Agrafola, where although the only SS officer he was elected—a remarkable compliment—as camp leader. Here even General von Senger could acknowledge 'warm thanks for his concern' adding in his memoirs: 'He was correct and polite, which was in keeping with the conduct enjoined on all SS officers. They were very punctilious in such matters and they considered themselves the elite of the Wehrmacht.' It is clear that the blond, intelligent d'Alquen, even then only thirty-five years old, exercised considerable fascination on interrogators, both British and American, to whom he was subjected for a large part of his five years as a POW. Being a top Nazi, holder of the golden party badge, a *Reichskultursenator*, many people wanted to get at him. He had a predictably unpleasant time at London District Cage before being eventually passed on to Featherstone Park. Sulzbach, realising that his stay was likely to be short and that he was no dangerous character, saw to it that he had the full freedom of the camp and could even go on outings. They had many friendly talks, d'Alquen recording him as 'an oasis in a desert of prejudice.' But he did not reveal to his good Samaritan a side of his nature that he did to Dr Otto John.* This escaped survivor of the 20th July conspiracy was now working for the P/W division of the Foreign Office as a screener, specialising in higher officers. In the course of several

* See also page 352.

conversations they naturally talked about the *Attentat*. D'Alquen, hearing how Dr John had been in the plot up to the neck, said, 'You were quite right really. Something had to be done. We too were having secret talks about how to end the war. If only you had come to us. You see, we had a pot in the middle—that was Hitler. This pot was untouchable, as we had to be loyal to Hitler —*Führertreu*. But the rest—they could have been done away with.' (Stürzbecher who sent a greeting to d'Alquen in his long letter to Sulzbach would surely have been shocked had he heard this. Conspiratorial treachery at the top was one of the things that had disillusioned him.)

Six weeks after his arrival at Featherstone Park d'Alquen was seen hovering near the IO hut. One of the officer typists told Sulzbach who said, 'Tell him to come in; he wants to say good-bye.' D'Alquen entered, clicked his heels, bowed and said halt-ingly, 'Herr Sulzbach, I only wanted to say—that you have freed me from certain prejudices.' He clicked his heels again and was soon on his way to the far north. It was a moment still cherished by Sulzbach. But perhaps it was not so difficult for d'Alquen to make this gesture before a man who was totally unlike other Jewish emigrants he had met and had, moreover, won two Iron Crosses in the First World War. Dr John saw him in different colours, as a man who had not basically changed his spots. When d'Alquen under the usual escort was taken to the far north, it was with a C plus against his name.

The single-track railway to Wick in Caithness winds far from the road between snow fences in the hills. Eventually, far beyond the furthest grouse moor and deer forest, it reaches a fertile farm belt with big stone-walled fields for cattle and barley. It is a tree-less, windswept country, desolate in winter. The camp at Watten,[91] four miles march away by the river, had two parts, one for C plus POWs conducted on war-time principles, the other for workers in this locality. Willi Leichner, who went there from Burford, helped build the road through the dunes at Wick, where they also enjoyed rabbit hunts and collected mussels which they cooked with herbs on the hut stoves. He remembers a commandant 'with bare knees and seven feet tall'. This was Colonel Murray, clearly a very decent officer, who spoke simple German and was referred to by some POWs as 'Irene' because he wore a kilt. The I.O. was a Pole, Captain Broekere, who was generally liked. There was a camp band, Leichner recalls, and courses in languages and type-writing; he also attended other lectures and took part in political discussion which apparently was conducted by two sergeant inter-preters who were social democrats. He had, he says, to be told what the word 'democracy' meant, but disruptive communist participation led to the discussions being suspended. Leichner was posted away in January 1946, unaware of the notorious compound in the heart of the camp for the C plus prisoners. The German camp spokesman was Colonel Unger who had been dismissed by Lord Napier from a similar position at Crewe Hall, after the beat-ing up of a 'traitor'. On the British side there was also an Austrian-born sergeant, known as 'Hermann', a veteran of the Spanish Civil War. He hated all Nazis and was hated in return for his vicious sense of humour which he exercised against his charges in what he called 'Little Belsen'. In the centre of the compound was a hut more like a ward in a psychiatric hospital for extreme cases of paranoia. It contained fanatics who believed that Germany had, in fact, won the war and that they, a specially selected elite, were being tested in loyalty to Hitler to the ultimate degree. As the Führer could not have been defeated, it followed that the English guards were puppets of the German occupying power. When Faulk visited Watten in 1945 and addressed the camp in his usual forthright manner, these people announced that they had informa-tion that he was one of their own intelligence officers pretending to be British to see if they would falter in the true faith. There was even a photograph that proved they were right! It was the famous one of Roosevelt, Stalin and Churchill at Yalta which, they exclaimed, had been doctored. Take off some of Stalin's mou-stache and you had Hitler; put back all the medals on to Churchill and you had Goering; both were conferring with a sick Roosevelt about the future of the world.

Men were sent to the C compound at Watten for a variety of reasons. There were not only the toughs and bullies—some, but perhaps not a majority, in the SS—who had terrorised other camps. There were U-boat crewmen who believed they were held illegally and had refused to work.* There were others who, out of high spirits or patriotic defiance, had given a screener an aggres-sive answer but who were not Nazis at all. One of these was the aggressive young man† captured by the Canadians and made to

* See page 194.
† See page 4.

walk towards the light. An interrogator in a vindictive mood had shouted, 'Come in, you son of a Nazi whore,' to which he had answered in a flash, 'I am not your brother'. A certain Richard Schneider sent a note to the Prisoner of War Aid Society to say he was at Watten because 'he gave the wrong answer'. The trusting, indefatigable Mary Foss, on the basis of this, at once wrote to the War Office about him. It is difficult to find people who will talk about Watten, which was a hot-bed of anger, hurt and suspicion. If they do talk, they do not wish their names to be mentioned. Some were horrified to find themselves *dans cette galère*, or had their minds changed by the shock therapy of being there at all. Young men who had till then little idea of the seamy side of the Third Reich, heard the grisly details. One highly educated Sudeten member of the *Leibstandarte* talked learnedly on art and poetry, but seemed to be in a permanent state of shock because of his experiences in Russia. The gifted friend whose ears he opened to Rilke and German expressionism was so beaten down by the fact of being at Watten that when he was recommended to go to the Youth Camp which had just been opened near Saffron Walden, he tried to reject what turned out to be the chance of his life. He and some other fortunates got away even as far as Wilton Park.

But even the rump at Watten had their outside contacts. James Collin, a Quaker, took his holiday in the Wick area so as to be able to visit the POW he had befriended in a camp in the south. On one occasion in d'Alquen's time the Thurso Salvation Army brought their band and a children's choir into the C plus compound. Lecturers were regularly sent up by Bush House. Dr Heinz Walz, refugee, academic and specialist on Anglo-German relations, visited Watten twice. He really believed he would make contact with the POWs there, especially with some of the SS, for when still a university lecturer at Heidelberg in 1936 he had experiences with two SS-men that were far from negative. He had lectured to a huge audience on 'British Democracy', receiving vociferous applause. At this an Austrian *Studentenführer* in the front row rounded on them. 'You are all a bunch of politically immature idiots. You don't know what you are doing. This man is a traitor to all the values our nation stands for.' At this one of Walz's best pupils, an SS officer in uniform, walked across the hall and slapped the *Studentenführer* in the face. Next day Walz was ordered to apologize to the Austrian; he refused and was dismissed, being held in prison for a brief while. During the moves

by which he and his wife then left Germany another member of
the SS, at risk to himself, played a secret and vitally helpful role.
This was the later Reich Youth Leader and Gauleiter of Salzburg,
Gustav Adolf Scheel. In 1946 when he was on trial in Nuremberg
a letter about him from Dr Walz may have saved his life.

On his first visit to Watten, Walz spoke on the possibilities of
Anglo-German friendship and was so popular that Colonel Murray
asked him to come back. But next time—it must have been after
the large outflow to the Youth Camp—the hall was almost empty:
the camp had been told not to attend. Only some seven did so,
obviously selected for the occasion, and they behaved in a mock-
ingly friendly manner, making facetious remarks. Even then, still
believing in the direct approach, Walz asked permission to visit
those in the 'worst' hut. Advised against it, he was nevertheless
allowed in with two guards outside the door. He found three men
there, two of them with thuggish faces. He said by way of opening, 'I'm sorry to find you here.' The answer came back, 'It's none
of your business; get out of here at once!' 'Is there anything I can
do for you?' 'Get out, you traitor!' Walz turned to the third, a
pathetic-looking, handsome youth who just looked back at him
sadly. Walz did not linger. He had seen the Watten camp described
in the screening report sent in May 1947 to Colonel Faulk.

One expected depression, animosity, defiance. But what one
found was, first, a deep hatred against everything British, which
exceeds their passionate contempt for Bolshevism. 'We'll go to
the Russians,' they say. 'They'll give us arms and we'll put paid
to these English dogs. Then it will be their turn.' Secondly, the
old arrogance hits you, particularly with the officers who talk
less than the ORs but behave 'correctly'. At interrogations they
are superior and contemptuous. Their answers are civil but the
tone is barbed. The ORs seem to be drilled in the answers they
give.

It was four months after this report that d'Alquen arrived at
Watten, a month later being made spokesman of the officers'
compound in place of Colonel Unger. How far it was due to his
firm control is not clear, but in December the camp in its outer
aspect was commended in one respect by the energetic Pastor
Jentsch who came there shortly before Christmas. 'The discipline
in the camp is excellent,' he wrote. 'There is a strong sense of

comradeship and no signs of bribery and corruption.' He noted
that it was the only camp where the SS were still preparing a Yule
Festival—a celebration of the solstice—instead of Christmas.
'Everyone who went there,' Jentsch continued, 'was struck by the
total cramp in the *Weltanschauung*, Christianity having virtually no
chance owing chiefly to the churches' declaration on war guilt.'
He found Pfarrer Sietges resigned to minimal activity. Jentsch
himself, practised at addressing young men on religion without
putting their backs up, had more success. D'Alquen noted down
that he spoke on 'What I have learned from the War' and that it
was 'the best sermon I've heard—I said some serious concluding
words.' And from Jentsch we have: 'D'Alquen to the general
amazement proposed that the usual discussion at the end of a talk
should be omitted on this occasion. He was no Christian himself,
but he had been so moved by the words of the speaker that he
felt it right for everyone to ponder what had been said on his
own.' A few days later, also noted by Jentsch, a certain Tietgen
committed suicide and d'Alquen records that the British on duty
came out of the guard room and paraded at attention as his coffin
was carried through the gates—a gesture that was much appreciated. On New Year's Eve some of these same guards got drunk
on the schnapps that the Germans made from dried apricots—
many camps seem to have had illicit stills which were often uncovered in searches. D'Alquen says that the night ended with him
keeping some of the guards' rifles beside his bunk to prevent any
untoward incidents with the paranoiacs, who still went around
believing that 'Hitler was fighting the war up on the Wartmann.'
Such a story coming from a talented journalist and propagandist
will be quite unbelievable to some. But it was a strange time and
Watten was a strange camp.

D'Alquen was repatriated in June 1948 with the last batch from
Watten. While they were en route, Colonel Murray, chivalrous to
the last, sent them a telegram wishing them good fortune in the
future.[92] Released by the British, d'Alquen was at once passed on
to the Americans who had asked for him as a war crimes witness
and to investigate his own past. A little later he was writing from
Nuremberg to Sulzbach: 'For a month now I have not been
interrogated . . . and, praise God, for some months I have had full
employment. You will smile understandingly when I say that I
work in the tailoring business, learn the secrets of ironing and
sewing in a straight line and am, once more, decently tired at the

end of the day.' He thanked him once more because 'in the bitter discrepancy between theory and practice you forced me to a real respect.' The trousers d'Alquen was ironing were those of the black American guards in the Nuremberg prison. But when two years later he was finally released, Sulzbach's testimonial did not soften the findings at his denazification by a German court. He was fined, had his property confiscated, was banned from being a journalist or publishing anything for ten years and also from own-ing a car. He took a course in business studies and remade his life as a company secretary. His reflections on his five years in Allied hands are sharp, often ironic and, to use Hoehne's expression, 'versatile'. He has no complaints about his treatment and claims to have suffered less from the ill-will of his interrogators, which he expected, than from their lack of intelligence. This was rarely the case, however, among American refugees in uniform whom he found frequently stimulating and never boring. He was disap-pointed that the apostles of humanity were so often inhumane. He has not been through any process of change, he insists, but he has learned a great deal. What exactly he has learned is, as with many an intellectual, hard to say. As a minor celebrity of the Third Reich he has no wish or need to step outside his own past.

Fallingbostel, a former *KZ* near Bremen, was the last camp for many Waffen-SS officers. It was not, in fact, a POW camp but rather an internment centre for security suspects, and under the Legal Division of the Control Commission. Colonel Vickers, Pastor Forell and Colonel Faulk were all concerned to prevent it becoming a backwater of anger and despair. Vickers, as we have seen, was posted there from Featherstone Park in the autumn of 1946, his firmness, fairness and caring personality being required for such a difficult job. Forell's journal records how he visited Fallingbostel camp in the following spring with Vickers greeting him like a lost son. He told him that among his charges were '600 wild men', but the others were decent men working hard at their educational and vocational training. Those who had been in the SS were sure that because of their past no one would want to employ them. 'Something must be done about this,' he insisted. When Forell told him of the plans for the new town at Espelkamp he was enthusiastic and relieved. A year later Forell returned to Fallingbostel and found there many members of the Waffen-SS whom he had known in England, all very depressed. One of them may have been Christiansen. Once more he addressed the camp and tried to give them hope for the future.

Faulk, who had a wide experience of Waffen-SS right across the POW board, was not aware of many vicious men. Indeed, at the end of repatriation he reckoned that there were as few as 300 totally recalcitrant men in Britain, of whom probably less than half were Waffen-SS. It was not too difficult, be believed, in the right circumstances to wean the others away from their former loyalties and beliefs. He had found this already at Carburton in March 1945 where more than one of the volunteer anti-Nazi staff were SS. Faulk tells two stories about Fallingbostel. In the first a British woman politician* was being shown round the camp by a guide in civilian clothes who was charming to her and spoke very good English. When the round of inspection was over she said to him, 'I am astonished that such a decent young man as you can bear to work among these animals.' 'It is not difficult, Madam,' he replied. 'You see, I am one of the animals myself.' The second story concerns Faulk himself. On one occasion he stayed talking to a group of Waffen-SS officers at the camp for so long that he was late for a summons to General Dunlop, head of the Control Commission in Hamburg. Dunlop was furious and ordered Faulk's departure from the area. Later there was a Committee of Enquiry at the Foreign Office about Faulk's attitude and activities in the camp, with German officials accusing him of being dangerously kind to the SS. 'The charges fizzled out, of course,' says Faulk, 'but the facts illustrate the feeling against the SS and their stereotype in people's minds. Years later General Dunlop went out of his way to make amends.'

It is surely one of the most just and salutary reversals of history that the special tattoo-mark inside the upper left arm which distinguishes nearly every SS man should become something to hide, while the identification number tattooed by the SS inside the left wrist of every *KZ* inmate and victim should now be a mark of suffering endured and survived. Hubris has been satisfied. But it is also sad that, in the process, hundreds of thousands should personally be maligned because of the blanket condemnation of

---

* Could this have been Ellen Wilkinson, the Minister of Education in Attlee's cabinet, who was investigating the German educational situation about this time? It might be added, however, that charm can go with the ability to act ruthlessly.

the whole organisation. It did not happen in England—but it did in Germany. At Nathenberg, the notorious American-run detention centre, Ernst von Salaman,* certainly no Nazi, noticed how the Waffen-SS 'grew increasingly hardened beneath the constantly growing pressure of a monstrous slander, till at last they had nothing on which they could fall back except their honour as soldiers (not a fruitful concept any more).' What seemed a 'monstrous slander' to Salaman was the decision of the Allies to lump the whole of the SS together as one body. It was rough justice in keeping with the mood of the time; there was no inclination to draw a line, both because of the way the Waffen-SS was formed and because of what the whole of the SS represented.†

Nor were there anything like enough Allied screeners and qualified lawyers to sort out, examine and bring to justice the tens of thousands retained in the camps, mostly Allgemeine-SS and Gestapo, who had been actively involved in the dark deeds of the Third Reich. In 1955 the Adenauer Government took over the responsibility of carrying through the unfinished work of unearthing and trying war criminals. The holding camps had already been dissolved and large numbers had simply slipped out of the net before investigation. The position of the Waffen-SS as a whole remained unclarified. Indeed, they were between the devil and the deep. The Allies had declared them an illegal body, so it was quite impossible for the Bonn government, for instance, even to consider allowing them pension rights for the period as POWs after the Nuremberg judgment against them. That would have appeared as being soft on the Nazis. The Social Democratic opposition was even less inclined to have any sympathy for their 'rights'.

But it is significant that an honest man like Kurt Schumacher in

* Author of *The Questionnaire* which exposed the blunders of much Allied de-nazification. See FitzGibbon, op. cit.

† The facts of the distinction between the Waffen-SS on the one hand, and the Allgemeine-SS, Gestapo, Totenkopfverbände, and SD (Security Service) on the other, were in fact known at the Nuremberg Trials, especially through the evidence of Eugen Kogon, author of *Der SS-Staat*. In the event the Allies convicted some fifty to sixty thousand war criminals, sentencing 816 to death, of whom 486 were executed. German denazification courts, supervised by the Allies, brought one million members of the Nazi Party to trial, sentences including imprisonment, fines, confiscation of property, disenfranchisement etc. After 1955, when the Federal Republic obtained full sovereignty, numerous further war criminals were discovered. In 1978 trials were still going on.

his sad last days after his defeat by Adenauer thought otherwise. Fresh from his eight years in a *KZ* he had been the first to speak up for the youth of Germany as not guilty for the state of their country. Now in 1952—admittedly in a private capacity—he wrote to a Jewish Socialist friend about the 'human and civil problem of the Waffen-SS, hundreds of thousands of whom were conscripted into it. The majority of the 900,000 men who returned from the war have got a role as pariahs. They are collectively answerable for the crimes of Security Services and the extermination commandos, although they hardly came in closer contact with these than many another Wehrmacht unit. . . . It seems to us a matter of humanity and good citizenship to break this ring and to open up prospects for the future for the great mass of former members of the Waffen-SS. They have endured without complaint the first years of helplessness and hardship which have borne heavily on their families. But gradually a feeling of revolt is growing up that derives less from their present troubles than from the fear that they are in a dead end. A close-knit body of 900,000 men together with their dependants without human and social prospects is not a good thing for a young democracy harrowed by great tensions between classes and ideas.'[93]

Schumacher may have overstated the stigma on the surviving Waffen-SS in Germany, and their numbers, and also how close-knit they were. But there is no doubt that it was highly convenient for the former Nazi adherents who became the main backers of successive Christian Democratic governments and also for the socialist opposition to have a scapegoat for the deeds for which Germany had had to bow down before the world in shame. Only a small proportion of them, however, deserve *personally* the brand-mark that world opinion and history has put upon the SS as a whole, and rightly so. For they were the chosen bearers of the master-race idea, and had Germany won the war all would have been used for monstrous purposes.

14

Camp for Hitler Youth

Ein unnützt Leben ist ein früher Tod—A life unused is an early
death.

Iphigenia, Goethe.

In the documentary films they march before us still, rank on rank
across the screen, chests puffed out, their faces glazed with loyalty,
patriotism and hope. Many had heard the call to sacrificial service
in the crisp lyrics of the best-selling Nazi laureate, Gerhart
Schumann: *Gefahr ist Hoffnung, Not ist dein Gewinn*—Danger is
hope, adversity your gain. Now in defeat, unless they had parents
or teachers who had inoculated them against total belief in Hitler,
they had little hope, little to fall back on. Re-education hardly
reached them. Henry Faulk, who after all was himself a schoolmaster, understood the condition of these young men, and in his
book *Group Prisoners* has written about them with empathy:

> Surrounded by a mass enthusiasm the boys had slipped easily as
> adults into the simple, convincing group slogans and distorted
> Darwinism of the National Socialist group ethos. As individuals
> in their inter-personal relationships within their group they
> were, given the exception of a normal percentage of anti-social
> and asocial elements, an ordinary crowd of youngsters, each
> with a personality of its own. But as a group bound by National
> Socialism they represented an a-human outlook and were a
> potential social menace. . . . The individual character was
> normal, the group motivation false. The outside world con-
> demned the individual on the basis of the group ideas. Hence
> the paradox that, among the young Nazis judged as the living
> incarnation of concepts detested by humanity, were some of the
> best human beings in a humanitarian sense. When Hitler's
> Germany finally collapsed, the immediate visible reaction of
> 'youth' was belligerent defiance. There were few camps from
> which they were not reported as a disciplinary problem

Mentally they were shocked. They talked of 'total emptiness', of 'standing on the ruins of their ideals'. They trusted no man, were often particularly mistrustful of the older generation, partly because the change in attitude of some older men transgressed their code of fidelity, partly because the moral superiority which some of the older men now adopted infuriated some of them, and partly because they blamed the older men for their condition. The younger the men, the more the symptoms tended to nihilism. They needed time to recover from the destruction of their belief in human integrity. The lovely bubble of a brave new world had burst.

It needed an unusual sort of man to reach the minds and feelings of these young men. Two such were Henry Faulk[94] and Herbert Sulzbach; another was a middle-aged Viennese businessman, born Karl Starnberg, now a staff-sergeant interpreter with the new name of Charles Stambrook. In Vienna in the late thirties when the Nazis were rampant and then took over, he had proved himself a brave and resourceful man. Modestly, he says this was largely because he was free to take risks, as his first much-loved wife had died in 1934. 'I hid people and smuggled them. I took my own goods from my small factory and sold them on the black market to raise money for desperate Jews driven from their homes. The more dangerous it was the more I liked it.' Escaping to England in 1939, he felt that he 'could not sit about as a guest while his hosts' house was on fire'. He at once joined the Pioneer Corps and went to France with the BEF, getting back just in time. He dug trenches, worked in a saw-mill, became a competent welder—all things far from his previous life—then, like Herbert Sulzbach, volunteered to be an interpreter. He found himself at Carburton, though reluctantly; he had no wish to be in contact with Germans but only a desire to be of service. It was March 1945, just at the time when Faulk had organised an anti-Nazi camp staff to confront the officers from Bridgend who had carried out a mass escape. Faulk has described how on the first day he took Stambrook to the camp gate and couldn't get him further; he had to put his hands on his back and push him in. Afterwards Stambrook told him what had been the matter: 'At the thought that I was about to come face to face with those who had been the ruin of my family and of my own life, I felt such a repugnance that my feet wouldn't move. After you pushed me in I could barely stop myself hitting out at the faces in front of me. But once I overcame the first shock I saw them as people and it was all right.' Stambrook confirms Faulk's recollection, adding that on first entering a hut he was told to give an order by the officer with him. No words came out. 'Do you speak German?' he was asked.

Stambrook however soon found his feet and began his very personal mission to reach those who would respond to human and democratic ideals. With Staff-Sergeant Werner he set up an information room with a sign at the entrance in big letters: JEDER SOLL DEN MUT ZU SEINER EIGENEN MEINUNG HABEN—Everyone should have the right to his own opinion. Two hundred and fifty of what were thought to be the most die-hard Nazis had been sent away, but the general spirit was only modified, not changed. Colonel Lemke, the camp spokesman who under Faulk's pressure had eventually stood up against the fanatics and had remained behind, asked permission to celebrate Hitler's birthday on 20 April. Stambrook advised Ellison, the Commandant, to agree on condition that attendance was voluntary. That evening two men were thrown out of their hut because they did not attend. Stambrook immediately showed his mettle by getting the hut cleared by the British staff. He put in seven anti-Nazis, including those thrown out, together with five ardent Nazis. When the latter asked to be moved out, numerous applications were made to move in. Soon there were three anti-Nazi huts, their occupants at last daring to express themselves. This was the beginning of a selection technique of his own that Stambrook steadily developed.

By the beginning of June Carburton was converted to a work camp and filled with other ranks, Colonel Ellison being posted away. All that stayed behind beside Faulk's original anti-Nazi staff were Stambrook and Werner, two doctors and two chaplains, including the excellent Father Lotz who had been forced by Faulk to stay in the camp under protection when his life was threatened. Stambrook says that 'Lotz agreed with me that for the moment it was not necessary to win Nazi youth for the Church but rather to give them human values.' The new Commandant was the regrettable Major J. whom Major Boughton replaced at nearby Norton and called an 'illegitimate'. Stambrook, too, thought him unfit to be a commandant or indeed to be commissioned at all—he had once been a provost-sergeant in the Indian Army. On occasions Stambrook simply counteracted his orders when he knew they would cause resentment, enjoying the fight and the risk of court-martial. When the Commandant arranged for certain selected staff to be posted away, Stambrook used Lotz's good relations with Major Boughton to get the latter to contact Faulk, who had the men brought back again. It was largely through Stambrook's force of character and capacity to care that Carburton was the unique example of a camp with a bad commandant that was a real success.

A POW with the unusual name of Ter Nidden also played an essential part. A student of theology and literature, he was a born teacher and leader. Stambrook made him head of one of the work gangs, selecting twenty young men to be with him. Nidden used the breaks to help them with their studies. Such was their enthusiasm that Stambrook saw the advantage of selecting by age and intelligence. When the flax harvest began he sent out two hundred youngsters with a single guard into a huge field where there were also Italians under Polish guards. The bailiff, who had lost relatives in the war, said he didn't want to have any more 'Nazi swine' on his land. Stambrook thereupon persuaded him to stay away for a few days, at the same time explaining the situation to the two hundred and giving them a pep talk. Three or four days later the bailiff came and saw that the Germans had done three times as much as the Italians, and wanted to express his gratitude. 'Give them a football,' suggested Stambrook. He gave them three and a day off on pay so that they could rest and play with them. This and other experiences convinced Stambrook that a special camp for Nazi youth could succeed.

Hitch, Faulk and others at Bush House had, in the meantime, come to the same conclusion. The 'lost generation' of the *Hitler-jugend* would obviously not be lost if they were given direction and new hope. It was decided, therefore, to open such a camp which could be both a working and an educational one. Stambrook and Werner from Carburton, with selected members of the staff there, would be transferred to it to act as yeast. The YMCA and the International Red Cross both backed the plan. But the War Office opposed it because its policy, based on the Geneva Convention, was that all POWs must be treated alike and none specially catered for. The Ministry of Agriculture objected because such a camp would interrupt its dispositions of labour. Even when the camp was scheduled to open in April 1946 the War Office remained adamant. The Foreign Minister, Ernest

Bevin, who had approved Wilton Park, generally left all POW matters in the hands of the ineffectual John Hynd, Minister for German Affairs. It was only when Major John Gwynn,* whose attitude to German youth had been inspired by Kurt Hahn, brought the difficulty privately to the ears of Sir Stafford Cripps, that the blockage was removed. Cripps, then in the Cabinet as President of the Board of Trade, went straight to Attlee who at once gave the go-ahead. The War Office retaliated by allotting the project a poor camp at Radwinter, Saffron Walden, that had been empty for the last thirteen months.

The plan was for young men aged eighteen to twenty-six to spend at least three months in the camp. The oldest of them could only have been thirteen when Hitler came to power and a high percentage were to be from the Waffen-SS. The hope was to give them in those three months 'a human perspective on life to fill the emptiness left by the collapse'. Camp 180 was at last opened in June 1946 with an initial intake of 542—eventually it would hold 1,300. The contrast with Wilton Park, started five months earlier, was complete. At the Beaconsfield camp 300 'white' or 'near-white' POWs were invited to a six weeks university-type course, with high-powered lecturers, personal tutors and relaxed living conditions. At Radwinter the initial intake was mostly 'black' and drafted and included 300 men from the unhappy camp at Lodge Moor, Sheffield. There were no proper paths, the hutments were shabby, the quartermaster unpleasant. It was basically a day release work camp—one day in five being free for lectures, study and discussions. Everything depended on the quality of the cadre from Carburton which acted as camp staff and on the Commandant. The former, belonging to a camp which over a year had developed a strong democratic spirit both politically and culturally, went to Radwinter with a quiet missionary purpose instilled in them by Father Lotz. Before they left he asked them to put on paper how they saw their task ahead when confronted with mainly nihilistic youth. They were all very firm about how they would seek to convince people not by words, but by example. One said he would look out someone from his own district and talk to him in dialect, and another would begin by talking about his own life and share

* John Gwynn was at the time head of the Religious Affairs Branch of the Control Commission, British Zone, and later became the first executive director of the Outward Bound Trust, starting up the original Outward Bound schools.

both the good and bad things in it; one would try to show that there were still people who had ideals but also their feet on the ground; one would try to get to know a depressed man by working alongside him; several would try, above all, just to be a good comrade. They could all expect suspicion and even hostility; they would keep their ears and their feelings open to everything they heard, and not condemn anyone. Another's intended attitude arose from an experience during the flax harvest when he had slipped away into an English church. Having let the atmosphere of peace sink into him, he had opened the Bible on the lectern and found himself reading a passage about love. He was brought face to face with the power and meaning of the death of Jesus and with the remembrance of his own mother whose love and care he had never returned. He had found the way to God and from that he could find the way back to mankind. 'Therefore, I say, give youth faith and everything else will come from that.' Another wrote, 'One should not anticipate their own views. They should learn to recognise democracy for themselves and make their own judgment. One should not say, "It is good or bad"; one can only give them a very small push by saying they should look into it and think about it objectively, making comparisons with Communism and National Socialism, and recognise for themselves the difference and the advantages of democracy.'

The little essays by the twenty Carburton men read like a group homily on Christian ethics—very German and very earnest. The Commandant, Major F. I. Woodnott, also believed that so-called 'black' youth were basically biddable and would respond to a non-authoritarian approach. An imperturbable man, he used regulations in a human way and punishments sparingly. When a POW struck a superior he naturally gave him twenty-eight days, but quite soon had him fetched out of the cells and for two days made him accompany him on his rounds to demonstrate how much care and trouble it took to maintain an orderly camp. Once he gave a lift to a man who turned out to be one of his own prisoners in civvies trying to hitch to the London docks. 'You'd better get a lorry back to the camp,' he told him, and on his return he said to the camp spokesman, 'Count more carefully next time, and when the man gets back see that he changes his clothes.' No one tried to get away twice. The camp leadership, in fact, asked for more discipline, promising to give the Commandant their full backing. But Woodnott refused. In his final report he comments that he could not have acted as he did with British troops: he would not have dared give them so much latitude.

The key figure at Radwinter was, however, Stambrook himself, now promoted to captain. Kelvin Osborne, who has German blood and was a language master at the nearby Quaker boarding school at Saffron Walden, became the local YMCA visitor. He got to know Stambrook well and recalls a sensitive, laconic man, quite without Viennese *Schmalz*, worldly-wise from all the bitter experiences he had been through, a man with great strength of character and steady common sense. Inevitably, perhaps, he was called 'Max' by the POWs—a name from the Jew-baiting paper *Der Sturmer*, but not unaffectionately. The name stuck and he effectively redeemed it in their eyes. One reluctant, untamed prisoner who was sent from Watten recalls his first encounters with 'Max':

We arrived and there was this extraordinary man, the complete Jew from Vienna. There was a raven in the camp which was a great joke, because it used to land on his shoulders when he didn't wish it at all. It always embarrassed him, because we used to take the mickey out of him. He gave us an introductory speech about how we were going to learn the way England functions. He then spoke to each of us singly and told me I would have to go and work in the fields like everyone else; and after so long I would be able to have two or three days in Cambridge. I said I wouldn't work and if they didn't like me, they should send me back where I came from. I finished by saying, 'I don't trust you because you're a Jew. You have no reason to like me and all your do-gooding is phoney.' Instead of losing his temper he said, 'You're just a young idiot', which I was. Next morning a farmer was showing me how to chop the heads off sugar beet which I knew from a child, but I just stood there and was still standing when his wife brought out tea and there was a cigarette break. Then there was lunch—they supplemented ours with something from the farm and I felt bad about it but wasn't going to budge. I told the farmer, 'Put me down as an absolutely undesirable worker who is costing you money', which he did. But the extraordinary thing is that Max just accepted it and left me alone—and at length suggested I go and work on the camp newspaper. A little later he was introducing us to democracy in this way: we, the POWs, were the House of Commons—each hut electing its member—and we could debate a variety of proposals, usually to do with camp life. The British lines were the House of Lords and had the veto. Proposals came very much from us and if they were tolerable the Commandant fell in with them. Max acted as Speaker. It was a very good thing, though not really related to life at large.

Early on 'parliamentary practice' was the main re-educational technique. There were also lectures in geography, history, economics, astronomy, largely by the POWs themselves. In the afternoon there were vocational courses in languages, stenography, technology, agriculture and horticulture, the last being the most popular. Since the instructor was a professional gardener the POWs not surprisingly won seven firsts out of eight in the local flower and vegetable shows. Captain Stambrook had the advice and backing of two training advisers, Macdonald and Reynolds, who were almost permanently resident. But during that first winter, one of the coldest in the century, things did not go too well at Radwinter. The POWs were meant to be working every day but one, but there was not enough local employment, which meant that the men did not get their shilling a day; this, in turn, reduced the welfare fund and thus morale. Repair work was then brought into the camp, but there were not enough work huts. With no proper paths, there was mud everywhere. The level of education of the second intake was lower than expected. The huts set aside for lectures and discussions were cold and the men would huddle with the teacher round an inadequate stove, their feet freezing in wellington boots, turning up their collars to protect their ears. The voluntary evening lectures were badly attended. Kurt Jaeger, coming over from the Belfast Camp, found that one of the instructors was his former corporal who had been a political officer and used to preach that a good soldier never gets captured. He told this man that as long as he remained in the camp as an instructor he would not attend any lectures. Jaeger was deprived of all privileges and sent back to Belfast.

Nevertheless, until the Carburton core was repatriated there was a good feeling in the camp. A training adviser reported 'a noticeably high standard of politeness and courtesy, the POWs being frank and outspoken'. He recommended that the intellectual level should be raised and 25 per cent intelligent 'greys' be introduced with enough personality to make themselves felt in the community. He added, 'Teaching the POWs to be decent individuals does not go far enough. Active social re-education is essential. . . . There are many decent youths who reject the excesses of the Hitler regime but still believe that the basic ideas were good —because they do not know what the basic idea was.'

In January 1947 the 320 Carburton 'whites' were repatriated and a crisis ensued. A large new intake grouped itself round its black activists. For a while Woodnott and Stambrook lost touch with their camp, which reverted to the old dual pattern of control, an outer one by the British and an inner, communal one by the POWs. Some thieving took place. In February a new 'white' staff was brought in from Colchester and the previous spirit was gradually restored. The human composition of the camp was altered and a new educational policy introduced. *Mein Kampf* became a discussion text book. A few months later F. J. Bell, Secretary of the Cambridge Board of Extra-Mural Studies, gathered together a group of German refugees with considerable experience in public service, representatives of the University, and training advisers, and produced a fourteen-week course on 'Citizenship'. It was largely practical in character, using film and other visual aids and visits to industrial, administrative and cultural institutions. Only a few lectures were given, the emphasis being on discussion and a daily press review. Tom Driberg, the journalist and Essex MP, took great interest in the Youth Camp, giving talks on Parliament and getting the 'Braintree Experiment' going, a way of combining contacts with the civilian population and local government, by which POWs were introduced to democratic practices. Other camps followed suit. Places were also reserved for POWs regularly at Cambridge Union debates.

It is sometimes said that Quaker women really come into their own in their sixties. Bessie Midgley was approaching seventy when the camp at Radwinter was opened. She is remembered as strikingly good-looking with white hair, china-blue eyes and a pink and white complexion. She was unmarried and walked with sticks because of a severe road accident. She was the daughter of a well-off public-spirited townsman of Saffron Walden and an Australian mother. The family were active Liberals and pacifists and, though their wealth came from brewing, had become militant teetotalers. They cultivated foreign friendships and when the First World War broke out, had had their windows broken

11*

because they had two Germans staying with them. Bessie Midgley had a lively mind but little education and, like her unmarried sister, till her parents died did not recover from her Victorian upbringing. But then she had stayed on in the family house, living the life of a local *grande dame*, dabbling in painting and pottery, travelling a little. When the war came she put up a note outside her house, 'Forces from Overseas Welcome!' When people asked her why not English forces she would say, 'They don't need it so much.' She received many Poles and from 1943 many Americans of the Eighth Air Force who found a second home at Larchmount. Then on 12 December 1946—the first day it was allowed—she put up a notice, 'German POWs Welcome!'

The first dozen who knocked on her door found themselves sitting down at a table spread not only with good things but with the family silver. For the next eight months till the camp moved nearer Cambridge she held open house, entertaining in all some two thousand men, this being greatly helped by the stream of parcels sent to her by American airmen she had entertained earlier. Larchmount was a mansion with a classical portico and an old coach house. It had well-proportioned rooms full of dark oak furniture, stuffed Australian birds in cases and much blue and white pottery made by Bessie and her sister. 'She largely looked after herself,' remembers Kelvin Osborne, 'and did nearly all the work, being by then not so well off. She got on much better with men than with women and had real insight into the disturbed backgrounds of some of her Germans, and also their talents and knew how to draw them out and help them. She had unfailing courtesy which sprang from the depths of her personality.' Charles Stambrook says simply, 'She was a saint'. Her pride was her extensive sloping garden with its pergolas and old fashioned walks. It had become thoroughly run down during the war, and out of gratitude to her, in that spring and summer of 1947 prisoner guests reclaimed a large part of it.

One of these guests, today a distinguished painter, remembers her vividly and with affection.

She used to hold court, sitting with her gammy leg on a couch and giving her views on life and the troubles of the world. She taught me manners. One afternoon she was handing round cucumber sandwiches, and I refused saying 'I am fed up'. Without a smile she said quietly 'Karl means he has had enough.' It was not till later when I realised my mistake that I understood how delicately she had spared me embarrassment. To a boy brought up in a children's home it was an unforgettable lesson in what true manners are. She was never a do-gooder. She never hammered her Christianity. Very practical too—there was a shortage of salt in the camp and she got us some. She was a dilettante painter and let me use her studio; I'd never had one before. She had some lovely old wood-carving tools and with them I made a war memorial, the first big thing I ever did. It was the head of a flier looking up into the sky and was made out of an old elm trunk. I dedicated it through the authorities to the pilots of all countries who had died. It was meant to be unveiled at Stansted Aerodrome, but then there was some trouble. The Commandant of the station wanted it, but the British Legion intervened, or maybe there was a Polish squadron there at the time. Anyway, some people thought it wrong for a German to do this memorial, and I have no idea what happened in the end. It was written up in the local paper, with a big smudgy photo of a big lump of wood and how this fantastic prisoner had only used razor blades and bits of glass—which would, of course, have made no impression on the wood at all! That was my first confrontation with the media.

From December 1946 onwards all the local churches were active and supported the local vicar, the Reverend Roy Sinker, when he called the POWs 'ambassadors in chains', and asked church-goers to have them in their houses, as this would accomplish something that books, lectures and discussion groups could never do. There was some criticism in the town, from parents of sons who had been killed and from a serviceman who was one of the first into Belsen. But every Sunday the parish room became a club for POWs with dancing, chatting, conjuring, tea and sandwiches, and with Captain Stambrook taking the lead in bringing the two sides together. In January the inter-denomination Youth Fellowship put on a concert with POWs. Stanley Wilson, later Mayor of the town, speaks of 'shy prisoners in the streets, whom people did not speak to as much as they should have.' But Kelvin Osborne thinks that the 'insulting ugliness' of the patches on their backs and backsides aroused sympathy for them. He reckons that his own family must have had 200 POWs in their small house, with the children doing the most effective entertaining.

Once I saw a couple walking about, free but lost. One was a rough type, the other had a really surly face. I took them home and John aged six and Jean aged four of course accepted them at once and got the two men to play with them, to mend things or even make a toy. They came, I think, after that every day for a fortnight and at the end their faces were transformed. The docility of the prisoners we met amazed me. Only one was an overt Nazi, who insisted that the British were robbing Germany of clothes. So I took him to the Friends Meeting House and showed him the pile of clothing that had been collected in the town to send to Germany. Meeting him later I asked him why he had not accepted our invitation to visit us. He said, 'I don't want to lose the convictions by which I have lived.' He went back to the camp in Scotland. Yet years later he wrote to me asking to arrange a pen-friend for a relative of his!

Bessie Midgley's international garden party on 31 May was a high point in that fine and brilliant summer. An eight-piece band from the camp played on the lawn, four hundred attended, with the vicar writing in his diary, 'All the men so happy and contented'. Five weeks later there was a two-day sports festival up at Radwinter. Five neighbouring camps sent teams each fifty strong for football, hand-ball and volley-ball events, light athletics and table tennis. There was an open-air concert and finally a revue. English guests were numerous. Behind the scenes was a great deal of feverish fun. The artist already mentioned designed and painted the stage:

The Commandant said we could go ahead as long as we used only materials on the camp and at the same time enlarged the cook-house. Well, an air-force camp nearby did lose quite a lot of roofing from its Nissen huts, a certain builder lost a pair of bloomers from his washing line. And there was that hole under the stage where you could retire to and find some fried chicken leg and some hooch made out of potato peel—a cross between lab alcohol and meths—but it kept you going. I worked for three days running till I fell asleep. The revue had a bit of *La Bohème* in it and a bit of Karl Valentin with some bitter anti-English and anti-Nazi humour in it, and all the things we dreamed about in our situation. There was a bit about a POW who was caught by a farmer standing in a bale of hay and affectionately accosting a cow; it was a great joke in the camp, so we said on the stage that there was someone who ought to be sent to a pastoral psychiatrist. Then came the performance and there in the front row was the Commandant and some Cambridge dons. Suddenly it all seemed very high-brow. You, the artistes, face the elite, as in the old days of the courts, and the paid entertainers have their party afterwards. . . . That's the sort of thing that ought to go into a film of POW life.

And yet at this very time a Training Adviser was reporting several negative factors. Half the new arrivals were thoroughly apathetic. No activists for re-education had replaced the repatriated 'A' prisoners. Knowing exactly when they were due to leave for home, others in their last months tended not to join in activities. Pastor Werner Jentsch, who came on a three-day visit on behalf of the YMCA in June, put his finger on a deeper factor. A specialist in youth counsellings, he took a group of some hundred POWs one morning. He first won their ears by talking about his own experiences as a POW in Italy, putting in some humorous anecdotes about his return to the *Heimat*. He started speaking about the problems that exercised young Germans at home, and at once met with a cool reserve. Only one man asked a question. They did not know where to begin and had become, because of their bitter disappointment in National Socialism, wary of the challenge of ideas of an alternative ideology. He then asked—a more successful approach—how many knew what career they would take up; a third did and two thirds did not. Next he gave them a psychological test: to continue a story which began with the words which he dictated to them, 'I lay awake in my darkened room. It was some time since I'd gone to bed and then . . .' His audience responded eagerly and set to on the spot with pen and paper. Their unspoken wishes, fears, hopes were released obliquely as they pondered and wrote. He selected six pieces at random and read them out. The ice was broken and discussion followed. In the next session he read a letter from a POW which dealt with extra-marital sex. This was 'topic number one' and led to lively interchanges into which he could drop some words about masturbation. At this, some frank talk broke out and people were grateful that a subject that many worried about was brought into the open. Jentsch, in analysing the test-pieces, saw clearly how it was private and personal problems that really concerned the men at Radwinter: their value as human beings, the anxiety about home or their

screening.* Whereas normal youth is more extraverted than intro-
verted, this sample showed a big preponderance of introversion.
His conclusion was that it was hopeless in most cases to awaken
interest in public matters unless one first took a man seriously in
his private capacity, just what the ideology of the Third Reich had
discouraged. But the Christian churches could make a similar
mistake if they harped on big issues; it was important to care on
a small scale for the personal needs of people, both inner and
outer. Such an approach has always been one of the strengths of the
YMCA.

In August 1947 the Youth Camp moved ten miles to the north
to Trumpington on the outskirts of Cambridge. By now all
participants were volunteers. In July the final screening had taken
place. Compared to the previous December when over half were
'black', and because of the Carburton intake about a quarter
'white', the new assessment was: 23 A, 215 B-plus, 533 B, 193
B-minus, and 40 C-plus. The conditions in the new camp were
much better, though the barbed wire had still to be removed. The
proximity of a University town meant more contact with hospit-
able residents. The Vice Chancellor, Canon Raven, took a special
interest in laying on facilities for POWs which included tours of
colleges and attendance at extra-mural courses. The young protégé
of Bessie Midgley attended art lectures by Professor Wahnfried, a
disciple of Barlach, and dined at St John's more than once. At the
same time the camp 'parliament' was replaced by a council which
had certain powers in that it could call members of the POW staff
to account; or, for instance, make representation against Germans
only being allowed to sit in the cheapest cinema seats—why such
undemocratic discrimination? In November Stambrook started a
special parcels operation. Groups of ten to twelve men undertook
to send out a package regularly to unknown individuals or families in Germany. The addresses were supplied by the Quaker relief
teams in the British Zone and from the Salvation Army. Each
member of the group gave up so much smoking or his weekly
cinema visit to raise the money, or was encouraged to go out and
find a little job with a civilian. The kitchen invented a cake which
would keep at least four weeks and withstand primitive packing.
Within three months fifty parcels were sent. The operation had a
good effect on morale and continued.

* In fact all screening officially ended at this time.

Every Sunday afternoon a well-attended social was held at St Columba's Hall. Two of the moving spirits were Norie Towers and A. S. Harris. The latter had been a wounded POW in 1918 and had been nursed back to health at the Eppendorf Hospital in Hamburg. He never forgot how he had been entertained when the war ended by the Hugo Zeisse family of Blohm and Voss and by Herr Otto Beit, and wished to do the same in return. His diary records that on 7 March 1948 the local churches, the Quakers, the UN Association and the Fellowship of Reconciliation provided and prepared the food for a social and supplied the necessary bread ration units: 100 sausage rolls, 250 buns, 100 scones, six slab cakes cut into 250 pieces and 4 lbs coffee. Afterwards many POWs were invited back into private homes.

In Cambridge another remarkable woman was playing her part, equivalent in many ways to that of Bessie Midgley at Saffron Walden. Lala Kaden was brought up in Dresden where her parents had a large circle of friends among artists, writers and musicians. She was drawn into Christianity at school when, being Jewish, she listened outside the door during scripture classes, and learnt by heart many passages of the New Testament. Later she was in the department of philosophy at the university under the famous theologian, Paul Tillich. A naturally joyful person, she felt closest to the mystics and Meister Eckhart. She was particularly fond of a line of Eckhart, which her son Herbert, a Cistercian monk, says also describes her: 'A burning soul in which yet reigns an unperturbed calm'. When they emigrated, however, she was ill for a while with home-sickness. But they found refuge and supportive friends at Cambridge where she worked for the Institute assisting refugee academics, becoming known as 'Mutter Kaden'. When mother and son one day heard prisoner of war voices through a hedge and then talked again their own language to ordinary Germans, they were filled with a sense of possible reconciliation.

She was now secretary of the Cambridge International Club which warmly welcomed POWs. She also used to cycle out to the camps bearing useful gifts she had collected—books in German, mending materials, pieces of cloth, an accordion. Prisoners would come to her house in Cambridge, singly or congregating in her small sitting room, sitting round on the floor. The evenings would have the semi-formal style beloved of Germans: someone would give a prepared talk on a topic of interest and then, after coffee, there would be general discussion. Men opened their hearts and troubles to Mutter Kaden and she herself finally opened hers in a farewell letter, as the last POWs were about to leave for home. In it she described how her efforts had changed in quality as they became more and more personal:

> Whereas at the beginning I was the giver, I noticed with astonishment that I became more the receiver. My new friends brought me an expanding wealth of warmth, fun and happiness, the stimulation of a world unknown to me. Suddenly it was quite clear to me from this experience that apart from purely material objects one cannot give without being in the same measure the receiver. The help that one gives to another is returned to one in other ways.

The most successful camps from the British point of view were Shap Wells (dissolved by the end of 1946 through repatriation), Carburton, Wilton Park, Norton, Featherstone Park and the Youth Camp. In the case of the last, its unique relationship with a university town was a key factor; the caring, fatherly attitude of Charles Stambrook another. At Trumpington morale did not decline as it did nearly everywhere else through boredom, frustration or bitterness. Courses had no fixed terms; so there were not such sudden turn-overs as at Wilton Park. The peer group image became established, newcomers quickly sensed it and tended to conform. Whereas there was normally an equality of intelligence at the black and white extremes, in the Youth Camp the residual blacks were below average intelligence and their motivation almost wholly instinctive. There was almost no backlash in the camps to which POWs returned, some 90 per cent giving favourable reports on it. At Romsey, however, a camp well-run on traditional lines, it was reported that some men from Camp 180 did not salute officers, lounged in late to roll-call and went out sloppily dressed in the evening. Called to account, they said that they had been at a democratic camp and were against militarism. On the other hand, the Youth Camp was also for not a few a stepping stone for Wilton Park for which they could not have qualified without going through the process of real inner change which was the aim, and often the hallmark, of Radwinter and Trumpington.

1*a* Lt-Col Henry Faulk *b* Pastor Birger Forell *c* Capt Herbert Sulzbach *d* The Revd Dr Herbert Hartwell *e* Capt Charles Stambrook *f* Capt Ted Lees.

2*a* Heinz Koeppler *b* Werner Lauermann *c* Dr Waldemar von Knoeringen *d* Lord Napier and Ettrick *e* General Heim *f* B. H. Liddell Hart.

3a Mary Foss   *b* Lala Kaden   *c* Father Theo Lotz, SJ   *d* Dr Kurt Schwederski   *e* Pfarrer Josef Jansen (in 1962)   *f* Gen von Ravenstein (in Canada).

4a An intake of POWs being addressed by the chief interpreter at Kempton Park and b German Pastors and Anglican Clergy in St Alkmund's Room, Shrewsbury.

a Grizedale Hall, a painting presented to Field-Marshal von Rundstedt and *b* Generals handle their own luggage on arrival back from Nuremberg. *Left to right*, Capt Lees, Gen Blumentritt, FM von Rundstedt, Sgt Strauss (interpreter), FM von Kleist, Gen Heinrici (obscured), Adm Krancke.

6*a* Education at Featherstone Park: a candidate undergoing a *viva voce* examination for Abitur and *b* A performance of *Troilus and Cressida* at Featherstone Park.

7a Puppeteers at Norton Camp (Wolfgang Kaftan in the centre behind) and *b* Visit of Cardinal Frings to Norton. On his left the Catholic Bishop of Birmingham, and Major Boughton.

8a Late stayers at Watten Camp, among them SS Colonel d'Alquen (back left) and *b* Teenagers from Bremen tending the German cemetery at Cannock Chase.

15

The Myriad Threads of Peace

Such is oft the course of deeds that move the wheels of the world:
small hands do them because they must, while the eyes of the great
are elsewhere.

J. R. R. Tolkien[95]

From Lands End to the dunes at Wick, from Dover to Limavady,
from Norwich to Harlech, the 400,000 German prisoners of war
mixed their labour with the land of Britain and for a time became
thoroughly mixed up with the people of Britain. There were innumerable personal encounters that could be servile, resentful,
hopeful, friendly, touching, amorous, comic, compassionate. But
it was the farmers who had the longest, closest and most fruitful
contact with the prisoners, who at one time provided a quarter of
the total labour force on the land. Since the relationship was
economic, it was not without friction; since it was human, bonds
of mutual respect and sometimes friendship grew up, some of
which have lasted to this day.

At first almost only gang labour was used, for instance by Roger
Davies in Breconshire: 'They came for potato picking and such
like, under one of their own sergeants who took my orders and
handled them firmly. If a Welsh tractor-man told any of them to do
something, he got a tongue-lashing from him in understandable
guttural English.' Marjorie Booker, then a landgirl, recalls, 'They
came in open lorries with wire sides and two or three guards.
They were never late and marched from the farmyard to the place
of work. They brought their own food and at dinner time relaxed
a little, but never like the Italians. It was rare for one of them to
talk to any farm-hand.' This was before the end of the war, at a
time when comparatively few Germans were used on the land; the
Italians were the farmers' mainstay, though with their sunny
volatile temperament they never did more than they had to. The
Germans at first worked well, for work was seen as a way back
into the community, even as a kind of personal therapy, an attitude

that persisted to the end in a few camps. Productivity was also generally boosted by re-education. But during 1946 morale declined and with it output. By March 1947 it was officially reckoned that POW labour was half as productive as that from British workers.[96]

Thomas Brasnett was Drainage Officer for South Norfolk and had previously served in the RAF. He writes:

To my amazement I had to supervise several thousand Germans. I was harsh and hostile to them at first, perhaps for a fortnight; after all, we had been killing each other for years. Then I found what wonderful workers the Germans were—the Eyties were useless. In each German gang a sergeant was in charge and to him I gave orders. I began to get friendly with them and did my best to ease their lot. When they realised I had been a regular for ten years we got on very well. They lived in the huts on the airfields where the Yanks had once been, the camps being mainly run by the war agricultural labour officers, with civilian supervisors under them. I had the use of the men during the winter months and at odd other times; for the rest of the year they were contracted out to farmers. Their rations for a long day's work were appalling and many is the row I had about this. I encouraged the farmers to give them what eggs and poultry they could spare. Since I was the man through whom the farmer got his subsidy it wasn't difficult. There was some trouble about this; but the output of my gangs was double that in the rest of Norfolk. There was no corruption where I ruled, but elsewhere there was a good deal, with questions being asked about the scandal of the Norfolk labour officers in the House of Commons.

The Germans, according to Brasnett, were more popular with the Norfolk farming community than the Americans had been. They were sober, not having the means to be otherwise; they were conscientious and did not interfere with women—which was forbidden. And if they stole, it seems they were discriminating:

It was just about the time when they read that Goering in his cell at Nuremberg had had chicken for Christmas dinner, which infuriated them. A certain lieutenant colonel's manor house lay over the fields. He had a small pedigree poultry farm and called me in to prepare a scheme for ditch cleaning with a 50 per cent grant towards the cost. I sent some thirty POWs to do the job,

but he continually harassed them, finding fault and trying to get
more work done than contracted for. I was forced to tell him
that unless he kept away from the Germans I would withdraw
the men, charge for the work done and he would forfeit his
subsidy. The men took three times as long as they should have
done—and had their revenge. They sneaked out of camp,
making their way two miles to the manor house in the heart of
the village, removed the pedigree birds, carried them back
across the fields and killed and plucked and cooked them without leaving a feather. It was real Commando stuff; they could
have stolen poultry from the ordinary farmers, but they were
their friends.

On the subject of killing, one group of prisoners in the same area
were not above holding a sheep under water during sheep dipping
till it drowned, so that they could take the carcass home to their
cookhouse. But Fritz Pons was deeply shocked when Mr Saxby,
a Leicester farmer, killed a hen by putting his boot on its neck and
pulling on its legs. 'We have a law against that,' said Pons. 'We
have to stun before killing.' 'How strange,' said Saxby; 'you have
such humane animal laws and yet are so cruel to human beings!'
The remark went home, and was the beginning of a friendship.

The folk humour of the POW language describing their food
amused Peter Lowe, a conscientious objector who supervised
labour in Essex. Any form of meat paste was referred to as
'Mussolini pasta', alluding to the dictator's end, while plain slices
of bread were spread with 'Horst Wessel pasta'. An old caretaker
in a depot at Preston which the POWs were converting into a
department store used to sit with them at lunch for which they
often had cold English sausages. He couldn't understand why
when they were eating it they kept referring to Churchill. 'We call
the sausage *Churchillpimmel*' they said, and demonstrated. Then he
understood. 'Ah, Churchill's tool!' He roared with laughter and
said, 'Kaputt! Kaputt!' It was 1947.

A member of Brasnett's gang in Norfolk was without doubt the
twenty-five-year-old P. A. Hoffmann, captured in the last Tunis
round-up in 1943 and therefore an 'American'. By April 1946 he
was back across the Atlantic and on the former American base at
Seething near Norwich.

Our work began with cleaning out marsh dykes round Reed-
ham, the only man responsible for us being the driver. It was

quite a change not to see an armed guard keeping an eye on us. On our journeys to and fro the population hardly took any notice of us, but one or two of the younger generation waved to us, which meant a great deal as it made us feel we were members of the human race once more. Although fraternisation wasn't allowed, we began to swap clothing for food, because our camp food was poor and inadequate. We would give our driver a pair of socks or trousers and he would give us loaves of bread in return, which we would eat by spreading Camp Coffee on it. If we had a good day in the fields the driver would ask the farmer, if he was satisfied with our work, to spare a few potatoes which we would boil and eat in the skin. . . . Eventually I was given the chance to become billetted on a farm and I took it without hesitation, for the people who took me in saw in me not a former enemy who could be exploited as cheap labour but another human being like themselves. The very first day I was invited to sit at table with them and gradually became one of the family. At weekends when friends were visited, I was taken along and received with the same warm hospitality as I received from the farmer's family.

On Christmas Eve we were threshing two stacks of corn and extra help from the camp was called for. At the end of the day the farmer said, 'All you boys are invited for dinner tomorrow —all six.' Came Christmas Day, we had not seen a table like it for many a year. There was food in abundance and a present for each of the POWs. We could hardly believe it was possible to treat us in such a way. There were one or two who were still hostile. I could understand their feelings but also wished they would understand mine. As time went on I fell in love with the farmer's daughter who was a war widow. We could not risk being seen together or the authorities would have taken a very dim view of our relationship. I had no wish to go back to Germany as my home was in Russian hands. We were given the chance to stay on in England for a limited period, and then we could stay on indefinitely provided we stayed on the land for three years. I went to an interview where my political past was probed, the result of which was that I was given permission to stay. At long last I was free and in November 1948 I married my English sweetheart. I have never regretted my decision to stay in this country although I love my country and my family at home. At heart I will always be German. One encounters the odd person who still shows a bit of the old hostility, but over the years I have made many friends among the British people.

Gerald Andreas, another of 24,000 POWs who stayed on in Britain, would be a conspicuous character in any setting. His mother was German, his father Greek, a circus strongman and a great Nazi. He shamefully neglected his son who inherited a Mediterranean shrewdness, a German toughness and also the cheek of Old Nick—which frequently got him into trouble. The first farm job he had was from the White Cross Camp at St Columb Major near Newquay. He volunteered to be billetted out, as he thought he would have a bit more freedom, and was sent to a farmer at Sennen near Land's End.

You could really see that that farmer hated Germans; I stayed eleven days and lived in the stable beside the horses. He came to me one morning: 'Charlie, you go out and put in some broccoli and don't come to eat till the broccoli is all in.' Three thousand plants to dib in, all by hand! I came back about quarter to four in the afternoon. 'Fine job done!' he said, and for the first time asked me indoors. Everything laid on the table—ham, cream; all I was allowed was bread and jam. We were a different class. Seven o'clock in the evening, we go to Penzance and fetch some more plants for the morning. Another twenty thousand, and without telling a lie we were putting in plants next day till midnight with a lantern. Next day when he and his son came out, I said, 'You're going to get a shock!' I'd set out hundreds of plants with all the leaves in the ground and the roots upwards. He chased me across the field with his digger, then rang up the camp and said, 'Send someone else!' But they told him, 'Tell him how to do it, he's never worked on a farm before.' The next morning I was milking. The cow kicked the bucket over and the milk went down the drain. The farmer's son who was there got hold of me by the neck. I broke loose and got hold of the milk-churn lid and said, 'One step and you have this right on top of your head. Any cow can kick.' So I walked the forty miles back to the camp, taking two days. I was put on a charge but got away with it. I'd rather be forty days in the cooler than three on that farm. I've had some good farmers too. . . .

But Gerald Andreas' picaresque tales are nearly all about the bad ones he hoodwinks and gets the better of. Not for him the grading book that U-boat man Karl Becker kept in Derbyshire at Swanwick Camp, assessing each farm he worked at against 100. One was put down as 'hungry farm—no food' and rated zero, but the Willards of Manor Farm, Brailsford and the Murrays of Slade Hollow Farm, Hollington, were 150 and Mrs Allen of Sturston Farm, Ashbourne, got the maximum 200 rating.

Kurt Schwederski is a man who makes human contact wherever he is. In the last winter of the war in Jersey he had shared the hunger of the population, glad at lunch-time to find a few crumbs left over from his breakfast to pick up with a wet finger. More than once an islander gave him part of the Red Cross parcels (which the Germans did not touch) in return, perhaps, for a little fuel which he provided. He was also frequently hungry at Llanmartin Camp.

Walking out one day I passed some Welsh roadworkers. The first time they just greeted me. The next time it was, 'How's that Commandant up there? Bit of a swine, isn't he?' The next time one of them came round, very delicately, to the question of food which was short at the time and, standing apart from the others, said quietly, 'When are you coming again? I've talked to my wife . . .' A few days later, so that the others didn't have to notice, he gave me a sandwich. I thanked him and he said, 'In this country we have a saying: the poor help the poor.' This man then invited me home and for the first time I ate with a family. I wanted to pay him back. There were some officers very clever with their hands and I exchanged some cigarettes for a lovely little wooden car. But how was I to get it out of the camp? The Commandant said that all the wood used in the camp was 'King's property', including all the toys we made. He used to put his sergeants out on the road to see if we didn't have any contraband on us. So I reached my friends by taking a roundabout way through a wood and gave them my little present.

In some camps a veritable light industry was conducted—in slippers, brushes, trinkets, lighters, caskets, chessmen, ships and toys—above all toys: ducks, dachshunds, acrobats on bars, pecking hens. Men made them for the joy of it, as a therapy against boredom and sadness, to have presents to give to British friends, or simply to sell and make money. The first problem was to get

the material, which usually meant pilfering; the second was to get
it into the camp; and the third to get the finished product out
again. At any stage a POW could be caught and any commandant
who kept to the letter of the regulations had to harry his charges
continually. At Swanwick there was a group making full-rigged
ships, eighteen inches long, that were worth £2 to £3 or a large
number of cigarettes if sold to farmers. It was no problem to hide
their tools under the linoleum in the old YMCA building at the
top of the camp;* it was more difficult to bamboozle the guards
who searched each group of twenty and the trucks that brought
them to and from work. One trick was, having hidden a ship in
the lunch canteen, to divert attention with a suspicious-looking
sack filled with scrap wood and shavings, which the guard duly
tipped on to the ground.

Makers of brushes needed horse-hair. Gerald Andreas worked
for a Cornish farmer who had some dozen horses. Just as he and
some comrades left, they clipped their tails short and put the hair
in their dinner bags. But the pick-up lorry had to visit another
farm afterwards, the farmer noticed the missing tails, phoned
through and the sergeant was waiting for them. 'You German
bastards! Kallabouche for you!' They got ten days, but Andreas
says, 'It was nothing! Look, you're behind wire anyway. So, as
long as you had a good time it was worth it!'

Slippers were easiest to make and sell, but it meant stealing
potato or corn sacks, picking them apart, dying the fibres in different colours and weaving them together. Twine was also useful,
while old driving belts might be used as soles. Gerald Andreas
was naturally into slipper trading, walking round St Colomb, St
Dennis and Newquay with samples and taking orders. He had a
group making sixty pairs a week for five shillings which he then
sold for twelve shillings. 'Of course I got caught in the end, walking through the town with a sack on my back. "What are you
doing, Johnnie?" said the copper pleasantly enough. "Making a
bit of money for a packet of cigarettes. We only get a bob a day.
Can't you turn a blind eye for once?" "Sorry." I had all the pound
notes in my shoes inside my socks and the loose change in my
pockets. He took the three pairs of shoes left in the sack and the
change and led me back to the camp. I got ten days.'

In the Loughborough districts such a big trade in slippers developed that Captain A. D. Burgess, in charge of the Knightthorpe

* Still part of the well-known Hayes Conference Centre in 1978.

Camp, appealed to the public through the Derby *Evening Telegraph* to report all cases of hawking slippers. At this Robert Hughes of Littleover wrote back that it was 'despicable to try to prevent the poor chaps from earning a little extra money. I understood that we Britishers had a decent way with all opponents after a fight and were ever ready to shake hands at the conclusion, but it would seem that this trait is missing from some people's make-up. One or two of these POWs have called at my house and I have been struck by their politeness and smartness, etc., and the excellent character of their handwork. . . . Sportsmen of Derby, don't kick a man when he is down. Assist him up!' This letter made a tremendous impression on all the POWs at Loughborough and farther afield. Paul Seufert wrote and thanked him in the name of his comrades and was invited to the Hughes house where he was well entertained. The slipper trade went on.

Most commandants were tolerant or made occasional examples. During routine searches guards tended to turn a blind eye— especially to toymaking—sometimes helping to provide materials. In December 1947 the toy workshop at Tonbridge featured in the local press with a photo of the craftsmen at work, though shortly before the MP for Westmorland, William Fletcher Vane, was protesting in the Commons that POWs were not even allowed to send toys to be put round Christmas trees in local hospitals. Such un-Christian regulations should, he demanded, be ended. The Minister of War's civil servants told him to answer blandly that exceptions could be made, but that 'there was considerable objection while the output of the British toy industry remained restricted.'[97] But there could be no restriction on personal gifts. Some of the toys made by prisoners out of old butts of wood with a penknife are today prized possessions, almost museum pieces. Josef, a professional woodcarver from Sudentenland, and Werner, a hefty blond engine driver, made a crocodile on wheels for Albert and Mary Steel of Croydon. It was two feet long with green scales and a fearsome set of teeth in a red mouth; this opened and shut as it was pulled along, but always just missed a little black boy in red trousers. Guards had helped them get the materials. Josef hardly ever carved again; having no home to return to, his talent wasted away in a picture framing works in Bavaria.

Possibly the most remarkable artistic effort by a POW came from Wolfgang Kaftan of Hanover. He was a puppet-master in his mid thirties, a language teacher and interpreter, and already

solidly anglophile when he was captured in March 1945. He had
been able to practise his art spasmodically while still in the Wehrmacht and within two months had written his first glove puppet
play in England, *Kasper Becomes a Prisoner of War*. Kasper is the
traditional central European figure of Punch or Pulchinello. His
cruel and sardonic streak had been, so to speak, 're-educated' out
of him within the idealistic German Youth movement before the
First World War and Kasper became more of a general fun-poker
—a droll fellow, a sharp critic but on the side of the angels.
Kaftan's Mr Punch is always optimistic and occasionally sentimental. First at Shady Lane Camp near Leicester and then at
Norton he developed a remarkable repertoire of original plays.
Among his comrades, who in the first days had virtually no other
entertainment, he found ample talent from which to make up an
eventual team of ten: artists, musicians, theatre experts, electri-
cians, good English speakers. The puppet heads were made of
papier mâché, later of wood, the first paint brushes of sticks and
sweepings from the barber's floor, the paint from crushed crayons
and engine oil. Searchlights from the camp perimeter provided
the lighting. After the first performance at Shady Lane the
Canadian interpreter sergeant was so happy that he came behind
the scenes and took Kaftan in his arms. In the end they had such
a brilliantly contrived stage that today it is in the famous puppet
museum in Munich. At Norton Major Boughton furthered
Kaftan's activities as much as he could. Early on he invited local
children in to see it. A worried War Office bureaucrat heard this
was going to happen. 'Imagine! He rang up and told me to make
sure the children did not come in contact with the prisoners! I
replied ironically: "Of course not, they might get an infection." '
The puppeteers were soon visiting neighbouring schools as well
as other camps. The plays in German included *Kasper Goes
Fraternising*, *The Sleeping Beauty* and *The Captain of Koepenick*. *Sleeping Beauty* had its première in English in three successive, rap-
turously received performances at the Middle School, Warcop.
The children wrote enthusiastic letters and criticism and Miss
Buckley, the remarkable headmistress, a sort of genius in her field,
was made an honorary member of the troupe. Soon a *Dr Faustus*
after Marlowe was adding weight to their repertoire, with Mr
Punch bringing in some sharp comic touches. All in all, the Norton puppeteers played before some 25,000 people, giving 108 performances, 78 of them in English. As repatriation thinned down

the team, Kaftan carried on alone, taking shows to infant schools as far as Sheffield and beyond. A group of teachers and Nottinghamshire education officers were so impressed by Kaftan's art that they petitioned he be allowed to stay on and do contract work for a further year. The War Office and the Ministry of Education apparently agreed, but at the last moment the Home Office ruled that it was against policy: for the time being the only work available to former POWs in Britain was on the land. In later years Wolfgang Kaftan would say that his years in England as a POW were the happiest and, in fact, the freest of his life.

The widespread friendliness when fraternisation was finally allowed totally surprised many POWs, and it was shown nowhere more than in Lancashire. 'Public opinion and the press had won,' records Father Jansen, then at Bury. 'But even before that the population had been good-natured to us, illegally giving us sweets, fruit and cigarettes and even rationed foodstuffs in 1946.' Contacts were at first tentative. 'Do you want to be seen with me?' said Engelbert S. to Daphne Rickard, then a young telephonist at Aylesbury, as they walked out near Aston Abbotts. 'Why?' 'I was in U-Boats and have helped to sink many British ships.' 'It is what you are now,' she answered firmly, 'and what you will be that matters to me.' They still write to each other. When Paul Seufert first walked freely through an English town he felt eyes upon him because of the patch on his back. His mind went back to the streets of Germany during the war and the Jews who had to wear the yellow Star of David on their clothes, and to the Poles in their own country who had to wear the mark of being a second-class citizen. 'How many of us,' it occurred to him, 'ever gave a thought to the pang in their souls?' Not long after this to his amazement a Mr Mann, head of a local college for art and design, called for him and a friend and transported them to his house at West Hallam. 'Feel yourself as free as you would be in your own home,' said Mrs Mann. The white tablecloth, good food, inspection of rare books and travel photos, the children taking them by the hand and showing them round the town helped to open up an invisible England to Seufert, who reflects that 'many of us had formed a completely one-sided view of the British and their ways. We discovered they had qualities the German lacks. I think especially of their extreme politeness which embraced us prisoners as well.'

On occasions German manners caught the English unawares.

When Pike and Crissie Jarvis of Barnstaple first entertained three Germans after Quaker Meeting one Sunday, they gave them a good meal and cordial relations were established over washing-up and photo albums. When the time came to go the Germans seemed to change character so much that the astonished Crissie Jarvis, now over eighty, says, 'It was like having Hitler in the house!' All they had done was to stand rigid, click their heels and bow.' German cleanliness, smartness and punctiliousness often made a good impression. A Dorset paper wrote that the POWs walking out on Sunday with their spruce jackets and pressed trousers were the smartest young men in the district. At Brook-wood Mental Hospital the Germans working there may have been called 'ruddy square-heads' but a land girl, Monica Montilla, noted how at the lunch-break they all plucked a bunch of grass to clean their hands, which she could never imagine an English or Irish gang doing. Colonel Ponsonby, in charge of a camp in Norfolk, was woken one morning by boots crashing to attention outside his room. There was a knock on his door. He opened it and a sergeant saluted and handed him a small parcel. At a signal, the troop of men lined up behind him burst into a well-drilled 'Happy birthday, dear Commandant, to you'. Another order and the Germans turned smartly away, this time at the double so as not to be a second late for work.

Germans are remembered for countless little unasked for ser-vices, like cutting and stacking logs, making a toy windmill for a garden, mending things. Using tools he had made himself, Helmut Rheinhardt got all the broken clocks in the Skevington family going again, after which the villagers of Astwood, near Newport Pagnell, had the benefit of his personal service. At Bwlch in Breconshire Conray Pryce had a mechanic coming to repair a tractor on Monday. Wilhelm begged to be allowed to do it instead, and spent his whole Sunday taking the tractor to pieces cleaning each part so that it ran like new. He refused any reward, but a few days later the officer in charge turned a blind eye when a barrel of beer was sent in. Not that all farmers were open-handed. Herr Balsten was a lay reader and became so good at English that when the elderly Congregational minister at St Andrews was ill, he asked the German to take his place. As he waited in the vestry a farmer entered with a smile and outstretched hand. 'I am the Sessions Clerk!' 'We know each other already,' said Herr Balsten. 'I have been working in your fields all week.' The Session Clerk's face got redder and redder, for the German, wanting to earn money to send a parcel to his wife, had worked over-time and been much underpaid.

Bernhard Harms from Bremen found the south-east English, though the schoolbooks said they were cousins, surprisingly alien. The men in the brickworks were Anglo-Saxons all right, self-controlled and at the lunch break scarcely raising their voices, rather exclusive, but fair and straightforward. But how much more vigorous, lively and versatile Germans were! 'The Tommies of Kent, Surrey and Sussex,' he concluded judgmatically, 'belong to a nation that lost its enterprising men to America and the colonies, a nation which had its prime in the past and in many ways backward. Where was the artisan who has in the German fashion been a true apprentice and taken his master's exam? As regards safety precautions and washroom and toilets they are behind the Germans. The boss at the brick-works didn't greet his men. Compared to the Prussian Junkers the gentleman farmers had little social awareness or sense of responsibility.' Would Harms, one wonders, have got a different impression in the north or in Scotland?

On the other hand, his archaeologist's eye was unforgettably impressed by the half-timbered buildings of Kent with roofs shingle-tiled or thatched, uniquely grouped in asymmetrical and organic units. For the Parachute Leutnant and poet, Jorhen Garster, it was the Yorkshire landscape that made a strong impression; one of its frequent aspects mirrored his own moods of frustration:

> A rigid net of black walls
> Splits the land with thin shadows.
> The wind from the sea brings showers
> that veil and vex the meadows.
> The fields in motley shapes
> Lie boxed-in up to the ridges.
> Occasional pale roofs glance
> Up valleys at ancient bridges.
> The landscape's repeated greens and greys
> are sombre as an oil painting.
> Everything has meaning and tries
> To sing out in clear colours.
> But the tenacious mist drapes the land,
> Then long cold rains descend.[98]

The freedom the POWs had in Britain did not include sexual access to women. The rules about this were very plain. But, of course, many longed for it, and some achieved it. Hans Freiberger remembers being marched from the station late in the evening to the Devizes camp. Inviting voices called out, 'Hullo, boys,' from the pavement. Just to be called at in a not unpleasant manner made them feel they belonged to humanity. At Glen Mills, Bury, early in 1945 Dr Mayenfels was still treating some three hundred cases of syphilis, picked up usually in France. But subsequently there was virtually none. G.M. recalls how when the non-fraternisation ban was lifted they were told firmly that they were not allowed into 'public houses'. At this, they went round looking in vain for places with a red light outside, for translated into German the words simply mean 'brothel'. Easy girls later on could be lured into unguarded hostels, especially when repatriation had thinned the occupants. The police used to look out for camp followers who found vigorous young Germans more exciting to know than local boys. At Coleshill they warned one girl away—who turned out to be a POW dressed for theatricals and taking a breather on the road. Elmar Tremmel recalls that they used to say that 'if you were caught with a girl it was a great advantage to speak English, as you could explain yourself; if not, you might be accused of attempted rape!' Plenty of bolder spirits contrived amorous adventures—even from the C plus compound at Watten. *The Times* reported how T. H. Verborg and A. Nohr were caught with two girls in a cinema in Thurso. Taken back the sixteen miles to Watten, they immediately escaped again through 'several locked doors' and next morning met up again with the two girls on the river bank. They were noticed, chased and shot at and were last seen disappearing, as on the films, into a convenient Scottish mist over the railway embankment. They were carrying two parcels containing food and shaving equipment which the girls confessed to have given them. Down in London a certain Eileen G. had Joachim K. to stay in her Kensington flat and some friends told the police. They came and went straight to a cupboard where they found him hiding. The *Daily Mail* was waiting after he was taken away. 'It will be ruin for me now,' Mrs G., who had left her husband, told the reporter. 'I shall lose this flat and a relative will probably cut me off without a penny. Joachim is a sensitive artist and the very sight of the barbed wire jangled his nerves.'[99]

There were many genuine romances and marriages. Willi Runkel served a sentence of eighty-four days detention for illegally consorting with Rosemary Vinall and wedded her on 4 August 1947, by which time marriages were allowed. Konrad Braun, a distinguished German Quaker who settled in Britain, once took great trouble to write a letter to persuade the Home Office to let a POW marry an English girl. He set down all his merits, his knowledge of English and good political record and his professional qualifications. The official response gave him great pleasure: 'Tear it all up,' he was told. All that was needed was for the girl herself to apply for permission for her fiancé to reside in Britain permanently so that they could marry. That was her inalienable right, which she took advantage of—along with seven hundred and ninety-five others. By no means all such unions were happy. Francis King wrote a poignant radio play about Christine, an Oxford undergraduate who gets herself pregnant by a POW, Thomas, a musician who is working on the land. They marry and settle down in a little cottage, he having to remain a labourer for the time being—a poor start to their marriage. At the end of the play a friend of Christine remarks to Thomas: 'You've been made a prisoner twice over.' The German denies it strongly three times, but in their hearts they all know that it is true.[100]

Sometimes invitations were politically motivated. Germans who were themselves Communists or inclined that way, might find themselves invited out for the weekend by members of the 'Heine Club', which was on the extreme left at the time. There are said to have been British Nazi sympathisers who organised an escape route for POWs. Indeed, slipping away from billets or unguarded billets was so easy that it is a wonder that more POWs were not at large. One got back home from Devizes, unguardedly sent a letter back to friends at the camp and was nabbed. Norman and Evelyn Cox, a Quaker couple near the Billinghurst camp, twice had absconding Germans in their house, without feeling they should turn them in. They lent them bicycles to get to Southampton, which were duly returned to them. It was two years after the war and it seemed wrong to retain prisoners so long. One of them, when next heard of, was working in a sausage factory in Spain. The case of Hans Muller is both authenticated and the subject of fiction.[101] Frustrated by the long wait to be repatriated, he slipped out of the camp at Colchester, and stowed away on a ship from Harwich to Bremen, swimming to the shore from the Weser estuary. Making his way to Dresden, he was arrested on suspicion of being an SS man on the run. He escaped from a Russian camp and, like the legendary Captain of Koepenick, realised that he could get nowhere in the world without the necessary papers. He therefore made his way back by the identical route, all the way to Colchester, discovering his release documents had been waiting for him all the time; they were to have been given him the very day he absconded!

Germans could be angered, puzzled or delighted by the British attitude to rules. Pastor Forell and Dr Hartwell worked out a list of rights which POWs had in order to clarify their relations with commandants. They called it their 'Magna Carta' and submitted it both to the Red Cross and to the War Office. Most of their suggestions were approved, but Hartwell's personal advice when introducing the Magna Carta to a camp was also important: when you find a commandant breaking a rule, do not rush to him with the rule book in your hand, or you will fail. To insist on your rights or the law is typically German. Put what you want to him as a petition and that will please him. The commandant is a little king in his camp and the War Office like it like that. If the petition is not granted, put another in four weeks later.

If commandants interpreted rules in their own way, the public often broke them, most frequently in regard to clothes. The director of the Wisbech Museum used to provide prisoners with civilian suits and take them off to the sea for the day. The I.O. at Horsham lent Private Botho Kirsch (captured at seventeen and perhaps the youngest POW) an overcoat to cover his patches, so that he might go up to London and the British Museum. Dr George Betts of Queen's University, Ontario, is today writing a history of German POWs in Canada, partly because when a teenager his family at Skipton used to lend clothes to young Germans so that he could take them cycling across the moors. The risk of being caught was half the fun of it. A naval officer called Davies in Newport lent Kurt Schwederski one of his suits so that he could take him to the rugby ground—just out of bounds. Returning home, the police were waiting—a neighbour had informed them—and Schwederski got his twenty-eight days from the Llanmartin Commandant. Eva Koch in Nottingham knew what she was doing when she gave Heinz her husband's housecoat, slippers and flannels to wear: he could begin to be his real self again. To change out of stale uniforms for a while was to leave behind the meaningless, for the German army no longer existed: it was either literally dead in battle or had been proscribed. The occasional family who gave a POW a key to their house, or left them in when they went out, lifted them right out of their present circumstances and could see the effect in the amazement and pleasure on their faces.

Gradually, however, rules were relaxed. POWs could travel in buses, go to the cinema, spend weekends with friends. Kurt Schwederski, having returned to Featherstone Park, was contacted by a Miss Jacobs, a German immigrant. Twice she arranged for the lecturers—he was teaching in the law school there—to go to London.

She could not do enough for us, especially those who were studying. If you needed a book she would try to get it for you. We were given a few pounds and ten of us set off with a sergeant. At Euston he said he'd expect us at such and such an hour in three days time under the clock. I was wearing some black American trousers obtained for cigarettes, a Luftwaffe jacket with insignia and a large cape. We stayed in an OR camp in a suburb, but merely slept there quite unsupervised. I just wandered round to the LCC, twice to a concert, twice to Parliament. Simply by showing my POW identity card I was let into the gallery of the House of Commons.

A high proportion of POWs, however, never made contact with the British population. Resentment and suspicion were fed by their being kept so long. More than one young Nazi, conditioned by being brought up in an authoritarian society, thought that the British people 'had been ordered by the government to be friendly'. Such men looked everywhere for evidence of the cliché 'perfide Albion' that Goebbels had drummed into them. 'Look at the insincere way the English greet each other,' they would point out. 'They say "How do you do?" to each other and don't even care to get an answer. *Typisch Englisch*!' Kaftan affectionately lampooned what the logical German found incomprehensible by making his Mr Punch answer, 'How do you do?' with 'Yes, I do!' Some saw proof of insincerity and lack of strong convictions in the very custom that British democrats thought so civilised and essential: dining with the opposition and drinking a beer with someone you have just been passionately arguing against. Father Jansen found the formula 'I'll do what I can for you' so frequently on the lips of interpreter officers that he had them using it in a jokey way.

Even the anglophile Kaftan highlights the lengths to which the British go in order not to give offence. In a letter home he wrote of five English characteristics alien to German culture, one of which was 'their emphatic politeness which can conceal dislike'. Others were the rejection of the abstract and rhetorical, emphasis on everything to do with business, avoidance of the 'fundamental decision' and a lack in wide areas of society of artistic education (which he believes may no longer exist). He added ten qualities which struck him positively and which may be seen partly as a critique of German characteristics:

1. Their strong sense of discipline—in traffic, shopping and at school.
2. Their strong sense of humour which allows many problems to be solved in a light spirit, when Germans would bungle them.
3. Their sober realism that takes life as it is without transforming it according to abstract theories.
4. Their enterprise (*Tatkraft*) with emphasis on the positive and on fun.
5. Their healthy common sense to the great advantage of everyday life.
6. Their openness to other opinions.
7. Their skill in treating children in a way that pleases them.
8. Their emphasis on the practical.
9. Their diplomatic way of getting people to do things.
10. Their uninhibited joining of religion with ordinary life.

This last observation may arise from the fact that it was the churches that took the lead in helping POWs. It might be added that the degree of class difference in Britain was frequently a source of surprise. 'If you spoke with a good accent to a man, he'd answer, "Yes, sir", even though you were a POW.' The prudery in hospitals amused both Colonel Borcherdt and Peter Brugger— as when a nurse kept a sheet over their bodies when washing them.

The flowing of feeling towards the POWs had two channels that were not muddied or blocked by national characteristics or problems of personal communication: parcel sending and music.

12

For the tens of thousands of German families who received parcels from England, it was not at all like the English receiving food parcels and gifts from America which were a supplement to a by no means poor ration. The parcels arrived in families which were living in wretched conditions usually without wage-earning menfolk. They came out of the blue from the former enemy. The sign of the English for years had been the approaching scythe of four-engined bombers striking deeper and deeper into their homeland, and now their cool, firm presence as occupiers was associated with the dismantling of German heavy industry. Yet suddenly from an unknown, far-off English family came parcels—waves of unexpected mercy and hope. Let two typical letters in halting English stand for all the thousands of others still fondly preserved in desks and little bundles.

Dear Family Martin,
Today I received a letter from my wife. She told me she had got your kind parcel and was the happiest woman. She told me she was weeping for happiness and gladness. In such a difficult time when all these things always be as a dream to have them is a great present. Two pair of shoes are quite right now for Joachim and the third paar is him still a little to bit. The slippers are very well now and beautiful. The coat will be for Heide and my wife will make him ready for her. . . .
                    Yours Heinz

Crissie Jarvis heard from Paul—after he had returned to Mecklenburg in the Russian Zone:

I want to send you many many many thanks for the parcels of food and white glue. You can't understand how happy I am as I get your parcels. Dear family Jarvis, I don't know how I can indemnify you. . . . The best surprise is the parcel with the sweetness. . . . Now, of my life in Germany, I work fast in my calling as tailor. Is it possible to send me some machine needle. You get them in Barnstaple at the Singer-shop. The no: 16 × 1 round. We don't get them here. I live by my parents. I don't tell you many because the letters censor.

Helen E. Woods, then Congregationalist minister at St Andrews, writes that it is very hard today to convey to younger people who have experienced no hardship the enhanced quality of life in those days. 'One felt more, one noticed more, and one entered more deeply into the feelings of others, a wider circle of others, than at any other period I have known. I don't think I have ever felt happier than when I have come out of the post office with one, perhaps two, parcels safely sent off. . . . The letters that came back made us cry.'

Music could be the greatest single comfort to POWs segregated and exiled in their camps. Being such a musical nation, Germans had even surrendered to it—as when a band played at the Massicourt Road in Tunis.* In a huge round-up camp in Holstein with ten thousand men arriving every day, Michael Siegel was walking with a friend; 'What did we hear coming from a fir copse but that familiar favourite for male chorus—"What made you rise, oh beauteous forest, upwards so high?" And we thought that when the end of the world comes, the last thing we'll hear will be a German male voice choir. A funny, macabre experience.' On the Atlantic Wall the crews of the heavy batteries, who were a long time together with time on their hands, formed choirs among themselves. In the camps in France and Belgium they at once became the nucleus of larger choirs that helped to keep up morale.

When the war ended, however, singing ended or became muted. The rousing tunes that had taken the German nation to war stuck in the throat, or offended the ears. Many songs that the *Landser* had sung to guitar, accordion or mandolin wherever he bivouacked, even the peaceable *Volksmusik* celebrating *Liebe, Heimat, Wein* and *Natur*, either brought an unbearable yearning for what was lost or seemed infected by having been adopted into the Nazi mythos. It would be a generation before the spontaneous singing of many traditional favourites would be renewed, and then only cautiously. All the more necessary, therefore, was the private inward solace that music could bring.

At Featherstone Park an old wind-up gramophone played an important part, as Herbert Schmitt's journal records:

It's almost 23 hours. The regular notices have been given out. Bunks are made, blankets pulled down. A shout from the duty officer: 'Lights out in three minutes!' Quickly the last cigarette of the day is rolled and laid aside, to be smoked later in the dark. Jokes fly across the hut, laughter flares up; contentedly one pulls the blanket up to one's chin and legs are gingerly stretched into the icy foot of the sleeping-bag. . . . Sigi in the next bunk

* See above page 5.

opens the gramophone. 'Tonight you will hear the Fifth Piano Concerto of Beethoven, known as the Emperor, performed by Walter Gieseking and the Berlin Philharmonic Orchestra.' Conversation dries up. Goodnights are exchanged now, so as not to have to speak after the concert. The needle scratches lightly on the surface of the record, reaches the first groove . . . Strings, bass, woodwind, with the piano on top. Gieseking is playing. Perfect stillness reigns. . . . You cannot imagine the experience of such a concert, you at home. You have other troubles, but for us it was a fragment of Germany that was not destroyed.

If music could have such importance and power with Germans in general, what of musicians? Interrogators and screeners used to discuss a special problem here. Musicians seemed to come, though on a higher level, in the same category as chefs and cooks who prepared meals for mouths without considering the views that came out of them. They were therefore morally fickle, for their job also was to give pleasure: the piper plays for whoever pays; but at the same time they felt they were 'above politics'. So it could be hard for musicians to prove that they had not been Nazis, which many of them wanted to do in order to get on with the new masters. The camps contained many a player or minor conductor unnecessarily worried about their grading because it would, they feared, affect their future at home. But for the most part they just got on with making music when and where they could, and often very well.

As early as October 1945 the OR Camp at Colchester performed Schütz's *Das leben Christi* that much impressed Norman Roffey, no mean judge. People in Bury still talk of hearing the Warth Mill's orchestra playing *Eine Kleine Nachtmusik* by candlelight in a local hall and how they followed the attractive German custom of only applauding at the very end of the concert. On a later occasion the Radcliffe Quaker Meeting House, a piano having been inched up narrow stairs, was more crowded than ever in its history. All the windows were flung open and instead of the *Horst Wessel Lied* boomed out by 4,000 voices, the *Kaiserwalz* and *Cavalleria Rusticana* permeated the warm July air. 'I don't think,' says Oswin Casdick, 'that the town of Radcliffe has ever been so well entertained.' In the end, German choirs and orchestras were delighting audiences up and down the country. Thanks to the prisoners at Featherstone

Park, Hexham Abbey enjoyed some of the finest music in its history. The band from Nutley in Sussex went to a parish hall in East Grinstead and raised £20 for children at a convalescent home. But then, when they wished to perform for another charity, the Musicians Union intervened: foreigners were potentially taking work away from their own members. It was not the only time this powerful and sometimes petty-minded body stifled goodwill and sent POW observers of this country to their homes with an unpleasant view of the British Trade Union movement. At Sale, when a highly successful joint concert with the Marbury Hill Camp Orchestra raised a large sum for 'Save Europe Now,' the Union stopped further such concerts as they did not approve the playing of 'military orchestras' in public; and POWs counted as soldiers.

Music and the arts were the field where reconciliation could flourish most easily. They were an international currency without the language barrier and could be boosted with gifts of instruments and materials. Forell carried hundreds of thousands of kroner worth of instruments in his van, the gift of Sweden. The Quakers alone presented seventeen pianos and harmoniums to the camps, as well as violins and cellos—and in a typically practical way set up a small fund for their repair. In 1947 a thousand mouth organs were sent over by American Friends. A rich elderly music teacher, Miss Mouncy Thomas, heard that Erich Schutz, a shy young violin maker from Breslau, wounded in Russia, was a labourer at Wye Agricultural College. 'He must have a violin,' she decided, and had him fetch one from Hills, the famous shop in Bond Street. He was flabbergasted, and still more so when she invited him home to play her Stradivarius. The touching part of the story is that he could not play well: what he really wanted was proper wood to make violins with, which at that time could not be got for him.

Self-help was also impressive. Many guitars were made out of chance materials, and one POW did play a violin he had made himself in the *Messiah* in Chelmsford Cathedral. Most remarkably, at Rimini in Italy, German prisoners actually constructed a whole organ out of tin cans which was later moved on to the cathedral there. Gifts to local churches of cribs, candlesticks, paintings of the Virgin were not infrequent. Dr Martin Baring, a Berlin judge, was deeply grateful for the courteous way he and his comrades at the Penketh Hostel were treated by the people of Widnes; he, therefore, organised a collection to put up a window in the local church depicting St Boniface, the English monk who became the Apostle to Germany. At East Chinnock Church in Somerset there are several modern windows installed personally in 1962 and later by Günther Anton. He had been shot down over England and later inherited his father's stained glass factory at Leonberg near Stuttgart. The windows are dedicated to the Glory of God in appreciation of the friendship shown him as prisoner of war.

The arts played an incalculable therapeutic role in many camps, especially early on before contact was made with the British. Those who could sink themselves into some artistic endeavour were generally the happiest.[102] Many men discovered unsuspected talents in themselves as actors, producers, stage-designers, puppet-makers, carvers, artists, musicians, singers—amateurs in the best sense of that word. Not a few, surrounded perhaps by a bevy of admirers, believed that their ephemeral triumphs were an earnest of more to come at home, but their dreams of a career in the arts were usually shattered. Some moments of glory were created by the highly-charged atmosphere during first contacts with the former enemy. Hans Eisermann, an organist from Hanau, composed a four-part unaccompanied Mass which he was asked to conduct at the Jubilee of the Catholic Church at Horsforth, near Leeds. The *Kyrie* had come to him while filling a cement mixer of Messrs Higgs and Hill and he jotted it down in the pause while it churned round. He rehearsed the Mass with the choir he had formed at Butcher Hill, till the mostly Lutheran singers understood its spirit.

The church on 6 September 1946 was packed solid as the spruce Germans arrived in trucks at the last moment. Willi Wolf recalls how as he sang a tingling feeling ran through him and that he could barely suppress tears. As they left the church they were enveloped in calls of appreciation and showered with packets of cigarettes. Once again music had created a bridge for true human relations and for the POW themselves 'the pain, misery, abandonment, despondency which they had undergone was transformed into hope, strength and inner peace.'[103] Yet Eisermann hardly ever composed again; his work as organist at Hanau and secretary of the music society took all his time. But the festive volume containing his Mass and his part-songs celebrating his love for his wife and *Heimat*, with colour illustrations and exquisite graphics and bound in an old piece of tarpaulin with a used cello string, is one of the most pleasing POW artifacts imaginable.

The myriad deeds and moments of human feeling through which true peace is made are seeds sown in Eliot's 'significant soil'; they are also like threads that reinforce each other, but must be held at both ends by people regarding each other as equals. For it can be difficult to be at the receiving end of goodness of heart. 'We used to say among ourselves,' said one POW to the author, 'that the English are kind to dogs and kind to cats and very kind to prisoners of war. We were another sub-species they were kind to.' Only the light touch is acceptable, the condescendingly well-meaning or do-gooding all too apparent. Dante in Purgatory, turning the stair near where the peace-makers were, felt himself being fanned as though by the stroke of a wing.

Kelvin Lawrence, the former Quaker language master at Saffron Walden, is well aware of the problem of being in a helping situation. 'We tried never to think of ourselves as "befrienders". That word is suspect. There was something obvious that needed doing. One asked the POW in to enjoy their company—one took them seriously as fellow human beings.'

Those who do good most effectively do not feel it to be an act of will or a moral task.* They are clear inside themselves and are responding rather than making a special effort. People find unexpected extra energy for this, just as a tired and jaded person can dance for hours because he or she is simply responding to the music. Nowhere is this naturalness and spontaneity of real goodness better described than in the famous words of the Emperor Marcus Aurelius:

> What more dost thou want when thou hast done a man a service? Art thou not content that thou hast done something conformable to thy nature? And dost thou seek to be paid for it, just as if the eye demanded recompense for seeing and the feet for walking?

* Iris Murdoch, in her stimulating study *The Sovereignty of Good* (Routledge and Kegan Paul), finds the fact that people are good against the odds, even heroically so, genuinely mysterious and the neglected central problem of philosophy. The moral task, as she sees it, is to overcome illusion and selfish fantasy in order to respond to the real world.

16

The Twilight of the Generals II

When the generals were moved to No 11 'Special' POW Camp at Bridgend in January 1946 nothing had been decided about their fate. Nonsensical rumours were around. Colonel Borcherdt picked up one (from a visiting Swiss officer) that all generals and SS were to be sent to Mexico for twenty years; but this plan was abandoned because of the proximity of the Panama Canal—they might one day escape and blow it up! Already at Grizedale Hall the generals feared some concerted action against them and before they left had asked Liddell Hart's advice. What could they do if there were a collective indictment against all members of the Supreme Command and General Staff? Would they be allowed counsel? 'They do not want to stir up trouble needlessly,' reported Liddell Hart, 'but they naturally want to defend themselves if included in a general court-martial.' One drastic solution was, in fact, under discussion at the Allied Control Commission in Berlin, namely that all officers with the rank of colonel and upwards should be interned in Germany for fifteen years. This was then linked with the proposal of the War Office that all the 6,000 officer POWs who were not working should be repatriated, including generals, as this would bring about a saving of one million pounds a year. Ernest Bevin, the Foreign Secretary, personally agreed to this, provided that the proposed internment were carried out.[104] However, the whole idea was dropped after being heavily attacked in a minute to the Foreign Secretary from Nigel Lawson of the P/W Division, who questioned the figures and pointed out what the effect on the morale of the POW work force would be if officers were repatriated first. No more was heard about internment.

During the thirty months until the general repatriation in May 1948 there were two Commandants at Bridgend. The first was Major Topham, a much respected elderly reservist who had been in charge of Trent Park when it had housed the unconsciously helpful high officers during the war.* He was succeeded for the

* See page 222.

last seven months by the much younger Lieutenant Colonel C. M. L. Clements, a cavalry officer who had himself been a prisoner of war in Germany. Each of them, writes General von Senger, 'was carefully selected, both personifying the British gentleman—polite, sympathetic, courteous, in short disarming towards any inmate.' Clements says that at his briefing by the War Office he was told 'to take complete responsibility, make all decisions and not refer anything to them.' He took this to mean that the authorities were bound by red tape and political opinion to treat the German generals with a severity the War Office did not agree with, being thus inhibited from making any official relaxation. He, however, as Commandant, could do what he thought right, the important thing being to avoid publicity. The German-born interpreter, Captain Ted Lees, was also an imaginative choice. He had been sent to Britain in the care of the Quakers at the age of twelve by his father, a strong anti-Nazi, who was in a KZ. He was given a home by a Manchester family whose name he took. Finishing his schooling, he joined up. Being a brave man he volunteered for special service behind enemy lines and was dropped in North Italy. The generals were both intrigued and impressed by this tactful young officer who wore a parachutist badge, spoke perfect German and said nothing about his background. He warmed to his unexpected assignment, finding the generals to be like other POWs with the same worries and troubles. 'I felt no inclination to continue my personal vendetta against the Nazi regime by making life unpleasant for them. . . . Those who needed help with their families and affairs got help. Those who had a chip on their shoulder were ignored.'

There was no problem in leaving the entire running of the camp in the hands of the Germans, among whom traditional hierarchy and pecking order still prevailed. But if von Rundstedt was the undisputed monarch of Bridgend, this stemmed as much from his highly disciplined personality and prestige as from his age and rank. He remained aloof, almost a hermit in his two cell-like rooms, but everyone was aware of his presence. The actual camp leader was a Luftwaffe general, Hans-Georg von Seidel, an able, diplomatic officer with a sense of humour. He was one of the few non-career soldiers in the camp, giving his profession as 'farmer'. The liaison officer with the British was the Catholic Rhinelander and engineer, Vice-Admiral Voss, who made such a good impression at Grizedale Hall on John Trevelyan. The atmosphere of

12*

Island Farm camp was both static and restless, boring and riddled with anxiety. There were frequent comings and goings. In June 1946 a large batch of 'Italy' generals arrived from Rimini and in the same month the three long-stay generals from Canada: Georg Friemel, captured when Holland was invaded, Hans von Ravenstein, and his Cairo companion Artur Schmitt. The luckless Heinrich Kreipe, the general abducted from Crete, had come back from Canada rather earlier. He was twice moved to Hospital Camp 99 at Shugborough Park in Staffordshire to have his diabetes treated. His hurt pride, because of the indignity of those eighteen days in the Cretan mountains, would dog him the rest of his life: he would one day take out an injunction against both the book and the film about the kidnap appearing in Germany, on the grounds of defamation of character: he had not, he claimed, given his word of honour not to try to escape, as was maintained. He won his case.[105] Kreipe was among the forty-six generals judged medically to be 'crocks' or compassionate cases and sent home early. Among the others were the Afrika Korps general, Ritter von Thoma, who had dined with Montgomery. He was much hospitalised, and had had a leg amputated, making several visits to the artificial limb centre in Cardiff. Another was von Ravenstein, who suffered from a heart complaint which had been aggravated by the rigours of service in North Africa.

Nearly all movements involved the relatively unpleasant stay at London District Cage which was ambiguously not only the war crimes interrogation centre but a staging post for all higher officers. When the parachute general, Kurt Student, went there in March 1946 it was on its way to be handed over to the French; his death sentence, due to the atrocities carried out under his command, was commuted to a number of years in prison. Two months later General Ramcke, the fanatical defender of Brest, was also handed over to the French. In October Field Marshal Kleist went via London District Cage to stand his war crimes trial in Vienna at which he received a sentence of eight years. Three months later the Waffen-SS General Max Simon left to be tried in Germany and was sentenced to death. Eight generals were at some time either loaned or transferred to the American historical section at Allersdorf. Some absences were educational—two generals and a vice admiral went on a course to Wilton Park. A small Rhinelander, General Kurt Pflieger, went to Camp 99 to be trained as a masseur and stayed there four months—a unique personal initiative.

General Heim, after Sulzbach interviewed him in May 1946, went away permanently and very happily to Featherstone Park.

One day in the autumn of 1946 at Bush House René Halkett, head of lectures, noted that Camp 11 was not on his list. Its inmates, he was told, did not need speakers as they were beyond 're-education' and he was shown a roll of some who were regarded as hard-core Nazi and militarists. To his astonishment one of these was his cousin, Major-General Freiherr van der Hoop. Halkett knew at once that there must be something odd about the list for he had grown up with his cousin, and at the time when he was last in Germany in 1938 he had been the one man he had trusted. Halkett, therefore, went down to Bridgend both to see if lecturers would be welcome and to investigate the suspicious 'black' list. Major Topham told him there had been no proper screening, the names having been provided confidentially by a general no longer there. This man, a Catholic, had been in a highly emotional state and during the welcome to Monsignor Godfrey, who visited the camp, had broken ranks and with tears in his eyes had clasped the Nuncio's knees. He had shortly after this been removed to hospital. Topham himself thought most of the men on the list were all right. Halkett then had a happy reunion with his cousin. Afterwards Topham mentioned that van der Hoop, who had been captured in Norway, was also on another list, namely of those wanted by the Russians, having fought as commander of German troops on the northern front. Knowing what that meant, Topham suggested that Halkett should go to CROWCASS* in London and tell what he knew of his cousin. This he did at once. 'Can anything be done?' he asked. 'Very simple,' was the reply, 'Van der Hoop is for technical reasons also on the Norwegian list. I'll pass on your information to them and they will then ask us to deal with him.' In due course the general, with cleared name, was in the first batch of Bridgend releases in October 1947.

Halkett's own return was less successful. Having fulfilled certain commissions, like obtaining a book on bee-keeping requested by an admiral, he wrote a report on his visit ending with a suggestion that the Bridgend POWs were mainly professional men whose opinions might carry a certain weight when they returned

* Central Registry of War Crimes and Security Suspects.

home; it would be wrong to leave them out in the cold as regards re-education facilities. His reasoned case, which echoed Liddell Hart's earlier report and was backed by several colleagues, was rejected out of hand, whereupon Halkett resigned and this highly gifted man was lost to Bush House. Ironically the policy he advocated was in part followed in 1947.

The official screening at Bridgend was conducted by a man with a special qualification and inclination to do so. This was Dr Otto John, who had grown up in the sharp shadow of the Prussian military caste. He had been deeply involved in the *Attentat* of 1944 and was one of the few conspirators to survive— having a pass as legal adviser to *Lufthansa*, he had been able to slip away to Spain. He had then put his wide background knowledge at the disposal of the Foreign Office. Some of the generals he knew personally and many others indirectly, in some cases through their families. Now and then he was therefore asked favours. An order had gone out to hand in every medal and order bearing the Swastika, which meant all those won in the last war. They had handed them in personally to Captain Lees, whom they trusted more than the War Office, and he kept them in a large cardboard box. (Indeed he still has them—all but two sets, the only ones which have been asked for again.) General von Seidel had thus been able to keep an Argentine decoration which had precious stones in it. His property in the east having been lost, this was his last capital. 'Please sell it for me,' Seidel begged John, 'so that my wife can have something for the children.'

Over many months Otto John re-screened virtually all the Army and Air Force generals (the admirals were left to another interrogator). He usually checked his opinion against those of five others whose confidentiality he still (1978) respects. He also picked the brain of General von Senger, who had come straight from Italy, having been held there to be a witness at the trial in Rome of General Doster, who was executed in connection with hostage shooting. Von Senger's former chief, SS-General Karl Wolff, who had secretly negotiated the surrender, was also at Bridgend. He had with him his all-white summer uniform which higher SS-officers wore in the Mediterranean and used to preen himself in it, like the playboy he had once been, to the annoyance of most of the others. This handsome, once very popular Hussar known generally as 'Karlchen', had even charmed Hitler twelve days before his suicide out of believing the evidence of his treachery.

John happened to know a good deal about Wolff's character and personal past, including his family life and shady tricks with money. Wolff also, like other SS, indulged in paranoiac fantasy. 'We were the first,' he told John, 'to fight for Europe against the Russians and one day we will be needed again. The world needs good German stock. I want to send instructions to all SS men in prison camps or wherever they may be that they are to masturbate, retain the sperm, have it preserved in any effective way and get it sent to the Fatherland.' Wolff even added, 'Dr John, will you help me do this?' If this was a perverted leg-pull in the unreal atmosphere of the time John could not be certain. Wolff is recorded as being transferred to LDC in November 1946 as a 'witness and affairs expert at Nuremberg'. He was later sentenced by a German court to four years imprisonment for his connection with the use of Dachau *KZ* for medical experiments on human resistance to low pressures.

John's reports turned out to be of benefit to the generals; so long as they were not on the CROWCASS list, they were free individuals as soon as they reached Germany, as Faulk had been able to persuade the Control Commission to accept all PWD screening. John recalls the many pathetic, troubled men before him, with no prospects and deeply concerned about their families. 'We were all unpolitical,' they would tell him. And 'We weren't even allowed to conduct strategy properly—that was done at the *Kaminklub*.'* Sometimes the generals' self-pity exasperated him. '*Wissen Sie, Dr John, ich bin nur ein kleiner General*!' said one. John exploded. 'So, you're only a poor little general, are you? When I was in Berlin not so long ago, I was travelling in the underground. At the Wittenbergerplatz a general stepped out of the train. You should have seen the people gawk at him! A general, travelling by underground—unheard of! A poor general—in Germany there was never such a thing.' The denial of past Nazi beliefs he found astonishing. One day he said to Ted Lees, 'You know, it's marvellous, out of a hundred people only Demelhuber says he is still a Nazi.' Karl Demelhuber was a Waffen-SS general who had once commanded the XVI Korps. He was repatriated with the main body officially as a 'member of a criminal organisation' and automatically a 'security suspect'. Dr John was in a curious position at Camp 11. He clearly got on well with many of the inmates; at the

* Fire-side Club—their name for the late-night sessions when Hitler addressed his entourage in long monologues.

same time he knew a great deal more than many thought was for their good. With a group of seven broad-minded generals he conducted over several months a seminar on recent history. John wistfully speaks of his own return to Germany in 1948, still at that time working for the British, and of the often sickening way people tried to get him to provide the so-called *Persilschein*, the magic testimonial that would wash their past clean at a denazification tribunal.*

With views of the Glamorgan hills to the north and south and to the sound of traffic on the Cardiff–Swansea road that passed the camp, the Island Farm generals eked out their day, suppressing their anxieties and homesickness, trying to kill boredom. Faulk found a high degree of irritability; one general had sowed some radishes, accused another of stealing them and they had a fight over it. Lees observed how some walked compulsively round the sports area a precise number of times and at precisely the same time each day. Others would stroll around as if pretending to be in Berlin on the Kurfürstendamm. Ritter von Thoma never adjusted to his new limb and always exercised with his peg leg. At the time Halkett arrived the camp was split by a controversy as to which of two field marshals was the senior. On that day in July 1940 when, after the fall of France, Hitler had created nine field marshals off the reel, one had received his baton some minutes before his rival. The latter, however, claimed that he was still the senior because he had originally been commissioned first. The whole camp, Topham said, had become neurotic over it. Could Halkett help? With his encyclopaedic knowledge of such matters he at once knew the answer: the date of the commission always had the priority. General Heinrici was trying as late as August 1947 to get satisfaction on the manner of his arrest and loss of property two years before and sent in yet another affidavit to the War Office. One general spent weeks making deerhorn buttons out of hickory to convert his uniform into a hunting jacket. Others made toys which found a ready market in local villages, their entrepreneurs being a guard, Fred Alsop, and a bricklayer, Ken Jenkins, working in the camp; both confess to giving the

* Dr John's subsequent career as Intelligence Chief in the Federal Republic ended with his controversial abduction into East Berlin, and a dubious prison sentence in West Germany. Juridical revision of his case hangs in the balance. (Leibholz to author, 1978.)

makers twenty cigarettes apiece and getting three times the equivalent on the market.[106]

Escape from the claustrophobic atmosphere of the camp was possible and increased under Colonel Clements, one of whose first acts was to remove the ammunition from the guard company, another being to permit unescorted walks. In the last period there was a good deal of local hospitality, especially at Merthyr Mawr, the pleasant, spread-out, thatched village just to the south of the camp. Here Jack Fowler invited four generals to Christmas dinner. They came in dress uniform wearing medals (which could only have been from the First World War). A few days later a small camp-made jewel box arrived as a modest souvenir 'with our best thanks for all the trouble you have taken about us!' Dandelions were picked from the lanes to make tea (or wine?). Once when the MO discovered some mysterious cases of high blood-pressure in the camp it was from 'cocktail parties, at which Camp Coffee was drunk neat.' Some generals worked voluntarily at the hay harvest and others are reported as delivering milk in Bridgend. The vicar of Merthyr Mawr, a genial local scholar, often entertained to tea and music the young Luftwaffe General Walter Grabmann, who hoped to become a concert pianist. His colleagues in fact clubbed together to hire him a piano on which he practised in the big hall in the British lines. General Dittmar worked as a gardener in the local park; when Liddell Hart next saw him he found that his command of English had greatly improved but he had acquired a Welsh accent which he kept for the rest of his life. The Nicholls at Merthyr Mawr Place had von Senger as their gardener for at least a year, though they found him very solemn compared to his mate, who was removed for trial as a war criminal. Soon von Senger was writing to his wife that he could no longer mend his socks as the holes had become too big but that a young woman had just put ten shillings in his hand. This was Helen Nicholl, who never had him into the big house but arranged it so that on Saturday afternoons he was free to take long walks alone along the lonely coast. One day in autumn he heard an almost forgotten sound that thrilled him to the marrow: a hunting horn and the distant thunder of hooves. On another occasion he suddenly found twenty couple of hounds tearing towards him in full cry by the scattered field, all against the background of blue Atlantic waves. The squire was silent and reserved and hated horses, but Helen Nicholl when a meet was in the vicinity would give him leave of absence for a whole day. Colonel Clements who rode with the Glamorgan Hunt himself was delighted to agree. The sport was not fast, so he could follow on foot or with a lift in a car. Members of the hunt used to greet him with, 'Hullo! Sorry we haven't got you mounted yet.'

After Mass on Sundays von Senger out of curiosity would visit one or other chapel of the twenty-four sects in the vicinity. 'The Plymouth Brethren,' he writes,[107] 'were the first to appear in the camp bringing cakes and coffee and holding forth on religious subjects.' His old friend from Oxford days, Dr Kurt Hahn, founder of Salem School and Gordonstoun, visited him and promised him a job in Germany when he returned. Von Senger was the obvious man to be press officer and, through his commentaries, was, as he put it, 'able to exert a certain amount of educational influence. I felt it my duty to explain to those of my comrades not versed in languages how profoundly we had been defeated and how the civilised world had become estranged from our Fatherland. Nor did I conceal from my audience that one of the first to subscribe to the relief of the hungry population of Germany was the Jewish publisher, Gollancz. There were many opportunities of inconspicuously encouraging the small circle of men of good will towards the "way back"—back to the normality of civil and civic life, back to a respect for essential moral standards, back to law and order—for this was the only possible basis for the new life of our nation within the community of nations.' It seems, however, that von Senger's highly civilised and urbane manner and feeling of being 'different' did not make him popular with most of his colleagues, devoted professional soldier though he was.

The past had infinitely more meaning for most of the generals at Bridgend than the future, and this past was represented for them supremely by von Rundstedt. Though he emerged but seldom from his double cell and hobbled on a stick, he was the living emblem of a tradition that might be vanishing but could be kept alive in that corner of Wales till the last moment. The tradition held them together. Colonel Clements, like Major Topham before him, used to visit him informally once a week. 'At the appointed time I knocked at his door; he answered, "Herein!" and rose to greet me. We sat down and he offered me a cigarette from his slender store. Having discussed the business of the day, we continued with a general conversation and when I rose to leave I left a packet of decent cigarettes on his table, as his canteen supplied a very inferior quality. I also occasionally brought him a little alcohol which, of course, he could not obtain.' On the first occasion Rundstedt, noticing Clements was a cavalry man, went out of his way to explain that though he himself was an infantry-man his family had been in the cavalry and that—evidently an honour—he had once himself commanded a cavalry brigade. The Field Marshal had not only a strong sense of dignity but also one of caste. When Sir Brian Horrocks, the distinguished soldier then at the head of Western Command, made one of his official visits to the camp, Rundstedt told him, 'It is most unpleasant for us members of the old general staff to have to associate with people who are not real generals at all.' He was referring to those who were Labour Corps Commanders, technical generals (one was a meteorologist), or in the Waffen-SS, or someone like the upstart General Ramcke who, in Rundstedt's view, 'would have made a good sergeant major'. He even thought fit, to the Englishman's astonishment, to ask that such men be moved elsewhere. Sir Brian, who went over old battles with him, knew what it was that he was too proud to ask for and, like Colonel Clements when he said goodbye, also left some packets of cigarettes behind.

Von Rundstedt kept very withdrawn, meeting only his close friends like Blumentritt, his Chief of Staff through most of the war, and later his biographer. His librarian son, Hans Gerd, did not stay long as he was invalided back to Germany. Rundstedt wrote no historical papers and took little interest in the future. This was in contrast to the next most senior officer, von Brau-chitsch, whom Dittmar described to Liddell Hart as 'the most active and thoughtful of the older prisoners' and who presented Professor Leibholz with a commendable paper on a new German constitution. The genial Leibholz, an always acceptable lecturer, could not resist challenging Rundstedt on the Ardennes offensive. 'You knew it was a forlorn hope?' 'Yes.' 'Yet you came out of retirement and accepted Hitler's invitation to lead it?' 'In the atmosphere of the time I would, had I refused, have been accused of obstructing the regime and been shot.'* 'How many German

* This is extremely unlikely. In that same month, December 1944, General Zeitzler, having continually opposed Hitler's military decisions out of his conscience to the German people and having four times asked to be allowed to resign, simply stopped doing his military duties

lives were lost in the offensive?' No answer. In June 1946 Rundstedt was required to give evidence at the first Nuremberg Trial. His departure was the most dramatic moment in the history of the camp. Captain Lees recalls how 'as he came walking slowly towards the main compound gate he found the entire complement of 185 or so generals and admirals lined up at the salute. One of the senior among them then delivered a short speech asking him "to uphold the honour of the German officer corps at Nuremberg." ' Captain Lees remembers his return very well. 'He wrung us all by the hand and assured us that he was glad indeed to be back at his "Hotel Island Farm". Later he intimated that he would be quite happy to remain there till his dying day—as long as he was not handed over to the Americans at Nuremberg again.' Aging and ailing, Rundstedt made one more visit to Germany, a sad one, at Christmas 1947. His son was dying of cancer at a Hanover hospital and he was allowed to go and see him, but had to return.

Every act of kindness weighed heavily in the scales against boredom, anxiety and yearning for home. Great trouble might be taken for someone in need. Karl Wilhelm von Schlieben, the defender of Cherbourg, has won a small niche in history by refusing to defend it to the last cartridge, as Rommel had instructed him to do. After fierce fighting he signalled 'I must state in the line of duty that further sacrifice can alter nothing' and surrendered to the Americans with 39,000 men. This humane and rather sentimental man had a son of four whom he had hardly seen, and had become one of the worst depressives in the camp. Colonel Darling on an inspection visit noted this and arranged a penfriend for him, Kate Greene, who was in her early twenties, and half German. She wrote to him faithfully every week and sent him cigarettes, biscuits and an occasional cake. She also wrote to Mary Foss and got his name on the list of the Prisoners of War Aid Society, asking hopefully and innocently, 'Could it be arranged for someone to take him out to lunch?' When the general, who always wrote back charmingly, was eventually supplied with a

---

and reported sick. He was dismissed from the army and deprived of the right to wear uniform, but nothing beyond this. Zeitzler's was a unique case. Such an act was, of course, quite out of keeping with Rundstedt's character.

demob suit, it lacked the all-important hat. She sent the money for one, but—the adjutant wrote to her all the amusing details—he had an extremely large head and it became a competition for all the English staff to find one large enough for him, which they finally did. General von Seidel and Field Marshal von Manstein are also in Mary Foss's ledger which recorded that when in No 99 hospital the latter was to be helped to transfer some money from himself to his brother-in-law in payment of a debt. Such can be the minutiae of POW assistance.

The generals could not at first send parcels home but the benefactors could. The Liddell Harts, who recorded everything, were very busy. Thus Frau von Tippelskirch at Christmas 1947 received two jumper suits, three pieces of knitted silk, two pairs of brown shoes, Ovaltine and halibut oil tablets, aspirins, toothpaste, toothbrushes, soap, lanoline, a tin of talcum powder. Frau Dittmar received a blue suit, a brown overcoat, a shirt, black shoes and underwear. On 21 March 1948 the Liddell Harts, when passing through South Wales, were at last permitted to take a few generals out to lunch. Though it was a Welsh Sunday Mrs Thomas specially opened an upper room in the Blue Bird Café at Bridgend. The wine had to be smuggled in by the hosts. The guests were Admiral Engel and Generals Seidel, Weckmann, Heinrici, Dittmar and von Senger, the last looking wistfully different from the others. Others present were the Vicar of Merthyr Mawr and Kathleen Liddell Hart—to whom Dittmar was able, as a park gardener, to present with a clicking of heels an indispensable *Blumenstrauss* of daffodils picked on the way. She brought her daughter Judith and both were wearing the full-skirted 'new look' which their guests, long deprived of any female company, much admired. Talk did not flow easily, there were so many subjects which were taboo. But an animated discussion did manage to develop on whether there actually were teddy-bears in Germany! Afterwards there was a small gathering in the Merthyr Mawr Vicarage for tea, at which General Grabmann played 'divinely well' on the decrepit piano.

Von Rundstedt, now seventy-two, was not permitted to join the Liddell Hart party. It was known that his trial was on the cards and the press were interested in him above all. Two movement orders for him, according to Colonel Clements, were not carried out 'because our excellent medical officer made out a certificate that he was unfit for travel'. On the third occasion he was routed to the military hospital at Diss in Norfolk. Just before the Field Marshal finally left, the whole British mess 'dined him out' with several of his close friends. This must have been the occasion when von Rundstedt made a typically chivalrous gesture. In appreciation of the good treatment that he and his colleagues had received, he presented his field marshal's baton to Major Topham who had been specially invited back to this dinner as the Commandant whom Rundstedt knew best. Topham, in return, promised to leave the baton to the Rundstedt family in his will. Rundstedt also presented a carved crucifix to the church at near-by Norton where many generals had worshipped, in gratitude for the friendly attitude of the neighbourhood.

The holding of trials by Britain of any German generals for permitting, or not preventing, war crimes in their areas of command had now become a controversial issue between the British and USA governments. The Americans wanted Britain to keep in step with the agreed policy on war crimes although feeling was turning against it in London. There was also the attitude of the Russians, who had several generals on their list who were held in Britain. Might it not be better to try them in the West, rather than create a breach by refusing to hand them over? It was, in the end, decided that four should be indicted: von Rundstedt, von Brauchitsch, Manstein and Strauss. To the last, it seems, they expected the trials not to take place because of the friendly treatment they had received in English hands. They were to have a rude awakening.

On 8 May some seventy-seven of the remaining fully cleared generals with a few admirals entrained to Colchester on their way home. 'Like emigrants,' wrote von Senger, 'we packed our kit-bags and with melancholy thoughts I left my old great-coat on the bed of my cell. It had been with me in many a battle and was worn to a thread.' Colonel Clements was instructed to accompany them all the way home, taking a small escort, which he thought unnecessary. Almost throughout the journey the generals were in a happy mood and he mixed freely with them. At Hook of Holland they were all fed in the British officers' transit camp, the officer on duty giving each a drink before dinner—a gesture much appreciated. They then travelled through the night, reaching the German border early in the morning. Here, remembers Clements, their mood abruptly changed as they observed the scarcely repaired war damage all along the line. He withdrew into his own private compartment. It was Whit Sunday and the under-nourished children were dressed up as smartly as could be managed and houses were decorated with oak leaves. The discharge formalities at Münsterlager were quickly gone through. The Colonel then wished them well and, having a car laid on to take him to Hanover, gave a lift that far to three of the party, among them von Senger.

At midnight the former Rhodes Scholar and Panzer General found a train to take him the seventy further miles to Göttingen. 'The kit-bag seemed heavy as I walked through the dark on that long, gently rising road. I wondered how I would summon P. (his wife) without rousing all the others in the house. Then I was there, at "Hohe Weg". Very quietly I stepped into the garden behind the house and gave the low whistle that was our special signal. P. appeared on the verandah.' From that dawn a new life began for the fifty-eight-year-old von Senger at last. Before long (his friend Kurt Hahn keeping his promise) he was acting as head-master at the Junior School at Salem where, two years later, the Liddell Harts visited them. Kathleen Liddell Hart remembers the disdain of the aristocratic Hilde von Senger when faced with a huge basket of boys' socks waiting to be darned. But soon they had moved up in the world, the ex-general being much in demand as a military commentator and expert, both in print and on television, in England and America. He died in 1962.

The four generals for trial were first transferred to Diss. Von Brauchitsch had already been in hospital the previous Christmas with a thrombosis, his wife being specially allowed to come and nurse him there. They had both been touched when English friends sent them a decorated tree. He and Strauss left Diss in mid-July, a reporter[158] observing how a famous Field Marshal, wearing a raincoat and trilby hat and with a parcel under his arm, walked by other prisoners who did not even take their hands out of their pockets. They went by train, along with many stretcher cases, to Southampton where they joined the hospital ship *Oxfordshire* which was bringing German POWs home from the Middle East. Rundstedt and Manstein followed by another route. Frau von Brauchitsch was waiting on the quay at Hamburg when the *Oxfordshire* docked, but her husband and Strauss were imme-diately put on a train for Münsterlager, where they were delivered to the security section of the camp. This meant barbed wire at the windows, lights always on, a British guard always in the room or at the door, special watch while shaving, and razor, knife, fork, spoon locked away after use. Brauchitsch protested strongly and went on hunger-strike for thirty-six hours. He sent a despairing letter in halting English to Liddell Hart beginning 'I am in severe prison'. They were, in fact, being treated according to the current regulations for war-criminals: they had forfeited the status of prisoner of war and were considered to be high-risk defendants awaiting trial. The legality of this procedure was contested by the Socialist MP Reginald Paget, KC, a year later at the Manstein trial, but he did not deal with a main factor behind such treatment: further suicides of leading Third Reich personalities had at all costs to be averted.

For Rundstedt the shock was greatest. The sick old man had not only recently lost his only son, but his wife had collapsed under the strain. His despair was complete. He wrote to his widowed daughter-in-law, Editha, forbidding her to visit him, adding, 'I don't think that now even my trust in God can help me any more.' She took these words as a danger signal and a cry for help, and got permission to see him. The humiliated state she found him in showed her that, being the man he was, he could not want anyone to see him like this, degraded in front of the German orderlies who had been soldiers in the great Afrika Korps, accompanied even to the lavatory which had no lock on the door. When she arrived a British soldier stayed in the room; every word they spoke was listened to by a Dutch interpreter officer, who, fortunately, was a delightful man. Editha von Rundstedt and the other three wives started a co-ordinated effort to appeal to any Englishmen they knew for better treatment. Things changed rapidly. First, a peep-hole was substituted for the continual surveillance, then they were moved to a highly-guarded wing of the Barmbeck Hospital at Hamburg. Here the four men were allowed to have their wives living on the floor above, but Rundstedt barely spoke to the others. A small solace were the visits of his twelve-year-old grandson from his boarding school in Hamburg.

On 20 October Brauchitsch died at Barmbeck just when the whole issue of further war trials was being hotly debated in Britain. At the end of the month Churchill, who spoke with more feeling and personal authority than any member of the government, said in Parliament, 'Retributive persecution is of all policies the most pernicious', and pleaded that 'apart from exceptional circumstances, British policy should henceforth be to draw a sponge through the past—hard as that may be—and look for the sake of all our salvation to the future.' Meanwhile, the Brauchitsch affair did not slumber. His widow's revelations, including the fact that her condolence mail was censored, was relayed further by Liddell Hart to the *Manchester Guardian* in November and the liberal press began to demand a more humane policy, for the sake of the good name of Britain. The trials of Rundstedt and Strauss, who were both found unfit to plead, were quietly dropped, but that of Manstein was not. Twelve years younger than von Rundstedt, he seems to have faced his troubles with cool disdain. Churchill himself was one of the first to subscribe to the fund raised in Britain for his defence, led by Reginald Paget. Manstein was sentenced to twelve years imprisonment, but, in fact, only served three.

Manstein's trial brought one of the last public appearances of Rundstedt, who was a witness. He sat in an armchair in the middle of the court, probably in pain. At one point he was asked if he had any questions and he started cursing out loud: *All dies ist eine Schweinerei, nur möglich weil dieser Besatzungsdreck keine anständigen Soldaten sind*—All this is a damned disgrace, only possible because these dregs of the occupation aren't decent soldiers at all. Otto John, who as an international lawyer was acting as trustee of the Wehrmacht documents, was standing beside von Rundstedt. He said to him, half under his breath, 'Herr von Rundstedt, can you tell me what you would have done if, when you were commander-in-chief in France, a Frenchman had spoken like this?' He didn't answer. The presiding judge asked what the fuss was about. 'Oh,' said John, 'we've just been discussing some minor matter.'

For the remainder of his life Rundstedt remained a closed-up, bitter, almost silent man, bowed before the moral imperatives of his Lutheran God: not to vindicate himself, not to reproach any nation or particular individual, not even to contemplate the past. For, and this was his final conclusion, 'We have all made mistakes which we should not have made and must forget.' It was beyond him to contemplate the danger of treating honour and loyalty as absolutes. He ended his brief introduction to Blumentritt's biography of him with the words of a crushed man who had no will to penetrate the cause of his private tragedy: 'Destiny is stronger than man.' Rundstedt, the last Prussian of an old mould, saw the mould broken for ever. At his funeral in Hanover on 28 February 1953 'not a drum was heard, not a funeral note.' There was no firing party and only a handful of former officers in top hats accompanied the coffin to the grave-side.

Von Rundstedt's marshal's baton is today prominently displayed in a glass case in the German Museum of Military History at Rastatt in Baden, together with his Knight's Cross with Oak Leaves and Swords. Ironically, this is the heavy gold-embossed Third Reich baton which he had received from Hitler's hand and so much disliked. The only true and soldierly baton for him was the simple field service baton, identical with the one which Marshal Blücher had carried at Waterloo. This he had chivalrously given to Major Topham. But when the Major died it could not be traced, and so has not been handed back to the Rundstedt family as intended. Strangely enough, von Brauchitsch's baton has also disappeared in Britain. All attempts to trace it failed, his distraught widow even sending a petition first to Churchill and later to Queen Elizabeth about it.

17

Heimatland

'Tell me,' Father Nikon then turned to Roderich . . . 'tell me, dear Count, will your fatherland, will your Austria,' and then including both of us, 'will your two unfortunate fatherlands ever be restored to health?' Then, without properly attending to our replies, but all too clearly exercised by homesickness for his own unhappy land, he followed through his thought with, '*Heimat*, homeland! Who can live without it? *Gott ist in der Heimat.* Always. It is hard to find it in a foreign place.'

Father Nikon, an old Russian monk in Mount Athos, to Erhart Kaestner.[109]

'For the last time we got into step, marched in columns through the suburbs of Guildford, in clean clothes, well-nourished and proud. Someone started up the old Silesian marching song, *Kehr ich einst zur Heimat wieder* (If ever I get home again) and the streets echoed with our robust singing. This so alarmed the much-liked young interpreter sergeant that he ran up and down the ranks telling us to stop, which we did. We had at last learned the lesson we had had to go through.'

So Lance Corporal Bernhard Harms from Bremen set out on his way home. Preparations would start weeks before. People would give up smoking in order to return with the maximum number of cigarettes allowed (300) for, till the currency reform of June 1948, these remained the chief means of exchange. Two pounds of soap were permitted but no articles of rubber, wood or leather unless they had been previously obtained in America. Officers were allowed a total weight of 112 pounds, other ranks half that amount. Not more than three kit-bags or suitcases could be used. There were angry scenes when over-weight luggage had to be unpacked at a strict camp, having been let through before. The whole transit experience, indeed, was not a pleasant one. Prisoners who had been working out on farms and generally enjoying a good deal of liberty had to go behind barbed wire again

as they passed through the staging camps. As they were not working, rations fell to 2,000 calories. Rumours, now and again with
substance, of heavy thieving on the way had spread back and
many is the story of the battle of individuals to keep possession of
their luggage en route or to arrange for guards for it from among
their own comrades. The German personnel at the other end were
generally more dreaded than the British and a quite false rumour
spread back to the Youth Camp that two of the former had been
strung up by enraged repatriates at Münsterlager, the destination
for all those returning to the British Zone—the big majority.

Home-coming: a thing yearned for yet also feared, dreamed
about and bolstered up with fantasies. The moment of crossing
the frontier might be a solemn one, but there was no welcoming
crowd or placard and little room for sentiment in the crowded
trains: rather the shock of the first sight of the stricken homeland. Landing at Cuxhaven men were seen to kneel for a moment
and in *pietas* kiss their native soil. Some POWs went at once to
their local church to pray and perhaps if a candle could be found,
light one. More than one Bavarian went to the Chapel of Maria
Eich at Planegg and put up a small plaque to the Virgin Mary in
gratitude for his safe return. Forell tells of a pastor at Cuxhaven
who felt strongly, as Forell himself did, that more should be done
to soften the bleakness of so many home-comings, but was
arrested by the British on the quayside when he personally tried
to put this in practice. Not a few, however, returned with resentment that the first sight of their country only made more bitter.
One man, obviously an 'American' or 'Canadian' recalls:

> Exhausted, tubercular women came up to us and many children
> begging a little bit of bread. It became very quiet in our com-
> partment. We're going to rot away, are we? Those swine, those
> criminals! Why did they make us work an extra year in England?
> It was here we were desperately needed. From this moment on
> many of us began to doubt the good-will of our western
> conquerors.

Münsterlager, a huge military complex in the training area of
the Lüneburg Heath was used for processing and discharging
POWs from all countries, including Russia. This involved docu-
mentation, a medical examination and the provsion of a personal
document which was at once an identity card, a certificate of
release and a ration card for food and clothing. Forell was first

there in July 1947 when it had been going some time. He found a friendly Commandant who was a strong Methodist, an excellent adjutant promoted from the ranks and an extraordinary character called 'Mr Charlie'—a Sudetenland salesman who had with his hearty evangelical helpfulness transformed the atmosphere of the place. 'He has already converted me to the true faith six times,' the amused Commandant told Forell. A dynamo of a man, he organised a whole staff of POWs into a long-stay welfare force and was always trying to find work for those who came from the east. It was on the same visit that Forell saw returning POWs from Russia for the first time—only those no good for work any more were at that time being sent home. No misery he had seen exceeded theirs, with 'boys called up at sixteen and seventeen looking like men of forty and fifty'. There was much hunger oedema among them, and some amputations had to be made without narcotics, for though the 2,000 calories could be supplemented for the sick, there was a great shortage of every kind of drug. Again and again the shock of seeing the POWs from the east made those from the west less self-pitying or angry at their own 'wasted years'. Schwedersky writes of men pale as corpses with shaven heads, and Pastor Gursky describes how his own group of repatriates, when they saw them, spontaneously divided cigarettes and other good things with them which they had brought from England.

At Münsterlager the YMCA made one of its biggest humanitarian efforts. A notice was put in camp newspapers in Britain: 'The YMCA helps the homeless', asking those with no home to go to, to write in advance giving personal details. Having the address in one's pocket of a friend who had promised a bed was not to be relied on. The large YMCA hut also housed the Salvation Army and the German Red Cross. There was an advisory service about new laws and employment regulations, and consulting rooms for the Protestant and Catholic chaplains. In addition there was a library, recreation room, cinema and church hall. There were so many cases of healthy or rehabilitated men who could not leave the camp because they had no clothes fit to wear, that the YMCA set up a store for the purchase of clothing at a low price, the funds being mostly provided by the Church of the Brethren and the Mennonites in America.

Of the characters who have appeared in this book the 'white' officers from Shap Wells were the first to go home, along with miners, forestry workers and radio technicians, and certain other special categories. The ebullient Bavarian artist, Josef Karl Huber, went freakishly early along with a batch of journalists, printers, radio and other technicians, in the first autumn. He found his house at Seeshaupt ransacked by the marauding *KZ* inmates from Dachau who caused a brief terror in the neighbourhood that summer. With his fellow-artist wife, Hildegard, he built a new life and a new home and on his front door, which looks out over the moorland and lakes to the Zugspitze and the Karwinkel Alps, he made a great carving of the sun with spike-like rays. Soon he was painting frescoes in the restored ceiling of the Wiesbaden theatre and, as the wave of church building got going, left his mark in the Stuttgart area with stained glass, altar figures carved in wood and a bronze Virgin on a monastery well-roof. Only after many years did he burn his old uniform tunic stained with the blood of the comrade who died in his arms at Le Havre.

By midsummer 1946 Joachim Ritter, centre of the intellectual life at Shap, was writing back to those remaining. He has been through seven camps on the way, plunging back into the mêlée of men and passing 'through the infamous Belgian camps with their demoralised and nihilistic populations'. Then, searching as ever for the real, permanent values of life, he describes how he walked the last stretch to his home on the Elbe:

Everywhere people were gathering wood and gleaning. One was even doubtful of being on the right path, so thinned out had the trees become. But then the children came to meet one, wife and parents, and everything is much brighter and gayer than one dared to expect; one takes a deep breath and the ground beneath one's feet is stable again. There are still slit trenches on the banks of the Elbe. This was the first direct evidence that the madness of war had penetrated right through the land. Although one knew it, it came as a surprise. But the troops didn't shoot any more, and as a result the English spared the hospital and the hamlet. For this one was grateful to them. It is strange that one does not register what has been lost, but accepts what is still there as an unexpected gift, especially books which appear as a treasure. The townspeople are always on the move. But it seems astonishing that they, too, haven't crumpled. One finds much bravery and resolution, even hope and gaiety, without being able to distinguish when it is real, and when put on. . . . The world outside one's small immediate circle remains remarkably unreal. One is unconnected with it. The need to keep to oneself is great. Yet pain, joy, concern, helpfulness are things that people really experience physically in their feelings and also what stands in opposition to these things is bad. An inner sense puts people on their guard against those who just go through the motions and 'fix' things their way.

Ritter's correspondence with Geoffrey Forrest, after his first letter of gratitude to him and Norman Roffey, continued. He wrote of the charms of 'a quiet life, the loveliness of the landscape, the old trees of childhood which still protect our house, the long river, the wide sky—all this is my homeland I longed for. Spinoza left the community and became a glass-maker; Kierkegaard sought anonymity . . .' In the first mood of homecoming Ritter was half tempted to do likewise. In the next letter he spoke of translating Eliot: 'Who can be more our helper than the great T.S.E.?' But he never got round to this; that autumn he was offered the chair of philosophy at both Tübingen and Münster and accepted the latter. On the edge of the ruined city he was soon gathering teachers and pupils around him, including several from Shap—Staudinger, Wagner, Heiks and Woetzel—enabling the last of these to join his seminar, though without any outer means of support. Ritter would in due course become Rektor and in the sixties play a leading part in the creation of the new universities of Bochum, Dortmund and Konstanz. As a teacher he became leader of the revival of philosophic discipline as a practical guide in life and the great defender of German idealism and especially of Hegel, against the attacks of Popper and his school.*

Of Ritter's Shap pupils, Hugo Staudinger became a professor at a young age and a director of the Institute for Education and Knowledge at Paderborn, an independent research foundation which he has helped to make into the most important institution of its kind in the Federal Republic. He is a leading exponent of the political philosophy of the pluralistic state. Characteristically he has been setting a significant thesis-theme to his pupils: they have to make a detailed historical study of the Jewish communities in the small towns of Westphalia and their fate under the Nazis.

* It seems likely that Ritter's discovery while at Shap of T. S. Eliot as a powerful corrective to the weakness of German romanticism helped to pave the way for this defence.

Wagner and Heiks both became grammar school teachers, while Woetzel has devoted his career to teaching and teacher-training at Dortmund. Hubert Walter, as a specialist in languages, has had a similar career in Münchengladbach, after spending his first period of freedom helping farmers to compose letters in English that would get a son or worker repatriated early. 'There's a goose for you if your letter gets him home,' he was promised once. The man duly arrived; 'Will you take a rabbit?' he was asked, and answered, 'Not on your life!'* Prinz von Urach entered business and founded a family but died tragically early of leu-kaemia. Clemens Podewils became the Secretary and then the President of the Bavarian Academy of Arts, while Werner Dütt-mann had a brilliant career as the leading German architect of the new Berlin, and became President of the Academy of Arts in that city. At St Agnes Catholic church in Kreuz, which he designed, there is an altar painting in the side chapel of a Madonna and Child. Done at the specific request of the congregation, its style and feeling unmistakably go back to the wood-cuts and water colours that flowed from him so spontaneously at Shap Wells.

When in 1945 Prussia ceased to exist, either on the map or as a concept, it was not lamented by many who were not born there. The provinces of East and West Prussia became part of Poland as did most of Mecklenburg. Silesia became Wroclaw, and the Russians installed themselves in Königsberg. Except for West Berlin, the rump that was left became the core of the new com-munist state. Repatriation for the older Junkers was therefore hardest and for none more than Colonel von Lindeiner, the anglophile Commandant of Stalagluft III. Court-martialled by the Nazis, held and interrogated by the British for more than two years as a war-crimes witness, he had ended up at Featherstone Park, where his caring, gentlemanly character was much appre-ciated. When he returned home his real woes began. He had lost his estate in Silesia, his Berlin home was in ruins, and he and his wife eked out a poor living in Frankfurt. Then came the unkindest cut. Paul Brickhill began publishing his best-selling books about escaping from Germany, the first of the line of sagas that cul-minated in the Colditz stories. In Brickhill's stories Lindeiner and

* A spot check by POWD in September 1947 revealed 55 per cent of cases to be well-deserved, 26 per cent to be acceptable and 19 per cent to be unjustified and due to lying. (Faulk op. cit. (English) Chapter 3.)

his staff figured in a disparaging way. He was deeply hurt and in 1953 wrote wistfully to Geoffrey Forrest, 'Not only have I had to take humiliation as a German officer and Junker from my own side, and then impoverishment; but also this defamation from those we tried to be decent to. But it is wise to remember the old Roman proverb, *Vae Victis*.'*

The resilient Colonel Borcherdt had also lost his home in Silesia but for the second time he had to start from scratch as a small-holder on Ochter Moor, near Minden. After 1918 he had made his way there taking as his trophies of war a pair of *Reitsprecher* riding boots and a walking stick made out of an old propeller, along with Spengler's *Decline of the West* to pore over. This time he had a dyed battle-dress, two hundred cigarettes, two pounds of coffee and two bottles of Bovril. Although put down as 'unfit', he had to work as a labourer for the Moor authority, as it was two years before a tenant could be got off his land. His wife, a general's daughter, had brought their furniture over from Silesia, together with—a great joy—the Wehrmacht Ranking List. She had also found in an old jacket of her father five gold pieces over a hundred years old, bearing the motto of Freidrich Wilhelm III *Lerne Leiden ohne zu Klagen* (Learn to suffer without complaint). With them the colonel bought some heifers, just as he had done in 1919. In spite of his gammy leg from the wound in Belgium and being past fifty, he once more pulled his life together.

For younger Prussians like Dieter Hankel and Botho Kirsch who had got something out of England, there was only oppor-tunity. 'For the last time,' writes the Brandenburger Hankel, 'I walked round the familiar ways of Featherstone Park, looking back on the bitterness I had felt—amazed that out of a time of despair and deep inner need I could derive principles to live by, and regard the land that held me captive as a second *Heimat*.' His parents had come across to the American zone. This meant he was processed through Dachau which, with deliberate intent to point the lesson, had been turned into a demobilisation camp. He be-came a working student, earning cigarettes which were the cur-rency then by teaching English to displaced persons. He believes that 'if less of Germany had been in ruins, if the war hadn't been as radical as Goebbels wanted it to be, we couldn't have rebuilt Germany as we did. Everyone was ready to muck in because of the total destruction in the big towns. We were ready to give

* Woe to the vanquished.

things up in order to go forward. Otherwise we might have muddled through'. Harking back to Sulzbach as a model he became a dedicated grammar-school headmaster at Sindelfingen, holding as he does that there are 'certain Prussian qualities which are worth transplanting into the rest of Germany: our incorruptibility, our practical responsibility towards others, our doing things for their own sake—and these combine well with the thoroughness and exactness of the Swabians.'

Botho Kirsch from Königsberg was only twenty years old after three years in captivity. He had used them to learn Latin, Russian and Italian, and had read all the forbidden émigré literature in the library at Diss where he also edited one of the better camp newspapers. At Münsterlager he met the captives from Russia; 'Beside them we were like millionaires.' This provident scholar had managed to possess a Bank of England cheque for £20. He kept it first as a souvenir, then a year later when a student in West Berlin he cashed it in East Berlin and lived off the proceeds for a whole year. Getting his degree, he was soon being sent as correspondent to Russia—the beginning of a dynamic career as an *Ostexpert* in politics and the media. He eventually became head of the Russian Service of the *Deutsche Welle*.

Another East Prussian, Werner Leichner, found a welcome at his cousin's in Gelsenkirchen. His parents were still missing. His earnings in Britain converted into 35 DM—a month's wages for a skilled man. This Ruhr city was sixty per cent destroyed and for a while he felt conspicuously well dressed, even on Sunday, in his English clothes. But over at the racecourse things were getting going again and soon he was employed there at his old trade of farrier.

Hans von Ravenstein's return led to the happiest part of his married life. Knowing his inner support for the 1944 *Attentat*—they had been friends of the Stauffenbergs and Witzlebens—his wife Elisabeth had always regarded his being a prisoner as a kind of protective custody, for she believes he would have been drawn into the conspiracy. Their last meeting on leave in Rome, together with the Rommels, just before the British 'Crusader' offensive, had been difficult, as she was aware of his inner tensions. Now, as she saw him after six years on the platform with a comic-looking Red Indian rucksack, it was 'as though he had been away for three days.' He had returned expecting the worst, even to see starving people lying in the streets. Admittedly they had to queue in turns

that winter for eight hours to get a loaf of bread, but they had
saddlery to sell; she kept on working as a seamstress in a laundry
and he got a little job in a Düsseldorf display firm for a while. He
applied for a post with the YMCA whose work he had much
admired in Canada, but was told that they 'could not encumber
themselves with a general'. Then to his astonishment the Ober-
bürgermeister of Duisburg, where till 1933 he had been traffic
director, offered him his old job back again with further activity in
public relations. Soon he was an important man in the rebuilding
of that city, the largest inland port in Europe. To younger men he
was still the tolerant, encouraging father figure, *Der letzte der
Ritter*—the last of the knights. To the British and especially to the
Control Commission Resident, Captain Colin Hutchison RN, with
whom he got on extremely well, he was known simply as 'von
Rav'. Together they and the Social Democrat Oberbürger-
meister, August Seeling, connived at the procrastination—a frequent practice at the time—of the dismantling of the steel works.
He helped to create the friendship link between Duisburg and
Portsmouth, a 'twinning' which has gone from strength to
strength. His strong Lutheran faith and the fact that his wife was
a devoted Catholic drew him to ecumenism. Much loved, honoured
equally by young and old, by former comrades in arms and new
friends, his life not, like von Rundstedt's, burdened by the past,
he died in 1962. Captain Hutchison gave one of the two funeral
addresses. The last of a distinguished Prussian line, Hans von
Ravenstein, more than any of his kind, pointed to the future.

For those whose parents lived still in the old Prussia or in
Thuringen or Saxony there was often a difficult choice. Only a
small percentage of prisoners opted to go through the camp at
Friedland. One was the senior medical orderly Karl Heinz Knoop.
He could have had a job as a gardener at an Oxford college, and
the professor on Boar's Hill whose garden he had been tending
offered him a bungalow in his grounds. But he felt he must visit
his mother in the Soviet Zone. From Friedland he travelled in a
goods truck for two days to the quarantine camp at Gustrow.
'The desolation I saw did not really surprise me. I had been in
Russia myself, but the treatment of the Germans remaining made
my blood boil. Some of our transport got into fights with Russian
soldiers, mostly from Mongolia, and one never saw them again.'
Regretting he had come, he worked as a lorry driver, then was

'denazified' without trouble—he had avoided the Hitler Youth and been in the church fight against the Nazis. He joined the police but continued to write frank letters to Britain which were censored. With the aid of Swiss and English friends he crossed the frontier again after twenty months, leaving all his possessions and diaries behind. He came back to the people among whom he was most at home, joined the Society of Friends, married a Quaker and became a British citizen in 1963.

Knoop's experience was hardly typical, but 1950 when he came back was the year of the show trial of Willi Bründert, who was accused of having been trained in the 'Wilton Park Spy School'. Two years earlier the *Daily Telegraph* correspondent in Berlin heard that all officers, on being repatriated to the Soviet Zone, were being sent to Sachsenhausen *KZ*, which may have been true in that jittery time.

Two lawyers of very different characters have appeared several times in these pages: Dr Günter Geisseler and Dr Kurt Schwederski. The former was the self-styled 'caged lion' of Crewe Hall and Llanmartin, and likes to recall an incident in his final days in England that took place at Colchester. 'A comrade and I were fetched by an Englishman who had received permission to take two prisoners home with him. He entertained us, then invited us to an open-air concert where he had to request that we as German POWs could occupy certain seats. He did this in a most affecting way, asking if his German *guests* could join the company. This last experience in Britain expunged many things in my captivity that I did not like.' Geisseler was soon down at Nuremberg acting as the second defence lawyer in the trial of Alfred Krupp von Bohlen in the third American tribunal. He argued that his client had to obey the orders of his government. But the multi-millionaire owner of the famous steel firm which had used and treated in an appalling way slave-labour from Auschwitz and Lublin was given a heavy sentence that was, however, like many others, commuted in 1951. Geisseler, a solid establishment figure, became one of the several former Wehrmacht staff-officers who helped to build up Mannesmann of Düsseldorf into such a formidable industrial power. He is also a promoter of the arts and owns several works by his friend Huber, captured with him at Le Havre.

Dr Kurt Schwederski too returned to Düsseldorf and at once got back his old post on the land judiciary. At that time a good deal of the preliminary investigation of war crimes was taking place in Düsseldorf and he became involved in it as an independent activity. His view was that 'we Germans had to make a stand on the recent past. This meant that crimes committed by a very small percentage of the population had to be atoned for. I wanted to make my contribution to this as far as I could.' Over the years Schwederski has interrogated a great number of witnesses representing the victims of Nazi crimes.

More and more I wanted to show that those who acted with such viciousness and hatred are not the true Germans. Around 1957 I once had to question a young Jew at the German Consulate in Edinburgh. He had lost all his family at Treblinka. I shall never forget how gradually the ice melted between us and at the end of the second day when it was all over it was he who stretched out his hand to mine and laid his other hand over it, as if to say, 'You are not one of those who are responsible.' I have questioned over a hundred witnesses in this way and in all but two cases it was they who held out their hand to me.

On 11 March 1948 a march group of twelve hundred set out on the seven miles from their transit camp to Leicester Station; five hours later they were at Harwich. Among them was a Bavarian Lutheran Pastor, H. F. von Freilitsch, whose destination was a small town, Presseck in Oberfranken, which he had not seen for four and a half years. Ten days later he wrote (in English) to his friend the Reverend William Rees, Baptist Minister at Northampton:

We shipped that afternoon on a wonderful quiet sea to Hoek van Holland. It was beautiful sunshine and we looked back a long time to the slowly vanishing British coast. I thought of all the kindliness I found in your country and promised within myself never to forget how much your very Christian fellowship did to alleviate all the unavoidable hardships of captivity, blessing all my British friends and their country. The 'welcome' on the continent by the British police was not very pleasant—a bit too much of the sounds we heard in the bygone days in the first months of our involuntary stay in Britain—I only found it a pity that the last impressions our men had from the British army were a bit rough. At dawn we arrived at the frontier of Germany. There we had to change the train. We came now in waggons without any sitting accommodation, crowded at about

110 men in each waggon. For 10 hours we traversed German country in an easterly direction. Destroyed houses and factories, the lesser bombed partly in repair; a very great number of men in old prisoner clothes; men, women and children a bit pale and exhausted looking; small boys on the station begging us for a piece of bread; but, taken in all, not as bad as I feared. . . . At Münsterlager, where a weekly average of 6,000 pass through, things ran with great efficiency much better than the rumours ran and sooner than we hoped we climbed in a sitting-less train which was now our 'home' for 24 hours. On the Monday in Holy Week I stood on the railway station next to Presseck. As soon as I could I rang up my dear wife. She fetched me with the car and about 9ʰ I was in my parish expected by my parish council, my confirmands and a small crowd, summoned at very short notice, for nobody expected me so soon in the morning. Then later on the whole day and the next people poured in for greeting. Tuesday evening was a big meeting in the Parish Hall, music, choirs, speeches. . . . I had never thought of so much attachment to my humble person.

Three months later Father Jansen also sailed from Harwich, having been a prisoner for nearly four years. He had by then made many English friends, and indeed become so anglophile that one of them believes he was tempted not to return to Germany, but did so because of his mother.

At Hook of Holland there was a real risk of losing your baggage, the main cause of our considerable excitement. The food and drink provided on the Dutch side as well were good. After a longish journey (at least 24 hours) we reached Münsterlager, where we were reduced to a few more weeks of sickening camp life. Rows were always in the offing, especially against the German camp staff; a few of the repatriates recognised the same people who had shoved them off to England two years before, after they'd been told they were on their way home. In our transport the Poles were the chief brawlers. An imperturbable camp chaplain named Bettinger, who had come with us, diverted the malcontents with a story about the man who held his dachshund by the tail and kept swinging it round and round. The poor dog howled out and he was accused of cruelty to animals. To this he said, 'I only want to give him some extra pleasure—don't you think he's going to be happy when I let him go? You see, comrades,' Bettinger went on, 'that's just what Tommy has done with us! You're going to be really happy when you're finally free'. This story was more appreciated than all the talks we got put together. . . . After yet another medical examination, an assistant nurse asked me if I had any claims for sickness benefit. 'No.' She indicated a bunch of sick reports. 'Then you are perfectly well?' 'I have come through alive,' I said. 'I only want to go home. I don't want to take a penny from this derelict, defeated country. I'd be ashamed to. I've had enough.' She shook her head and let me go. That's how idiotic a homecomer can be. But it was a fairly common attitude among us.

[*He has reached Duisburg*] Weeks and months in this country. I am pursued by the faces of local officials. For earlier arrivals, Birger Forell once assured me, it was worse: 'So you're one of the people who prolonged the war—you could have been here a lot sooner!' Now what one heard again and again was: 'So you were in England, were you? You've had it good!' I don't know where they got this idea. In the long run one kept out of people's way. One didn't quite belong. I can understand the 'leave me out' attitude of many POWs. . . . I was at home; but I had become old, prematurely, at forty. Former interests didn't return. Certainly my experiences contrasted with those of many repatriated comrades who—I had not expected this—brought their troubles to me. Or their wives did. Newly-won freedom was a strong enticement along with the chaos all around them to throw over the traces and quite ignore the bond of morality in regard to their marriages. Most prisoners of war I knew went through this. Young people too, from whom I hadn't expected it. Even in myself I recognised the uncanny power this first flush of freedom could have over one and had to wrestle with it. An example was my over-sensitivity towards my superiors. Fortunately, I found in them great understanding for my peculiarities—they gave me the friendliest support in my plans for future work, the building of churches, and so on.

Father Jansen settled down as a parish priest in Dürren, but he never recovered from the circulatory troubles that began during the Normandy fighting and the subsequent retreat. He died in 1974, aged sixty-six.

For returning generals there was an extra shock. They faced

not only the fall of their nation, but their own fall from any kind of importance in their own country. On the contrary, they were blamed for the extent of the disaster. 'It is astonishing,' wrote the *Deutsche Rundschau* 'that the generals always speak of their duty towards their superiors and not of their duty to the soldiers entrusted to them, most of whom were the flower of the people. The reproach of not having prevented the slaughter of many hundreds of thousands of German soldiers must weigh heavily on the conscience of every single German general.'[110] Their whole profession was in eclipse; indeed the very idea of there being a German army again seemed remote. They retired into the circles of their families, the new unemployable, except for a few like von Senger or von Ravenstein, or the practical Admiral Voss who wrote to Captain Lees that he had a job as a plumber's mate. But even the family circle might not be the place to nurse one's wounds. The story is told of the ex-general who returns to his wife living in two rooms in a little suburban house. They greet each other lovingly and soon he is sitting down to some orange juice, crisp bread, real butter and real coffee.

'Isn't Gisela living at home still? You wrote me she is being such a help.'

'Oh yes, she'll be in soon.'

'Is she well?'

'She's thriving. You'll see for yourself.'

'She has a job?'

'She'll tell you about it when she comes.'

Presently a long car with a military driver and a large white star on it draws up in the street outside. Gisela jumps out, buxom and blooming, wearing a smart new costume and nylons. Her father, standing at the window, at a glance takes it all in. Gisela runs into the house and flings her arms round his neck.

'Oh, daddy! I was only fourteen when you saw me last. I've grown up. Look at me!'

'I am looking at you—very closely.'

'I have a present for you. I remembered how you loved cigars. A whole box full. And they're the best—all the way from Havana! Aren't you pleased?'

At that moment the ex-general experiences his most shaming moment of defeat. The cigars go into a drawer and he never smokes a single one.

For a while yet, until the quite generous German military pen-

sion system was created, many senior officers had to live on pit-
tances. The Liddell Harts, travelling to Germany in 1950, took
with them useful gifts. Sometimes they realised the intended
recipients would be too proud to accept them. An American staff
officer suggested to them the tactic of leaving a pair of nylons—
precious in those days—in the corner of a sofa: it would be discovered after their departure and honour would be saved. Not a
few high officers were forced to apply for official relief. General
von Schlieben did so in June 1948, as he told his pen-friend and
benefactor, Kate Greene: 'Never in my life could I have imagined
that as a former general I could have got into such a situation.
Don't be cross if I can't write often in the future as it has got so
bad that I cannot afford the stamps. Life is not worth living any
more. The Lord giveth and the Lord taketh away.' Kate Greene
had mentioned that some friends of hers were looking for help in
the house. This gave Frau von Schlieben the idea that, though she
had a child, she might apply for the post. 'But, of course, your
friends might shy away from having the 44-year-old wife of an
ex-general as help in the house. But should they not think twice
about it, please write and tell me the conditions of employment.
My son is seven years old. The hat which you went out of your
way to give me is still the best item in my wardrobe and keeps
reminding me of you, dear Katy. With affectionate greetings,
Karl Wilhelm von Schlieben.' The two never met, but till he died
the grateful Thuringian continued to send a small gift to his young
friend every birthday and Christmas.

On 9 August 1948, the day after the last German POW left
Harwich, a notably uncomplacent editorial appeared in the
Manchester Guardian, beginning 'The story of their long captivity
in these islands does not do us any particular credit.' The writer
mentions the good work of Wilton Park, the facilities offered by
universities and municipal councils and the effect of much private
hospitality. But 'although we have given them their freedom we
have not usually succeeded in giving them also a new faith to face
the future. If re-education had been undertaken earlier and the
work of repatriation conducted more swiftly, these prisoners, only
a minority of whom were ever convinced Nazis, might have returned to their homeland better prepared to face the appalling
difficulties which undoubtedly await them.'
The editorial makes a typical mistake of the time, at once

idealistic and patronising: it assumed that it was the task and responsibility of the British to provide the new faith for the future. It is true that at the time evidence of the great moral and physical resilience of the German people was hard to see. But the degree to which the POWs wanted and tried to work out their own salvation was not appreciated, nor was the suspicion with which nearly all POWs regarded, rightly or wrongly, the whole re-education project. It was partly the word 're-education' itself that brought such antagonism; Robert Birley, then Director of Education in the British Zone, gave orders that it was not to be used at all in his department. Most of the Bush House personnel avoided the word too and, indeed, thought of their work more as assisting a reorientation, as helping the Germans to help themselves. Those Germans who also saw it in those terms bore no resentment and returned friends of Britain.

But the majority did not do so, especially—as one would expect —those held longest. Just as first impressions of a new country stand out most boldly afterwards, they fished up for official German investigators their bad early memories. The sanitary and ration system of the Wehrmacht had, in typical German fashion, functioned well till near the end. All the more inferior or punitive were, for instance, the Belgian camps. The short rations of 1945 were, similarly—and falsely—regarded as a penance for the *KZ*: the long isolation from the British population was brought up, and the 'Americans' added their rankling grouse. Among the most negative were, naturally, the 100,000 captured in North Africa and Greece and held, most of them, in Egypt until 1948.* They could not understand or believe that the Allies who had landed armadas in Europe could, due to the great shipping shortage at the end of the war, be having difficulty in even bringing their own troops back from the Far East. Those who were still Nazi-minded —and there were not a few of these—brought up standardised stories of the way unpleasant Jews had treated them. If one adds the sheer length of most captivities, the shock or disorientation at returning to a shattered fatherland and a need to strike out at someone or something, these attitudes among average POW are not surprising.[111]

* On 10 March 1947 the Cairo correspondent of *The Times* wrote on the 100,000 prisoners in Egypt who still did not know the date of their repatriation. A third were old Afrika Korps men who could 'easily be distinguished by their bearing'.

The British and American authorities were puzzled by this ill-will, reckoning that it should have been directed at countries which treated prisoners less well. One reason may well be connected with the discovery by psychologists in England that British POWs returning from the dreadful Japanese camps were generally in a better mental and emotional state than those who had been held in comparative comfort in German camps. They had had to develop a solid community spirit to come through at all and had a sense of achievement and pride when they did. Similarly, perhaps, Germans who sweated it out in French labour gangs, in Belgian mines or who helped to rebuild Leningrad, supported each other through thick and thin and bore grimly the frank fact that they were being used as reparations labour; they knew too, that the Third Reich had relentlessly used forced labour from occupied countries. The British were different in their eyes: for one thing, they had not been occupied or suffered devastating destruction; and secondly, they never came out with a forthright policy statement on reparations labour. The government was sensitive about this point, partly because it did not easily marry with re-education.

But when all this has been said, the other side of the picture appears much more significant than the negative response from the average POW. In a fluid situation, without norms of loyalty of behaviour, quantitive assessments are less than ever important. For in human terms something unparalleled had been taking place. Victor and vanquished very soon after a terrible war had rubbed up against each other in an increasingly human way. It was not just a form of words when Lord Pakenham, as Minister in charge of German Affairs at the Foreign Office, said that the German POWs had been their country's best ambassadors. The British people, on their side, could see that many German qualities, which in the service of an evil regime had made their nation powerful and hated, were valuable and positive in themselves. Stereotype differences which had been divisive appeared more as acceptable alternative ways of being a human being. For those Germans who did not succumb to despair the protracted experience of England widened horizons more than today's 'packaged' foreign travel can. All this helped to create a ground and growing point for a common future which future political and economic stresses will find hard to disturb.

By 1950 travel to Germany was possible and there began the first of innumerable visits from Britain by men and women to the families of POWs whom they had become fond of. In that summer the Hope Gills were renewing friendships they had made at Fishers Camp—from where the Germans, as it was closed down, had hired the largest hall in Alton and given a splendid concert to the local people. The two Quakers visited the camp leader, Kurt Meinel, and the chaplain, Pastor Becker. 'When, at a remote hamlet, we reached the home of the boy who had been the camp baker, his family and half the village ran to greet us. In fact, the parents of all six boys whose homes we went to literally fell on our necks and wept—just because we tried to show humanity to their sons in their time of trouble.' Also in 1949 Mary Foss travelled for three weeks to trace families in need and even visited Field Marshal Manstein in prison in Nuremberg. In the following year the petite white-haired Quaker, Marian Edmundson, was being driven 2,000 miles to pay a return call to a string of the 'boys' who had visited her cottage on the North Yorkshire Moors. She was repeatedly fêted with flowers and gifts and wonderful meals. She even flew to Berlin so that she could meet her favourite, Albert the watchmaker, who had returned to the Soviet Zone. Some delayed the trip to Germany for decades. It was not until 1976 that the Yorkshire housewife, Clare Floyd, flew to Munich airport where retired policeman, Walter Schmere, had no difficulty in recognising her after thirty years. The Schmeres then entertained her for two weeks, giving her a party for her 76th birthday, all in return for her hospitality once given in Guiseley. The Baptist minister from Northampton, William Rees, has six times been to East Germany to visit Bernhard Mohr. His friend, however, cannot expect to be allowed to come to England till 1985 when he will have reached the officially safe (and useless?) age of sixty-five. But such trips to the DDR, like those of Margaret Owen, have been exceptional. Most personal links with former POWs in East Germany did not last; but some of those which remain, if cautiously expressed, are all the stronger because of the forces which try to prevent them.

An account of contacts maintained with West Germany would fill a small book. It would include friendships kept up to the third generation, as with the Freemans in Broadway; wedding and holiday visits, naming of children and god-parenting; au-pairing and even now and then the sending of food parcels in reverse, as when sugar was rationed in Britain. Later, and especially in the seventies, more and more Wehrmacht veterans have come to

England to show their wives and children scenes from their youth, the farms they worked on and perhaps meet the farmers and others who were good to them. A notable sentimental journey was made in 1977 by the seventy-six-year-old Berlin high-court judge, Dr Martin Baring, on the thirtieth anniversary of the dedication of the 'German Window' at Widnes for which he had been responsible.

Werner Düttmann came often to England, and likes to recall an incident in 1948. He had been awarded a scholarship to study architecture at Durham, and seized the opportunity of a trip to London to make a thank-you visit to Betty Jenkin at Jordans, and took the train from Marylebone to the nearest station, then called Seer Green Halt.

> In the compartment there were two men opposite me, a young man in the left hand corner and an older man in front of me. I said, 'Good afternoon'. There was no answer. After a little the pleasant-looking man on the left said, 'You're German, aren't you?' 'Yes—how do you know?' 'Englishmen don't say "good afternoon" when they get on a train.' We got into conversation. At this the older man was clearly annoyed and said presently, 'How can you be so friendly with a Hun after all they did!' I wanted to get out of the compartment but then the train started. Both men disappeared behind their papers. After a while the one on the left reached over a portion of his *Times* to me, which helped to calm me down. A bit later I noticed that he had some paper on his brief case and was writing something. Deep in thought, he continued doing this for the rest of the journey which lasted about 40 minutes. As the train slowed down for Seer Green he said, 'This is your stop', folded the piece of paper and as I got out handed it to me. It was a long and wonderful letter, addressed to me. He explained why he had not taken issue with the gentleman opposite me or continued the conversation. The war was not so long over, and the man might have lost all his family in an air-raid. Such bitterness which he did not wish to rouse up any more was understandable, and I must try to forgive him. He went on to talk about England and Germany and what he believed in and gave me some good tips. I sat there on the deserted wooden platform at Seer Green reading that letter with moist eyes, for the words of that unknown friend really reached into me.

The motives for staying on in Britain—and in the first instance

25,252 elected to do so—were very varied. A man's home had become Polish territory, or was in East Germany and he did not want to live under communism, or he simply had no family to return to. (These were the most frequent reasons.) He had an English girl; he had grown to like the English way of life; he did not believe that Germany had a future and saw an opportunity in Britain; he wanted to leave Europe for America or one of the Dominions and Britain seemed then the best launching point for this. (Canada in 1946 refused all applications from POWs to settle there.) He had made a mess of his life, or had something to hide. Britain would give him a new start. There wsa often a combination of motives. Werner Cziborra heard that his wife and his two small children had starved to death in Königsberg; he had also as a child been fed after the First World War by the Quakers whom he sought out when a prisoner. He found among them what he had been looking for: 'thoughtful people with a feeling for their fellow men.' In Weston-on-Trent he had met Nellie Scaife, who had been working in Germany for UNRRA, and they married in the Meeting House there. Otto Erxleben, from North Schleswig, believing in the good of Nazism with all the stubborn national loyalty of a frontier German, could not bear to go back to such a changed *Heimat*. Being released for agricultural work in Scotland, he simply wanted to forget what had happened. For a while he worked with fanatical energy as much as ninety-five hours a week. His industry and dedication eventually made him a successful farmer in Kent.

All over England German POWs have integrated into the farming population especially, the Vale of Evesham and South Wales being favourite places. Many have become business representatives of German firms. The factory manager in Glamorgan, the Methodist minister at Darlington, the goalkeeper who broke his neck in the cup final and carried on—the fabulous Bert Trautmann, the ferryman at Kyle of Lochalsh: these are among innumerable POWs who opted for Britain and made their mark. But they do not form themselves into the usual German *Vereine*, or clubs; they rather keep up with small groups of friends, as if aware that they are usually well-liked as individuals, but would not be so acceptable if they had any kind of group presence. There is one exception to this: some nine hundred Transylvanian Germans have largely maintained their collective identity,* most of them former

* See page 289.

conscripts into the Waffen-SS. They were brought over to camps in East Anglia. Pastor Gursky recalls how hard it was in 1947 to comfort these men, as the news filtered through that their farms had been taken over and wives or mothers transported to Siberia, leaving the old people to bring up their children. These soldiers of good yeoman stock had in Rumania been among the prosperous. They started from scratch again in Britain and today (1978) 90 per cent own their own houses, having mostly left agriculture. They form small solid Lutheran societies, being still moved by the community spirit which held them together in a far-off alien land for eight hundred years. But their folk culture and language are being fast diluted, and in another generation their assimilation will be nearly complete. For the present, however, they meet twice a year at Cottenham Village Centre near Cambridge, for an evening of dancing, singing and modest drinking. With a band on the stage, the occasional folk costume still in evidence, and with the proceedings conducted by Michael Zeck, known as 'the King of Siebenbürgen', the occasion produces a spontaneous old-fashioned happiness, rather rare today. Nor do they seem weighed down by nostalgia as they sing the lilting national song about their green and fruitful homeland, ringed by the Carpathians:

> Siebenbürgen, süsse Heimat
> unser teueres Vaterland!

A number of the refugee lecturers, who contributed so much to the revival of the country that they had to leave, returned to Germany, notably Gerhart Leibholz who went back to his chair of constitutional law at Göttingen and for the next twenty years served the new state as a member of the Federal Constitutional Court at Karlsruhe. Waldemar von Knoeringen built up the Bavarian Socialist Party, soon became its leader and founded the College for Political Education at Schloss Alperstein. Fritz Borinski played a full part in the redevelopment of German adult education, residential and otherwise. Werner Lauermann, too, would have returned had he not preferred to see his children educated in Britain. He stayed on at Wilton Park till his early death in 1971. Of his colleagues George Greene stayed on there for a while, becoming Dean; retiring, he remained in the same field by opening with his wife an international finishing school at Beaconsfield, at the same time pursuing his civic duties and becoming Mayor of the town in 1976. Philip Rosenthal shook off his other name of

Rossiter, kept his dual nationality and returned to Bavaria. After 'my life of adventure', as he put it, he rebuilt the family firm of Rosenthal Potteries. He became a Social Democrat MP at Bonn and in 1977 President of the Advisory Board on Design. René Halkett became a star broadcaster for the German Service of the BBC.

Of the captain interpreters, Karl Stambrook, having sacrificed certain career opportunities in Britain, went to New York where he made a new life. Herbert Sulzbach returned to Germany after ten years to participate in the Berlin airlift of 1948. He visited the shell of his old house in the Prinzregentenstrasse and found the inevitable refugee family squatting in the cellar. At Frankfurt he stood under the long-delayed sign EMIL-SULZBACH STRASSE, which the city council had at last erected in memory of his father. For a while, in spite of a sheaf of almost embarrassingly commendatory testimonials, he was in a jobless limbo. Eventually while keeping his British nationality he received back his German citizenship and, as a member of the press section of the German Embassy in London, has served under five ambassadors, in his eighties surpassing his father both in energy and bonhomie. In 1978 he still works on passionately and individualistically for better understanding and trust between the two countries of which he has worn the uniform. To honour him the unique Featherstone Park Friendship Circle gather each autumn in Düsseldorf, attended by former POWs and their families even down to the third generation with distinguished speakers, British and German, taking part. General Heim, retired in Ulm, used to go; he died only in 1978, a year when his deputy, U-Boat Commander Jurgen Oesten, having started from scratch to become an expert in ventilation and air-conditioning for ships, was still running two businesses in Hamburg with success.

Of the commandants Lord Napier on leaving Crewe Hall was offered a full colonelcy but in Nigeria. He preferred to serve his native Selkirk as a J.P. and County Councillor, but died within nine years of cancer, aged only fifty-four. In 1978 Colonel Grondona, reverting to his civilian career, was still being listened to as a distinguished economist. The cavalryman, Colonel Clements, having returned the last of the generals to Germany, retired back to Eire and, aged seventy-three, was still riding to hounds as President of the Kildare Hunt. His young German-born intelligence officer, Captain Lees, having stayed on beyond demobilisation for the sake of his job, found no doors open to him in 1948. He joined the Fire Service at the bottom, rose to be divisional chief and became a thorough Welshman. Major Puleston of Butcher Hill who, when his POWs manfully kept the roads and railways open in the hard winter of 1948, became as fond and as proud of them as he had been of his own men, still treasures a folder full of greeting cards that increases every year. Major Boughton for a while went back to the furniture business in South London, then advanced cheerfully, vigorously and independently into old age, till, in his late eighties, he had a fall and died in 1978. Colonel Faulk returned to being a grammar school teacher in Scotland. Later—a remarkable compliment—he was commissioned to write an account of 'Re-education' in the British section of the huge twenty-two volume official history of German prisoners in the Second World War. His book, eight hundred close-set pages, was a labour of love and written in German, an essential source book for all studies such as the present one.

Pastor Forell and Bishop Bell died within two months of each other in 1958. Both had spent themselves to the limit in response to the suffering of the mid-twentieth century; the lives of both were closely bound up with Germany. When Forell, who was ten years younger, died aged sixty-four, Professor Joachim Ritter at Münster immediately thought of proposing him for a posthumous Nobel Peace Prize. He knew not only Forell's work among POW, but had witnessed the growth of Espelkamp and his work for refugees and expellees from the east. He would not have known that one of Forell's activities had been in a specially Gandhian spirit: his journeys round north-west Germany trying to get landowners to release land for new settlements was a mirror of what Gandhi's disciple Vinobha Bahve was doing in India at the same time, but with more success. Forell's efforts were ultimately frustrated by legal and bureaucratic difficulties. Over twelve years he had planned, persuaded, cajoled, lectured, inspired and shamed thousands to work for and support his causes. He helped create a trust to bring German children to Sweden to recover from the traumas, mental and physical, of war. He started the Swedish-German Aid Organisation for Refugees. He set up a sponsorship system for specific projects, making thousands of Swedish peasants aware of the plight of their landless opposites in Germany and he personally raised millions of kroner. Yet there was no question of his being given the Nobel Prize. As Bishop Bengt

Sundkler comments, 'The sad fact is that Forell was very little known in Sweden. You have to be famous in order to be famous; you must be highly placed in order to move another rung up the ladder.' Forell lived before the media came to seek out and build up such personalities and at a time of confusion when deeds such as his received almost no publicity.

Dr Bell said his farewell to Chichester in the spring of 1957 after an episcopate of twenty-eight years. During the turmoil of Europe there had surely been no truer place of peace than his Bishop's Palace with its rose-red brickwork, ancient panelled rooms and the great beech tree on the wide walled lawn over which the pile of the Cathedral seems to lean. Here came and stayed, and so are linked together, many of those who have appeared in this book, drawn to the Bishop by his rare combination of vision, goodness and intellect: Gandhi (in 1930), Dietrich Bonhoeffer (who would have joined Gandhi for a while, if the call back to Germany had not been stronger), Birger Forell, Gerhart Leibholz, Basil Liddell Hart, Bishop Dibelius, Rudolf Halver, Herbert Hartwell and Martin Niemo.

In May of 1957 Bishop Bell made the last of his numerous visits to Germany in order to deliver at Bonn and Frankfurt a lecture on 'The German Resistance' with which he had been intimately involved. But he was still a thorn in the flesh to some. A version was due to go out in the German Service of the BBC, but Lindley Frazer, its chief voice during the war and still its head, had a long memory and cancelled the broadcast on the grounds that 'an official voice ought to put the opposite point of view'—and none was forthcoming. The following year President Heuss came to Britain on his historic, reconciling state visit. He brought with him his country's highest decoration, the Grand Cross of the Order of Merit with Star and Sash, but Dr Bell died a few hours before the news of the award would have reached him.* He had, however, already received the token that linked him indissolubly with Germany—the gift, as it were from the scaffold at Flossenbürg *KZ*, of Dietrich Bonhoeffer's 'Imitatio Christi'. He was more deeply and appropriately honoured, it has been well suggested, by that authentic gift than he would have been by receiving the

---

* Among others who received the Federal Republic's Order of Merit, but without Star and Sash, were Birger Forell, Herbert Hartwell, Julius Rieger (Pastor of the Lutheran community in London) and Herbert Sulzbach.

archbishopric of Canterbury which he sacrificed through standing by the Germans in their most dangerous crisis.[112]

Among the war generation in West Germany Liddell Hart became a familiar and honoured name. Already in 1943 his clear mind told him that after the Allied victory a German army would be essential to counter the westward expansion of Russian power. For this pragmatic reason as well as for the sake of justice he was extremely critical of the war crimes trials, and especially of the precedent created by the death sentence on Jodl, Hitler's personal Chief of Staff, whom he called a 'first rate clerk'. In 1951 he wrote to *The Times* that few charges against the generals would have been upheld by an impartial court, and that opposition to the early release of those in prison was not the way to make good Europeans. These were unpopular views at the time, as was his verdict that in occupied West Europe the Wehrmacht at least had behaved 'correctly'. His instinct of chivalry made him speak up often for those who were not in a position to speak for themselves.

During his second visit to Germany in 1952 Liddell Hart had a long meeting with Adenauer. The German Chancellor had for two years been making moves, secret from a hostile public opinion but not from the Commissioners of the Western Powers, towards building up a German contribution to a European defence force. The chief theme of their talk was the creation of an atmosphere of confidence through releasing imprisoned generals—especially the much respected Field Marshal Kesselring who was held in British custody.[113] Three years later, the wheel which Liddell Hart had helped to turn had come full circle. After a limbo of nine years a fresh army, the Bundeswehr, was in being. The screening of suitable candidates for the new senior officer corps was conducted by a highly confidential expert committee of the Bundestag.[114] All traces of the old Prussian militarism were eliminated, each soldier retaining his rights as a 'citizen-in-uniform'. So unmartial is the style and presence of the new Bundeswehr, and so discreet, that it is widely wondered that the nearly total absence of military pomp and pageantry does not deprive the Federal public of a normal, necessary focus of national identity and pride. It is very different across the tightly sealed eastern border. Here the goose-step persists and—except for the Russian-style steel helmet—a uniform almost identical in cut and colour with that of Hitler's Wehrmacht, a sight that can give the viewer an uneasy sense of *déjà vu*.

Liddell Hart's influence, both intellectual and personal, continued to be felt in West Germany for the next two decades. His articles and historical writings, including *The Other Side of the Hill* based on his conversations at Grizedale Hall, and his *History of the Second World War* had wide currency. He got to know several of the creators of the new Bundeswehr, including Helmut Schmidt, who used to attend meetings of the Institute of Strategic Studies in London. So it was that when Liddell Hart died in 1970 Schmidt himself, then Defence Minister, could write to his widow: 'To many of us, soldiers and political leaders, Sir Basil was not only a mentor, but a living example of the fact that war offered not only experience of the military field, but also lessons to be learnt in the interests of maintaining peace.'

Epilogue:

Unfortunately we need to assume that the historical soil from which our state grew is incompletely known to the young generation.

President Walter Scheel of West Germany,
speaking at Würzburg in March 1978

During the fifties a new phrase was coined in Germany for dealing with the Nazi past: *die Vergangenheit bewältigen*. Linguistically it is very interesting, for the verb *bewältigen* is normally used for coping with a difficult problem, getting on top of a difficulty, managing or mastering an unruly horse. The immediate past had, understandably, to be 'overcome'.

When Sir John Hunt, as he then was, wrote his book on the first climbing of Everest the publishers wished to call it *The Conquest of Everest*. He insisted on the factual word 'Ascent'. Similarly, how can the mountain of the past be *bewältigt*? It is always massively there, to be surveyed from different angles, visited and learned from and experienced again and again. To keep the same image, one might climb up out of disaster and chaos, at first wisely not looking back over one's shoulder, and this most Germans instinctively did in 1945. But once safety is reached a look downwards reveals both the shadows left behind and the distance travelled—a measure of one's achievement. "Dwell on the past and you'll lose an eye," says the Russian proverb; "Forget the past and you'll lose both eyes."[115]

A generation after ignominious defeat and total prostration, Germany—or rather the free part of Germany—has recovered its strength and dignity as a nation and is an essential factor in the maintenance of world stability. It has been an amazing transformation. Historians will differ endlessly about how far this was brought about by the Germans themselves, how far it was helped by acts of good will and statesmanship by her former enemies and how far by the switch of American strategy as the threat of Soviet Russia to the free world became plain. The economic advantages of defeat were grasped, making the first flutter of neo-Nazism look stupid. If the mood of the outside world remained watchful and the friends of the young Federal Republic for a while inclined to condescension, by the sixties all the remains of tutelage had disappeared. The admirable Institute of Contemporary History at Munich for a quarter of a century has been exposing in the best traditions of German scholarship the truth about the Hitler period. Willi Brandt went to Poland to kneel in prayer at the Auschwitz memorial and generous aid was given to Israel. These were events beyond the most sanguine expectations of 1945. But the past remained.

Once more thrustful German businessmen have penetrated to most corners of the world; and they are valued members of multinational companies. Spurred by the early pact with France and the European economic treaty, Germans have found a solution to the problem of national pride and identity in becoming 'good Europeans'. With the national eagle on their passports, formal and pacific compared with the Third Reich emblem, tourists from the Federal Republic have swarmed across the continent and beyond (sometimes forgetting how much they were but recently the hated occupier). A heavy inoculation of the American way of life has been absorbed and abroad the younger generation has happily linked up with international youth. But the past remains.

'What did *you* do in the great *Schweinerei*?' asked the children of the returned soldiers, and rarely got an answer that satisfied them. In a resounding silence the generation gap was widened to twice its usual size. After the slaughter of 1914–18 the war generation in Britain distanced itself from its ordeal.

> And when they ask us, and they're certainly going to ask us,
> The reason why we didn't win the Croix de Guerre,
> We'll never tell them, Oh we'll never tell them,
> There was a front, but damned if we know where.

The average Germans of 1945 had to distance themselves not only from the war but also, as far as they could, from a knowledge of what, in ignorant idealism or puffed-up chauvinism, they had fought for. It was too much for most to bear. The next generation felt bitter about what Germany now stood for in the eyes of the world:

'Germany, my country, unholy heart of the nations . . .' wrote one of its leading poets, Hans Magnus Enzensberger, born in 1928, reversing a famous line of Hölderlin. Thirty years later has come a wave of genuine curiosity about the Nazi era, coupled

with one of partial nostalgia, memory selecting its own version.
But what is repressed remains.

Today we understand much more about the importance of
being able to mourn. But it is difficult for a defeated nation adequately to mourn its dead, for their sacrifice seems to have been in
vain. In the years after the First World War the Weimar Republic
was so determined to break with militarism and turn its back on
the chauvinist past that the presence of two million dead was left
hovering over the country, largely unmourned.[116] The immense
psychological trauma of that holocaust remained unhealed. It was
left to the nationalists and the Nazis to do a service to the nation
by reviving their memory and honouring their sacrifice. But as
they called for a return of the 'spirit of the trenches' they manipulated it for their own ends, preparing another generation of German manhood for a much more aggressive war, a greater, still
more useless sacrifice.

In one small way the Federal Republic has tried to remedy this
mistake. At the German military ceremony at Cannock Chase,
4,859 military and naval casualties are buried. Two fifths of them
are from 1914–19, including a communal grave of Zeppelin crews.
The rest are from 1940–48, airmen shot down, seamen washed up
on our shores and those who died in internment camps or as
prisoners of war (of the last there were 994). This corner of
Staffordshire that is for ever Germany is a strangely moving place.
With its heather and silver birches it resembles the Lüneburg
Heath. It happens, too, that the colour of the identical headstones
in Belgian granite, chosen for its lasting quality, is reminiscent of
the German field-grey uniform. A slender white cross thirty-five
feet high stands in the centre of the gently sloping rows. Each
stone bears the names of four men, with rank, date of birth and
death. The Hall of Honour is a large covered courtyard open to
the air on four sides, from which natural light falls on the bronze
sculpture by Hans Wimmer of a fallen warrior. In contrast to
similar monuments in the past, it carries no evidence that the man
has fallen for his fatherland or indeed is a soldier at all. There is no
weapon, or even a suggestion of a uniform. The figure is of a man
half draped, the hollowness of the body suggesting pain and
waste, the moulding of the head a suffering that has ended in final
peace. He is simply a man, a human being. These graves are not
forgotten. Each year a party of teenagers comes over from

Bremen to tend the graves and enjoy a holiday in the neighbourhood. Each year similar parties of schoolchildren are sent by the
Federal Republic on similar missions to other parts of Europe (but
not Russia) where there are graves of German war dead.

This is all to the good, but it seems sadly significant to the
writer that present-day Germans do scant honour, in history books
or the media, to the men and women who perished, sometimes
unspeakably, because of their opposition to Hitler. When General
von Senger heard of the 20th July he reflected that 'the future of
the nation now seemed to hinge on whether this liberation movement would succeed in acquiring the place in history that it
merited. It was the only liberation movement in German history
that—based on conscience—aimed at eliminating a criminal
despot.' Britain, the Netherlands and France had long established
the *droit de résistance*, the right to resist absolutism by any means.
Catholics and Calvinists have, since the Renaissance, acknowledged that tyrannicide is in certain circumstances permissible. But
in German territories political tradition and the doctrines of the
Lutheran Church had decreed otherwise. Ideals of loyalty and civil
obedience sustained the *Führerprinzip* to the end. But the taboo
was at last broken in a whole series of failed assassination
attempts. Churchill's deep-felt words on 'this heroic chapter of
German domestic history' have already been quoted. But the
resistance covered a much wider spectrum than the mainly right-
wing aristocrats behind the *Attentat* who today are not seen to be,
because of their political views, among the founding fathers of the
West German state. Christians, Socialists, Communists, students,
above all thousands of ordinary men and women made up the
internal enemies of Hitler who suffered and often died at the hands
of the Gestapo. It was inevitable, perhaps, that the *Restauration*
regime of Adenauer, seeking a national consensus for recovery,
found it impolitic to honour these victims adequately. In so far as
the memory of those who sacrificed themselves for a noble cause
is alive, it is almost only as receding historical figures. Yet to
one Englishman they seem to be like the sustaining pillars in a
cathedral crypt that is only visited by a few devout or curious
people, who like to linger there because of the quiet strength of
the place. Few of those that walk in the airy spaces above are
aware that a crypt exists at all.

The graph of the outer, material recovery of a nation can easily
be plotted; it is much more difficult to chart an inner and spiritual

recovery. To try to do so at all implies, if not taking a stand as a judge, at least some agreed criteria of measurement. One can start with the vast national trauma of 1945 and ask how much the wound has been healed—rather in the way one might ask how far Britain has recovered from the amputation of Empire. 'Give us time, and more time,' said many a German POW. 'Don't expect us to become good democrats overnight. Don't lecture us too hard—let us find out for ourselves.' Quite rightly, they rejected or suspected many of their comrades who at once started to sing to the victor's tune. But they frequently failed to distinguish these trimmers from those who, with complete clarity, saw along with the falseness of the old gods the new way ahead, and followed it. Some learn fast, some slowly.

The salve of history does not try to overcome what has happened, still less to cover it up. But rather it tries to assist a process of healing and understanding. It restores the connection of the present with the recent past, to which it gives meaning. It renews the roots of sound tradition and sustains links with the dead, with the all-important ancestral part. It also can give meaning to lives in old age and help people to see themselves as part of a whole. But the past can with time also become too painful to bear. This is, for instance, noticeable in the case of many refugees who were victims of the Nazis. The energy of youth and their middle years has enabled them to survive horrible experiences and make a new life and, in the most forgiving way, perhaps bring succour and hope to their enemies. But then the life force recedes and the horrors of what they saw or escaped from swim up from the unconscious and fill them with fear and anger again. Someone as sanguine as Herbert Sulzbach only has to put up with a recurring dream that he is on a station platform with the luggage waiting for the last train to safety, and his family does not turn up. Others are haunted by the past to the point of mental illness. In Germany itself psychological breakdowns are frequently traced back to the Nazi period and its terrible, shaming aftermath—that is, if the psychiatrist himself is free of it.

But maybe the years after total defeat dealt with in this book will also be seen as, in the words of Hans Carossa, 'the good growing years of a people', though in a far sounder way than the Weimar Republic achieved. Certainly many among those who were in POW camps in Britain look back on that period as one of hope and optimism, as a creative pause, as a new beginning and a seed time. And many of those who tried to guide them, or help them to help themselves, believe that the effort was important and sometimes fruitful. This was the generation of Germans that returned to cities that were still largely rubble, and as students had to clean so many bricks before they went into emergency lecture halls; who often sought in vain for their parents, for these were among the two million expellees from the eastern territories that died *after* the war (part of a terrible equation with the many more who were driven into the gas chambers). This was the generation which today, having worked itself to the bone, ages and dies early, suffers from ulcers and alcoholic breakdowns, sometimes hides guilty secrets, and feels its freedom and hard-won prosperity bewilderingly, continually threatened. Their children, taking material riches for granted, hardly know, because there is still a veil over 1945, at what psychological cost and from what degradation they rebuilt their nation. But the salve of history cannot operate quickly. Surely it will be their grandchildren who, when the truth of the past, both good and bad, becomes better known, will understand, forgive and thank them and perhaps even honour them.

Appendix

By the end of the war Germans captured by the British or for whom the British were responsible totalled some 2,788,000. They included 30,000 in Austria, 35,000 in Norway, 40,000 in North Italy and 1,620,000 in North Germany, Denmark and Holland. In addition, there were those already held in the Middle East, North Africa, Canada and Australia, in all 170,000. The Americans passed on to the British 300,000 Germans who laid down their arms in the Magdeburg Bulge (before occupation by Russia). 368,000 (half of those held in the Rhine camps during the summer of 1945) were likewise passed up into the British Zone. In addition, there were the 123,000 held on behalf of Britain in the USA and discussed in Chapter 8.

Of the round 400,000 POWs dealt with in the present study, 43 per cent were ferried straight to Britain, 17 per cent after a period in camps in Belgium, 26 per cent and 7 per cent came via camps in USA and Canada respectively, 4 per cent were transferred from US custody in Britain and 3 per cent were SEPs from Germany.

Repatriation was carried out in six separate groups, mixed together in each monthly transport:

1.	Men graded 'A'	37,580
2.	Sick	43,301
3.	Economic priorities (i.e. miners, forestry workers, operators of earth-moving equipment). Others sent home early included local government officers and radio technicians	15,135
4.	Compassionate cases	19,761
5.	Special cases	18,835
6.	General repatriation by length of captivity, beginning Sept. 1946 at a monthly rate of 15,000, increased later	234,843
	Elected to stay in Britain	25,252
		394,707

(Details from Helmut Wolff op. cit. and Faulk op. cit.)

Notes

1. Items in order provided by K. H. Boettger, Gerald Andreas, Hugo Staudinger, H. D. Borcherdt, Werner Düttmann, Richard (now Michael) Crewdson, Erich Leverkus and anonymous.
2. Moorehead, op. cit.
3. *Seven Pillars of Wisdom* Ch. CXVII.
4. Heinrich von Trott would give much to be able to shake by the hand the British officer who saved his life. (Letter to the author.)
5. Hansard 8.2.47. See also page 280.
6. *Gulag Archipelago* Part I, p. 246.
7. A full account of the *Osttruppen* and *Hiwis* in the West is to be found in Rohrwald, op. cit., balancing that in N. Tolstoy, op. cit.
8. Collected by Victor Gollancz in *God of a Hundred Names*, Gollancz 1962.
9. Revision of Prisoner of War Accommodation in Holding Countries, P.R.O. File WC/32/10727.
10. *Zur G.d.d.K.* XIV, pp. 31–2.
11. Faulk op. cit. pp. 772–773.
12. Re Belgian Camps, Faulk op. cit. pp. 691–4; also *G.d.d.Kgf* XI, pp. 75–9.
13. Further information provided to author by G. J. O. Tunbridge.
14. Told to Henry Faulk.
15. Colonel Scotland's book on LDC was so heavily censored by the War Office as to be of little value.
15a See McLachlan op. cit. Ch. 8.
16. See A. J. Barker op. cit.
17. Details taken from *G.d.d.Kgf.* XIV, p. 45 and *Quick* 12.7.72.
18. Information from Viola Gollancz.
19. Story as in Faulk op. cit. (English) Ch. 2, with additional material from S. Bandelow and C. Stambrook. The official German *Wissenschaftliche Kommission* at first did not accept the truth of Faulk's account, but did so fully after questioning some of the witnesses, including Father Lotz.
20. See Kersten *Memoirs* (Hutchinson 1956) introd. Trevor-Roper.
21. The main source for Forell is his copious diary, long passages of which were translated for the purpose of the Koenigswald biography by his son, Professor Urban Forell, who retains the diary. Further material is held in the *Bundesarchiv* in Koblenz.
22. Further influence seems to have come to Forell through his grandmother from Karl Olof Rosenius, the nineteenth-century

evangelical prophet and also through the Salvation Army. (Urban Forell to the author.)

23. Taken from Forell op. cit. and also *Collected Works* of Gandhi, Vol. 35, pp. 461–4. See also Louis Fischer *Life of Mahatma Gandhi*.

24. In a Foreign Office minute (8.7.44) 'I see no reason to encourage this turbulent priest.' F.O. 371/39087/C9091. Dr Bell had continued to urge support for resistance circles in the Evangelical Church in Germany ever since his meeting with Dietrich Bonhoeffer on 31 May 1942 at Stockholm.

25. Churchill in the US Congress (19.5.43), speaking just after the Axis collapse at Tunis, said, 'It proves the truth of the old saying, "The Hun is always either at your throat or your feet".'

26. Cordell Hull *Memoirs* Vol. II, p. 1617 (Hodder 1948).

27. Reported in Sir A. Cadogan Diaries p. 402 (Cassell 1971).

28. Quoted in Purnell Vol. VII, 'Germany and Austria: A Question of Survival' by H. W. Koch.

29. Koch and Sullivan op. cit. *Die Stunde Null*.

30. *The Listener* 28.4.77.

31. *Das böse Zauber hielt nicht länger als der Zauberer*. The word 'spell' (*Zauber*) is reminiscent of Klaus Mann's father's famous short story about the Nazi danger, *Mario the Magician*. Dr George Bell used the word *Hitlerspell* in a letter to Sabine Leibholz 2.2.46 (Bettge op. cit. p. 1024).

32. Hibbert Journal July 1944 pp. 135–48, in reply to an article by E. F. Allnutt which advocated the setting up of education boards under the United Nations to control with its help all educational activities in the Germany of Tomorrow.

33. Quoted in *Germans against Hitler*, 3rd ed. 1960, Berto-Verlag, Bonn.

34. See Faulk op. cit. pp. 23–5. Brooks remained with POW/D till August 1946, but during that year was increasingly inactive as he was moving back into his old profession of literary agent.

35. Published in H. C. Ansbacher *Attitudes of German Prisoners of War. A Study in the Dynamics of National Socialistic Fellowship* 1948. Quoted in Faulk op. cit. pp. 25–6.

36. In a letter to Gunther d'Alquen 5.4.66.

37. A German TV film *Ausflug von Bridgend* was first shown on 31.5.77, and a BBC radio programme on July 1977.

38. Deposition made to Hubert Sulzbach at Featherstone Park 30.8.46.

39. Story from the late Major J. Boughton.

40. *G.d.d.Kgf.* XIV, pp. 77–82.

41. Reprinted in Joachim Ritter's posthumous collection of essays *Subjektivität* (Surkamp 1974). He was particularly attached to this essay because of its association with his circle at Shap Wells (Henning Ritter).

42. *Erkenntnis der Gefangenschaft*, Merkur 1948, pp. 137–40.

43. *Gedanken über die Gemeinschaft unseres Lagers* Shap Wells 1.12.45. A shorter version published in Faulk op. cit. pp. 696–700.

44. Pablo Neruda, *Childhood and Poetry.*
45. One of them, Berit (now Katherine) Lloyd tells the story.
46. Darter op. cit. p. 46.
47. See German Chaplaincy Services (POW) Protestant (UK). (Papers of the Reverend Charles Cranfield) Report to Deputy Chaplain General 15 August 1945.
38. Ibid.
49. Ditto, Visits to Camps, 7 Dec. 1945–3 Aug. 1946.
50. See Martin Gilbert, op. cit.
51. Liddell Hart, Notes for History 18.2.47. A similar line had been put personally to the Foreign Office by Cardinal Frings in Nov. 1946, and can be found in the British Press during 1947 (viz. *Spectator* 12.9.47).
52. Menuhin to Sulzbach Dec. 1967.
53. Unconfirmed. Reported in long article by Peter Dürenmatt in *Baseler Nachrichten* 28.4.47, entitled 'Eine Zelle des Wiederauflaus'.
54. Text and bottle in possession of John Clark of Featherstone Castle.
55. Details on Espelkamp from Forell's Journal and *Visit to Espel-kamp* by Herbert Hartwell in *The Bridge,* journal of the German–British Christian Fellowship, Sept. 1951.
56. G. F. Horedt in *Die Zeit am Tyne,* March 1947.
57. *Manchester Guardian* 2.5.47: 'German Prisoners in Britain—Political Enlightenment'.
58. Butterfield, op. cit. p. 122.
59. In 'Wölfe und Tauben', Karl Hanser Verlag.
60. I have followed Ryder op. cit., except that Schmitt was not, as stated, released in Oct. 1947. Facts are in Camp II Personalia file.
61. de Guingand op. cit.
62. Taken mainly from Grondona's account of Wilton Park in the *Royal United Services Journal,* and from conversation with the author.
63. Information from Dr Albert Hollaender.
64. Information from Professor Eric Birley.
65. R. V. Jones, op. cit.
66. Details in this paragraph recalled by Geoffrey Forrest. The transcriptions of the reports of bugging at Cockfosters, Latimer and Wilton Park have not been released.
67. See also *History of the US Army in World War II, Cassino to the Alps,* p. 529, which differs slightly from General Clark's autobiography.
68. The account of *The Surrender* by John Keegan in Purnell Vol. VI has been followed, with additions from Speer *The Third Reich.*
69. Deposition sworn to Captain Lees, Bridgend 13.8.47.
70. R. V. Jones, op. cit.
71. Information from Dr Editha von Rundstedt.
72. Hoffmann op. cit. p. 260.
73. Information from Dr Otto John.
74. Heinrich Koeppler: *The Purpose, Aims and Methods of Wilton Park.* Based on an address given on 21.6.71.

75. Information on Waldemar von Knoeringen provided by F. Borinski.
76. Harold Nicolson *Spectator* 1.3.46.
77. *Neues Deutschland* 26.4.50.
78. *Evening News* 12.12.46.
79. Keezer op. cit. p. 31. Helmut Schmidt spoke at the 133rd Wilton Park Conference, 20 June to 3 July 1971, commemorating the 25th anniversary of its foundation.
80. Faulk op. cit. pp. 96–8.
81. Observed by the Reverend Edwin Robertson, Deputy Head of the Religious Affairs Branch CCG, British Zone.
82. Letter to J. Sulzbach.
83. *Der Monatsbrief* (Norton Camp) August 1947.
84. *Manchester Guardian* 24.10.47.
85. Information to Otto John, then serving with Lufthansa.
86. From his *Fugue of Death* 1945. Paul Celan was born Paul Anczel in Rumania, in 1920.
87. Information from Fritz Körner, then stationed at the former *KZ* Sandbostel, which was filled with SEP.
88. See Anthony Terry, 'How the SS Alter History', *Sunday Times Magazine* May 1977.
89. A.E.'s story provided through Professor Jentsch.
90. Heinrich Fraenkel to the author.
91. Information on Watten comes from those mentioned and anonymous sources.
92. Information from Herbert Christiansen.
93. Wesermann op. cit. p. 237.
94. Faulk op. cit. IV/2 used also extensively in this chapter, supplemented by correspondence.
95. *The Lord of the Rings*, Book II Ch. 2 (J. R. R. Tolkien considered this the most important sentence in his famous trilogy).
96. Faulk op. cit. p. 617.
97. Hansard 27.10.47.
98. Original in Gerster's *Du Stimmst mich wie ein Saitenspiel* published in England. Provided by Seigfried Bandelow.
99. *Daily Mail* 29.4.47.
100. BBC Home Service (See *Radio Times* 20.7.67).
101. 'The Man Who Came Back' by James Follett. BBC Radio 4, 26.9.77.
102. See *Dilettantismus und Kriegsgefangenschaft* by Erich Wesselow. Faulk op. cit. pp. 521–3.
103. The words of the Benedictine camp chaplain at Butcher Hill, Father Sigismund Biedermann.
104. Memo in Bevin's hand reads: 'I am of the opinion that all prisoners not working should be sent home.' (F.O.371/C3940). Bevin always emphasised their work value for the food supply.
105. See Dilys Powell, *The Villa Ariadne*, on her visit to Kreipe in Germany after the war.
106. Information in Williams op. cit.

107. General von Senger appears to be the only high officer on the German side who has written a detailed account of human experiences in captivity.
108. *The Times* 14.7.48.
109. *Mount Athos—the Call from Sleep* by Erhart Kaestner. (Tr. Barry Sullivan, Faber 1961, p. 124.)
110. Deutsche Rundschau *Die Schuld der Generäle* Jan. 1949.
111. Information from Helmut Wolff, also in Mitcherlich, Haas, Seeman's Report on questioned homecomers at Münsterlager, 25 May to 9 July 1948. See Faulk op. cit. p. 43.
112. 'The Controversial Bishop Bell' by Professor D. M. Mackinnon. BBC Third Programme 18.11.67.
113. Liddell Hart *Notes for History* 11/1952/8.
114. The files used in the investigation were destroyed after the Committee ceased to exist; therefore 'anyone is lost who is interested in how the German forces succeeded—and they did indeed—in fishing out of the former Wehrmacht pond those generals and colonels whose loyalty could be relied upon'. (Col.—ret.—Hans Joachim Kraaze to the author.)
115. Quoted by Alexander Solzhenitzyn in introduction to *The Gulag Archipelago*.
116. See Hubertus von Loewenstein: *The Tragedy of a Nation*, 1934.

Sources

The essential starting point is the German official history, especially the volume by Henry Faulk (with its much shorter version in English). No official account has been published in Britain, but there are many relevant documents in the Public Record Office. The files on the German generals in captivity were only opened in 1979, too late for the writing of this book, but a last-minute inspection shows that no fundamental textual changes are called for.

The greater part of material used comes from correspondence with the author, tape-recorded interviews, diaries and private or unpublished memoirs, and newspaper cuttings. The rest derives from the books listed.

GERMAN OFFICIAL HISTORY (referred to as *Zur G.d.d. Kgf.*)
Zur Geschichte der deutschen Kriegsgefangenen des Zweiten Weltkrieges (22-bändige Dokumentation der Wissenschaftlichen Kommission für deutsche Kriegsgefangenengeschichte herausgegeben von Universitätsprofessor Dr Erich Maschke. Gieseking Verlag).
Band XI Helmut Wolff: *Die Deutschen Kriegsgefangenen in britischer Hand —Ein Uberblick.*
Band XI/2 Henry Faulk: *Die deutschen Kriegsgefangenen in Grossbritannien —Re-education.*
Band XIX Kurt W. Böhme: *Geist und Kultur der deutschen Kriegsgefangenen im Westen.*
Beiheft 2 *Aufzeichnungen über die Kriegsgefangenschaft in Westen.*

BOOKS CONSULTED
Balfour, Michael: *Four Power Control in Germany* (OUP 1956).
Barker, A. J.: *Behind Barbed Wire* (Batsford 1974).
Bettge, Eberhart: *Dietrich Bonhoeffer, Exil und Martyr* (Chr. Kaiser Verlag, München).
Blumentritt, Günther: *Rundstedt, the Soldier and the Man* (Odhams 195-).
Bond, Brian: *Liddell Hart: A Study of his Military Thought* (Cassell 1977).
Butterfield, Herbert: *Christianity and History* (Bell 1949).
Clark, Gen. Mark: *Calculated Risk* (Harrap 1951).
Cooper, Matthew: *The German Army 1933–1945—its Political and Military Failure* (Macdonald and Janes 1978).
Cooper, Matthew and Lucas, James: *Hitler's Elite* (Macdonald and Janes 1972).

Dammann, Ernst: *Contribution to Tradition-Krisis-Renovatio aus theoligischer Sicht* (N. G. Elwert Verlag, Marburg 1976).

Faulk, Henry: *Group Prisoners* (much shortened version of *Zur G.d.d. Kgf* XI/2) (Chatto and Windus 1976).

Fitzgibbon, Constantine: *De-nazification* (Michael Joseph 1969).

Forell, Birger: *Från Himalaya till Ceylon* (SKD Stockholm 1929).

Frings, Josef, Kardinal: *Für die Menschen Bestellt* (J. P. Bachen Verlag, Cologne 1973).

Gilbert, Martin: 'Winston S. Churchill' Vol. IV, 'Companion' Vol. 2 1917–1919 (Heinemann 1977).

Gollancz, Victor: *Shall Our Children Live or Die?* A Reply to Lord Vansittart on the German Problem (Gollancz 1942).

de Guingand, F.: *Operation Victory* (Hodder and Stoughton 1947).

Hearnden, Arthur (ed): *The British in Germany* (Hamish Hamilton 1977).

Hoehne, Heinz: *The Order of the Death's Head, the Story of Hitler's SS* (Secker and Warburg 1969).

Hoffman, Peter: *History of the German Resistance 1933–1945* (Macdonald and Janes 1977).

Horrocks, Lt. Gen. Sir Brian: *A Full Life* (Leo Cooper 1974).

Jasper, Ronald C. D.: *George Bell, Bishop of Chichester* (OUP 1967).

Keezer, Dexter M.: *A Unique Contribution to International Relations— The Story of Wilton Park* (McGraw Hill Books U.K. 1973).

Kaestner, Erhart: *Zeltbuch in Tumilad* (Fischer Bücherei 1956).

Ketternacher, Lothar: *Die britische Halting zum deutschen Widerstand während des Zweiten Weltkrieges* (Klett Sonderdruck 1977).

Königswald, Harald von: *Birger Forell: Lben eund Wirken in den Jahren 1933–1957* (Eckart Verlag 1962).

Liddell Hart, B. H.: *The Other Side of the Hill*, revised ed. (Cassell 1951).

McLachlan, Donald: *Room 39: Naval Intelligence in Action 1939–45* (Weidenfeld 1968).

Moorehead, Alan: *The End in Africa* (Hamish Hamilton 1943).

Nicolson, Nigel: *Alex: The Life of Field Marshal Earl Alexander of Tunis* (Weidenfeld and Nicolson 1973).

Nielsen, Walter Henry: *Germany Re-armed* (Simon and Schuster 1972).

Powell, Dilys: *The Villa Ariadne* (Hodder and Stoughton 1973).

Purnell: *History of the Second World War*, especially Vols. V, VI (BPC Publishing Ltd.).

Ryder, Rowland: *Ravenstein: Portrait of a German General* (Hamish Hamilton 1978).

Scott, Peter: *Eye of the Wind* (Hodder and Stoughton 1961).

Senger und Etterlin, F. von: *Neither Fear nor Hope* (Macdonald 1963).

Shedd, Clarence Prouty: *History of the World Alliance of the Young Men's Christian Association* (SPCK 1955).

Speer, Albert: *Spandau: The Secret Diaries* (Collins 1976).

Speer, Albert: *The Third Reich* (Weidenfeld 1970).

Spender, Stephen: *European Witness* (Hamish Hamilton 1946).

Stewart, Herman: *Rebirth of the German Church* (SCM Press 1946).

Sulzbach, Herbert: *With the German Guns—Four Years at the Western Front 1914–1918* (Leo Cooper 1973).

Sulzbach, Herbert: Ch. in *Total War to Total Trust* (Oswald Wolf 1976).
Sykes, Christopher: *Troubled Loyalty, a Biography of Adam von Trott zu Solz* (Collins 1968).
Thorwald, E. Jürgen: *Die Illusion—Rotarmisten in Hitlers Heeren* (Droemer Knaur 1976).
Tolstoy, Nikolai: *Victims of Yalta* (Hodder and Stoughton 1977).
Vogler, Hilde und Will: 'Birger Forell', a chapter in *Durchkreuzter Hass* (Käthe Vogt Verlag 1961).
Wenzel, Fritz: *Single or Return* (Kimber 1954).
Wesermann, Fried: *Kurt Schumacher* (Herkul, Frankfurt o/M 1952).
Wheeler-Bennett, Sir John: *Nemesis of Power; The German Army in Politics* (Macmillan 1953).
Williams, Herbert: *Come Out Wherever You Are* (also title of joint NDR–BBC TV programme, 13.9.77 on Bridgend Escape) (Quartet Books London 1976).

UNPUBLISHED SOURCES

Borcherdt, H. D.: 'Gast bei Weiland Sr. Majestät König Georg VI' (family memoir).
Darton, Lawrence: 'An Account of the Friends Committee for Refugees and Aliens' (Friends House 1954).
Forrest, Geoffrey: Assorted papers and journals.
Hartwell, Rev. Dr Herbert: 'Die Geschichte der Evangelischen Lagerseelsorge in Grossbritannien 1944–48'. Lecture given on 30.3.48.
Hitch, F. H.: 'The Activities of the PS/W Division Oct. 46 C.I.(d)' COGA.
Hunt (formerly Foss), Mary: Assorted papers.
Jansen, Josef M.: 'Rabauken, Bakeleuten und Menschen "Guten-Willens" in West England 1944–1948, Kriegsgefangenschafts-Eindrücke' (Copyright held by Dr Peter Mayenfels of Düren).
Kaftan, Wolfgang: 'Als wärs kein Kopf aus Holz (Abenteuerfahrten eines Puppenspielers in Deutschland, Frankreich, Grossbritannien und anderswo in der Welt)'.
Koch, Herbert and Sullivan, Barry: 'Stärker als Stackeldraht—die sogenannte Umerziehung deutscher Kriegsgefangene in England und was aus ihr wurde' (A joint radio programme BBC German Service—WDR, 2.10.62).
Koch, Herbert and Sullivan, Barry: 'Die Stunde Null—Die Begegnung von Engländern und Deutschen Anno 1945' (A joint radio programme BBC German Service—WDR, 28.8.65.)
Liddell Hart, Sir Basil: Archives now at King's College, London.
Monatsheft, Der: 'Christliche Zeitschrift für Deutsche Kriegsgefangene 1946–48'.
Siefert, Paul: 'Hinter Stackeldraht in USA und England, ein Kriegs-gefangenen-Schicksal'.
Sulzbach, Herbert: Memoir and assorted papers.
Zeit am Tyne, Arbeit im Anfbau and other POW camp newspapers.

CONTRIBUTORS AND CORRESPONDENTS (including Germans living in England)
*Those marked * were tape-interviewed by the author*
Dorothea Abbott, Lesley Ainslie, Gerald Andreas,* The Ven. Sydney D. Austerberry, Leonard L. Baldwin, Robin Barker, Bertram Barnes, Alan Barth, John and Marjorie Bateman, J. K. Benthall, Dr George M. Betts,* Prof Eric Birley,* Mary Booker, Major J. Boughton,* Thos. R. Brasnett, Thomas Braun, Gerald and Norah Brown, Rev. Lionel Brown, Dr Michael Brown, Peter Brugger,* Canon Maurice Brunsden, P. Alan Burtt, Rita Campion, Rev. G. Carr, John Carruthers, Mrs M. A. Carter, Oswin Castick,* Joan H. Cautherley, Enid Chadwick, Rev. Peter Chandler, Rev. O. E. Charlton, Lt-Col C. L. M. Clements, Katharine Collacott (Greene), James R. V. Collin, Rev. Charles Cranfield,* Hubert (formerly Alan) Craycroft, Michael (formerly Richard) Crewdson,* Marjorie Dandie, Roger Davies, J. A. Dent, Charles and Stella Desforges, Mrs B. B. Curry, Werner Cziborra, George E. Dixon, Bernard Doherty, E. M. Dubrau, Rev. Alan Ecclestone, Elgiva Edmonds, Leslie L. Edwards, Cecil Elbra, Otto Erxleben,* Henry Faulk,* Ruth E. Fisher, Prof Urban Forell,* Marjorie Francis, Brother Edward Franey, A. V. Freeman, Dr Martin Gilbert, Prof W. Glyn Jones, Gerhardt Goersdorf, Viola Gollancz, Lawrence A. Green,* George Roundell Greene,* Lt-Col St Clare Grondona,* Alan Haigh, René Halkett,* The Ven. A. G. Hardie, A. S. Harris, Rev. Dr Herbert Hartwell,* Joan Hewitt, H. E. Hiley, Wing Commander F. H. Hitch, Dr Albert E. Hollaender, Charlotte Hollingworth, Prof Michael Howard, G. William Hope Gill, Lt-Gen Sir Brian Horrocks, Margaret D. Horwill, Ronald Howe,* F. Lyth Hudson, Mary Hunt (Foss),* P. Huxtable, Crissie Jarvis, Brother Herbert Kaden, O.S.B., Dr Lothar Ketternacker, Karl Heinz Knoop, Eva Koch, Sir Heinz Koeppler,* Werner Kuwerz,* Daisy Lane, Hannah Lauermann, Wynne Lawrence, Edward Lees, Lady Liddell Hart, Albert F. Lindley, Catherine Lloyd, Frances Longman, Peter Lowe, W. McArthur, Mrs M. W. McBain, Canon Alexander Macleod Murray,* Lilian Martin, Herbert and Minnie Mayman, Monica Montila, Kenneth Morgan, Lord Napier and Ettrick, Canon Robert P. Neill, Rev. A. P. Nichols, Helen Nicoll, Ronald Oehlke,* Robert O'Neill, Kelvin Osborne,* Margaret Owen, Muriel Palmer, Mona Pehle, Cyril A. Philips, Elsie Pickvance, Ruth Plant, Dr Alfred Plaut, Major J. C. Puleston, Rev. Dr Eckart von Rabenau, Rev. William Rees, Daphne Rickard, Helen Roberts, Rev. Edwin Robertson, Norman Roffey,* Alfred Rosenberg*, Peter Rowe, Heinz Rummler, Eleanor Rugman, Brenda Thomas, John Trevelyan, Kathleen Sandow, John W. Scaife, Godfrey Scheele,* Reg Shephard, Sheila M. Sinman, Rev. D. E. Simpson Baird, Rev. Roy Sinker, Geoffrey Skevington, Patricia Smith, Rev. H. D. Speakman, Charles Stambrook, Albert and Mary Steele, Frank C. S. Stevens, Richard L. Sturge, Herbert Sulzbach,* Prof Bengt Sundkler, P. H. M. Swan, Henry Swanzy, Heather Tanner, Frances-Marie Thacker, Elmar Tremmel,* G. J. O. Tunbridge,* Bruno Ullrich, Ben Vincent, Cliff Vincent, Prof Hans Walz,* Canon I. F. F. Webb, Geoffrey Wedlake,

Dame Rebecca West, Eva R. White, Mary Whiteman,* W. David Wills, Rev. I. T. Wilson, Mrs R. Wilson, Stanley Wilson,* P. Witterer,* Michael Zeck,* Norman and Evelyn Cox.

CONTRIBUTORS AND CORRESPONDENTS IN GERMANY

Siegfried Bandelow, Dr Martin Baring, Karl Becker, Dr Kurt Blohm, Oberst D. Borcherdt, Prof Fritz Borinski, Oberst K. H. Böttger, Rudolf Bradatsch, Herbert Christiansen,* Prof Werner Düttmann,* Diether Ebbecke,* Hans Eisermann, Hans-Georg Frieberger, Prof G. D. Friedrich, Dr Joachim Friese, Dr Günther Geisseler,* Pastor Karl Gursky,* Willi Gutmann, Pastor D. Rudolf Halver,* Dieter Hankel,* Bernhard Harms, Frau Gotthard Heinrici, Dr Heisig,* Prof Freiherr von der Heydte, Karl Hildebrand,* P. O. Hoffmann, Karl Heinz Huber,* Dr H. V. von Hulst, Prof Werner Jentsch, Dr Otto John*, Wolfgang Kaftan, Botho Kirsch,* Dr Max Kobbert, Helene von Königswald, Hans Joachim Kraaz, Hermann Kreis, Prof Gerhart Leibholz,* Werner Leichner, Dr C. Erich Leverkus,* Kurt Lichdi, Dr Peter Mayenfels,* Lilo Milschsack, D.B.E., Hans-Georg Moschallski, Herbert Mott, Jurgen Oesten,* Otto Peschel, Clemens Graf Podewils,* F. T. Pons, Herbert Quoss, Elisabeth von Ravenstein, Edith and Henning Ritter, Philip Rosenthal,* Dr Editha von Rundstedt, Prof Kurt Sandig, Herbert Schmitt,* Karl Schneider, Dr Kurt Schwederski,* Frau von Senger und Etterlin, Michael Siegel, Heinrich von Trott zu Solz, Superintendant G. Wallmann, Dr Helmut Wolff,* Dr H. Ziock.

Index